KENNEDY AND GREAT BRITAIN

Also by Christopher Sandford
★

FICTION
Feasting with Panthers
Arcadian
We Don't Do Dogs

PLAYS
Comrades

MUSIC BIOGRAPHIES
Mick Jagger
Eric Clapton
Kurt Cobain
David Bowie
Sting
Bruce Springsteen
Keith Richards
Paul McCartney
The Rolling Stones

FILM BIOGRAPHIES
Steve McQueen
Roman Polanski

SPORT
The Cornhill Centenary Test
Godfrey Evans
Tom Graveney
Imran Khan
John Murray
Laker and Lock

HISTORY
Houdini and Doyle
Summer 1914
Macmillan and Kennedy
The Man Who Would Be Sherlock
The Zeebrugge Raid
Summer 1939
Victor Lustig
Midnight in Tehran
1964

KENNEDY AND GREAT BRITAIN

THE SPECIAL RELATIONSHIP

CHRISTOPHER SANDFORD

The
History
Press

To Barbara Dungee

★ ★ ★

First published as *Union Jack* 2018
This paperback edition published 2023

The History Press
97 St George's Place, Cheltenham,
Gloucestershire, GL50 3QB
www.thehistorypress.co.uk

British Library Cataloguing in Publication Data.
A catalogue record for this book is available from the British Library.

ISBN 978 1 80399 533 5

Typesetting and origination by The History Press
Printed and bound in Great Britain by TJ Books Limited, Padstow, Cornwall.

MIX
Paper from
responsible sources
FSC
www.fsc.org   FSC® C013056

Trees for LYfe

CONTENTS

Acknowledgments   7

1   "Father Does Not Always Know Best"   11
2   My Trip Abroad   35
3   Why England Slept   73
4   A Very Broad-Minded Approach to Everything   120
5   Europe's New Order   156
6   John F. Kennedy Slept Here   180
7   Family Feud   205
8   Special Relationships   231
9   "We Are Attempting to Prevent World War Three"   268
10 Harold and Jack   307

    Notes   347
    Selected Bibliography   383
    Index   388

Democracy may be a great system of government
to live under, but its weaknesses are great … We must
realize that democracy is a luxury. We may be able to afford
it due to our particular position, but we must be continually
aware of the lesson we have learned from our study of England
and Germany's armament history from 1937–1939. We have
seen that a democracy cannot successfully compete with a
dictatorship on even terms. Our foreign policy, therefore,
should be directed to taking advantage of certain economic and
strategic advantages that we now possess, and making sure that
we never reach a position of having to compete with a dictator
on their home grounds – that is both starting on an even basis –
or the dictatorship will win.

JOHN F. KENNEDY
Why England Slept (1940)

★　★　★

The British Empire and the United States will have
to be somewhat mixed up together in some of their affairs for
mutual and general advantage. For my own part, looking out
upon the future, I do not view the process with any misgivings.
I could not stop it if I wished; no one can stop it.
Like the Mississippi, it just keeps rolling along.

WINSTON CHURCHILL
House of Commons, August 1940

★　★　★

All educated Americans, first or last,
go to Europe.

RALPH WALDO EMERSON
The Conduct of Life (1860)

ACKNOWLEDGMENTS

THIS IS NOT A BIOGRAPHY of John F. Kennedy. Anyone interested in reading more about the subject will find some suggestions in the bibliography at the end of the book. Instead, I've written a study suggesting the ways in which Kennedy reacted to certain experiences he had of Britain and how these may have shaped some of his basic thinking as president. That's not to say that he instinctively sympathized with British policy, particularly when it came to colonial affairs, or that he invariably sided with Britain in presenting a united and coordinated front to the world. He did not. Kennedy was of course motivated first and foremost by American self-interest as he saw it. His intellectual and sentimental (if not romantic) attachment to the aristocratic British political tradition he so thrillingly read about in David Cecil's book *The Young Melbourne* was neither the determining factor nor the principal ingredient in the Atlantic special relationship as it played out from January 1961 to November 1963. But Kennedy did, nonetheless, understand the hard fact of Britain's steady course of national decline management in the postwar years and, all else being equal, proved himself ready and willing to help ease his country's historic ally through its

sometimes painful passage from the first to the second division
of the world's great powers. It's also true that at an intellectually impressionable age in his early twenties, Kennedy thought
deeply about issues of appeasement and armament, and that
these same issues resonated with him in determining his attitude
to the Soviet Union a generation later.

No gift of psychiatric interpretation is needed to see how
far John Kennedy differed from his own father, Joseph, the
US ambassador to Great Britain from 1938 to 1940, in his admiration of Britain's initial stand against Hitler, and how far he was
later prepared to go to accommodate the country's lingering
ambitions to enjoy a seat at the international top table. An example of this came at Nassau in December 1962, when Kennedy
agreed to continue to provide Britain with its own independent
nuclear deterrent, a decision taken over the vocal objections of
most of his senior staff. Later explaining this arrangement to the
queen, British prime minister Harold Macmillan wrote, "It has
been a hard and at times almost desperate struggle to maintain
the two concepts of interdependence and independence. But I
must pay tribute to President Kennedy's sense of fairness and
willingness to be persuaded by argument and over-rule those
of his advisers who were not sympathetic to our views." This
was a significant moment in Anglo-American relations, and
its strategic consequences remain with us today. It's perhaps
the chief example, but not the only one, of the way in which
Kennedy's deep-seated affinity for Britain and the British people
sometimes overcame the more pristine logic of a man like his
defense secretary Robert McNamara, a supremely rational systems analyst not given to emotional effusions on behalf of even
a close ally. Britain was extremely lucky that the outcome of
the November 1960 presidential election went as it did. This
book hopefully shows why that was so, and how it was that
the youthful John Kennedy developed a unique and intimate
relationship with certain British figures whom he later turned
to during the most critical period of the Cold War. Even today,

it seems Britain has yet to resolve the central dilemma of the postwar "special relationship": whether it should best be seen as a loyal but financially strapped European ally, a key nuclear superpower, or what amounts to the fifty-first American state. No US president has stamped a more profound imprint on that debate than Kennedy.

For archive material, interviews, or advice, I thank the following: Abacus; Alibris; the *American Conservative*; Connor Anderson; Laurie Austin; the Avon Papers at Birmingham University, United Kingdom; Andrew Baird; the Bodleian Library, Oxford; Book Depository; Bookfinder; the British Library; British Newspaper Library; *Chronicles*; the CIA; Companies House, London; Stephen Cooper; the Devonshire Collection at Chatsworth House; the Dwight D. Eisenhower Presidential Library, Abilene, Kansas; the FBI Freedom of Information Division; Tom Fleming; General Register Office, London; Tony Gill; Maryrose Grossman; *Hansard*; Tess Hines; Steven J. Hull; the John F. Kennedy Presidential Library and Museum, Boston; Barbara Levy; Antony Lewis; the Library of Congress; the Massachusetts Historical Society; Millbanksystems.com; National Security Archives; Hugh O'Neill; Renton Public Library; Scott P. Richert; Rebecca Romney; the Salisbury Papers at Hatfield House; Sam Satchell; Seaside Library, Oregon; the *Seattle Times*; the Seeley Library, Cambridge, UK; the 1776 Coalition; the *Spectator*; Andrew Stuart; James Towe; UK National Archives; the Us National Archives and Records Administration; the University Library, Cambridge, UK; University of Montana, Missoula; University of Puget Sound, Tacoma, Washington; Vital Records; Harold Waters; James Waters; Emily Watlington; the late Auberon Waugh; the late Harold Wilson; and Aaron Wolf.

And on a personal basis, I thank the following: Lisa Armstead; Rev. Maynard Atik; Pete Barnes; the late Ryan Boone; Hilary and Robert Bruce; Jon Burke; Don Carson; the late Pat Champion; Changelink; James Clever; Common Ground;

Christina Coulter; Tim Cox; the Cricket Society; Celia Culpan; the Davenport; Monty Dennison; Micky Dolenz; the Dowdall family; John and Barbara Dungee; Rev. Joanne Enquist; Malcolm Galfe; the Gay Hussar; Gethsemane Lutheran Church; James Graham; the late Tom Graveney; Jeff and Rita Griffin; Charley Grimston; Grumbles; Alex Guyver; Steve and Jo Hackett; Masood Halim; Alastair Hignell; Charles Hillman; Alex Holmes; Hotel Vancouver; Jo Jacobius; the Jamiesons; Lincoln Kamell; Terry Lambert; Belinda Lawson; Todd Linse; the Lorimers; Robert Dean Lurie; Les McBride; Heather and Mason McEachran; Charles McIntosh; the Macris; Lee Mattson; Jim and Rana Meyersahm; Sheila Mohn; the Morgans; John and Colleen Murray; Kaiyo Nedd; Greg Nowak; Chuck Ogmund; Phil Oppenheim; Gary O'Toole; Valya Page; Robin Parish; Owen Paterson; Peter Perchard; Greg Phillips; Chris Pickrell; Roman Polanski; Premier Tutors; the late John Prins; Robert Prins; the Prins family; Ailsa Rushbrooke; Debbie Saks; Sam; the late Sefton Sandford; Sue Sandford; Sandy Cove Inn; Peter Scaramanga; Seattle C.C.; Fred and Cindy Smith; Rev. and Mrs. Harry Smith; the Stanley family; the late Thaddeus Stuart; Jack Surendranath; Danny Tetzlaff; Cynthia Tyrrell; Mary Tyvand; the late Robert Valade; Diana Villar; Lisbeth Vogl; the late Peter Way; Karin and Soleil Wieland; Debbie Wild; the Willis Fleming family; Heng and Lang Woon.

Copyediting of the manuscript was performed by Lee S. Motteler. The index was prepared by Robin B. James, MLS.

And a low bow, as always, to Karen and Nicholas Sandford.

1

"FATHER DOES NOT ALWAYS KNOW BEST"

FOR THE PAST SIXTY YEARS, the British have occupied a subsidiary role in the much-vaunted Atlantic partnership. In fact, the basic terms of trade were already at work in the last days of World War II, when, over its ally's strong military objections, the administration of President Franklin D. Roosevelt unilaterally laid down the strategy for the final conquest of Nazi Germany, although it would be more than a decade before the Anglo-American balance of power assumed its modern tone. It took the Suez crisis of October 1956 to fully execute the mid-twentieth-century role reversal that would see London essentially act as a branch office of its Washington headquarters. The story of how Britain, in league with France and Israel, took armed action against the Egyptian dictator Colonel Gamal Nasser following his nationalization of the Suez Canal Company, and how President Eisenhower's anger at his allies' intervention was sufficient for Prime Minister Eden, in Downing Street, to recall picking up the transatlantic phone and hearing a flow of soldierly language at the other end "so furious I had to hold the instrument away from my ear" illustrates the harsh truth that national self-interest will usually, if not always, triumph over a fuzzy concept such as the so-called Special Relationship.★

Similarly, in 1965 differing views on Vietnam led Lyndon Johnson to assess the British premier Harold Wilson as "a creep," while Richard Nixon in turn privately considered Edward Heath "weak" and "as crooked as a corkscrew," which was surely high praise coming from that quarter. Nor did the British relinquish this peripheral role when Ronald Reagan found himself in power at the same time as Margaret Thatcher in the 1980s, frequently ruffling her feathers on issues ranging from the Strategic Defense Initiative to the us invasion of Grenada. In more recent years, we've seen Tony Blair pandering to George W. Bush and Gordon Brown agonizing over the most "culturally correct" gift to take Barack Obama and receiving some hastily acquired DVDs (in a format incompatible with British technology) in return. This has been roughly the state of affairs in the Atlantic alliance right up to the time of President Biden and Prime Minister Sunak in 2023.

The one significant exception to the rule of postwar Anglo-American relations is the presidency of John F. Kennedy. It's true that there were moments of mutual exasperation in Kennedy's dealings with his British counterpart Harold Macmillan, both on a personal and a strategic level. Although the specific details are in some doubt, it's agreed that the libidinous young president once turned to the monogamous, if not celibate, prime minister (born under the reign of Queen Victoria) at the end of a long meeting and mildly enquired, "I wonder how it is with you, Harold? If I don't have a woman for three days, I get a terrible headache."[1]

Then there was the occasion, in August 1962, when Macmillan returned from an afternoon's grouse shoot on the Yorkshire moors to find a telegram awaiting him to casually announce

---

★ In some versions, it was William Clark, Eden's press secretary, who had the misfortune to take the president's call.

that Washington was about to supply a consignment of Hawk surface-to-air missiles to Israel, so preempting a possible sale of Britain's own Bloodhound rocket. Macmillan's immediately cabled salvo to Kennedy was not notable for its deference or restraint. There was no salutation. "I have just received the information [about the missiles]," it began, "and that the decision will be conveyed to the Israelis tomorrow. This follows two years of close co-operation during which we decided [the sale] would be unwise." After some more in this vein, Macmillan went on to get personal. "I cannot believe," he fumed, "that you were privy to this disgraceful piece of trickery. For myself I must say frankly that I can hardly find words to express my sense of disgust and despair. Nor do I see how you and I are to conduct the great affairs of the world on this basis."

Four months later, the same two leaders went on to have a contentious meeting at Nassau on the question of Britain's continued right to possess an independent nuclear deterrent. Following the discussions, the president archly remarked that "looking at it from the [British] point of view – which they do almost better than anybody – it might well be concluded" that they were entitled to such a weapon.[2] One of Kennedy's final acts in office was to commission a report on the whole affair, which he read over the weekend of November 16–17, 1963, as he prepared to leave for campaign trips in Florida and Texas. The First Lady recalled him saying ruefully of the task, "If you want to know what my life is like, read this." It was the only government paper he ever gave her. An annotated copy of the report – mischievously suggesting it might be sent on as a Christmas gift to Macmillan – was found on top of the files in Kennedy's briefcase following his assassination.

But on the whole, John Kennedy's story is remarkable for the distance that he put between his views and those that forged his father Joseph's notorious World War II isolationism (if not his clinical Anglophobia) and the way in which, with variations of technique and tempo, the young, Democratic president came to share a common purpose and vision of the world with his seemingly decrepit, Conservative British counterpart. Of course, there were compelling tactical reasons for the exceptional closeness of the Atlantic alliance in the years 1961–1963. This was the era of the Berlin Wall and the Cuban Missile Crisis, among several other Soviet-inspired threats to global peace and security. But there are almost always human factors behind political relationships. Kennedy and Macmillan liked each other, in general admired each other, shared a mutual connection to the superbly aristocratic Cavendish family and their ancestral home, and each of them was prepared up to a point to bend his nation's policy to accommodate the other's needs – for example, in Kennedy's guaranteeing the continued British nuclear arsenal over the objections of most of his cabinet and senior advisers at the Nassau summit in December 1962, which was, as one American observer said, "a case of 'king to king,' [which] infuriated the court."[3]

Kennedy was surely unique among American presidents not only in the depth of his personal prior experience of Britain and Western Europe, but in the almost Shakespearian struggle he waged for some twenty-five years in order to distance his Atlantic policy from that of his still living father. Joseph Kennedy, at least in his tenure as us ambassador to Britain, did not always make a sympathetic figure. He was authoritarian and brusque both with British officials and his own staff (one of whom was found to be a pro-Nazi spy), and while becoming increasingly isolationist and defeatist about Britain's prospects in the war with Germany, he showed little concern for the sensibilities of the host government once hostilities were declared and even less for the feelings of the British people as they came under a rain of enemy bombs. While still serving as his nation's representative, Joe argued strongly against giving military or economic aid to the United Kingdom. "Democracy is finished in England. It may be here," he notoriously stated in an American newspaper interview in November 1940.[4]

At the time Ambassador Kennedy made these remarks, ordinary British citizens were being killed on a nightly basis in German incendiary bombing raids. Just forty-eight hours later, the English midlands city of Coventry was subjected to a sustained terror assault by 515 enemy aircraft, with the loss of an estimated 650 civilian lives and 5,300 buildings, including the town's medieval cathedral. His comments, consequently, were not well received by the British public as a whole. Kennedy in fact contrived to spend much of his time while in office on home leave in the United States, including a four-month sabbatical in the critical period from November 1939 to March 1940, and even when compelled to remain in England he increasingly preferred to inhabit a seventy-room mansion (today the home of the Legoland theme park) in the western countryside around Windsor rather than to risk personal harm in London.[5] As one unattributable but popular quote of the day had it, "I thought my daffodils were yellow until I met Joe Kennedy."

It has to be said that as ambassador, Kennedy also exhibited a consistently poor sense of timing and protocol. In September 1940, he was once unavoidably close to the scene of a Nazi bombing raid, and his essential contempt for the British people was seen in the offhand remark he made at the time to an embassy colleague named Harvey Klemmer. "The first night of the blitz," Klemmer recalled, "we walked down Piccadilly and he [Kennedy] said I'd bet you five to one any sum that Hitler will be in Buckingham Palace in two weeks."[6] According to the ambassador's generally forgiving biographer David Nasaw, it reached the point where "the British Foreign Office began to monitor [Kennedy's] activities as if he were an enemy agent … They were so concerned by his endless badmouthing of British war efforts that they debated whether to notify [the United Kingdom ambassador] Lord Lothian in Washington and, if necessary, ask him to speak to Mr. Roosevelt."[7]

It may well be, as has been argued, that Joe Kennedy's attitudes to Britain in her hour of peril were founded less on the principle of American isolationism per se than on the fear of a worldwide economic collapse in the event of a prolonged war. In late July 1939, as Hitler planned the further realization of his dream of Lebensraum – the occupation of Poland – Kennedy in turn arranged to take an extended family vacation on the French Riviera. "I am leaving tomorrow on a holiday," he wired President Roosevelt, "and before I go, I would like to tell you about what I regard as the makings of the worst market conditions the world has ever seen ... I feel more pessimistic [about] this than ever."[8]

Kennedy's despondency would seem to have been moved by considerations of racial theory as much as pure economics. "I get very disturbed reading what's taking place in America on the Jewish question,"[9] he wrote in November 1938, voicing his concern that a concerted "Hebrew lobby" would conspire to force the United States into a war with Germany. The following year, Kennedy was agitating, possibly on what he considered humanitarian grounds, for the widespread resettlement of European Jews in remote parts of Venezuela, Costa Rica, and Haiti. More than a decade later, he still seemed bemused at the negative reaction to many of his pre-war policies and initiatives, blaming it in part on "a number of Jewish publishers and writers" who had somehow wanted to provoke a fight with Hitler.[10]

★　★　★

AS THIS BOOK hopefully shows, John F. Kennedy made a long, arduous, but ultimately successful journey to free himself from the taint of his father's attitudes and prejudices as seen in the critical years leading up to World War II. Although he took longer to outgrow some of those beliefs than others, the younger man came of political age with astonishing speed. Barely two decades after his father's inglorious departure from London, Kennedy was elected president – an office to which he brought an obvious and profound sympathy for the British position on almost every substantive issue. (Even then, the seventy-two-year-old former ambassador retained his sense of presumed authority, briskly informing his son, the president-elect, that he should nominate his younger brother Bobby to be attorney general, for example.) It remains to be fully seen how much of Jack Kennedy's path to power was the result of conscious opposition to his father and how much was simply a brilliantly shrewd reaction to changing events and circumstances. In either case, it's also worth noting that there was a part of America's thirty-fifth president, whether innate or acquired, that was "more English than the English."

Time and again in the Kennedy–Macmillan partnership, it was the "cocky young Yank" (as a Foreign Office minister once called him) who proved to be the cool and phlegmatic one and the avuncular Briton who often worked himself up into a nervous state to an extent that made him physically ill before delivering a major speech. In July 1963, on hearing the news of a successful outcome to nuclear test-ban negotiations in Moscow, Macmillan, having waited anxiously by his phone all day, promptly burst into tears of relief. Kennedy's own published schedule for the day in question notes only some routine meetings with cabinet officers and visiting Ethiopian dignitaries, although it's thought he may have allowed himself a celebratory cigar following his mid-afternoon swim. Similarly, Kennedy loved British historical literature and political gossip; although afflicted by a whole series of truly debilitating illnesses, he apparently thought it bad form to speak of such things in public. As his close British friend David Ormsby-Gore, son of Lord Harlech, remarked, "He was somebody who didn't like the display of undue emotions … His character told him that people who become hysterical and get overexcited don't usually have good judgment – it's not actually an emotion for which he had any great admiration."[11] In short, Kennedy – the embodiment of the American New Frontier – was in some ways more stereotypically an Englishman.

In London, Joe Kennedy's popularity had reached the lowest point of its curve with his notorious "Democracy is finished" outburst in 1940. "While he was here his suave monotonous smile, his nine over-photographed children and his hail-fellow-well-met manner concealed a hard-boiled business man's eagerness to do a profitable deal with the dictators and deceive many English people," A. J. Cummings wrote in the London *News Chronicle*.[12] It wasn't just that the soon-to-depart ambassador had appeared to betray the trust of his nation's closest ally. His perfidy also seemed to undermine the political prospects of his two oldest sons, Joe Jr. and Jack, both of them frequently resident at the embassy in London and each, in his own way, with ambitions of future public service. It was a case of "the old name be[ing] mud in England for the next generation," Jack noted ruefully to a local friend.[13] The twenty-three-year-old was even sufficiently moved to write to his father in December 1940 to complain that he found himself being personally attacked in the British press as "being an appeaser and a defeatist." That sort of reputation could prove ruinous to Kennedys both young and old, he went on to warn. "It must be remembered continually that you wish to shake off the word 'appeaser,'" Jack told his father. "It seems to me that if this label is tied to you it may nullify your immediate effectiveness, even though in the long run you may be proved correct."[14] "We regarded the [former] ambassador with some contempt," Harold Macmillan confirmed following the American presidential election of 1960. "It was generally thought he was unfriendly, and defeatist … I had no particular reason to have any affection for his son."[15]

In all, then, John Kennedy's legacy from his father was mixed: he enjoyed certain contacts and points of access in the higher echelons of British society not normally open to a young American undergraduate. But set against this, he was tarred with the same brush as the ex-ambassador – "Jittery Joe" – whom many in England saw not only as a self-centered and crooked "twister," but also as positively ludicrous in some of his social affectations. Longing to be accepted as a shrewd and progressive businessman, Joe was at the same time touchingly gratified to mingle with the ancient British aristocracy. Never a martyr to false modesty, he shamelessly exploited all the prerequisites and privileges available to him as his country's envoy, while complaining that people accepted him only because of his official position. One diary account remembers him as "almost endearing ... There [was] a sort of childlike innocence in the way he crashed through the stately homes of England, addressing his hosts as 'Hiya, Dook,' etc, and frequently jumping up to offer to buy their family heirlooms, or to pass round their own food and drink in front of the fireplace at teatime ... An absolutely negligible individual in everything except money."[16]

Without delving too far into the briar patch of psychology, it seems fair to say that the young John Kennedy was deeply conflicted in his formative views about Britain. On the one hand, there was his father's bedrock belief that the British as a whole were effete, corrupt, and essentially decadent, as perversely stubborn in war as in peace, and that their best bet in the dark days of late 1940 would have been to graciously accept defeat. On the other hand, there was the fact that neither of the younger Kennedy's parents was immune to the charms of British high society in general and to her ruling elite in particular. Time and again, we see this curious mixture of condescension, if not open contempt, coexisting with a marked degree of respect and even hero worship on the part of the Kennedys while in England. "We came up in an embassy car ... and drove through a large and beautiful park to arrive at the castle at 7:00 pm," the ambassador's wife Rose wrote, a shade breathlessly, of an April 1938 house party spent with King George and Queen Elizabeth at Windsor. "We were met by the Master of the Household, who conducted us to our rooms. There were numerous servants in evidence, in full livery. One of them soon brought us sherry. That weekend was one of the most fabulous, fascinating experiences of my life."[17]

Of course, it's not the case that Jack Kennedy's parents single-handedly determined his later attitude to Great Britain or to anything else. Faced with a loud, brash, indefatigable father like Joe, a child could reasonably be expected to go one of two ways: inward or outward. There's little evidence that the senior Kennedy was ever physically violent or even particularly "abusive" to his family in the modern sense. But Joe certainly impressed his views forcibly enough on his two oldest sons, whom he treated more as promising if occasionally wayward business apprentices than he did their seven younger siblings, and whom he clearly saw as destined for public service in some capacity. "Since my two boys are eventually going to make their homes [for electoral purposes] in Massachusetts," the recently retired ambassador wrote in February 1942 to his associate David Sarnoff, the president of RCA, "I would be interested in purchasing any radio station that you might have for sale in Boston ... My energy from now on will be tied up in their careers rather than my own."[18]

All of this was to lead to the outcome *Kennedy and Great Britain* seeks to grasp. Essentially, it's a tale of two Kennedys; of how a father and son reacted so differently to the coming of a world war, and how some of the younger man's sympathies and responses at that time of crisis directly informed his policy positions when he came to enter the White House just twenty years later. Unlike his father, for example, Jack actively backed President Roosevelt's "Lend-Lease" shipment of food, oil, and materiel to the beleaguered British people starting in March 1941. "There is a real feeling," he noted, "that outright and total support for Great Britain is not only preferable but essential for long-term survival and stability [here] in the States ... We have no choice now but to make ourselves, and our friends, strong."[19] This "granite truth," as he called it, would find its counterpart not only in President Kennedy's later insistence that the British be indulged in their desire for their own nuclear capability but also in his recall of seventy-one-year-old Averell Harriman, the chief broker of the Lend-Lease deal, to join with the British delegation in three-way strategic arms limitation talks with Nikita Khrushchev's Soviet Union.

Contrast this with the stated opinion of Ambassador Kennedy, writing in terms of confidence (perhaps wisely) at the time of the Lend-Lease program to his friend J. J. Astor: "I hate all those goddamned Englishmen from Churchill on down."[20] Speaking in November 1941 of his father's decision to arrange a lobotomy for his mentally challenged sister Rosemary (a procedure that had the effect of reducing her to a human vegetable for the remaining sixty-three years of her life), John Kennedy told a friend that the tragedy "confirmed that vital part of me, that has always been, at heart, a fatalist." It was an outlook, the twenty-four-year-old added, that had made him "confront unavoidable facts, grim realities, and awful possibilities about the times in which we find ourselves abandoned. It has also made me realize something more simple. Father does not always know best."[21]

★ ★ ★

LIKE MOST American presidents, John Kennedy has attracted the interest of psychiatrists, and several works have been published paying particular note to his early family circumstances, which were both materially privileged on an epic scale and predicated on the idea of future public duty. It is not the contention of this book that Kennedy's whole subsequent career was somehow the outcome of a "father complex" as the Freudians define it. The degree of sheer pragmatism obvious in his time both as a congressman and president clearly outweighed any other single factor. But it could be plausibly argued that Kennedy absorbed early on his parents' mutual confidence that he would prove to be someone special who would achieve great things; and that from around his early twenties he was on an intellectual and moral quest to distance his views of America's place in the world from those of his father. The combination was to prove a powerful legacy.

"Jack," a close British friend noted, "was obsessed by his father. The old man was his god, the sense of his life. In [later] years, Jack always thought of the other world leaders he met as either the 'get-along,' or the 'unrelenting' and 'uncompromising' type. The irony was that the latter were obviously more of a known quantity, as he could at least call on about twenty years of childhood experience in dealing with them."[22] By the same logic, it could be said that Harold Macmillan was a patriarchal figure to Kennedy, in the more benign sense of the term. In contrast, there was the "fat, vulgar man with his pig eyes and his ceaseless flow of talk"[23] – at once ludicrous and terrifying – who ran the Soviet Union. "He treated me like a little boy, like a little boy!"[24] the US president and commander-in-chief complained, pacing the floor of his Viennese hotel bedroom, after meeting Nikita Khrushchev for bilateral talks in June 1961. "It was like being chewed out by the old man," Kennedy added later that week to a friend in London.[25]

John Kennedy may have inherited his father's values in some ways, then, but from early adulthood he showed a refreshing willingness to go his own way when it came to what was then widely considered the proper and consistent means of assessing an American statesman: his attitudes to his country's historic ally Britain and, conversely, to the threat of Soviet communist aggression and subversion. This independence of spirit wasn't one invariably shared by other members of the Kennedy clan. The ambassador's heir-apparent, Joe Jr. (1915–1944), maintained the family tradition during the depths of Britain's darkest wartime hour by declaring in a January 1941 speech that the United States should refuse to supply her old friend with food or other commodities, even if this policy resulted in a Nazi victory. In the latter event, Joe believed, "a barter trading system should be devised between America and Hitler to preserve the economic status quo."[26]

Three months later, in the face of published evidence of German atrocities against Jewish civilians in Poland, France, and elsewhere in Europe, Joe Jr. informed an audience at the Hebrew temple of Ohabei Shalom in suburban Boston that it would be "perfectly feasible for the United States to exist as a nation, regardless of who wins the war," and again condemned the "folly" of the Lend-Lease program or any other form of material supply to the British people.[27] Although time and events might have conspired to modify some of these opinions, we can only speculate on what might have become of the Atlantic alliance had the oldest Kennedy son, rather than his sickly younger brother, ultimately become US president.

Similarly, Robert Kennedy (1925–1968), too young to comment authoritatively on the origins of the world war, later proved only a critical friend of British interests. In December 1961, for example, as the ranking member of his brother's cabinet, he argued against the grant of any American financing of the Upper Volta Dam project – a scheme Prime Minister Macmillan had championed tirelessly over the course of many months, arguing that to avoid the issue would be to drive Ghana – like Egypt before it – into the Soviet camp. Eventually announcing that the United States would furnish some $95 million toward the construction costs, President Kennedy acknowledged that it was not a universally popular decision within either the administration as a whole or his own family. "I can feel the Attorney General's hot breath of disapproval on the back of my neck," he admitted.[28]

In terms of the Atlantic alliance, we need linger only briefly over the career of the fourth and youngest Kennedy son, Edward (1932–2009), who in 1971 likened the British presence in Northern Ireland (a democratically established part of the UK) to the American invasion of Vietnam, among other similar effusions over the years. The constitutional historian Andrew Roberts expressed a widely held view when he wrote that Britain's 2009 decision to grant the then mortally ill Ted Kennedy an honorary knighthood was "nothing short of obscene."[29]

Besides Jack himself, the one obvious exception to the rule among the Kennedy siblings was Kathleen, or "Kick" (1920–1948), who for the last ten years of her life made England her home, and who in May 1944 went on to marry William "Billy" Cavendish, heir to the tenth duke of Devonshire, who as a captain in the British army died in action in Belgium only three months later. Cavendish being both a Conservative and more importantly a Protestant, the bride's parents were unmoved by this union with one of Britain's oldest established families, the inheritors of a stately home tradition it may be difficult to imagine outside of a PBS costume drama. As marchioness of Hartington, Kick would spend much of her brief married life at the 175-room Chatsworth House in the English Midlands. The property included twelve thousand acres of parkland, an estimated twenty-three kitchens, seventeen staircases, and a full-time staff of between fifty-two and seventy. Impressive as it was, this was only one of a half-dozen Cavendish family estates scattered throughout the British Isles, which they moved around between on their private train. Rose Kennedy nonetheless wrote bitterly of the "defection" of her daughter, and later expressed her "horror" at Kick's marriage: "I thought it would have such mighty repercussions in that every little young girl would say if Kathleen Kennedy can, why can't I? ... Everyone pointed to our family with pride as well-behaved, level-headed, and deeply religious." Rose concluded sadly, "What a blow to the Kennedy prestige."[30]

Even Jack, if on less narrowly priggish grounds, had his doubts about Kick's choice of husband. "After reading the paper, I would advise strongly against any voyages to England [to] marry any Englishman," he wrote her in March 1942. "For I have come to the reluctant conclusion that it has come time to write the obituary of the British Empire. Like all good things, it had to come to an end sometime, it was nice while it lasted." Jack's essential position, which had more than a ring of his father's about it, was that Britain had been in a slow and painful decline for many years before the outbreak of hostilities with Germany. "It goes back, I think, fundamentally, far beyond any special event," he wrote. "It goes back to a state of mind really, which is a phase of its organic growth. When a nation finally reaches the point that its primary aim is to preserve the status quo, it's approaching old age. When it reaches the point where it is willing to sacrifice part of its status quo to keep the rest, it's gone beyond being old, it's dying – and that is the state of mind England reached some time ago."[31]

Just four years after her husband's death, Kathleen herself was killed in a plane crash while on her way from Paris to the French Riviera in the company of another wealthy English aristocrat, the Earl of Fitzwilliam. Because Fitzwilliam was both outside of the Catholic faith and married, this particular liaison had driven Kathleen's parents to fresh transports of fury. In time, Rose would privately advise her daughter that she would be disinherited were she not to immediately break off the affair and return to Boston. Ambassador Kennedy, who had been on business in France at the time, was the only member of the family to attend Kathleen's funeral. There were no public memorials, endowments, or charities established in her name. Fifteen years later, John Kennedy, on an official visit to Britain, ordered a last-minute detour to Chatsworth, where he paid an impromptu visit to his sister's grave. As an Anglo-American entourage watched at a discreet distance, the president knelt and prayed there in the rain – surely the most vivid single image in history of the human face of the Atlantic special relationship.

It's not known how, if at all, the decline of the British Empire disqualified Billy Cavendish as a husband for Kathleen Kennedy, but it may be remembered that Jack wrote his letter at a time of profound Allied gloom at the recent loss of Singapore to the Japanese, with the surrender of some eighty thousand British, Australian, and Indian troops, a blow Winston Churchill characterized as the "worst disaster" and "the largest capitulation in our military history." It was certainly not the empire's finest hour.

Nor was John Kennedy's disquiet in March 1942 entirely typical of his views on Britain and the British people as a whole – just the opposite. His note of regret to Kathleen was caused not by disillusionment with Great Britain itself but by the failings of the British military planners. Elsewhere, he wrote, "I have the highest respect for [Prime Minister Churchill] and the great sovereign people of that island." It was more than respect. As we'll see, when it came to Churchill, it was almost a case of infatuation.

In August 1943, after his PT boat was rammed by a Japanese destroyer, Lieutenant John Kennedy and his shipmates spent a week on an inhospitable Pacific island before he was able to scratch an SOS message on a coconut with a pocketknife and have it taken to the nearest Allied base. At that stage, the odds appeared to be strongly against the success of Kennedy's mission or the rescue of a ship's crew that had survived thus far largely on a diet of leaves and palm oil. The next morning, however, a native wearing a loincloth appeared in a canoe, marched smartly up to Kennedy, saluted, said in Oxford English, "I have a letter for you, sir," and handed over a sheet of paper. It was from one Reg Evans, an Anglo–New Zealander coastguard officer attached to the Royal Navy who was currently stationed in a small hut concealed behind the Japanese lines. Neatly headed *On His Majesty's Service*, Evans wrote, "Have just learnt of your presence … I strongly advise you return immediately here in this canoe, and by the time you arrive I shall be in Radio communication with authorities." The native bearer stood to attention, a Union Jack tattoo swelling on his naked forearm, while Kennedy incredulously read this news of his salvation from what had seemed to be an inevitable slow death by starvation. A mug of strong tea was then poured out from a crested flask and ceremonially handed to the young American, along with a plate of dry, Admiralty-issue ships' biscuits, when he embarked on the canoe. "You've got to hand it to the British," Kennedy remarked admiringly.[32]

Jack's real affection for Britain and for certain trappings of the "faded [but] glorious" old empire would make an important contribution to his later policy. There's also the significant fact that he was present in London during some of the most critical weeks of the gathering international storm of 1938–1939, and that he later used the experience in his Harvard thesis-turned-bestseller *Why England Slept*, which can be read both as a timely call for American rearmament and an intellectual rebuke by a twenty-two-year-old undergraduate of his appeasement-minded father. In fact, with the timing of a Leonard Zelig, the younger Kennedy managed to show up at some of the most seminal moments of twentieth-century British history. On September 3, 1939, to give just the most obvious example, he was seated with his family in the strangers' gallery of the House of Commons to hear Prime Minister Neville Chamberlain announce, in terms that again conveyed a certain quintessentially British coolness under fire: "Our ambassador in Berlin hand[ed] in at 9 o'clock this morning a note which read, 'Sir ... I have the honour to inform you that, unless not later than 11 am, British Summer Time, today 3rd September, satisfactory assurances that the German Government has suspended all aggressive action against Poland ... have reached His Majesty's Government in London, a state of war will exist between the two countries as from that hour.' ... No such undertaking has been received by the time stipulated," Chamberlain continued, "and consequently this country is at war with Germany ... I cannot tell what part I may be allowed to play myself. I trust I may live to see the day when Hitlerism has been destroyed and a liberated Europe has been re-established."[33]

Both of Kennedy's parents later spoke of how moved they were by Chamberlain's speech and how deeply sorry they were for him personally. For Jack, however, the "high moment of the day" was when Winston Churchill rose to his feet to announce, "Outside, the storms of war may blow and the lands may be lashed with the fury of its gales, but in our own hearts this Sunday morning there is peace. Our consciences are at rest ... This is no war for domination or imperial aggrandisement or material gain; no war to shut any country out of its sunlight and means of progress. It is a war ... to establish, on impregnable rocks, the rights of the individual, and it is a war to establish and revive the stature of man."[34]

It would be hard to think of a more character-forming experience for the lean, sandy-haired boy from Boston crouching forward in his seat just a few feet above the chamber (close enough to be rebuked by an usher for taking notes "within sight of Honourable Members," in contravention of parliamentary rules) where these words were spoken. Nearly six years later, John Kennedy would again witness history in the making when he came to report on the San Francisco conference that established the United Nations, before in turn flying on to the devastated capitals of England and Germany. On a visit to the Allied summit at Potsdam, the twenty-eight-year-old had the opportunity to see the likes of President Truman up close with Churchill's successor Clement Attlee, as well as a Soviet delegation that included the trio of Stalin, Molotov, and Gromyko. As Dwight Eisenhower was also present in his role as supreme Allied commander, the same Berlin suburb thus played host to three present and future American presidents. As part of his tour, Kennedy was able to visit both Hitler's bunker and his ruined mountain retreat at Berchtesgaden. At a nearby alpine hotel, the visitors enjoyed a "six-course dinner – Rhine wines and champagne – [and] some cigars taken from Goering's armored car."[35] In this rarefied atmosphere, Kennedy seemed to be philosophical and even guardedly respectful toward the late führer: "[Hitler] had a mystery to him in the way that he lived and in the manner of his death that will live and grow after him ... He had in him the stuff of which legends are made," Jack wrote.[36]

From September 3, 1939, onward, John Kennedy would routinely run a sharp eye over the transactions of the British House of Commons, focusing on a tight circle of leading politicians and subjecting it to his fascinated and lingering scrutiny even after he assumed the leadership of the free world and had other things on his agenda. At the height of the Cuban missile affair in October 1962, the president invariably took the time during his nightly hotline calls to Prime Minister Macmillan to ask him how he was coping with his domestic opposition and often to inquire at length about the precise figures in that day's parliamentary vote. Kennedy placed one such call at midnight, London time, on October 25. He had spent most of that day discussing with his advisers whether or not to "take out" Cuba and thus risk a full-scale nuclear exchange with the Soviet Union. The first thing he said on the phone was, "Harold, how did you do with your debate?"[37]

It's been said that Kennedy was temperamentally more of a parliamentarian than a congressman, better suited to the cut-and-thrust of cross-party debate than to the set-piece orations and soaring rhetoric of the US Senate, whose denizens would probably wear togas if they felt they could get away with it.

Of course, Kennedy was also "an Irishman," at least by sentimental family tradition. A pathological distrust of the British has been almost an article of faith for long stretches of Irish history, and Kennedy was well aware of the part played in his family's story by social and religious inequality. In fact, it was one of the points impressed on him during his brief time in 1935 studying under Professor Harold Laski at the London School of Economics. "In speaking of Boston, he [Laski] said, 'Boston is a state of mind' – and as a Jew, he could understand what it is to be an Irishman in Boston," the eighteen-year-old overseas student wrote in his diary. "That last remark reveals the fundamental, activating force of Mr. Laski's life – a powerful spirit doomed to an inferior position because of race – a position that all of his economic and intellectual superiority cannot raise him out of."[38]

Thomas Kiernan, Dublin's notably perceptive ambassador to the United States during the Kennedy administration, felt that the president avoided the "misty" view of Ireland represented by "prancing little green elves" or "Bing Crosby hamming his way through some movie." Instead, the president was "more British than Irish … It's the New England attitude in him, I suppose, it's the Harvard attitude … Kennedy's first reaction, if there were any even minor dispute between Britain and Ireland, would be to side with Britain."[39] The long-serving Washington journalist and Kennedy confidant Hugh Sidey put it simply: "He was an Anglophile. Kennedy … delighted in the romantic accounts of the rise of the British Empire and the great figures on the battlefields or in parliament who made it possible. When he was in the White House and I asked for a list of his ten favorite books, the top three were about British history."[40]

In time, this affinity not only influenced and molded Kennedy's core belief in the Atlantic special relationship. It also fuelled his unshakable admiration for the way the British – or at least a certain kind of Briton – reacted to adversity. In the 1930s, "Kennedy saw the consequences of the Depression at first-hand, and was struck by the manner in which Westminster politics sought to combat them," the historian David Nunnerley writes. "He held a fascination for British political society, with its seemingly casual combination of deeply held concern, steadfast commitment, dry and sardonic wit and above all sheer knowledge."[41] Comparing the laid-back but generally effective approach of certain rising young English politicians of his own generation to their American counterparts, Kennedy observed, "It's like watching a Rolls-Royce purring along on one side, and a bus being driven downhill by the Marx Brothers on the other."[42] He took special interest in the British Whig statesmen of the late eighteenth and early nineteenth centuries. "The Whig lord," wrote David Cecil in his study *The Young Melbourne* (the top of the list of ten books Kennedy gave Hugh Sidey), "was as often as not a minister, his eldest son an MP, his second attached to a foreign embassy, so that their houses were alive with the effort and hurry of politics."[43] There was an obvious resonance to Kennedy's own upbringing, where the premium was on constant hustle and a spirited competitiveness between all nine siblings.

In a way, Kennedy's respect for the British political class was one of temperament and character. He liked the sense of aristocratic languor that permeated the great stately homes, where it was such an important part of the ethics that one should never seem to be working. "He was terrifically snobbish, you know," the columnist Joe Alsop wrote. "But not what people normally call snobbish. He was terribly old-fashioned, almost like, sort of English grandee kind of snobbishness. It was kind of a snobbery of style." Even at moments of acute crisis during his presidency, Kennedy tended to treat men and events alike with a kind of polite irony. Anything but an armed assault on Cuba would be "as bad as the appeasement at Munich," the bluff, cigar-chewing air force chief Curtis LeMay told the president at a White House meeting on October 19, 1962, a possibly ironic rebuke to a man who had once written a bestselling book on the subject. When LeMay proceeded to inform his commander-in-chief, "You're in a pretty bad fix at the present time," Kennedy allowed himself a sardonic smile and replied merely, "Well, you're in there with me."[44]

In private, Kennedy sometimes extended his Anglophilia to a consideration of the more obvious visual differences between the political classes of London and Washington. "Half my cabinet look like they're about to go play in a suburban bowling league," he once complained.[45]

★ ★ ★

PRESIDENT KENNEDY set out his foreign policy aims in his first State of the Union address on January 30, 1961. "It is vital," he said, "that we are never lulled into believing that either the Soviet Union or China has yielded its ambitions for world domination … Our task is to convince them that aggression and subversion will not be profitable routes to pursue these ends."[46] A few days later, Kennedy went on to tell his ambassador to Peru that Latin America was "vital … and require[d] our best efforts and attention."[47] Relations with France and West Germany were also "vital," he added in cabinet, because those countries were close allies in the "drive for peace in Berlin, in Germany, and in Europe."[48] But what did "vital" mean? Did it necessarily involve a "special relationship"? Or merely a strategic alliance to help secure Europe's peace and freedom? On February 6, 1961, Kennedy sent a personal note to Harold Macmillan telling him that, while us undertakings elsewhere in the world were currently under review, "I am happy to confirm the continuance ... of Anglo-United States Understandings ... Needless to say, I personally welcome this continuing evidence of the intimacy with which our countries work together in all matters."[49] Kennedy did not come out in public and announce that any one country or region was more "vital" to American interests than any other one. All were equally important in their own way when it came to the larger framework of us foreign policy, he said. But it is possible that some were more equal to him than others.

Kennedy persisted with the Atlantic special relationship for more than just sentimental reasons that resulted from his youthful experiences in London and elsewhere. He wanted such a close alliance with Britain primarily because he believed that the ussr would continue its rolling campaign of imposing carbon copies of its regime on Central and Eastern Europe. He was also well aware of Britain's diminished but still impressively widespread colonial influence in territories ranging from Guiana to Ghana, where, left to themselves, local tensions might be escalated to the point that threatened to trigger an East–West nuclear event. No other nation provided the distinctive and positive support to us interests around the globe that Britain did. The relationship as a whole "rested and flourished to a large degree upon the extension by Great Britain to the United States of a determined assumption of common interest that had – and still has – no equivalent elsewhere," David Nunnerley writes. "The cohesion of the alliance was similarly enhanced by a degree of confidence, openness and reciprocity rarely equaled in international relations."[50] To many Americans and Britons alike, of a certain generation, it must seem as if their whole lives have been spent in the shadow of repeated official assertions of the unique partnership that exists between their two nations. As recently as the UK's general election of 2015, the Labour leader Ed Milliband made it a centerpiece of his keynote campaign speech on foreign policy that, were he alive, President Kennedy would "argue fiercely that Britain should stay in the European Union," before noting that Kennedy had a "deep affection for the traditions and people of Great Britain," an uncontroversial slogan.

But it wasn't just mutual strategic self-interest or a common assumption about communist ambitions that so dramatically strengthened the Anglo-American alliance in the early 1960s. It also took a personal commitment by the man who above all others helped to shape events and to determine policy, the British-loving president of the United States. Anyone doubting Kennedy's lifelong attentiveness to Britain or his almost obsessive concern about what ordinary Britons thought of him should consult the archive at his presidential library, which still contains some five thousand letters written to him by individual British citizens, or read his instruction, shortly after taking office, that the US Information Agency conduct a poll to determine his personal popularity in Britain as a whole. (The agency's gratifying conclusion: "The reactions to your [inaugural address] were overwhelmingly favorable, with 80 per cent voicing [a] good to very good opinion and only 2 per cent [an] adverse opinion … The aspects of your speech which look to have most favorably impressed British auditors were the elements of challenge and inspiration, and the candor about current problems and the difficult times ahead.")[51]

Some of the friendships Kennedy made in Britain during the late 1930s and early 1940s later had a direct bearing on American foreign policy. There was the president's instant acceptance of his fellow London swinger David Ormsby-Gore's advice on the "quarantine" aspect of the Cuban missile crisis, for instance, or the private White House dinner he held for the British Conservative MP Hugh Fraser, a family friend since 1939, during which Fraser persuasively laid out the options for future Western policy in British Guiana. One senior us official noted ruefully that Kennedy "gave more of his undivided time to his old British chums than he did to his own cabinet officers." At the height of the Cuban crisis, Vice President Johnson similarly complained that "the limey" (uk ambassador Ormsby-Gore) was seated front and center at a meeting of a steering group in the White House situation room, while he, the nation's second-ranking executive, was "down in a chair at the end, with the goddamned door banging into my back."[52]

In 1961, amplifying in the London *Sunday Times* on his "deep affection" for Harold Macmillan and, by extension, the British people, as compared to other friendly states, Kennedy established for all time the true nature of the Atlantic special relationship as he saw it: "I feel at home with Harold because I can share my loneliness with him," the president said. "The others are all foreigners to me."[53]

2

MY TRIP ABROAD

ON JANUARY 25, 1933, five days before Hitler came to power, the Oxford University debating union passed by a large majority the motion that "This House will under no consideration fight for its king and country." It was far from the only such anomaly in British public life, as it may now seem to us in the light of future events. Three weeks later, speaking at the Queen's Hall, London, Winston Churchill praised the Italian fascist dictator Benito Mussolini as "the Roman genius." He was "the greatest law-giver among living men," Churchill added, a veritable titan who "has indicated the path that a nation can follow when courageously led."[1] In June of that year, Mussolini orchestrated the Pact of Four between Italy, Great Britain, Germany, and France, a means by which a "numerically small but powerful elite of like-minded states" could act outside of the cumbersome machinery of the League of Nations. Later that week, David Lloyd George, Britain's former wartime Liberal prime minister, told the Italian ambassador Dino Grandi of his "sincere admiration" for Mussolini: "Either the world follows the Duce or the world is doomed ... only your leader has clear vision," the Welshman rhapsodized.[2]

Later that autumn, forty-five-year-old Joseph Kennedy
sailed to London to negotiate an exclusive distribution deal
for Haig and Haig whisky, among other British liquor brands,
taking the new American president's son Jimmy Roosevelt
along with him as a sidekick. Kennedy's traveling companion could only admire his chief's sales patter, he recalled.
"'Mr. Smith (or Brown, or Jones), have you ever considered
the *millions of thirsty Americans*?,' Joe would begin, flashing a
toothsome smile. Then he would invite the hapless mark to
look over a beautifully prepared color manifesto under the
reassuring title, 'Somerset Importers.'" Was the very name not
redolent of pleasant British associations? Kennedy wondered.
By the same process of flattery and smooth talking, he invariably charmed the hardheaded businessmen into compliance,
"and came away with the signature he required."[3] Until he sold
it thirteen years later, Kennedy's liquor wholesale company regularly generated annual gross profits of between $550,000 and
$2.5 million, which respectively translates as some $9.7 million and $43.75 million in today's money. He divested himself
of Somerset Importers in 1946 only because by then certain
American newspapers had begun to raise questions about the
propriety of first-term congressman John F. Kennedy apparently being subsidized by foreign liquor revenue. The original
1933 sales tour had proved a spectacular coup on Joe's part, and
all the more so given that Prohibition still remained legally in
force at the time he and the president's son were sitting down
across the oak-paneled boardroom table from some of Britain's
oldest established scotch and gin executives.

Of course, Kennedy's personalized and highly lucrative version of the Atlantic special relationship didn't mean that either
he or his family invariably took the British side against that of
her European neighbors. His only concern was what was good
for business. Enrolling at the London School of Economics
later in 1933, eighteen-year-old Joe Jr. wrote to his father that it
seemed to him Hitler had "things well under control. The only

danger would be if something happened to Hitler, and one of his crazy ministers came into power, which at this time does not seem likely."[4] Perhaps curiously for a Roman Catholic, young Joe found particular words of praise for "the [Nazi] sterilization law, which I think is a great thing. I don't know how the Church feels about it, but it will do away with many of the disgusting specimens of men which inhabit this earth." In time, Kennedy's father wrote back to announce that he was "very pleased and gratified at your observations of the German situation. I think they show a very keen sense of perception, and I think your conclusions are very sound." It was possible, the future ambassador allowed, that "Hitler went far beyond his necessary requirements in his attitude to the Jews," but in general he was delighted by his firstborn son's grasp of the world situation. "I think you show a great development in your mind in the last six or seven months. It is most gratifying to both Mother and me."[5]

It's worth touching on these views, shocking now but only part of a much larger isolationist movement in America at the time, if only to show that there was nothing inevitable about John Kennedy's later attitudes to Britain, Germany, and the whole future destiny of Western Europe. If anything, Jack spent his formative years in a household – by no means alone in this belief – where European fascism was on the edge of being respectable. As late as June 1938, Ambassador Kennedy would seek out his German counterpart in London, Herbert von Dirksen, who cabled back to Berlin of their talks: "Kennedy said that most [Americans] were afraid of the Jews and did not dare to say anything good about Germany ... He [said] that it was not so much the fact that we wanted to get rid of the Jews that was so harmful to us, but rather the loud clamor with which we accompanied this purpose. He himself understood our Jewish policy completely."[6]

★ ★ ★

IN OCTOBER 1931, John Kennedy, aged fourteen, enrolled as a boarder at the Choate School in Wallingford, Connecticut. His time there was less distinguished by high scholarly achievement on his part than it was by his only variable health (he always seemed to be the "thinnest and palest among us," and in the grip of "constant flu-like symptoms," a classmate recalled) and a perhaps compensatory love of pranks, the most spectacular being his explosion of a toilet seat in the junior lavatories with a powerful firecracker. Jack attained a certain celebrity status among the student body when, next morning, Choate's venerable headmaster George St. John brandished the toilet seat aloft at a school assembly and referred to those who had perpetrated the outrage as "muckers" – a term of abuse for particularly coarse or unskilled Irish laborers of the time. Young Kennedy promptly turned the insult to his advantage, forming a cabal of like-minded souls he called "The Muckers Club."

Kennedy, then, was neither an outstanding academic student nor a popular one with the school authorities. "Jack couldn't or wouldn't conform," his mother Rose was later forced to admit. "He did pretty much what he wanted, rather than what the school wanted of him."[7] As a whole, his problem seems to have been one of application rather than of raw mental firepower. Kennedy was intellectually gifted and sharp tongued ("I've never known anyone in my life with such a wonderful humor," his closest friend LeMoyne "Lem" Billings recalled),[8] with a taste for the satirical wisecrack. According to Jack Maher, another faculty member at Choate, "His attitude was, 'You're a master or a sixth former and I am a lively young fellow with a nimble brain and a bag full of tricks. You will spoil my fun if I let you, so here I go; catch me if you can.'"[9]

It's easy to glimpse in the precocious young Kennedy some of the qualities and attributes that dominated his later life. Never one to pander to authority, he was not entirely a rebel either. Almost comatose in math or modern language classes, he came intensely alive in school debates, civics, and politics and could knock out a convincing two-thousand-word essay on current affairs in about half the time it took anybody else. Almost all his papers were well written; most were rich, uninhibited, and crisply phrased, with sudden and surprising jolts of insight; some bore the imprint of a true author. Kennedy's friend "Rip" Horton remembered that their English teacher once "called Jack aside. We'd all had to write essays or papers. He told Jack that when he went to college and graduated he ought to go into something like journalism because he had a very fluid, mature style for someone his age."[10]

We can also see some of Kennedy's adult foibles in the making during his years at Choate. Tall, gaunt, and seemingly in perpetual motion, he could "light up a room" with a smile like that of a boy in a toothpaste advertisement. It only added to Jack's charm that he seemed to take no interest whatever in his personal appearance or the impression he made on other people. There was a running joke at Choate about his preference for a pair of "cheap, rubber soled sneakers" even during the winter months, and one contemporary remembers him "lurch[ing] into Chapel, tie askew," his feet flapping down the aisle in his outsize shoes "like Charlie Chaplin waddling on his way down a street."[11] For all that, Jack had also given notice of the healthy libido of later legend. Lem Billings (who was bisexual) told the Kennedy Library for the record of a letter his fellow seventeen-year-old had written him in July 1934: "I still have your shaving brush, which I shall return when I get back my seer-sucker coat you slimy fuck," Jack observed. "Have you had Pussy yet? You bitch."[12] According to their mutual friend Rip Horton, around this time Kennedy and Billings "got in a cab and went to a whorehouse in Harlem. First they saw a dirty show and then they went off with the girls. It was about $3," although it was thought that the subsequent medical visit added to the cost of this.

Joseph Kennedy Sr. was then forty-five years old and had been recently appointed as chairman of the Securities and Exchange

Commission by his friend President Roosevelt. It was in some ways a curious sinecure for a man who had amassed a truly fabulous fortune largely on the basis of stock market manipulation. Like his wayward second son, Joe allowed himself a certain leeway in his personal code of conduct. A devout Catholic and outwardly puritanical in his ways, the elder Kennedy had long been in the habit of exploring the limits of his wedding vows to Rose. In December 1927, he'd begun a passionate affair with his protégé, the actress Gloria Swanson, only one of many such moral lapses. The old man later appeared to see it as a form of male bonding to regale Jack with "intimate details of Swanson's body, particularly her genitalia, making fun of Swanson because, he claimed, she was sexually insatiable, having orgasms not once but 'five times a night.'"[13]

In another curious parental choice, Jack once returned home from Choate to "find his bed covered by sex magazines, all open to display the female anatomy at its most immodest. 'I think it's Dad's idea of a joke,'" the teenager was left to conclude.[14] Well into his sixties, the former us ambassador to Great Britain would flirt outrageously with his sons' wives or his daughters' girlfriends. One of John Kennedy's premarital lovers recalls that "the minute Jack was safely out of the room, or even called to the phone, old Joe would try and hop in the sack with me," and he had once gotten as far toward achieving his goal as "scraping his hands up and down my thighs" – an experience like "hav[ing] some dead leaves itching painfully against your skin."[15]

★ ★ ★

EVEN IN 1934, Jack Kennedy had his eye trained on Great Britain. By then his brother Joe had enrolled at the London School of Economics, from where he was able to enjoy an extended field trip to fascist Italy and Germany. Now Jack wanted to follow in Joe's footsteps, but he acknowledged that his latest headmaster's report at Choate might not help his cause.

"Dear Dad: I thought I would write you right away," Jack opened a letter of December 4, 1934. "[Billings] and I have been talking about how poorly we have done this quarter, and we have definitely decided to stop any fooling around. I really do realize how important it is that I get a good job done this year if I want to go to England. I really feel, now that I think it over, that I have been bluffing myself about how much real work I have been doing."[16] A sign of respect for the old man was the untypically neat handwriting Jack displayed in the note. One can admire the charm and modesty of the teenager's appeal, although sadly it failed to win the day. "I have always felt that Jack has a fine mind," Joe Sr. in turn wrote to George St. John. "But I still feel that what he needs to be trained in most is the ability to get a job done."[17]

Jack, in his elliptical, ironic way, later referred to his early home life as "not uncomfortable" and dominated by a series of domestic staff, always of impeccably Catholic origin, who maintained the high standards of order and punctuality his parents demanded of their children. When he was eight, the family drove seventy miles down the coast from Boston in Joe's chauffeur-driven Rolls-Royce and rented a three-acre compound overlooking Hyannis Port harbor. It soon became the Kennedys' permanent summer home. The following year, this time traveling in a private railway car, they moved to a fourteen-room furnished mansion in Riverdale, an exclusive and then quaintly rural suburb of Manhattan. In 1929, the Kennedys took possession in turn of a sprawling, neo-Georgian estate set among ten acres of landscaped gardens, complete with a small working farm and two staff cottages, in Bronxville, New York. Before long, they added a red-tiled, Spanish-style hacienda in Palm Beach, Florida, which became their preferred retreat during the winter. From time to time, Joseph Kennedy supplemented these quarters by renting various discreet bachelor apartments for himself in Boston, New York, Los Angeles, or elsewhere around the country, according to the demands of his fast-moving business or amorous pursuits at any one moment. A Hollywood actress with whom he "walked out" for a while recalled that Joe proudly showed her a shaded rooftop patio at one residence, where he said he liked to sunbathe in the nude and conduct business deals on the phone, later introducing her to a "downstairs room completely padded out in some sort of black leather material," which he informed her was soundproofed for their heightened enjoyment.[18]

John Kennedy, then, was materially privileged on a regal scale. The seven-room house on a tree-lined street in Brookline, Massachusetts, where he was born on May 29, 1917, was to be the most modest family home of his life. Kennedy's generally admiring biographer Robert Dallek has written that in the 1950s, "Jack's interest in civil rights was more political than moral. The only blacks he knew were chauffeurs, valets, or domestics, with whom he had minimal contact." Joseph Kennedy's lifelong quest for money and power dominated the household far more than the vivid, larger-than-life caricature of him as the tyranni- cal, bellowing father storming around the pages of more than one Kennedy biography. As a child, unseen hands had drawn Jack's bathwater and squeezed just the right amount of tooth- paste onto his brush for him before he awoke each morning; had carefully ironed the newspapers awaiting him at the breakfast table; and generally ushered him through a daily routine that combined some of the bucolic charms of a P. G. Wodehouse tale with a peculiarly immigrant American emphasis on competi- tiveness, knowledge, and self-improvement.

Born in 1890, Rose Kennedy, the children's mother, was the eldest daughter of Boston mayor John Francis "Honey Fitz" Fitzgerald and his wife Mary. Her father was not pleased when at sixteen she fell in love with Joseph Kennedy, who happened to be the son of Fitzgerald's long-standing political rival. As a result, Rose was dispatched for a lengthy period of contem- plation at a series of American and European convents (at one time enjoying a private audience with Pope Pius X) before eventually emerging from her exile, undaunted, to marry Joe on October 7, 1914. She had waited nearly eight years to do so, and Honey Fitz had relented in his opposition only after it was learned that he had been conducting an affair with a New York prostitute named "Toodles" Ryan, effectively marking the end of his time in elective office.

Rose gave birth to the couple's first child, Joe Jr., nine months later. What affection she had for any of her offspring remains a matter of debate. On the surface she was a supremely dedicated homemaker with an almost manic zeal for education, both civil and religious, yet she was also authoritarian, priggish, and what would now be called emotionally absent. Preoccupied with clothes, scent, and jewelry – her haute couture wardrobe the match of her future daughter-in-law Jackie's – Rose can plausibly be said to represent a lingering female archetype to her impressionable, sex-mad son Jack. "He was obsessed by it," Kennedy's biographer Nigel Hamilton has written. "Yet his disgust at women who wore heavy perfume, as well as his embarrassment at normal public gestures of affection, spoke volumes ... Except in sexual excitement he hated to be touched, hated the very idea of loving attachment to a woman involving lasting commitment or affection."[19] Rose's piety is not in doubt, but religious observance has never ruled out material acquisitiveness. On a 1929 visit to Paris, accompanied both by Joe and his mistress Gloria Swanson, Rose sat "fascinated as the beautiful mannequins slinked and slithered the length of the ornate [dress] salons," the beginning of an obsession with couture and jewelry that would match that of any royal princess.

As we've seen, both Joe and Rose were observant Catholics, and this fact naturally permeated the close-knit, regimented Kennedy clan. It is sometimes hard to equate the pious married couple and their outraged public opposition to their daughter's marriage outside the faith with the laxity of some of their own social life. In an unpublished essay entitled "Joe Rosebud," Gloria Swanson tried to rationalize this apparent contradiction.

"Joe believed in hell and he believed in Purgatory. It didn't worry him too much because he also believed in confession and the forgiveness of sins. He believed you could wipe the slate clean just by going to confession. It worked for him like sleeping pills for other people."[20]

Rose knew about her husband's infidelities, and in time Jack knew that she knew. The stagelike farce of their 1929 visit to France, with Swanson and her male companion occupying a suite in the Paris Ritz and the Kennedys installed in the adjoining one, was the first but not the last such signal that Joe's views on marriage might stray from the traditional monogamous ideal. Rose was by no means alone among highly educated women of her era in believing that it was essentially unrealistic to expect faithfulness from a man. It was an attitude that can only have buttressed Jack's later belief that sexual fidelity was an optional extra rather than a moral requirement within marriage. In due course, Rose would come to prefer travel rather than confrontation as her technique for coping with her family circumstances. According to Nigel Hamilton, "she ventured abroad 17 times in four years" while her children were all still minors.[21] Rose herself cheerfully related in her memoirs that when in 1923 she was about to leave on another extended trip, five-year-old Jack had exclaimed, "Gee, you're a great mother to go away and leave your children all alone."[22] The rebuke struck her as a priceless witticism. Nine years later, Jack was taken from Choate by ambulance and rushed to the hospital in New Haven with a blood condition severe enough for prayers to have been said for him in the school chapel. "He came very close to dying," his friend Lem Billings remembered. "It was diagnosed at one time as leukemia."[23] Rose was then spending the winter in Palm Beach, after again vacationing at length in Europe, and she made no effort to visit her son during the month he lay stricken in bed.

It might be a stretch to say that Rose was apt not just to occasionally deny approbation to her children, but to advertise her preference for being thousands of miles away from them. But it could fairly be said that she was literally a distant mother. In fact, she seems to have acted more like the tirelessly commuting manager of a chain of luxury hotels, in which her young family members happened to be occasional guests, than to have adopted the normal role of a full-time parent.

The Kennedy children "didn't have a real home with … their own rooms where they had pictures on the walls or memorabilia on the shelves," Billings later noted, "but would rather come home for the holidays from their boarding schools and find whatever room was available. 'Which one do I have this time?' Jack would ask his mother, if she was there."[24] Always on the move, often ill, aware that parents could as easily withhold their affection as give it, if not vanish altogether, Jack developed an unsentimental realism about life – "the abyss under everything," as he later put it to Harold Macmillan.[25]

There is no doubt that John Kennedy enjoyed female society, and that he made something of a career of his later sexual conquests. But these were almost invariably transitory affairs. One of his many casual partners later spoke of him fondly as a "wine and roses at night, pat on the ass in the morning" type, who had a "permanent apparatus of self-containment." Kennedy himself seemed to allude to this latter trait when he said, "Once I get a woman, I'm not interested in carrying on. It's the chase I like – not the kill."[26] Several of his companions have said that women lined up – sometimes literally – to make love with him, and that the act itself tended to be brisk. "He didn't even take his shoes off," one date later sighed.[27]

Around 1935, then, when he was lobbying to make his first Atlantic crossing, John Kennedy was a gifted if underachieving student, a bibliophile, athletic yet frail, and seemingly determined to follow his father's example as a seducer of women on an industrial scale. As usual, it seemed that there were two conflicting personalities present in him: one, the diligent bookworm, serious, anxious to excel; the other, a sort of post–Jazz Age swinger, dissolute, chronically late, untidy, and with a bitingly caustic wit. It's also worth remembering that Kennedy, for all his iconic status as the most invigorating and modern of American presidents, was born barely fifty years after the end of the Civil War. There was a part of him that came out in his speech and public manner that was a thoroughly conventional product of his times. Greeting Harold Macmillan at Nassau in December 1962, Kennedy stepped to the microphone to remark that he had "benefitted greatly from the sage counsel and friendship which you have shown to me, Prime Minister, to my predecessor, your old friend General Eisenhower, and also to the sovereign American people, who have a heavy claim laid upon you from earliest birth." It was one of those slightly prim official pronouncements that reminded Kennedy's audience that this emblematic figure of the 1960s in some ways remained a typical political product of the 1940s, or even earlier.

★ ★ ★

IN THE SPRING of 1934, Kennedy again became seriously ill. It began with recurring nausea, followed by a loss of appetite that was written off as indigestion. When the discomfort persisted for several weeks, Jack was sent to the Mayo Clinic in Minnesota for further tests. His confinement there played out several of the themes that dominated his early life. For one, there was the twinned pleasure and revulsion he always found in intimate physical contact with a woman. Jack's letters to his friend Lem Billings dwell at some length on the specifics of his treatment. "I am suffering terribly out here and I now have gut ache all the time," he wrote on June 19. "I'm still eating peas and corn for my food and I had an enema given by a beautiful blonde. That, my sweet, is the height of cheap thrills."[28] There was more in this vein, particularly about the enemas. On June 27, Kennedy playfully rebuked Billings: "Please do not write to me on toilet paper anymore. I'm not that kind of boy" – evidently a reference to Billings's personal orientation and the practice of those seeking same-sex liaisons to express their sentiments on toilet paper, which if needed could be quickly or easily discarded.[29]

When not fixating on the nurses and their "charmingly cut little tops," Kennedy passed the time by reading all five volumes of Winston Churchill's *The World Crisis* and any other history books with a specifically British flavor he could lay hands on. For a while Jack's symptoms retreated and, although it was only a remission, he was thought well enough to join his family for the summer at Cape Cod, where he told Billings, "I am now sporting around the beaches in flesh-color silk bathing trunks acquiring that chocolate tan which is the rage this year at Newport and Hyannis Port. Hot Screw."[30] The following year, doctors in London diagnosed Jack's condition as agranulocytosis, an acute imbalance of the white blood cells that puts sufferers at risk of major infections due to their weakened immune systems. If Kennedy was aware of how ill he was, he appears not to have shown it in his social life. He wrote to Billings in bawdy terms about his friendships with several young women. "Trox Box is coming down, so that should be rosy," he noted later in July.[31] But it was not an exclusive arrangement. A cable to Jack in Hyannis Port reads, "Will arrive tomorrow about noon … Has my prey [*sic*] arrived yet, Kisses and love, Ruth."[32]

Kennedy went back for a final year at Choate and passed out sixty-fifth in a graduating class of 110 – combined with a tactfully phrased headmaster's report, and Harry Hopkins, a member of President Roosevelt's cabinet, as a character reference, enough to win him a place at Harvard.

Before going up, Jack was at last able to follow his elder brother's lead and spend a year under Professor Harold Laski's supervision at the London School of Economics. The eighteen-year-old was understandably excited at making his first-ever trip abroad. "Send gray hat immediately," he wired Billings before sailing, among a long list of other characteristically last-minute details. Kennedy's British visa, for which he paid $8, arrived just a day before his departure.

If England was pure Shangri-La to Jack, Laski himself represented more of an acquired taste – "a P. T. Barnum figure always selling the promise of a revolution." Then aged forty-two, he was a fiercely opinionated socialist economist, historian, and essayist whose stringent political views – ultimately to prove too strong even for the tastes of Clement Attlee's Labour Party – were somewhat offset by a passing facial resemblance to Groucho Marx. Laski had taken a shine to young Joe Kennedy and later remarked, "He often sat in my study and submitted with that smile that was pure magic to relentless teasing about his determination to be nothing less than President of the United States." Laski seems not to have known about the glowing reports that Joe was then sending home about the Nazi regime in Germany. On the face of it, it was curious that the devoutly Catholic, unapologetically capitalist, and socially conservative Kennedy parents should have allowed their two oldest sons to study abroad under a left-wing, atheistic Jewish intellectual whose wife Frida (nine years his senior) was a prominent leader of the birth-control movement. Joe Sr. seems to have looked on it as a further opportunity to broaden his children's minds, if not to better familiarize them with their enemy. It was a transitional time for the Kennedy clan as a whole. Joe had resigned as chairman of the Securities and Exchange Commission after only a year, complaining that he had lost at least $100,000 while in public service, and had decided to take a European vacation while considering his next move. As a result, he, Rose, and their fifteen-year-old daughter Kathleen (en route, like her mother before her, to a convent) accompanied Jack when he boarded the SS *Normandie* on September 25, 1935, bound for England.

Authors searching for early signs of political genius among the Kennedys use Joe Jr.'s obvious determination and occasional vindictiveness, freedom from self-doubt, and unflinching belief in his own destiny – very much his father's son – as evidence. Joe's Harvard tutor, Kenneth Galbraith, recalled him as "slender and handsome, with a heavy shock of hair and a serious, slightly humorless manner. He was much interested in politics and public affairs" and "would invariably introduce his thoughts with the words, 'Father says,'" while Jack "too was handsome but, unlike Joe, was gregarious, given to various amusements, much devoted to social life, and affectionately and diversely to women."[33]

Jack, while talented, appeared to be squarely in the "second-son" tradition, someone who might have gone on to a career as a globetrotting, playboy journalist or an eventual celebrity television correspondent, something like a more self-aware Geraldo Rivera. The odds at this stage were that, while Joe Jr. was destined for the top, his kid brother would have made a successful chronicler of human-interest stories about international events and world leaders, possibly also running to a popular if undemanding book or two; a long and comfortable early retirement; a stream of well-upholstered young mistresses to discreetly coexist with an extensive, ostensibly close-knit family; some memoirs; illness; death; appreciative but not long obituaries, followed by a footnote in the dictionaries of national biography – that would have been it. As it was, John Kennedy arrived in England in the fall of 1935 promising his father that he would "think seriously, not just about capitalism and socialism," but also about the "very nature of international relations between states,"[34] even if, in practice, he fell some way short of these lofty ambitions.

The Atlantic crossing itself was ill starred. "This is the fourth day out and it is getting pretty goddamned rough," Jack wrote Billings from his suite on the *Normandie*. "The food here is very pimp-laden and my face is causing much comment from the old man, and it is getting damned embarrassing."[35] Being a Kennedy, there was also a certain amount of descriptive detail about the female passengers, as well as about a "fat Frenchie aboard who is a 'homo.' He has had me to his cabin more than once and is trying to bed me." Earlier in the summer, the *Normandie* had beaten the transatlantic speed record, and with a ratio of one crew member to each passenger it was considered the ultimate in seagoing luxury. But that was not the case here: heavy gales blew the liner off course, and as a result the Kennedy party made landfall not in Plymouth, England, but in Calais, France. After an uncomfortable night at a local inn, they set off on an overcrowded cross-channel ferry to Dover at eight the next morning. "Soon everyone began to yawk," Jack reported. "I was on deck singing to one of the women in the party. I was singing 'The Man on the flying trapeze,' and when I came to the part where you break into the chorus with O O O Ohhhh, etc, a woman behind me retched all over me with 'oh my God that's the finish' – you can imagine me covered from tip to toe with hot vomit."[36]★

Kennedy's undergraduate course at the London School of Economics (LSE) also failed to go fully according to plan. Although he attended some half a dozen lectures with Professor Laski on British government, economic history, and English legal institutions in the week of October 7 – arriving on campus in a chauffeur-driven Bentley from the family's local base at the luxurious Claridge's Hotel – Jack took ill on only his fifth day of class and had to be hospitalized. Rose, breaking off from her nearly permanent tenure among the dress shops on Bond Street, believed it to be merely "fatigue" or "jaundice," but William Murphy, the family doctor in Boston, soon cabled back his opinion concurring with the British specialists that it was a case of agranulocytosis: "Strongly urge injection liver extract every eight hours ... suggest consult Lord Dawson of Penn or Sir Thomas Horder," he recommended.

★ Although it was undoubtedly a bad crossing, Kennedy's imagination may have colored his account of his first arrival on British shores. The best available records give the weather on the south coast of England during the weekend of October 5–6, 1935, as only "rather changeable, with below average temperatures and rainfall, [but] near normal sunshine." See, for instance, UK Met Office 1935 records.

After appearing to be gravely ill, Jack then made one of those equally sudden overnight rallies that form the basic pattern of his life's medical history. "Am once more baffling the doctors," he wrote Billings around the middle of October. Before long, Jack's letters again fastened obsessively on the more sensual aspects of his ordeal. "There is a very good looking blonde whom Dad seems to know, about 24 ... She is studying here and comes to see me every day [but] I have not as yet laid her," he told Billings. "The nurses here are very sexy and the night-nurse is continually trying to goose me, so I have always to be on my guard."[37]

After several days, Kennedy felt well enough to return to his studies under Harold Laski. It's debatable whether he actually learned much of value about the socialist theory of world history from his eminent tutor. But before long he was showing a distinct interest in his more comely female classmates. Jack adopted a cynical tone in another letter back to Billings: "The night before I got in here I attended the 'Fresher's Social.' It was the strangest affair I have ever seen. The place was lousy with Boogies [persons of color] who were holding in their arms pimply faced English school-girls," he reported. Perhaps to tease his bisexual friend (a Protestant but rumored to have Jewish family blood), Kennedy added, "My most intimate pally [is] Hyman Purloff, a terrific yid. This would certainly be no place for you ... From your description and after talking it over with my night-nurse," Jack concluded, "you have sif. This will teach you a good lesson and will stop you from screwing every girl you meet." As well as health and sex, the two eighteen-year-olds regularly exchanged views on their contrasting financial circumstances. "Your economic worries have also upset me," Jack wrote, generously offering to loan Billings "the $500.00 Steelgram now as it is still intact and I won't need it."[38]

Kennedy reacted to the British social scene with much the same mixture of fascination and amused condescension he displayed throughout his life for members of the European ruling elites. "I met a cousin of yours, Prince Surloff, who is supposed to be the next Czar or some such shit," he wrote Billings, possibly another exercise of his vivid imagination. "He ran at Oxford and knew 'Charlie' Stanwood. The Prince stated that old Charlie was certainly a Prince among men and I agreed heartily that he certainly was. I have met a number of Earls + Lords here and I am getting rather royal myself."[39] Jack's dual nature allowed him to sneer, for Lem's benefit, at the young idlers he met at Claridge's receptions or in fashionable London drawing rooms. But his letters home also have to be taken with a grain of salt, for they were always seeking to entertain or shock. In reality, Kennedy soon made a number of lasting friends among the British upper classes, including the eighteen-year-old Anthony St. Clair Erskine, just down from Eton and described by one acquaintance as "exquisitely handsome, slight of build, mischievous ... he loved being admired and he was ... shallowly sophisticated, lithe of mind [and] a smart society figure."[40]

Like many American visitors, Jack was intrigued by the Bright Young Things personified by Erskine, all of whom seemed to be rich, intelligent, beautiful, and decadent, if not to have stepped straight from the pages of Evelyn Waugh. The English women were especially alluring. One lady born in 1919 remembers that she attended a "wear-nearly-nothing ball" held in the basement of "some huge Mayfair house" in October 1935. Passing herself off as eighteen, she arrived dressed as "a sort of classical peasant girl, draped in a fuchsia bedsheet," and soon made the acquaintance of an "American boy who was a bit self-consciously wearing white tie and tails, and carrying an ivory-topped black cane." The two of them had later enjoyed "a snog" in the darkened back garden, something about the young Kennedy's technique suggesting to her that "I wasn't the first girl he'd ever pounced upon in that way."[41]

However, it wasn't all fun and games for Jack, who quickly adopted his own working routine at the LSE. Although he made no pretense to be a great scholar, he continued to read voraciously on European history and politics. More than eighty years later, Kennedy's presidential archive still holds boxes of English newspaper cuttings he clipped in 1935, as well as transcripts of contemporary parliamentary speeches and even the reports of the Oxford and Cambridge universities' debating unions. As a result, his brief tenure at the LSE wasn't to be completely wasted. One contemporary student recalls that "Jack may not have been an intellectual giant, but he had all the facts and figures at his disposal, so that he could hold his own in supervisions, which frequently resembled miniature political debates with a running exchange of shouted objections and topical repartee."[42]

In a sense Jack had already fallen in love with London and its upper-class partying set. But the LSE itself had little to offer him. After consulting his father, Kennedy announced that he had reconsidered his plans and would now join his best friend at Princeton. On October 21, Jack wired Billings in typically brisk fashion: "Arriving Thursday afternoon. Hope you can arrange rooming – Ken." The following day, the dean of Princeton wrote to his opposite number at Harvard, inquiring if he could send him the academic files of "a chap by the name of John Fitzgerald Kennedy."

Although Jack had enjoyed his first taste of English nightlife, he clearly didn't take to Professor Laski's "cardboard socialism" in the way his brother Joe had.[43] There was also the troubling matter of his recurring illness. "They didn't seem to know what it was," Billings recalled thirty years later. "The thinking was that if Jack was going to be sick, he might as well be sick over here. So he left London and came home."[44]

John Kennedy had spent twenty-two days in England and probably a total of two weeks actively enrolled at the LSE. This was significantly less than his claim when later running for public office to have attended the LSE as a special student for three months, six months, or even a full academic year. Even in the brief time he was there, Kennedy's group studying often consisted of attending after-hours tutorials at Laski's home in

Addison Bridge Place, West Kensington, where bright young people sat on the floor swigging beer in front of a log fire and excitedly sharing views on everything from Stalin's purges to contraception. To bolster up his illusions, Kennedy later sought Laski's public endorsement of his Harvard undergraduate thesis *Why England Slept*, although his old professor's eventual review was guarded at best. "While it is the book of a lad with brains," Laski told Joseph Kennedy, "it is very immature, it has no real structure and it dwells almost wholly on the surface of things ... I don't honestly think any publisher would have looked at that book of Jack's if he had not been your son."[45]

★ ★ ★

KENNEDY LASTED just barely longer at Princeton than he did in London. Having arrived on campus on November 2, he left again on December 13, when a renewed outbreak of nausea sent him to the hospital in Boston. "My [white] blood count this morning was 3500. When I came it was 6000. At 1500 you die," he airily wrote Billings, among a wealth of more salacious detail about his nurses and their "fetching" uniforms of starched blue dresses and black stockings.[46]

Following a period of recuperation in Palm Beach, New York, and the unlikely backdrop of a dude ranch in Benson, Arizona, Jack decided to renew his application to Harvard in the fall of 1936. Although a willing member of the football squad and an enthusiastic participant in various displays of mutual hormonal abandon with the local coeds ("Went down with 5 guys from school ... four of us had dates and one guy got fucked three times, another guy three times – the girl was a virgin! – + myself twice," Jack wrote Billings back at Princeton),[47] he seems not to have applied himself to the same degree academically. "Exam today so have to open my book and see what the fucking course is about," he was forced to admit in another letter to Billings.[48] As at Choate, Kennedy did much of his studying in his own time, preferring to read (up to twelve books a week, he later claimed) on European and world affairs, rather than submit to the routine of organized classwork. We know from his letters home that he paid particular attention to the changing political scene in Britain, where in May 1937 Neville Chamberlain succeeded Stanley Baldwin as prime minister and set about a policy of "pragmatic accommodation" – later shortened to "appeasement" – of the fascist regimes in Berlin and Rome.

Jack had originally thought of spending that summer relaxing at Hyannis Port, but "the family do not want me to do it, because they think there may be a war soon and I should see Europe," he wrote Lem Billings. If so, this showed keener political perception on the Kennedys' part than that of the highest echelons of American government. After Joe Sr. generously agreed to help underwrite it, Jack decided it was time that he and the loyal Billings embark on a "grand continental tour," taking in "the usual architectural and cultural splendors etc," but also certain "more delicate" sights. The two twenty-year-olds would travel around in Kennedy's two-tone Ford convertible, which accompanied them on July 1, 1937, when they set out on the adventure of a lifetime aboard the SS *George Washington*, bound for France.

"Very smooth crossing. Looked pretty dull the first couple of days, but investigation disclosed some girls," Jack wrote on the first pages of the red, leather-bound journal he titled "My Trip Abroad." That early entry set the tone for a two-month tour that combined a sophisticated analysis of European affairs with a sometimes sardonic (and occasionally puerile) running commentary on national character as seen from the continent's cheapest boarding-houses and least salubrious restaurants. Kennedy later spoke convincingly of the friends having "roughed it" throughout that summer, and it's true that Billings's only modest budget forced a gesture to economy when it came to their daily lodgings and meals. But Jack's idea of roughing it also allowed for certain personal amenities. As well as the car, he got around Europe with six tailor-made suits, fourteen shirts, three pairs of monogrammed silk pajamas, and a letter of introduction signed by the US secretary of state Cordell Hull. There was also the bespectacled and curly haired Billings himself, a man whose teddy-bear-like devotion to his more exalted companion led him to play something of the role of Boswell to Kennedy's Dr. Johnson. As a result, while in Europe there was a certain amount of servile adulation on "poor old Lem's" part. "Jack Kennedy was intensely interested in [revolutionary Spain]," Billings wrote at one point. "I was quite impressed ... He spent a great deal of time talking to the refugees, making notes, and writing a good deal."[49] Billings, of course, was usually impressed by Kennedy. But there was genuine friendship, and a sort of exasperated affection, on the other side, too. "It's too damn bad about losing your scholarship," Jack had written to Lem back at Princeton in February 1936. "You have been a terrific ass, and unless you come around now, you haven't a chance. If you do good work now, maybe you can get the scholarship back" – a rare case of Kennedy advising a contemporary to simmer down.[50]

After a lengthy stay in Paris (where Kennedy complained of the relaxed local approach to personal hygiene), the young tourists motored south to within a few miles of the Spanish frontier. There they were horrified to meet streams of bedraggled refugees hobbling past them in the other direction, victims of the civil war that had broken out the previous summer. Attendance at a local bullfight served to confirm Kennedy in some of his new-found misgivings. "Very interesting," he jotted in his diary, "but very cruel, especially when the bull gored the horse. Believe all the atrocity stories now as these southerners, such as the French and Spanish, are happiest at scenes of cruelty. They thought funniest sight was when horse ran out of the ring with his guts trailing."[51]

On August 1, the boys' trip took a turn away from essentially recreational or cultural visits to such innocuous events as a champagne reception at Versailles or a day outing to Lourdes when they crossed the border into fascist Italy. Here Jack was torn between the powerful religious attractions – enjoying what he called a "semi-private" blessing (there were a thousand others present) from Pope Pius XI, who entered the fabulously ornate audience room on a litter – and the less welcome attentions of ordinary Italians. "Left Rome amidst the usual cursing porters," Jack wrote in his diary, among other unappreciative remarks about the town's "noisy" inhabitants. But there were compensations, too. "Took out some dates that turned out quite well," Jack dutifully recorded. "V. beautiful girls although our not speaking Italian was a temporary damper. Billings knew some Italian parlor tricks that were worth remembering and we went to bed tired but happy!"[52]

The next day, in one of those characteristically abrupt switches of tone and mood, Jack began making notes at the back of his diary on the philosophical nature and underlying causes of fascism. "Would [it] be possible in a country with the economic distribution of wealth as [*sic*] the US? Could there be any permanence in an alliance of Germany and Italy – or are their interests too much in conflict?" he wondered.[53] Kennedy added that he was "shocked and appalled" – terms he would use again twenty-six years later when visiting the Berlin Wall – after attending a rally of Mussolini's in Rome, although Billings later recalled the same event as "fantastic ... He was such an unusual speaker. You know, he'd talk, then he'd jut his chin out."[54]

Oddly enough, following this event, Mussolini, like Kennedy and Billings themselves, would go on to visit Nazi Germany, even if the Duce's own progress – climaxing in an open-air rally in Berlin attended by close to a million people – eclipsed theirs in pomp and circumstance. In fact, one of the trip's historical curiosities is the contrast between Jack Kennedy's distinctly muted reception in Germany and the scenes of wild adulation that greeted him on his return there quarter of a century later. In Munich, the two Americans had their first taste of the current regime when they came up against some young brown-shirted thugs at the Hofbrauhaus, a popular watering hole for the party faithful. "We had a terrible feeling about Germany and all the 'Heil Hitler' stuff," Billings recalled. "They were extremely arrogant – the whole feeling of Germany was one of arrogance: the feeling that they were superior to us and wanting to show it."[55] In his diary, Kennedy notes with approval the German flair for civil engineering, if not the civility of her people as a whole. Good at roads and bridges, he concluded, they were not otherwise greatly gifted. Leaving Nuremburg marked a new low. "Started out as usual except this time we had the added attraction of being spitten on," he wrote.[56]

Kennedy's European report card at that point shows an almost caricature record of national types: the French, dirty; the Spanish, cruel; the Italians, chaotic; the Germans, capable. On August 25, the two young Americans took the ferry back to England – which Kennedy now called his "home from home" – although thanks to a last-minute hitch on embarkation, Jack, somehow appropriately, went on ahead of his companion. "Had 5 minutes to get the mail boat," he wrote, "but due to some misunderstanding with Billings over the passports [he] missed it by 10 seconds." Waving gaily from the deck as he disappeared into the English Channel, Kennedy was able to see the positive side of the situation. "Billings managed to get a good work-out, which he badly needed."[57]

In London, the friends put up at a modest rooming house, today's backpackers' hostel, in the centrally located Talbot Square. Rather optimistically described in its sales brochure as "offer[ing] panoramic views of beautiful Hyde Park," the establishment in fact occupied two corner slums in a dark, almost impenetrable region, relieved only by a small communal garden, behind Paddington Station. It extended the essential poverty format of the tour. The boys weren't entirely without their creature comforts, however, as Jack's brother Joe and sister Kick were also in town, staying at the palatial Claridge's. A more than usually lavish dinner followed on the night of the 25th. The next morning Jack decided not to visit with his old professor

Harold Laski, as Joe wanted, and to go shopping with his sister on Bond Street instead. Always personally frugal on these occasions, in the course of the day he bought a packet of Irish linen handkerchiefs and an apple.[58]

Following dinner that night at the Dorchester Hotel, Jack and his siblings were up early the next morning to catch the train to Southampton, where around 11 o'clock, serviced by "a great conga-line of maidservants, stewards [and] porters," their mother Rose stepped off the incoming boat from France, where she had acquired an impressive amount of new furs and jewelry. Rose, Joe Jr., and Kathleen then embarked on the waiting liner for New York. For lunch that day, "helped myself to a liberal dose of chocolates and tomato juice," Jack recorded in his diary.[59] Alone again, and possibly relieved to be at liberty in his favorite foreign city, "after a quick poke" he caught the return train to London. When in Paris, Rome, or Munich, Kennedy and Billings had sometimes agreed to meet up after a brief interval apart at a centrally located monument. Lem was always punctual, Jack always late. Their rendezvous that particular afternoon in London was under the large clock at Paddington Station. This time Kennedy never showed up at all. "When I arrived back found myself with the Hives," he noted laconically in his diary. "Went home and was damn sick."[60]

"It was very worrying because we didn't know anybody, and we didn't even have a clue what kind of doctor to get," Billings anxiously recalled. "Jack broke out in the most terrible rash, and his face blew up, and [we] had an awful time."[61] Kennedy himself retained his sense of mocking irony even in the midst of this latest health crisis. "Saturday August 28 1937: Still sick," he wrote in his diary. "Had a very tough night. Billings got a 'neat' doctor who wondered if I had mixed my chocolate and tomato juice in a big glass. Finally convinced him I hadn't. Got another doctor."[62]

After three days, Jack's symptoms vanished as suddenly as they arrived. On the night of August 30, the two Americans stayed up late to listen to the broadcast of the Joe Louis–Jimmy Farr world-heavyweight boxing match from New York. Louis won a controversial decision. Some of the other boarders at Talbot Square had organized a little betting action on the outcome of the fight. "Won six bob [shillings]," Jack noted happily.

Characteristically, Kennedy was soon on the move again. The next stop on the itinerary was Herstmonceux Castle in Sussex, the home of Joseph Kennedy's business associate (and Conservative MP) Sir Paul Latham. This was more to Jack's taste than the boarding house behind Paddington Station. The thirty-two-year-old Latham, who had inherited first a baronetcy from his father and then millions of pounds from Courtaulds textiles, lived a life of gentlemanly privilege that included a rich vein of aristocratic eccentricity. He and his wife Lady Patricia "pottered around the estate, her dressed up in a sort of comic-gypsy outfit, him looking as though he'd just spent the night under a bush," their family friend James Lees-Milne remembered. "The two things I recall [Lady Latham] saying are: 'The peacocks are rather off colour this morning,' and 'If only we could get Neville Chamberlain committed to a loony-farm.'"[63] Herstmonceux itself was impressive. "Terrific big castle with beautiful furnished rooms," Jack wrote in his ever-present diary. "One room forty yards long – a bedroom. Had grouse for dinner and stayed up to about three." Like his sister Kick, Jack was beginning to take to the routine of leisured weekends spent among the more literate members of the British upper crust. It was all like a "great MGM musical," even if the "near lunacy" of some of the principal cast occasionally took things in a darker direction. Just four years later, Latham, having joined the British army, was arrested by the military authorities for "improper behavior" with three young soldiers and a male civilian. He then tried to kill himself by crashing his motorcycle into a tree. Latham survived his injuries, resigned his parliamentary seat, and was sentenced to two years' imprisonment. While he was incarcerated, his wife Lady Patricia divorced him. Once described as a "bounding retriever puppy," Latham emerged a broken man. He died in 1955, shortly after his fiftieth birthday.

On September 2, Kennedy and Billings spent an "uncomfortable" night in a third-class compartment on the Flying Scotsman express to Edinburgh, followed by an even more kidney-rattling ordeal on a local connecting train. Their destination was the "gigantic house" belonging to Sir James Calder, another of Joseph Kennedy's associates in the liquor trade. A classically Arcadian day of fly-fishing and grouse shooting followed, in both cases "without any success," Jack admitted.[64]

For any young American visitor, let alone Kennedy, life at a house like Calder's must have been extraordinarily stimulating. The sense of being on some grand theatrical stage returned when they sat down to dinner that night. Calder's ancestral dining room was lined with suits of armor, and antique weapons and heraldic banners were displayed on the stone wall, making it seem to another guest present "more like the lair of some ancient Scottish chieftain than a place of modern conversation."[65] Kennedy deemed the meal itself "very good," if not protracted. No sooner had the party finished their single glass of port than their host announced that it was time to turn in. "The bed hour is 10:00 and from then on it is quite perilous to move about as Sir James is very cautious on the electricity," Jack wrote. Billings went a step further in his account. "It was a great shock to us," he recalled, "that, in this enormous house, which probably had twenty to thirty bedrooms, there was only one bathroom ... [and] that was difficult to find because it was so far from our room. Sir James had the Scottish habit of turning off all the lights with a master switch at 10 o'clock. If you didn't get to the bathroom by that time, you were in deep trouble. Jack and I had one hell of a time getting to the bathroom during our whole visit."[66]

Returning to London, there was just time for Kennedy to enjoy another frenetic few nights on the town, including one spent in a front-row seat at a song-and-dance revue where "wailing young women high-kicked in short skirts, [and] a line of bongo drummers went into a kind of syncopated frenzy behind them."[67] Jack was later spotted dining with a young dancer, who was clad in an outfit said to be "more adapted to a Riviera bathing pool than an English public restaurant."[68]

On September 10, Kennedy and Billings boarded the ship back to the United States. Their summer in Europe had delivered in full on its recreational promise. But Jack had also used the time to develop his latent interest in the European political system and in Britain particularly. In true Edward Murrow fashion, he'd interviewed anyone who would stand still for him and rarely stopped writing notes during his ten weeks abroad. As Kennedy returned to Harvard that fall, his playboy image was tempered by a new-found appreciation of the way in which the world's older democracies interacted with each other. "Isn't the chance of war less as Britain gets stronger?" he mused in his diary. ("Laid B.D. – a knockout," he added elsewhere, lowering the tone a bit.) As the European storm clouds gathered, Jack's position on the whole issue of international relations increasingly put him at odds with that of his own father.

★　★　★

ON DECEMBER 9, 1937, President Roosevelt announced that Joseph Kennedy would serve as the next US ambassador to Great Britain, taking up his post there the following March. This was not just the most coveted diplomatic prize within the president's remit – it came at a time of acute European tensions, and thus when the job would seem to have called for a man equipped with a particularly high degree of tact and passing familiarity with the concept of self-abnegation. It has to be said that as ambassador, Joe Kennedy did not quite conform to this ideal. Neither training nor instinct had noticeably cut him out as one of life's conciliators. "Kennedy was entirely unprepared to serve [in Britain]," his biographer David Nasaw has written.

"His businessman's skills, his head for numbers, his negotiating talents, [and] his flair for publicity had served him well [domestically], but they would not help him in London."

On arrival, the new ambassador announced himself generally content with the basic fixtures and fittings of his fifty-two-room official residence at 14 Prince's Gate, just off Hyde Park, if less so with the available household provisions. According to David Nasaw, "Kennedy … imported plenty of Maxwell House coffee, tons of candy, dozens of cans of clam chowder. When he discovered that English freezers did not handle ice cream well, he had an American freezer shipped from New York … In May 1938, [Kennedy] ordered two thousand bottles of Pommery and Grena champagne, five hundred to be shipped to London at once."[69]

It is not only with hindsight that Joe Kennedy seems to make such a curious choice as an ambassador. Many observers thought so at the time. Even Kennedy's friend Boake Carter, a popular radio commentator (and later tireless exponent of the view that the British royal family members were the direct lineal descendants of the Ten Lost Tribes of Israel) wrote to ask him if he could ever be truly happy in a role that was essentially that of a glorified messenger boy between President Roosevelt and Prime Minister Chamberlain. "You are an honest man," Carter wrote charitably. "But the job of Ambassador to London needs not only honesty, sincerity, faith, and an abounding courage – it needs skill brought by years of training. And that, Joe, you simply don't possess."[70] Roosevelt himself justifiably looked on Kennedy as a potential rival for the presidency in 1940, and thus may have been happy to have him temporarily off the scene. There had once been a similar vogue for British prime ministers to dispatch troublesome colleagues to India or some other far-flung outpost of the empire. Indeed, Roosevelt privately referred to his nation's representative at the Court of St. James as "unscrupulous" and "a twister" and said he had him "watched hourly."[71] There was also the sense among the British press that the new ambassador was just a little too smooth, an impression he did nothing to alter when he managed to score a hole in one during his first-ever round of golf in England. Back at Harvard, Jack Kennedy good-naturedly wondered if "chicanery" had been involved in the old man's sporting coup.[72]

Like his father, who looked on his marriage vows as a tedious but necessary ritual component of the wedding service, to be affirmed once and promptly discarded thereafter, Jack too favored a policy of multiple, sometimes overlapping sexual arrangements. One elderly Englishwoman reflects that Jack's early technique had included "a lot of squeezing and stroking" in public places such as their dinner together at Simpsons-in-the-Strand, "rather making it clear where we were headed after the pudding course."[73] Though resistant to real emotional intimacy with his partners, he enjoyed its outward forms. In most other ways, however, Jack's relationship with his father would increasingly become more a matter of fear and admiration than of slavish emulation.

In fact, the "old man" would continue to besiege his famous son with a steady stream of phone calls, cables, and notes, offering his views on a wide range of state policy, even or especially after Jack entered the White House. According to the writer William Manchester, there had been a "family agreement" about the August 1961 erection of the Berlin Wall, for instance. Joseph Kennedy told Manchester that he had discussed the issue with his son the president, and they had concurred that trying to hold Berlin open for the West would be a "bloody mistake."[74] A White House staffer named Priscilla Wear similarly remembered that "JFK might have spoken to [his father] maybe four times a week … I think his relationship with his father was very strained. He once said that he could never be around his father for more than three days without having to get away. His father was terribly dictatorial, always giving him advice on things. I think he just never relaxed around him."[75] Although Ms. Wear (who went under the in-house name "Fiddle") was one of those surprisingly numerous female secretaries in the Kennedy White House not known for her typing or filing skills, there is no reason to doubt her essential thesis that the president regarded his father with a mixture of respect and trepidation.

Meanwhile, Jack pursued his deepening love affair with all things British. He still read everything he could on English history, ordered his suits from London, and in time came to experiment with a clipped, BBC-style accent, even if this last affectation "made him sound as if he were being slowly strangled" and was soon abandoned.[76] Jack's Anglophilia seems to have been important to him on a number of levels: it provided a distinct individual style; an implied touch of outsiderism and sophistication; and a viable apparatus for distancing himself from the old man. Like his sister Kathleen, Jack seemed to have been born for a life of grand country estates, relaxed sexual mores, and effortlessly urbane dinner parties where politics vied with equestrianism and the weather as conversational obsessions. "There was," Kennedy's friend William Douglas-Home recalled with nostalgia years later, "a perverse exhilaration among the British upper class just before the war."[77]

★   ★   ★

ON JUNE 18, 1938, twenty-one-year-old John Kennedy checked himself out of the New England Baptist Hospital in Boston following treatment there for "intestinal flu" and drove to Rockefeller Center in New York to collect his freshly issued red US diplomatic passport. The document would allow him to spend the summer vacation from Harvard working alongside his brother Joe as interns (or "Special Assistants to the officially accredited Legate," as the paperwork put it) at the US Embassy in London. It was Jack's third visit there in three years and his second within nine months. A few weeks earlier, Ambassador Kennedy had written to his chronically ill second son: "You really should give yourself plenty of rest. You really should take very good care of your health and you can only do that by getting lots of rest. I don't like to close a letter with an admonition, but it is for your own good, and I am sure you realize it."[78] It was sound advice, but it seems it was ignored. The journalist Arthur Krock accompanied the Kennedy brothers and their father on the Atlantic crossing on board the SS *Normandie*. "The ship was very gay ... and Jack was staying up pretty late at night," Krock recalled, "and he had a girl with him. The [agreement] was that Jack would be in his suite at midnight. Well, the next midnight, [he] arrived on time, and by arrangement with me, I let him out the back door of the suite and I don't know whether the old man ever found out about it or not. At any rate the curfew was not maintained."[79]

A twist of fate had placed John Kennedy in England that summer just as the European powers came to the brink of a general war for the second time in twenty years. The first night he arrived in London, he went to a public meeting in Westminster Hall addressed by the once and future Conservative foreign secretary Anthony Eden. Eden launched into a familiar theme: the folly of appeasing the "odious gang" in Berlin. Jack's visit differed from the one he had made with Lem Billings in 1937 in two significant aspects: he lived in greater comfort, but consequent to this he was there primarily to do Joseph Kennedy's bidding. As Jack wryly put it, "I guess Dad has decided he's going to be the ventriloquist, so that leaves me the role of dummy."[80] Regrettably, the ambassador soon forfeited the goodwill of much of the British press and public alike with a series of ill-judged pronouncements that advocated the further mollification of Hitler and Mussolini. A speech Kennedy gave that October on Trafalgar Day (typically the moment for a spirited eulogy on British arms) to the Navy League in London seemed to contain an almost pre-hippyish appeal for universal peace: "It is unproductive for both democratic and dictator countries to widen the division now existing between them by emphasizing their difference," he announced to an audience of serving and retired military personnel. "Instead of hammering away at what are regarded as irreconcilables, they can advantageously bend their energies toward solving their remaining common problems and attempt to re-establish good relations on a world basis … After all, we have to live together in the same world, whether we like it or not."[81]

But if the new American emissary thought that his Navy League speech would be widely hailed as an example of states-manlike restraint, he was to be cruelly disappointed. The next morning's headline in the *New York Times* was representative: "KENNEDY FOR AMITY WITH FASCIST BLOC: URGES THAT DEMOCRA-CIES AND DICTATORSHIPS FORGET THEIR DIFFERENCES — CALLS FOR DISARMAMENT." It would be fair to say that the ambassador never quite recovered the mutual feelings of goodwill that had greeted him on his arrival in London just six months earlier. Even fol-lowing the actual outbreak of war a year later, Kennedy advised President Roosevelt that sending aid to Britain "would just be throwing it down the drain."[82] Joe's local approval rating only fell further once these remarks were published in the London press.

★ ★ ★

FOR TWENTY-ONE-YEAR-OLD Jack Kennedy, international affairs were also "terrifically important," he insisted, but not to the exclusion of a vibrant social life. He was later to remark that "the English elite seem[ed] to have turned decadent" in the twenty years since the Great War. It was not an entirely disap-proving observation. As we've seen, Jack was particularly drawn to the sort of contemporary Briton who, like him, combined a rigorous intellectual approach to life with generally relaxed personal morals. That summer of 1938, he met his beau ideal of such a man in twenty-year-old David Ormsby-Gore, then in the midst of an academically glittering if debauched undergradu-ate career at Oxford. According to their mutual friend Deborah

("Debo") Mitford, Kennedy and Gore met at the Epsom horse races, although the writer Evelyn Waugh always insisted that the momentous first handshake occurred "over the supine bodies in a squalid basement bottle-party."[83] Gore himself was vague on the details but remembered that "we [met] when I was I suppose 20 and he was 21. We talked a good deal more about golf or what parties we were going to rather than getting into discussions [on politics]."[84]

Following wartime service in the army, Gore emerged as a socially well connected Conservative MP and in time a rising star at the Foreign Office. Some Kennedy biographers have speculated that he represented an idealized, smooth Englishman – a sort of James Bond with extra diplomatic training – to the future president. In fact, Gore was a rather diffident figure, with a tendency to ramble in his speeches – which he frequently punctuated with a sharp, snickering laugh – and proudly Welsh. He also had an affinity for the spirit of his age, a profound depth of European and American history, and a keen understanding of modern international relations, and it was these, rather than any more exotic qualities, that friends tended to remember in later years. Lean and sharp-nosed, with a silk scarf often tied nonchalantly around his long neck, Gore gave one observer the impression of an "animated ferret." Photographs taken of him in more formal settings around the negotiating table reveal a hint of steel in the eyes. Although his personal tastes ran more to jazz and sports cars than to fast women, Gore was within hailing distance of being a sort of Anglicized version of Kennedy in his fundamental outlook on life. Even when they came to sit across the Oval Office desk from one another, the American president affectionately referred to her majesty's representative in the United States by his adolescent nickname of "Boofy" Gore. The ambassador reciprocated with "Jack" in the course of their frequent family weekends together, or in the privacy of their handwritten letters.

That same summer, Kennedy also met the Oxford undergraduate and future Conservative politician Hugh Fraser. Bonding over "a well-built set of blondes," twenty-four years later they found themselves sitting together at dinner in the White House, earnestly discussing Anglo-American policy in Latin America. There were soon other lifelong friends, too, drawn from among that peculiarly bohemian-intellectual strata of the British peerage. Later that summer, Jack fell in with the twenty-six-year-old dramatist-politician William Douglas-Home, son of the 13th Earl of Home, who at the time was passionately in love with Kathleen Kennedy. "He liked to play golf," Home later told the Kennedy Library, recalling one of those faintly absurd adventures that confirmed Jack's view of life as something not to be taken entirely seriously. "The first time I ever played a round with him we went to the Royal Wimbledon Club," Home related, "and we asked for a couple of golf balls each. The assistant professional said we could take a box each. He gave us a dozen deluxe golf balls each in a box." Impressed and surprised by the man's generosity, the two young friends had later returned from their game to find "an ambulance waiting outside the club house to take the poor chap away."[85] Although denied political office himself – in part because of his cashiering by the army for disobeying a wartime order – Home's elder brother Alec would serve both as British foreign secretary and later prime minister during the final days of the Kennedy administration, thus becoming the government's principal mourner at the president's funeral.

★ ★ ★

IN 1938, JACK KENNEDY idealized and romanticized such figures – soon to be joined by his sister Kathleen's lover "Billy" Cavendish, marquess of Hartington – at this stage perhaps still seeing their rakish charms more than their aristocratic vanities and foibles. Jack seemed to possess an instant affinity for Britain, and in that affinity lay an almost instinctive appreciation for how at least one strata of its culture worked. While

Joe Jr. struck many of his English acquaintances as abrasive and grasping (a "typical yank money-grubber," in one withering comment made to the author),[86] Jack was everything his hosts could have wished of him – irreverent and charismatic, blessed with both a self-deprecating wit and the tranquil consciousness of his own superiority. As usual, he was also busy filling the gaps in his education with his voracious reading list: everything from John Buchan's biography of the seventeenth-century Scottish poet-warrior James Graham, earl of Montrose, to the popular Fleet Street papers, pamphlets by the Peace Pledge Union, *Hansard's Parliamentary Debates*, golfing and sailing periodicals, and Winston Churchill's two-volume life of his father Randolph. Jack had narrowly missed meeting Churchill himself at a country-house party in October 1935 when the young LSE student had fallen ill just the day before, although he had heard him speak in the House of Commons and claimed to have once caught sight of the old man's trail of cigar smoke as he disappeared into a train compartment at Waterloo Station. Perhaps Jack related to Churchill's book's central thesis of a precociously talented son, half-impressed, half-appalled by an overbearing patriarchal figure who was only nominally committed to a political ideology and was really a one-man party all to himself.

It was another sign of Joseph Kennedy's streak of independence that, as the newly installed ambassador to Great Britain, he chose to sit out most of the European crisis of July–August 1938, not close to the heart of events in London but in a palatial rented villa in Cap d'Antibes on the French Riviera. Although Jack drank milk in a commendable effort to gain much-needed weight, this seems to have been his one and only gesture to moderation while enjoying the "blue Mediterranean and the sun-drenched sands, the casualness of people in a holiday mood, luncheons, teas, dinner and golf" that long summer.[87] "Had J.K. in bath-tub," one attractive young Frenchwoman recorded in her journal on July 29.[88]

Back in London, Jack cut a more conventional figure to eigh-teen-year-old Debo Mitford, youngest of the six socially and, in time, politically prominent daughters of the second Baron Redesdale and his wife Sydney. At a ball given by Lady Louis Mountbatten, Debo danced with the tail-coated Jack. "Rather boring but nice," she wrote in her diary. They danced again the next night. "I don't think he was enjoying the party much," she recorded. Debo's mother Lady Mitford evidently saw some-thing in the waltzing young American the others missed. "Mark my words, I won't be surprised if that man becomes President of the United States," she announced.[89]

On August 29, 1938, Ambassador Kennedy returned from the south of France to his post in London. Jack accompanied him. Father and son were thus on hand when Prime Minister Chamberlain began the tortuous diplomatic gavottes that ulti-mately led to him prostrating himself before Hitler in Munich and gave tacit approval for the German rape of Czechoslovakia. Joe's central position, like Chamberlain's, was that Britain had no vital interest in defending the Czech people from Nazi ter-ritorial aggression. Jack appears to have demurred, because Arthur Krock remembered the ambassador dismissing his son as an "idiot" when they debated the point.[90] Here were the seeds of the Kennedys' generational clash that would follow on the whole wider issue of appeasement — Joe concluding that it had been a "swell, statesmanlike effort" on Chamberlain's part, Jack favoring something closer to the Churchillian line that Britain had got herself in an impossible position, unable to fight even had she wanted to because of her long-term neglect of her armed forces. Back in Washington, President Roosevelt seems to have increasingly aligned with the latter viewpoint. "That young man [Ambassador Kennedy]," he told Secretary of the Treasury Henry Morgenthau, "needs his wrists slapped rather hard."[91]

Jack Kennedy sailed home to New York on September 8, and so he followed the final convulsions of the Munich pact while starting his junior year at Harvard. He had clearly been impressed by his recent experiences in Britain, because he applied to the college authorities for permission to return to London "and study full-time there for six months" beginning the next February. Meanwhile, in a piece of unsurpassable theater, on the afternoon of September 28, Neville Chamberlain was speaking to the House of Commons about his now grave forebodings of war when, just after 4 o'clock, a colleague silently passed him a folded slip of paper. According to the politician and diarist Harold Nicolson, the prime minister "adjusted his pince-nez and read the document that had been handed to him. His whole face, his whole body, seemed to change. He raised his face so that the light from the ceiling fell full upon it. All the lines of anxiety and weariness seemed suddenly to have been smoothed out; he appeared ten years younger and triumphant. 'Herr Hitler,' he announced, 'has just agreed to postpone his mobilization for 24 hours, and to meet me in conference with Signor Mussolini and Signor Daladier at Munich.'"[92]

For a second the House was absolutely still as it absorbed this momentous news, some members apparently overcome with relief, others aghast at the perceived humiliation. Then, out of the silence, a roar of approval suddenly broke forth from the strangers' gallery. It was ambassador Kennedy, beaming down at his friend the prime minister, before racing outside to announce to waiting reporters: "Well, boys, the war is off."[93]

3

WHY ENGLAND SLEPT

JOHN KENNEDY HAD a rare gift for timing. While touring Europe in 1937, he had gained firsthand experience of the fascist movement that was still largely a mystery to most senior American politicians, let alone her ordinary citizens. In 1938, Jack took a ringside seat as his father conferred with the British prime minister about what response, if any, to make to Hitler's threats against Czechoslovakia. The twenty-one-year-old had even enjoyed privileged access to official embassy telegrams and dispatches both to and from the State Department in Washington, and in general he seems to have operated more as a de facto first minister than a summer intern. Jack was back in England early in 1939, just as German troops finally moved into Prague – the moment when even Ambassador Kennedy began to feel that "some sort of continental spat" was more likely than not. "Everyone thinks war inevitable before the year is out. I personally don't, though Dad does," Jack wrote to his friend Lem Billings that March.[1]

The timing of this latest trip was opportune, too, on a more personal level. During the previous winter Jack had engaged in a torrid love affair with twenty-year-old Frances Ann Cannon, a cigarette-slim, fabulously wealthy North Carolina textile heiress

whose family happened to be Protestant, which "presented difficulties" to the staunchly Catholic Rose Kennedy. Apparently
the reservations were mutual, because Frances Ann's friend Jane
Suydam later told a Kennedy biographer, "I had long talks with
her about Jack. She said it was a great romance, but her father
didn't want her to marry a Catholic."[2] As a result, Jack may have
looked on his six months' sabbatical in England as an opportunity not only to further study the darkening European situation
but to recover from a broken heart. On February 24, 1939, wearing a loose-fitting tweed suit and waving his "Anthony Eden"
homburg hat to a small group of reporters at the quayside
in New York, Kennedy – who struck one of the newsmen as
"looking about sixteen, not nearly 22" – boarded the SS *Queen
Mary*, bound for Southampton. As he stepped on the liner for
his fourth Atlantic crossing in as many years, he was handed a
telegram. It read:

> Great golden tears too plentiful for very famous last words.
> Can only say stay away from the hay. Goodbye darling,
> I love you.
>
> *Frances Ann*.[3]

If Jack himself had similar qualms on their parting, he seems
to have put a brave face on things soon after reaching Britain.
"Been having a great time … Working every day & going to
dinners etc. with Dad," he wrote Billings early in March. "Met
the King this morning at a Court Levee. It takes place in the
morning and you wear tails. The king stands and you go up
& bow. Met Queen Mary and was at tea with Princess Elizabeth
[the present queen] with whom I made a great deal of time," he
confided. "Thursday night am going to Court in my new silk
breeches which are cut to my crotch tightly and in which I look
mighty attractive."[4]

    It wasn't just that young Kennedy enjoyed swanning around
at court or emulating the gentlemanly life of the English upper

classes. He had an affinity for the sort of double-barreled young men epitomized by "Boofy" Ormsby-Gore (who thought Jack "by nature, and later on principle, one of life's true anglophiles"), but the place held an almost sensual appeal for him, too. As Kennedy later remarked, he found his batteries "greatly recharged" whenever he saw "a red bus, or Big Ben soaring into view."[5] The style of politics he was becoming familiar with in London – the comedy of understatement and irony, set amidst the knockabout exchanges of the House of Commons – laid the tone for a basic political operating style that would become his own hallmark when in office. More importantly, by early 1939 he already saw Britain as a bulwark between the "idle and decadent" races of southern Europe (in which he included France) and the "insufferable and dangerous" mood unmistakably wafting from "Germany and her slave states" to the east. By now something of an authority on British habits and customs, Jack labored ceaselessly to deepen that knowledge. He did so by quizzing the men and women he met in offices, at dinner parties, or in the street, by visiting them in their homes, and by taking his usual painstaking notes on all he saw and heard. Unlike his father, Jack was already beginning to wonder if the Munich agreement had succeeded quite as brilliantly as the appeasement bloc still fondly hoped was the case. After visiting Warsaw that spring, he returned to London convinced that Poland was serious about defending herself if attacked, and that Britain would ultimately make good on her pledge to fight in that event. As the young Kennedy once again moved around the great English country houses that summer, there was a "faint but distinct" echo, he felt, of the "strange, twilight world of 1914," a sense of "a ticking clock, of time winding down."[6]

Ambassador Kennedy, for his part, was never quite able to enjoy the easy social prestige among the British people for which he thought his long years of proven business success and political acumen perhaps qualified him. There was something almost tragicomic about his ill-conceived attempts to ingratiate himself with his hosts that put some in mind of Joachim von Ribbentrop's disastrous term as German envoy to London a year earlier. Faced with an increasingly hostile Fleet Street press, the elder Kennedy chose to spend increasing amounts of time at his rented villa in the south of France, or "on consultation" in Washington. Winston Churchill, on being told that the ambassador was unavailable to meet him one day in August because he was "away on holiday," retorted, "As opposed to what, pray?"[7]

Kennedy did, it's true, enjoy regular and apparently amicable meetings with the British royal family. But even here he was to be ultimately frustrated in his quest for social acceptance. The career diplomat Walton Butterworth served at the US Embassy in London in 1939 and later recalled, "Joe was the one who conceived the idea of the King and Queen of England visiting the United States that June. He prompted this venture, and then he was not allowed to accompany them. My recollection is that he got a message from [Roosevelt] that asked him not to come. He regarded it as a conspiracy of the leftish New Dealers, who didn't approve of him, to embarrass him."[8] Joe was to be further discomfited late that spring when the British publication *This Week* reported on his meeting in London with one Dr. Helmut Wohlatt, a deputy to Field Marshal Goering. According to the paper, the US ambassador had "used language which [was] not merely defeatist, but anti-Rooseveltian … Mr. Kennedy [went] so far as to insinuate that the democratic policy of the United States was a Jewish production, but that Roosevelt will fall in 1940."

Three months later, when war was actually declared, Joe Kennedy went to visit the king at Buckingham Palace. Here some discrepancy exists between the ambassador's memory of a "full and productive discussion" of world events and that of the monarch. "He looked at it all very much from the financial and material viewpoint," the king recalled in his private diary. "He wondered why we did not let Hitler have SE Europe, as it was no good to us from a monetary standpoint. Didn't seem to realise that this country was a part of Europe, that it was essential for us to uphold the rights of small nations."[9] To the former Wall Street mogul, it was as if the German leader was merely the head of a rival business concern, someone he could swiftly deal with if seated across from him at a boardroom table. In fact, within forty-eight hours of the outbreak of war, Kennedy had booked the first available berths out of Britain for his wife and children, and he would soon take to driving out to the western suburbs in search of a combined rural pied-à-terre and fallout shelter once the bombs started falling on London. The story that Joe had seriously proposed leasing Windsor Castle from the royal family for this purpose but ultimately decided against it because it had "too few crappers" is probably apocryphal, but it nonetheless expresses a view that some people had of him.

In the meantime, Jack pushed to conduct "direct, on-site research," as he called it, by proposing that he and his father travel through continental Europe and draw their own conclusions about the prospects of war. They could achieve this with just "a bag and a couple of notebooks," he remarked optimistically, reflecting his lifelong preference for personal observation over the niceties of diplomatic reports. In the event, the ambassador for once found himself unable to leave London, but Jack was soon on the move again, first joining his family for a private audience with the newly enthroned Pope Pius XII and then enjoying a month as a sort of glorified clerk at the US Embassy in Paris. It was the usual story of scholarly contemplation tempered by intense social activity; even when Jack relaxed, Ormsby-Gore once noted, "he seemed to do so flat-out."[10]

"Working hard these days," Jack wrote Billings from Paris on April 6. "Was at lunch today with the Lindberghs and they are the most attractive couple I've ever seen," he added, tactfully ignoring Charles Lindbergh's stated admiration for the Nazis. "Will only be in London a couple of days over the 4th [of July] as Dad is giving a party for the King and Queen, which I am going to go back for, and then I think I will leave for Poland, if things stay as they are now."

Speaking in September 1960, as the Democratic presidential nominee running in a tight race against the Republican challenger Richard Nixon, Senator John Kennedy told an audience in Portland, Maine, "As for experience ... I spent a good deal of my life before the war, at least in the last years, traveling. I was in the Soviet Union, I think, in 1939 and in Poland ... I have been concerned about foreign policy since my father was in London."[11]

In fact, this was a rare case of a politician if anything understating his experience of the world. In that summer of 1939, Jack Kennedy was variously in Italy, France, Switzerland, Poland, the USSR, Hungary, Lithuania, Latvia, Estonia, Rumania, Turkey, Palestine, Egypt, Lebanon, Greece, Germany, Austria, and Czechoslovakia. Along the way, there was plenty of the "direct research" he craved. Driving through Munich, Kennedy and two friends were attacked by brick-throwing storm troopers, apparently incensed by the car's British license plate. "You know," Jack calmly observed to his companions as they gunned the motor, "how can we avoid having a war if this is the way these people feel?"[12]

When Kennedy periodically returned to base in England, it was for a series of activities that ran the gamut from attending his family's reception for the royal couple to "debagging" his friend the sixth earl of Rosslyn during the course of a country-house weekend at Tichborne Park. On Monday, July 10, Jack went straight from a "hilarious party" given for Princess Cecile of Prussia, the exiled kaiser's granddaughter, to listen to Neville Chamberlain's statement on the "tinderbox of Europe" and, more particularly, the disputed control of the city of Danzig, in a packed House of Commons. It was a classic example of how the twenty-two-year-old American undergraduate seemed to straddle the worlds of politics and pleasure. Kennedy went on to a private reception held by Chamberlain at 10 Downing Street, where he met "all the great appeasers," including British foreign secretary Lord Halifax and R. A. "Rab" Butler, a future deputy prime minister in the 1960s. "Jack would carry a heavy ledger under his arm, and engage everyone he met in deep discussion about the history of their country, [and] whether it would come to war," Ormsby-Gore recalled.[13]

The Nazi era is viewed by posterity as one of darkness, and so of course it was for civilized people. But at least in mid-1939 it was also an invigorating time for an inquisitive, historically minded young American to further his political education. Throughout the summer, courtesy of his friends Halifax and Butler, Ambassador Kennedy was able to read official British cabinet papers, including the secret dispatches to and from Berlin, and to share at least some of these with his son. Jack later remarked to Ormsby-Gore that "the old man flung down one document and said that [Halifax] had asked him about forming a response to it, and what could I contribute from my experience of Germany?"[14] The document was the text of Hitler's latest ultimatum to Poland, among other things gruffly demanding the return of Danzig. Ambassador Kennedy went back to Downing Street, where he told the prime minister, "There are two great difficulties with the present situation. The first is that the English" – he spoke as if he were somewhere else than the seat of the British government – "thinking they have Hitler on the run, will get too tough. The second is that the Poles … thinking they have the French and the English all hooked up to help them, will get tough and make no concessions … I think the Cabinet should be firm but I think it should offer Hitler something to hang his hat on."[15]

For Joseph Kennedy, the international crisis of 1939 was at root all about capital. As he later recalled telling Chamberlain, "Propose a settlement that will bring Hitler economic benefits more important than the territorial annexation of Danzig. To put in a billion or two now will be worth it." It was an almost comic misreading of a regime which, while it had its share of the psychotically vain and materially acquisitive, was always more about the supposed moral superiority of National Socialism than mere monetary gain. If Kennedy was woefully misguided on Hitler's real motivation, he still had a shrewd idea of the popular mood in Germany as a whole, however, with Jack wiring back firsthand reports from his travels in Berlin as late as two weeks before the outbreak of war. One morning in mid-August, the young American opened the curtains of his room at the Hotel Excelsior and saw storm troopers marching down Hardenbergstrasse, a mile or two west of the Nazi chancellery, followed by a "gale of hysterical shouting about Danzig" piped out on loudspeakers hung from the nearby lampposts and trees. Jack later brought back a souvenir copy of the *Berliner Zeiting* whose headline read, "POLAND: LOOK OUT!"[16] It was an extraordinary higher education for the impressionable Harvard government and history student, and it provided him a ringside seat at events that shared at least some of the same politically charged and increasingly martial characteristics he confronted twenty-three years later in the Cuban Missile Crisis.

Back in England, Jack lived out the last days of summer in a burst of political activity and social hedonism among his upper-class friends, delighted, he later said, to be in a city now "bustling with marchers, [and] flags fluttering everywhere from buildings and cars, and pretty young girls kissing soldiers in the street."[17] He owed much of his immersion into the higher strata of English society to his sister Kathleen – "Kick" – who had come to think of Britain as her spiritual home. Though not, some sniffed, a conventional beauty, with her rather stout legs, prominent teeth, and a touch of the haphazard about her personal grooming, Kick was, nonetheless, widely admired for her natural exuberance, charm, and friendliness – and had gone on to make a catch of William Cavendish, marquess of Hartington, heir-apparent to the duke of Devonshire, or "Billy" to his many friends. Years later, Hartington's brother remembered, "It was her vitality, and that of all the Kennedys, that overwhelmed us." As the clock ticked down to war, nineteen-year-old Kick tearfully pleaded with her parents to be allowed to stay behind in England. They denied her request but granted the consolation prize of a glittering farewell party at Prince's Gate. Jack was there, along with his friends Hartington and Ormsby-Gore, both of them now in uniform. Many loyal toasts were drunk. It was possibly tactless of the ambassador to take the opportunity to remark that, in his opinion, the British were about to be "badly thrashed."[18] Jack seems to have prudently held his tongue, perhaps mentally weighing the issues of appeasement and intervention that he would soon take up in print. Later in August he wrote to Billings from Berlin: "England seems firm this time ... But as that is not completely understood here, the big danger lies in the Germans counting on another Munich and then finding themselves in a war when Chamberlain refuses to give in."[19]

Continuing his double life as a high-minded scholar of public affairs and a priapic womanizer, Jack had "developed a terrific crush" on his sister's best English friend, Sally Norton.[20] On a subsequent flying visit to the Riviera, he's said to have gone on to show a marked interest both in his father's next-door neighbor, the thirty-seven-year-old actress Marlene Dietrich, and in Dietrich's fifteen-year-old daughter Maria. Frustrated there, Jack and his friend Lord "Tony" Rosslyn had promptly styled themselves the team of "Ross Kennedy" and "made the rounds of London balls," "targeting blondes and slightly older married women."[21] The idea was to consciously shy away from any overnight partners who might expect some form of commitment and instead concentrate on "dames," as Jack called them. "Never had a better time," was his overview of the late summer of 1939 in another letter home to Billings.[22] Rarely sleeping more than five hours a night, Jack traveled restlessly around with a new color movie camera and a notebook, obsessively recording his impressions and helping himself at will to "literally scores" of beautiful women. History was unrolling before his eyes. "You had the feeling of an era ending," Jack later remembered of those dolce vita days, "and everyone had a very good time at the end ... The month of August was idyllic."[23]

★ ★ ★

HITLER'S TROOPS invaded Poland at dawn on September 1. Under parliamentary pressure, Chamberlain sent him an ultimatum: unless he evacuated Poland by 11 a.m. on the 3rd, the British would intervene. On the climactic Sunday morning, Rose Kennedy and her daughters went to the Brompton Oratory to pray, while the ambassador, Joe Jr., and Jack listened to the declaration of war on a small radio set at the American Embassy. As soon as Chamberlain stopped speaking, the ambassador recalled,

> I picked up the receiver and asked for him. To my surprise he came on the line at once.
> "Neville," I said, "I have just listened to your broadcast and it was terrifically moving ... It was really great, and I feel deeply our failure to save the world from war."
> To which Chamberlain replied, "We did the best we could," he said, "but it looks as though we have failed ... Thank you, Joe. My best to you and my deep gratitude for your constant help – Goodbye, goodbye."[24]

At noon the Kennedy family en masse was back in the strangers' gallery of the House of Commons to witness Chamberlain issue the formal announcement of war and Winston Churchill, speaking from the back benches, to reply, "We are fighting in defense of all that is most sacred in man." There was a good deal of vociferous support for this sentiment, although the ambassador himself "felt no wish to cheer. Chamberlain had mirrored my sensations better when he said, 'This is a sad day for all of us ... Everything that I have worked for, everything that I had hoped for, everything that I have believed in during my public life has crashed into ruins.' By then I had had enough and with-out waiting for other speakers, I made my way back through the silent crowds to my home."[25]

Kennedy's personal distress at the outbreak of war was not quite over, however. It was a mild and sunny afternoon, and he and his two older sons decided to walk the three miles from the Commons to the American Embassy building (adjacent to its modern premises) in Grosvenor Square. After being joined there by Rose and the other children, the Kennedys again set off on foot toward Park Lane, intending to cut across Hyde Park en route to their official residence at Prince's Gate. As they passed down the narrow streets of Mayfair, "the air-raid siren suddenly began to howl, and we ran for refuge into the nearest shelter we could find."[26] By coincidence, it happened to be the Grosvenor Street premises of Edward Molyneux, couturier, who provided Rose Kennedy with her London wardrobe. In the past she had often walked up and down the building's sweeping Georgian staircase as she tried on some "fabulously lavish" outfit for size. But it was to the store's unprepossessing brick cellar that she repaired now, where the family found themselves squeezed in with thirty or forty other "thoroughly frightened" ordinary British citizens.[27] It was to be a hectic and life-changing war for Jack Kennedy, as for so many others, but even he must have been struck at how it began for him: crouching in the basement of a fashionable English ladies' dress shop until the "All Clear" wailed overhead, signifying a false alarm.

★ ★ ★

JUST FIVE HOURS LATER, the unarmed British passenger liner SS *Athenia*, en route from Liverpool to New York, was torpe-doed by a German U-boat and sank in the icy Atlantic waters three hundred miles off the coast of Scotland, with the loss of 128 lives. It was the first Allied maritime loss of the war. John Kennedy's political career effectively began three days later, when he was sent post-haste to Glasgow to meet with the American survivors of the disaster. Jack was "there to represent his father because the Embassy staff in London was so rushed with work that no regular member could be spared," the *Boston Globe* reported.[28]

For the next few days, the fresh-faced Harvard undergraduate, so recently enjoying the nightlife of London, visited the injured in hospital and listened to the harrowing tales of the bereaved – "widows were crying, children clinging," he recalled.[29] Initially, Kennedy seems to have got by with his usual mixture of charm and good manners. He was especially popular with the single women, who responded to his athletic good looks and winning personality as he went around asking them about their ordeal and distributing mugs of tea. But when Jack met with 150 bruised and bloodied *Athenia* survivors at Glasgow's art-deco Beresford Hotel on the morning of September 8 to discuss their transport home to America, they did not give him an easy time. "People shouted demands for a convoy of ships to accompany them and guarantee safe passage," the press reported. There were "many interruptions" when Jack got to his feet to optimistically announce, "Everything will be all right. I talked to my father this morning, and he has spoken to America since. He asked me to tell you that the Government has plenty of money for you all … Ten thousand dollars has been allocated for your immediate wants, ocean tickets will be provided, and a ship is on the way. We do not know where she is going to dock, but you will all be informed, and returned together."[30]

"What about mines?" one woman shouted.

"We – " Kennedy began.

"What about submarines?" she continued. "We must have a convoy," cried another woman. "You can't trust the Germany navy, anyway," said a man, not unreasonably under the circumstances.

Kennedy patiently explained that President Roosevelt himself had personally assured his father the ambassador that there was no need for a convoy, as American ships would not be attacked. "The United States government guarantees this," he announced.

"That's what they said last time," retorted a woman.[31]

Another man stood up. "Twenty brand new cruisers and many destroyers are just in commission. The US government can spare a few of them. Women who have been through what these have in the last few days will not feel safe without protection.

"One female [Amelia Earhart] came down in the ocean a while ago," the man continued. "They sent out the entire Pacific Fleet from America to find her."

"Well, I'm sure we can resolve this," said Jack, still clinging to vestiges of his earlier optimism. "I will tell my father all you say. I know he will consider all aspects."

The meeting then ended with two minutes' silence for the dead.

Over lunch, a reporter asked Kennedy about his own family's plans for the duration of the war. "Oh," he replied, "we must get back to school, but we shan't go until all other American citizens have left."[32] (In fact, Rose Kennedy and three of her children sailed home on the SS *Washington* five days later, and Joe Jr. followed them within forty-eight hours on the *Mauritania*.) Later that evening, there was a somewhat strained display of municipal jollity in Glasgow City Hall, where Kennedy and the lord provost cohosted "a big tea, speeches, a bag-pipe outfit and a performance by music-hall star Harry Lauder," who entertained some of the still-traumatized survivors, many of them huddled together in blankets, with such popular airs as "Roamin' in the Gloamin'" and "I Love a Lassie." The temporary goodwill came to an abrupt end later in the night when the "schoolboy diplomat" – as the *Daily Telegraph* correspondent dubbed Kennedy – again rose to his feet to assure the audience that all would be well for their eventual return to the United States. At this, "there were further loud remonstrations ... One young lady declared: 'We defiantly refuse to go until we have a convoy. You have seen what they will do to us.'"

"Young Kennedy was taken aback," the Glasgow *Daily Record* reported, "but managed to shout above the din, 'You will be safe in a ship flying the American flag under international law. A neutral ship is safe.'"

The room looked "unmoved," the *Record* added, but Jack kept his composure. After again promising his audience, "I will tell my father all you say" and "I know he will listen," he "circulated round, shaking hands and posing for pictures ... When seeing an obviously distressed party he would stride over, ungainly in his haste, and nod attentively as they offered their views." Once again vowing to refer all such matters to his father, Jack then gave a final wave and left in a waiting car for Glasgow Central Station and the night express home to London.

Three days later, John Cudahy, the US ambassador to Ireland, wrote of the "exile or refugee problem in general" to President Roosevelt: "Of course all Americans in Europe are clamoring to get home," he acknowledged, "and most of them then fail to understand why they cannot be repatriated at once. The main thing is to calm them down and let them know that they have not been abandoned by their Government."[33] Cudahy felt that the *Athenia* disaster in particular "has been handled with the hand of experienced wisdom."[34] The press by and large echoed the sentiment, agreeing that Jack Kennedy had made the best of a thankless brief. The *London Evening News* called him the "ambassador of mercy," and remarked that "his boyish charm and natural kindliness persuaded those who he had come to comfort that America was indeed keeping a benevolent and watchful eye on them ... He displayed a wisdom and sympathy of a man twice his age."[35] Kennedy had come through his first political test bruised but unbowed, presenting himself to his audience as one of them – a concerned, patriotic, temporarily displaced American. In later years, Jack modestly downplayed his role in the *Athenia* affair, insisting that his father had sent him to Glasgow only after long hesitation and "because no one better was available" for the role. But the later release of Ambassador

Kennedy's papers showed that in fact he had thought of Jack immediately for the job and had no doubt of his burgeoning political skills. "I [can] get all my thrills and excitement watching [his] career," Joe would tell his friend Lord Beaverbrook, adding that as a result he now had no presidential ambitions of his own.[36]

Back in London, experience was soon filling out Jack's youthful idealism. Describing recent events in a memo for his father, he recommended that the city of Glasgow and the Royal Navy both be thanked for their relief work and that "a convoy be sent with the boat that is going to take [the *Athenia* survivors] back to America, because a) the natural shock of the people would make the trip to America alone unbearable, and b) because of the feeling that they will have that the United States government exposed them to this unnecessarily."[37] The ambassador in turn dismissed the idea of an escort as "impossible and unnecessary" and brusquely told Jack to get on with arranging for the immediate repatriation of these "hysterically demand[ing]" people.[38] At that point, Jack sat down to write to the dean of students at Harvard, mildly noting that he was currently "in charge of the committee for the evacuation" of several hundred US nationals, and politely hoping that his consequent late arrival on campus "will … not endanger my standing." (The dean proved sympathetic.) After a further flurry of signals between London and Washington, the World War I troop ship USS *Orizaba* duly left Glasgow on the morning of September 19 to return some four hundred *Athenia* survivors to New York. In the event, Jack arrived home before they did, having caught a Pan American flight from Foynes, on the west coast of Ireland, early on September 20.

With the war in Europe in full flow, back in Massachusetts Jack Kennedy (as always in his element among a female audience) gave a one-hour lecture to the local chapters of the YWCA and WMCA that seemed to go "very well," he modestly wrote his father.[39] The younger Kennedy would go on to become the one family member to emerge in 1945 with his anti-appeasement credentials fully intact. Yet, in October 1939 he followed up his YWCA talk by an editorial in the Harvard *Crimson* that sounded more like a draft speech of Chamberlain's at the time of the Munich sellout. Entitled "Peace in Our Time," it argued that Britain and Germany were "both painfully eager to end the fight after the first preliminary round," and it went rapidly downhill from there. "There is every possibility – almost a probability – of English defeat," Jack wrote, in an approximation of his father's voice, before adding some fond hopes about the prospect of achieving an effective thirteenth-hour compromise with "Hitlerdom." The logical outcome of this "would mean a free economic hand for the Nazis in Eastern Europe [and] a redistribution of colonies," he admitted.[40] Clearly, Jack's views would soon be modified, showing both a more realistic grasp of European affairs and a new-found willingness to break with the family line. But the fact remains that his words could – and did – offend many of those among his British friends, such as David Ormsby-Gore, who were already fighting in defense of their country. Perhaps it was just as well that editorials in the *Crimson* were unsigned, leaving Kennedy later able to distance himself from his youthful folly.

Within a month of his article's appearance in the *Crimson*, Jack wrote to his father, "I am taking as my thesis for honors England's Foreign Policy since 1931, and will discuss the class influence in England." Future presidential biographers and historians would come to debate this document with unusual intensity, facing off on Kennedy's intentions in writing it with all the fury of Swift's Lilliput and Blefuscu fighting over whether to break eggs at the big end or small end. Was he in fact appalled, like his father, at the collapse of appeasement? Could the ensuing paper, with its post-Churchillian title "Why England Slept" (later a book of the same name) be read more as a cautionary tale about Britain's slowness to rearm and, by extension, the apathy of the European democracies when confronted by the emergent Hitler? And if so, what were the lessons that Kennedy, as president, might have gone on to apply in broadly similar circumstances, in particular toward the threat posed by Nikita Khrushchev's Soviet Union? Whatever conclusions can be drawn from the 148-page thesis, it's surely significant that Jack – in contrast to other Harvard students, whose dissertations dwelt on such matters as the Massachusetts road network or Boston's municipal sewer supply – chose to write at such length about British social and political history. In later years, Rose Kennedy felt that her son had formed an almost romantic attachment to pre-war Britain. "I think Jack responded to all that," she said in a somewhat rambling filmed CBS interview following President Kennedy's assassination, "because he did like literature, and he did appreciate it, [and] of course, he did enjoy seeing all the beautiful homes, like the Devonshires' … There were different souvenirs of the years they had spent in government, in those houses, and all those things Jack responded to, and so he did enjoy himself there."[41] To David Ormsby-Gore, Jack's true intent in "Why England Slept" was more narrowly pragmatic: "His major interest, which never left him, was how democracy reacts to a bully."[42]

Jack began writing his thesis over the Christmas vacation of 1939 at Palm Beach. He developed a theme: that Chamberlain's accommodation of Hitler at Munich was only the logical consequence of Britain's failure to rearm earlier in the 1930s; and a style: stiff and pedantic for the most part, although with sudden and redeeming jolts of sardonic black humor. Jack's grammar and spelling were whimsical, at best, and he often struggled with his prose, which could be suggestive of a light fog moving over a hazy landscape. At one point he wrote of a particular era of British parliamentary inertia, "This is mentioned, as I want to bring home the fact, for example, in this group, Hitler's rearming would be little immediate cause for alarm – at least in the year 1934." Another passage read, "What is trying to be shown here is that while we may look back on Herr Hitler's rearming in 1933–1934 as calling strongly for

England, herself, to start rearming, we have to remember that for many people this meant merely asserting her rights of equality, or protecting herself against Russian aggression, not as an act directed against England." His paper's less-than-pithy subtitle was, "The Inevitable Result of the Slowness of Conversion of the British Democracy to Change from a Disarmament Policy to a Rearmament Policy." Nonetheless, all undergraduate gaucheness aside, it was an impressively detailed, cogently argued work that went far beyond the specifics of the immediate crisis in Europe to ask Americans to think hard about the sort of decisions needed to ensure their own national security. "[Democracy] may be a great system of government to live in internally," Jack wrote, "but it's [*sic*] weaknesses are great. We wish to preserve it here. If we are to do so, we must look at situations more realistically than we do now."[43]

For Kennedy, the thrust of the argument was the need for the thinking man in America to apply an "unflinching realism" and "cold, practical reason" in his view of the world. Anything less was to make him "the dupe of the tinpot dictators." Ignoring an obvious threat like that posed by European fascism was really akin to a form of national suicide. "If the tyrants win the present war, we are going to have to be prepared to make the same type of sacrifices [as] England," he wrote. Ironically, of course, Jack's thesis was also an implied criticism of the same sort of self-serving isolationist policies collectively flying under the "America First" banner long waved by the serving us ambassador in London. As such, it was the very moment when the younger Kennedy first demonstrated a fledgling but still coherent political philosophy independent of his father's. The Harvard professor Carl Friedrich privately told colleagues that Jack's thesis should have been called "While Daddy Slept."[44]

In a further twist, the older Kennedy went out of his way first to help Jack's work and then to circulate it to the widest possible audience. After putting his official public affairs staff at his son's disposal, Joe went on to arrange interviews for him with Lord Lothian, the British ambassador in Washington, and Sumner Welles, the undersecretary of state, with whom Jack "chatted cordially" for three hours. These were not the usual undergraduate resources when it came to writing a thesis. Some of the flavor of the research process as a whole can be seen in Jack's cable of January 11, 1940, to the long-suffering US press attaché in London, James Seymour:

SEND IMMEDIATELY PAMPHLETS, ETC, CONSERVATIVE, LABOR, LIBERAL, PACIFIST ORGANIZATIONS FOR APPEASEMENT THESIS DISCUSSING FACTORS INFLUENCING PRO CON 1932 TO 1939 STOP SUGGEST LASKEY [*sic*] AS REFERENCE ... THANKS, JACK KENNEDY[45]

Seymour found himself just then in the middle of a war-torn capital, coping with paper and fuel shortages, blackouts, and the demands of several thousand anxious Americans citizens still awaiting their passage home, but nonetheless he promptly replied that "a word from your father had already sent me scratching to find you some source material ... I am checking with Chatham House and Oxford University Press ... London School of Economics has evacuated to Cambridge, but I reached Laski by wire. I shall follow him up ... Also I have a couple of booksellers investigating for other publications on the subject and I am making a survey of articles and books listed at the British Museum Reading Room."[46]

Having begun writing what became "Why England Slept" only on January 3, 1940, Jack had completed the entire thesis by March 17, allowing him to enjoy a "muted" St. Patrick's Day celebration that night in Boston. In his conclusion, he wrote, "Our foreign policy must take advantage of every opportunity so that we can use our natural advantages ... We must keep from being placed on an equal keel with the dictator because then we will loose [*sic*] ... We must use every effort to form accurate judgments – and even then our task will be a difficult one." These were topical and even prophetic words in the United States, although to many of those already at war in Britain they must have seemed oddly redundant.

Although the Harvard faculty graded Jack's thesis cum laude – the lowest of the three passes possible – the Kennedys' family friend (and *New York Times* columnist) Arthur Krock insisted that it could be commercially published. After significant editing, in large part by the biddable Krock himself, it was accepted that June by the small firm of Wilfred Funk in New York. By then events overseas were assuming a new urgency, with the evacuation of the British Expeditionary Force at Dunkirk and the subsequent fall of France. Despite or because of the deepening world crisis, Jack wrote to his father asking to be allowed to return to London. It was the young man's natural impatience with being forced to watch unfolding events from the sideline. The ambassador declined his request. "Mother told me you didn't think it best I came over, which is probably right … I guess I shall go to the Cape," Jack responded, with just a touch less of his former deference.[47]

Soon, Jack wrote to the Harvard *Crimson* to rebuke those who still thought that the United States could stay out of the hostilities indefinitely. It was a marked departure in both tone and substance from his editorial line of the previous October. "The failure to build up her armaments has not saved England from a war, and may cost her one," he noted. "Are we in America to let that lesson go unlearned?" In a rare case of academic theory becoming policy, twenty-one years after he wrote these words, President Kennedy returned from a "very sober" meeting with Nikita Khrushchev in Vienna to inform the American people, "We will at all times be ready to talk … But we must also be ready to resist with force, if force is used upon us."[48] To demonstrate his resolve, Kennedy announced that he would ask Congress for a further $3.3 billion military buildup, including an increase of 125,000 in army manpower, a tripling of draft quotas, and an equivalent call-up of reserves.

★ ★ ★

LIKE MILLIONS OF OTHERS, Ambassador Kennedy was shocked and appalled when in July 1940 the German Luftwaffe unleashed its first extended bombing campaign against the British mainland. In his case, however, the widely shared revulsion at the enemy terror attacks on civilian targets was matched by a growing sense of exasperation that the British should stubbornly refuse to surrender when they were so obviously beaten. "If the [Royal] Air Force cannot be knocked out," Kennedy wired Secretary Hull on August 2, "then the war will drag out with the whole world continuously upset, with the final result the starvation of England and God knows what happening to the rest of Europe."[49] The ambassador candidly added in a cable direct to President Roosevelt, "I have yet to talk to any military expert … who thinks that England has a Chinaman's chance" of victory. The tragedy for the British people was not so much the German bombing raids, he added, but the delusion of the new prime minister Winston Churchill and others that the United States would, taking pity on their old ally, "come into this war and sign a blank check."[50] Joe was equally guarded when it came to his private investments, taking care to liquidate all his shares in British companies as the European situation deteriorated that summer.

Wiring the State Department on September 27, after a week of nightly terror attacks, Kennedy scoffed at Churchill's claims that British factories would continue to turn out enough munitions to take the fight to Hitler. "Production is definitely falling, regardless of what reports you may be getting," Joe wrote. "I cannot impress on you strongly enough my complete lack of confidence in the entire conduct of this war," he added, concluding that the only possible outcome now, barring an outright Nazi victory, would be if the United States came in "against Germany, Italy, and Japan, aided by a badly shot to pieces country which in the last analysis can give little if any assistance to the cause."[51]

The same coldly calculating qualities that made Joseph Kennedy such a poor choice as an ambassador also gave him clear-eyed and often startling powers of insight when it came to his son Jack's future career. The older man immediately realized the advantages for an ambitious Harvard graduate in the climate of 1940 in having a published book about the origins of the war to his name. "Whether you make a cent out of it or not," he wrote Jack, "it will do you an amazing amount of good. You would be surprised how a work that really makes the grade with high-class people stands you in good stead for years to come."[52] The ambassador was far too shrewd a businessman not to see that Jack's stock would rise appreciably as a result of his book, and from then on he seems to have watched over him much as an anxious employer might do a precocious but frail young protégé settling in to an important new job.

Pausing in his biblical prophecies of doom, Joseph Kennedy wrote letters to each of his children as the bombs fell on London that summer. Eight of the siblings got social chat about weekend parties, the scores of tennis and golf matches, or the difficulties of procuring fresh eggs under the new rationing provisions. By contrast, Joe favored Jack with a full report on "the situation here," which spoke at length about the prospect of Britain being bombed to the conference table, if not destroyed as an independent state.[53]

It was in this febrile atmosphere that *Why England Slept* went on sale throughout North America in early August 1940, with a British edition following in October. By and large, the critics were fulsome, and there was also a heartening initial response from the public. A total of 3,674 copies were sold in the book's first two days, a figure that most modern nonfiction authors could only dream of. Jack told the *Boston Herald* he was pleased by the success, "but irked by constant innuendo that he is his father's mouthpiece. 'I haven't seen my father in six months, nor are we of the same opinion concerning certain British states-men,'" Jack said, carefully distancing his view of Churchill from the ambassador's. While the "old man" continued to pour scorn on Britain's chances of survival, his sometimes wayward second son was quickly being taken up as a prophetic figure whose book pinpointed the moral lesson to America about the need to prepare for war while time still remained for her to do so. The British author and historian Paul Johnson adds the detail that "Old Joe and his men turned *Why England Slept* into a 'bestseller,' partly by using influence with publishers such as Henry Luce, partly by buying 30,000–40,000 copies, which were secretly stored at the family compound in Hyannisport."[54] According to figures provided by the book's commissioning editor Wilfred Funk, *Why England Slept* enjoyed roughly twelve thousand "recorded sales" in North America during the first twenty years of its publication.

Unlike most first-time authors, Kennedy went on to preside over several well-subscribed public speaking events for his book. His predominantly female readers flocked to them, turning the encounters into raucous literary-political festivals whose audience members toted handmade signs and banners, many of them customized with slogans indicating how positively they would react to any romantic overtures Jack might make to them and in general responding with a delirious enthusiasm that fore-shadowed in only slightly more muted form the "Sinatramania" furor of a year or two later. The book's more formal reviews were also warm. Many of the major metropolitan papers on both sides of the Atlantic praised *Why England Slept* as a timely call to American arms. In London, the *Times Literary Supplement* deemed it "a young man's book" but one that "contains much wisdom for older readers," the fifty-two-year-old us ambassador to Britain possibly among them.

Perhaps even more gratifying to Jack were the comments of individual readers who wrote to congratulate him, including President Roosevelt and Winston Churchill. John Pierrepont, the financier, announced that he was sending copies "to at least half a dozen hard-bitten isolationists" whom he thought would profit by reading it. Offers for Jack to lecture or supply magazine articles on world affairs flooded in to the young author's postbox. When the final figures were added up, *Why England Slept* sold some eighty-two thousand hardback copies in sixteen markets around the world (including those alleged not to have left the Kennedys' storage facility in Hyannis Port), netting its author some $25,000 in royalties. Jack donated his first British earnings to the recently bombed city of Plymouth, England, and used his American fee to buy himself a pale green Buick convertible. But more important than either sales or reviews was the fact that, overnight, the book's success made it possible to think of the twenty-three-year-old college graduate as a future contender for high public office, just as his father had predicted. It seems only logical that President Kennedy later kept a copy of *Why England Slept* prominently displayed on his White House desk.

The young man who had joked his way through high school, who had lasted only days at the LSE, and who had moved around fecklessly between American colleges was now a highly regarded author. The one significant exception to the chorus of approval that greeted *Why England Slept* was Jack's one-time tutor at the LSE, Harold Laski. Laski wrote to Ambassador Kennedy declining to supply an introduction to the book and warning him that its publication would cause everyone involved with it severe embarrassment. While it "would be easy to repeat the eulogies Krock and Harry [*sic*] Luce have showered on your boy's work," Laski allowed, "I choose the more difficult way of regretting deeply that you let him do it." Further twisting the knife, the academic noted that no one would even have looked at the book without the older Kennedy's influence. "And these are not the right grounds for publication," he added.[55] Both the number of editors who in fact turned down the original manuscript and the matter of Krock's uncredited contribution lend weight to Laski's thesis that the author of *Why England Slept* had "little personally to brag about." But set against this was Winston Churchill's view that the book showed a "rationality and reason" that had eluded Kennedy's father.[56]

Meanwhile, the speed of the German advance through the Low Countries and France in May 1940 had taken even Hitler by surprise, and there were divided views on how to pursue the Allied forces trapped at Dunkirk. While the High Command in Berlin debated the issue, the British were able to evacuate 340,000 troops (including 140,000 French) by a swarm of boats of every description in a remarkable improvised operation. At this desperate time, Ambassador Kennedy wrote "most urgently" to President Roosevelt to complain that the Bank of England was selling gold in the United States at $35 an ounce in order to pay for imports of food and military supplies, and that this might result in an unwelcome fall of Wall Street stock prices.[57] It's possible to believe that when certain British commentators later came to observe that Americans as a breed only care about money, it was Joe they chiefly had in mind. Even as the Allied troops were being hurriedly taken off the beach at Dunkirk, the ambassador cabled the president to announce, "Only a miracle can now save the [British] from being wiped out ... I suspect that the Germans would be willing to make peace with them now – of course on their own terms, but on terms that would be a great deal better than they would be if the war continues."[58] According to his colleague Selwyn Lloyd, this was the moment that Churchill gave it as his private opinion that the accredited US representative to Britain was a "callous, cunning manipulator, who tossed opponents aside like so many cigar-ends in the gutter."

"He's entitled to his views," John Kennedy later remarked when discussing his father. "He made himself."[59] But by the late summer of 1940, those views already differed radically from those of his son. The lionized young author told reporters who came to interview him about *Why England Slept* that Churchill was the voice of "British fiber" and of a "new realism" about the struggles that lay ahead before the inevitable victory over Nazism. The ambassador refused to credit it. "There is no question but that they are covering up a great deal in the English press," he wrote to Jack on September 10. "For instance, [NBC correspondent] Bill Hillman wanted to broadcast the fact that he had been down to Dover and had seen no British ships going through the Channel. The censors refused to let him say that … The [government] keep saying their chin is up and that they can't be beaten, but the people who have had any experience with these bombings don't like it at all."[60]

Joe Kennedy's own tolerance of aerial attack was also thought modest, and by the time he wrote his letter to Jack he was spending both his weekends and most of his weeknights in the relative safety of a seventy-room mansion in the capital's far-western suburbs at Windsor. After dinner there one night, Joe was summoned to take an urgent phone call from Herschel Johnson, his deputy at the embassy. Johnson laid out an "almost fantastic" story of espionage and high treason apparently being conducted from under their own roof. Tyler Kent, a twenty-nine-year-old Virginian "born into one of America's richest families," as he insisted, but currently working as a junior cipher clerk at the embassy, had been observed by British intelligence consorting with a shadowy group of exiled White Russians and disaffected right-wing politicians such as one Captain Archibald Ramsay, an anti-Semitic Scottish Unionist MP, broadly thought to be sympathetic to the Nazi cause. Now Scotland Yard was preparing to make arrests, "and would search Kent's rooms at the same time provided that we would waive any diplomatic immunity that might prevent this," Johnson added. The ambassador immediately agreed to the request. Johnson then asked his boss what his relations with Kent had been like. "He has always been solidly behind me," replied Kennedy.[61]

When the British police came for Kent at dawn the following Monday morning, he refused them entrance, shouting at them through the letter-box of his flat that they were communists who themselves deserved to be arrested. After breaking down the door and taking Kent into custody, the authorities found 1,929 official or semiofficial documents, as well as a quantity of

Swedish pornography, concealed on the premises. The former included copies of secret cables between Winston Churchill and President Roosevelt that would seem to have been in breach of the strict us neutrality laws. Kennedy was justifiably alarmed at the possible implications as they might apply both at the highest levels of government and in terms of his own career. An investigative team from FBI headquarters in Washington, joined by several of Roosevelt's inner circle, left for London posthaste. "It is appalling," Assistant Secretary of State Breckinridge Long wrote in his diary. "Hundreds of copies – true readings – of dispatches, cables, messages. Some months every single message going into or out from the London Embassy was copied and the copies found in Kent's room … It is a terrible blow – almost a major catastrophe."[62]

Three months later, Ambassador Kennedy was leaving a concert in London one evening when an usher handed him a note asking him to go immediately to 10 Downing Street. Arriving there at midnight, Kennedy was met by Winston Churchill, who congenially offered him a brandy and a cigar. The ambassador told the prime minister, "I'm not smoking or drinking for the duration of the war." "My God," the PM replied, "you make me feel as if I should go round in sackcloth and ashes."[63] Churchill then remarked that he was certain Britain would win the war, regardless of whether or not the United States joined in, and that as a personal favor to his friend Franklin Roosevelt he was arranging for the Tyler Kent trial to be postponed until after that November's presidential election, which could thus go ahead without any embarrassing release of "telegrams that showed too close a connection between the Prime Minister and the President." Kent was duly tried in camera, with brown paper glued over the courtroom windows, found guilty of offenses under the Official Secrets Act, and sentenced to seven years' imprisonment. At the end of the war, he was released and deported to the United States. Ambassador Kennedy had little to reproach himself for in the whole scandal – it could have happened to anyone – but it seems fair to say that it contributed to his being one of the most talked-about figures in high government circles both in London and Washington – and much of that talk was unfavorable. The State Department subsequently issued a statement indicating that it had acceded to British wishes in the affair because "the interest of the United Kingdom, at a time when it was fighting for its existence, was preeminent."[64] Ambassador Kennedy's term of office in London was later generally recalled with something closer to exasperation – and occasional grudging respect – than real affection. Tyler Kent lived long enough to denounce President Kennedy as a communist and to charge that his assassination had somehow been a result of this. Kent himself died in poverty in a Texas trailer park in 1988.

★　★　★

WITHIN A FEW WEEKS of the publication of *Why England Slept*, Jack Kennedy was openly praising Churchill's leadership and implying that it should be a model both to those in authority in the United States and by extension to his own father. In the charged atmosphere of 1940, many young men might have carped – and did – at the wrong-headed opinions of an older generation that had seemed to them to sleepwalk into war, but it took intellectual self-confidence of a high order to publicly contradict a man quite as opinionated and volatile as Joe Kennedy was. Still only twenty-three, and rather listlessly studying law at Stanford, Jack could convincingly present himself to the world as an expert on international affairs in his own right, not just as the mouthpiece of a controversial billionaire diplomat. When, later that year, the ambassador decided it was time to publish a major article on appeasement and the whole history of recent British foreign policy, he turned to his son for help. "Dear Dad," Jack wrote in a dictated letter on December 5, "I am sending along to you a rough outline of some points that I feel it would be well for you to cover … I don't present it in the form of a finished article, as I first of all don't know what your view point is on some questions, and secondly I think the article should be well padded with stories of your experience in England in order to give it an authenticity and interest … I think it is right for you to do this in order to clear the record."[65]

Jack's draft, among other things, attempted to portray his father as a visionary anti-appeaser in the Churchillian mold. "My views are not pleasant," he had Joe say, factually enough, in the article. "I am gloomy. And I have been gloomy since September, 1938. It may be unpleasant for American[s] to hear my views" – another phrase that was perhaps truer than intended – "but let me note that Winston Churchill was considered distinctly unpleasant to have around during the years 1935 to 1939." In another brave if forlorn attempt to salvage the ambassador's public reputation, Jack wrote in a sidebar, "Dad – I would think that your best angle would be that … you with your background can not stand the idea personally of dictatorships – you hate them – you have achieved the abundant life under a democratic capitalistic system – you wish to preserve it. But you believe you can only preserve it by keeping out of Europe's wars." Proof that Jack himself seemed to be aligned with the interventionist cause followed later that month when his number was pulled out of a glass bowl by a blindfolded Henry Stimson, the secretary of war, signifying his induction into the US armed forces. The young Kennedy's chief concern was that his long history of ill health might prevent him from serving his country. "They will never take me into the army," he fretted to Lem Billings.[66] Billings thought the whole matter of the draft, Jack now wanting to fight, the ambassador leading the negotiated-peace camp, "a sort of snapshot of the Kennedys' relationship" as it stood at the end of 1940. "It is my feeling," Lem remembered later, "and I'm sure I am right, that Jack absolutely disagreed with the ambassador a hundred per cent."[67]

Later that same week in December, en route to address a
meeting of the Institute of World Affairs in Los Angeles, Jack
took out a sheet of United Airlines stationery and scratched on
it in his nearly indecipherable handwriting what amounted to an
affectionate rebuke of his father:

> I realize that aid for Britain is part of it, but in your message
> for America to stay out of the war – you should not do so *at
> the expense of having people minimize aid to Britain*. [Emphasis in
> the original.] The danger of our not giving Britain enough
> aid, of not getting Congress and the country stirred up suf-
> ficiently to give England the aid she needs now – is to me just
> as great as the danger of our getting into the war now – as it is
> much more likely.
>
> If England is defeated America is going to be alone in a
> strained and hostile world. In a few years, she will have paid
> out enormous sums for defense yearly – to maintain arma-
> ments – she may be at war – she even may be on the verge of
> defeat or defeated – by a combination of totalitarian powers.
>
> Then there will be a general turning of the people's
> opinions. They will say, "Why were we so stupid not to
> have given Britain all possible aid. Why did we worry about
> money etc. *We should have put in more legislation*. We should
> have given it to them outright … We should have been ready
> to give England money – they were definitely another arm
> of our defense forces."
>
> Just as we now turn on those who got us into the last war,
> so in the future we may turn on those who failed to point out
> the great necessity of providing Britain in the crucial months
> of 1940–1941.[68]

Here was surely the first-person voice of a future leader of
the Atlantic alliance, putting the whole weight of his world-
liness behind an unspoken, or half-spoken, reprimand of the
"old man" and his ruinous policy of keeping America out

of the war at any cost, if simultaneously that meant the fall of Britain.

★ ★ ★

MEANWHILE, President Roosevelt had responded to Churchill's own increasingly dire warnings about British shipping losses by proposing to Congress the reassuringly named Act to Promote the Defense of the United States, or "Lend-Lease" as it soon became known. Among other things, this would supply America's beleaguered Atlantic ally with some $32 billion in food, oil, and materiel during the course of the war. A lively domestic political debate ensued, and on January 16, 1941, Roosevelt summoned Joseph Kennedy to the White House to canvass his views. After a fifteen-minute wait, the ambassador was "ushered into [Roosevelt's] bedroom, and found he was in his bathroom in his wheel chair. He was attired in a sort of grey pajamas and was starting to shave himself. I sat on the toilet-seat and talked to him."[69] While conversing with the president in this posture, Kennedy remarked simply that he would do everything possible in his power to keep the United States out of the war. Later that afternoon, Roosevelt was able to tell his cabinet only that "Joe would probably not go too far overboard [in opposing Lend-Lease], but he realized that he was always unpredictable and might say anything."[70]

In the end, it was Jack Kennedy who successfully advised his father to "swallow hard [and] back Lend-Lease." To do otherwise, Jack argued, was only to increase the danger of British defeat and a subsequent American war with Germany. According to this theory, the views of "well-meaning dreamer[s]" like the ambassador in themselves posed the greatest single threat to global stability. "Where I think [Charles] Lindbergh has run afoul is in his declarations that we do not care what happens over there – that we can live at peace with a world controlled by the dictators," Jack notified his father. "The point

I am trying to get at is that it is *important that you stress how much you dislike the idea of dealing with dictatorships*, how you wouldn't trust their word for a minute – how you have no confidence in them" (emphasis in original).[71] Shortly after he read this letter, Ambassador Kennedy went live on national radio to announce that it was "false and malicious" to claim that he was an appeaser, or that he would under any circumstances "ever advocate a deal with the dictators contrary to British desires."[72] In short order, the Lend-Lease program was passed first by the US House of Representatives (where, to give it a further patriotic twist, the bill was officially designated "H.R. 1776") and then the Senate. President Roosevelt signed the provisions into law on March 11, 1941. "Thank God for your news. Strain is serious," Winston Churchill cabled from London.[73]

By then Joseph Kennedy was home once again, this time permanently. He had told Roosevelt immediately after the 1940 election of his "irrevocable wish, whatever distress it may cause" to resign his post as ambassador, although it was thought that the president had met the decision with equanimity. During the previous two and a half years, Britain's opinion of Kennedy, at least as expressed in most government circles and in the popular press, had evolved from fascination and optimism to one of outright hostility. At his final meeting with Winston Churchill, the retiring ambassador had asked the prime minister if he still "did not want the United States in the war," as he seemed to think was the case. Churchill replied "sharply," Kennedy was later forced to admit: "Of course, as soon as they want to come in, I do want them in," the premier stated.[74] Kennedy had not only completely misread this critical British position, but he apparently believed that the PM continued to think of him personally as a "swell type" and "devoted friend of this besieged island."[75] Misapprehensions could hardly be much greater. For some months beforehand, Churchill's political aide Brendan Bracken had been instructed to keep a file containing Kennedy's more hostile comments about President Roosevelt and to ensure that this was forwarded to the White House.[76] A certain cool-ness ensued in the president-ambassador relationship as a result. In time, Roosevelt privately called Kennedy a "temperamental Irish boy," who was "terrifically spoiled at an early age by huge financial success: thoroughly patriotic, thoroughly selfish, and thoroughly obsessed with the idea that he must leave each of his nine children with a million dollars apiece when he dies."[77]

Nevertheless, the two men maintained their public pre-tense of civility until the end. "Today the President was good enough to express regret over my wish [to resign]," Kennedy announced, after mutually agreeing with him that it was the best solution. "I shall not return to London ... My plan is, after a short holiday, to devote my efforts to what seems to me the great cause in the world today – and means, if successful, the preservation of the American form of democracy. That cause is to help keep the United States out of war."[78]

In London, Winston Churchill celebrated Kennedy's depar-ture with a "particularly fine" bottle of Pol Roger champagne.[79]

★　★　★

"I READ YOUR BOOK and I thought it very good indeed," Kennedy's society friend Tony St. Clair-Erskine told him in December 1940. "It was beautifully written, though most Americans do not write beautifully."[80] The consensus in those rarefied British circles was that Jack had already far eclipsed his father as a political thinker and produced a work that was scholarly, objective, and full of practical good sense. Winston Churchill privately added that *Why England Slept* "had the courage to state the truth, at least as its author [saw] it," and "tell Americans what they needed to hear."[81] Churchill's lord chancellor John Simon, a notorious pre-war appeaser, told Joe Kennedy, "Your son is obviously trying to give a fair account in his book" and enclosed with his letter "a little pamphlet ... deal-ing with British diplomacy during the Manchuria business" – as

he called the 1937 Japanese Rape of Nanking – for Jack's edifi-
cation. "If Mr. John Kennedy is in England, perhaps he would
come and see me?" Simon wondered.[82] The chancellor's long,
self-justifying letter demonstrated the paradox, also shared by
Joe, where the most belligerent of characters could be the most
outspoken advocate of peace.

In January 1941, Jack Kennedy left Stanford and again
checked in to the hospital in Boston. It was the wearingly familiar story of back pain, digestive problems, and acute weight loss,
which he bore with his normal fortitude. While lying in bed,
Jack fashioned a writing board out of a cafeteria breakfast tray
and drafted an article for the *New York Journal-American* on the
troubled issue of whether Ireland should supply naval and air
bases to the English. In his first serious analysis of his Irish heritage, Jack took a careful politician's view of the matter. While
acknowledging that the bad blood between Dublin and London
went back over six hundred years, Ireland "would still stand a
far better chance of living in peace and freedom in a world free
from the menace of Hitler," he wrote.[83]

When not laboring on the world's great geopolitical problems, Jack still found time to lingeringly assess the nurses on
his ward, "with their crisply ironed uniforms and stockings."
It's not uncommon for hospital patients to develop warmly
appreciative feelings toward their caregivers, especially those of
the opposite sex, but in Kennedy's case it begins to go beyond
normal gratitude and resemble an obsession.

"There is a real feeling here," Jack went on to tell a peace
conference in California, "that outright and total support for
Great Britain is not only preferable, but essential for long-term
survival and stability in the States."[84] Showing that he had the
courage of his convictions, and despite having already failed
one set of army physicals, in August 1941 he managed to persuade a medical board that he was "exceptionally qualified for
appointment" as a probationary officer in the US Navy. Kennedy
had "leadership, purpose, and direction" the recruiters noted,

although in strictly nautical terms his experience had been limited to sailing lazily around Cape Cod on summer weekends.

Jack's term of service began in Washington, D.C., where he was required to put in long hours as a pen-pusher in the Office of Naval Intelligence (ONI), while continuing to enjoy a full social life. "Isn't this a dull letter," he wrote Billings in the week of Japan's attack on Pearl Harbor. "But I'm not sleeping much nights."[85]

Through his sister Kick, Jack met twenty-eight-year-old Inga Arvad, a blonde, blue-eyed Nordic beauty who wrote a popular gossip column for the *Times-Herald* newspaper. She had been born in Denmark as Inga Maria Petersen, but changed her name before coming to the United States, where she studied at New York's Columbia School of Journalism. Inga was, as one friend put it, "no rocket scientist," but both she and her column displayed a certain earthy humor. She had been on assignment in Berlin at the time of the 1936 Olympic Games, where she was on friendly terms, if not more than that, with several high-ranking Nazi officials. "You immediately like him," Inga wrote of her "great friend" Adolf Hitler. "He seems lonely. The eyes, showing a kind heart, stare right at you. They sparkle with force."[86] Like British Nazi sympathizer Unity Mitford, she seems to have experienced the thrill of the "Führer Kontakt."

On November 27, 1941, Inga informed her readers in the *Times-Herald* that Jack Kennedy was "a boy with a future." At twenty-four, he was already a successful author, and "elder men like to hear his views, which are sound and astonishingly objective for one so young."[87] Jack in turn extolled the charms of "Inga Binga," as he called her, even if his immediate superiors at ONI took a dim view of him consorting with a possible Nazi provocateur. After being transferred to a desk job in Charleston, South Carolina, Jack told a reporter in his newly salty language, "They shagged my ass down [here] because I was going around with a Scandinavian blonde, and they thought she was a spy!"[88]

Before going into exile, Jack enjoyed a dinner at the home of the *Times-Herald* publisher and outspoken isolationist Cissy Patterson, where he found himself rubbing shoulders with Undersecretary of the Navy James Forrestal, left-wing Democratic senator Burton Wheeler, and the Pulitzer-prizewinning reporter Herbert Swope, among others. Characteristically, Kennedy went on to write a five-page account of the evening, thinking he might later work it up into an article or a book. After some invigorating back-and-forth about Lend-Lease and the course of the war in general – this was shortly before Pearl Harbor – forty-nine-year-old Forrestal, a future us secretary of defense, paid Jack the compliment of asking him his views. "I replied that I had been an isolationist due to the fact that I believed that the effort necessary by the us to defeat Germany would be so great that in the end the us would have lost what they were fighting for," Kennedy admitted. "I said that my belief has changed somewhat … America's aid might become decisive, and if the situation reached that point and if a quick victory could be achieved, I would favor America going in."[89] It was a carefully nuanced reply, with that same mixture of intelligence, self-belief, and detachment that typified Jack's political views as a whole. "You know, I may run for president one day," he airily informed his sister Kick and some British friends that month.[90]

Meanwhile, the FBI had begun tracking his movements, the bureau's director J. Edgar Hoover reacting with a mixture of moral indignation and voyeuristic glee to the reports he read on Jack's affair with his foreign-born siren – one that "appear[s] to have involved engaging in sexual intercourse," Hoover noted incredulously.[91] On the whole, this was unwelcome attention for a prominent young American serviceman in the prevailing climate of 1942. Ensign (later Lieutenant) Kennedy soon applied for foreign duty, his libido held in check by patriotism and nascent political ambitions. "You are going away," Inga wrote him on Valentine's Day, 1942. "A thing I have known for months, and I suppose most women would be proud and say 'Go and defend your country.' I say the same, but somehow the pride is not there, only a hope that God will keep his hand safely over you. And more important than returning with your handsome body intact, to let you come back with the wishes both to be a White-House-Man and wanting the ranch – somewhere out West."[92]

By the following spring, Inga's letters had a more wistful, valedictory air about them. "Jack, dear," she wrote on April 23, "Life may be tough now and then, but you know how to hold the reins and steer your horses the right way ... So long, some day we will have a steak, mashed potatoes, peas, carrots, and ice cream again. It won't ever be like the old days, somehow the past is gone, but you have a great future ... Don't ever let anybody make you believe anything different."[93]

For most young men in Kennedy's position, the basic act of going away to war was enough. There was simply no point in them wasting time reviewing the long series of political missteps that had led them there. Jack, however, continued to be fascinated by Britain's pre-war foreign policy and, more particularly, by the isolationist sentiments of some of her ruling elite. Before embarking, he arranged a dinner with Lord Halifax, formerly Chamberlain's appeasement-minded foreign minister, whom Churchill had since sent to Washington as British ambassador. "Had a long talk with Halifax regarding Munich and its background," Jack noted in his diary. "He affirmed the thesis that I have always maintained: that Munich should not have been the object of American criticism, but rather the condition of British armaments which made it inevitable ... He said that if England had fought in 1938, she would have been licked immediately."[94] According to this view, it had not been cowardice at play in British pre-war desire to accommodate Hitler, but rather an unsentimental realism about the balance of military power. "Halifax believed that Chamberlain was misled, and defeated by his phrases as much as anything else – phrases which he did not really believe in — such as 'Peace in our time,'" Jack wrote. "When he returned home from Munich, Halifax rode in from Heston with Chamberlain. Chamberlain remarked to him that all the wild celebration, all the roses in the streets would be over in two weeks."

★   ★   ★

FOR JOHN KENNEDY, the year beginning in August 1943 was the seminal one of his career, not excluding any period of the early 1960s. He began it as the lieutenant in command of the thirteen-man Patrol Boat *(PT) 109*, part of an island-hopping flotilla deployed against the Japanese in the South Pacific. It has to be said that it was neither a glamorous nor, in strictly strategic terms, a particularly successful campaign. One PT commander later remarked, "Motor torpedo boats were no good … Whether we ever sunk anything is questionable … The only thing PTs were really effective at was with raising War Bonds."[95] There was a touch of the knockabout book *Mr. Roberts* to the generally relaxed protocol on board *PT 109* itself, where the dress code consisted of a shirt and shorts, sometimes with a sheath knife tucked into a belt, and where there was a generous issue most evenings of a "dynamite-strength" alcoholic concoction drawn from the torpedo tubes, known as "torp juice." Kennedy told his sister Kick in June 1943, "The glamor of PTs just isn't [there] except to the outsider. It's just a matter of night after night [of] patrols at low speed — two hours on — then sacking out and going on again for another two hours."

Yet just twelve months later, Jack Kennedy would be an authentic war hero, his ambition to succeed at something "really big" in life further intensified by the tragic flying death of his brother Joe at the age of twenty-nine. The failed lobotomy performed on his sister Rosemary and the deaths in action both of Billy Hartington, just four months after marrying Kick Kennedy, and several other friends and colleagues-in-arms can only have reinforced Jack's already acute sense of life's fragility. The man leaving the service in 1945 was not the same one who had entered it in 1941.

On the night of August 2, 1943, Kennedy's PT boat was rammed by a Japanese destroyer near New Georgia in the Solomon Islands. Two of the crew members were killed outright and the other eleven cast adrift. It remains a matter of debate whether negligence on Kennedy's part in any way contributed to the tragedy. Thomas Warfield, the navy's director of operations in the area, later speculated that *PT 109*'s crew were "kind of sleepy," and that Jack had essentially panicked when catching sight of the enemy ship bearing down on him out of the moonlight. "If [he] got bugged a little bit and shoved his throttles forward, he'd have killed his engines, and I think that's what he did ... He shoved the [engines] up too fast and killed them."[96] What's beyond dispute is the sequence of events that followed the collision. Despite reinjuring his back in the impact, Kennedy famously swam for five hours, towing a badly hurt shipmate with a life-jacket strap clenched between his teeth. He eventually landed on a small island, where, as we've seen, exhausted and half-mad with dehydration, he carved an SOS message on a coconut with a pocketknife. The natives agreed to carry this to a nearby US base. The subsequent *New York Times* headline conveyed the general domestic reaction: "KENNEDY'S SON IS HERO IN PACIFIC." Asked later how he became a national celebrity, Jack himself noted self-deflatingly, "It was easy – they cut my boat in half."[97] He eventually emerged from the service with a chestful of medals and a certain wariness of the Japanese military capability that never entirely left him. More importantly, in later years Kennedy was able to call on his personal experience of being under enemy fire when, as commander-in-chief, he came to decide whether or not to commit American troops to battle. He knew what it was like to be in the front line of a war.

In May 1944, while Jack was preparing for surgery on his injured back, his twenty-four-year-old sister Kick married Billy

Cavendish at Chelsea Registry Office in London. It's perhaps difficult today to convey the full horror expressed in Kennedy family circles, and elsewhere, that one of their own would tie the knot with a Protestant. "Heartbroken. Feel you have been wrongly influenced – sending [Cardinal] Spellman's friend to talk to you. Anything done for Our Lord will be rewarded hundred fold," Rose Kennedy cabled the intending bride from Boston. After a period of intense negotiation personally brokered by the archbishop of Canterbury, it was agreed that any sons of the union should be raised in the Church of England and any daughters as Roman Catholics.

While Rose Kennedy writhed with religious agonies, others worried more about the prospect of a lowborn Irish–American girl, the granddaughter of a Boston saloon keeper and daughter of an alleged one-time bootlegger coming to assume the title of duchess of Devonshire – and with it the ownership of Chatsworth House and half a dozen other family estates that formed part of an English aristocratic dynasty essentially unchanged since the Stuart era. From our modern perspective, it's possible to see certain fundamental differences in the background and personality of the bride and groom that might have come to transcend any sectarian considerations. Kick Kennedy tended to be brisk in manner, with a certain engaging frankness of speech, which was peppered with American colloquialisms such as "Making whoopee," for instance, and other phrases not customary in the average English country-house salon. Her husband, by contrast, was perhaps more of a stereotypical English "toff," tall, suave, languidly elegant rather than conventionally handsome, and, while politically ambitious, seeming to epitomize the kind of graceful, slightly sleepy British landed aristocrat who was as much taken with the gentlemanly pursuits of hunting, shooting, and fishing as with the vulgarities of policy. "The marriage is now providing a choice morsel of gossip for the dowagers, matrons and debutantes of Mayfair, as well as the crusty and tweedy set of the British squirearchy," the *Boston Globe* chuckled mischievously.

Jack took a typically dry view of the proceedings. "Your plaintive howl in not being let in on Kathleen's nuptials reached me this morning," he wrote Lem Billings. "It was certainly evident that you weren't irked so much by her getting married as by her failure to inform you. You might as well take it in your stride, as sister Eunice from the depth of her righteous Catholic wrath so truly said: 'It's a horrible thing – but it will be nice visiting her after the war, so we might as well face it.'"[98]

Tragically, there were to be no such visits. On September 9, 1944, while serving with the Coldstream Guards in the Allied breakout following the D-Day landings, Billy Hartington was shot dead by a German sniper. He was twenty-six years old. An army colleague, Captain Charles Waterhouse, told me of Hartington's last moments: "He was wearing a pair of light corduroy trousers and waving his cap in his hand to encourage the men. That may have rather marked him out to the enemy. I remember his last words as being, 'Come on you fellows, buck up!' Death came to him instantly."[99]

Mixed with Jack's natural grief and concern for his widowed young sister was another related emotion. Despite his proudly Irish–American family roots, he was coming to appreciate – and perhaps romanticize – what might be seen as a quintessentially English stoic attitude to life. In his four-page letter of condolence to the duchess of Devonshire, Jack wrote that the news of her son's death was:

> about the saddest I have ever had … It was so obvious what he meant to Kick and what a really wonderful fellow he must have been that we all became devoted to him, and now know what a really great loss his is. When I read … about the cool and gallant way Billy died, I couldn't help but think of what John Buchan had written about Raymond Asquith: 'Our roll

of honour is long, but it holds no nobler figure. He will stand to those of us who are left as an incarnation of the spirit of the land he loved. He has become eternal. Debonair and brilliant and brave, he is now part of that immortal England which knows not age or weariness or defeat.'"[100]

Even before Jack wrote this letter, his brother Joe had also perished. He had been flying a specially modified navy Liberator bomber on a raid to attack German V-1 rocket launch sites in Belgium when it exploded in the sky over eastern England. The intention had been for Joe and his copilot to steer the plane, which was packed with nearly ten tons of TNT, to within a few miles of its objective and then to bail out. A trailing bomber using remote control would then guide the Liberator to its final target. It was a near-suicidal mission, and we can speculate that there was a degree of competitiveness, as well as raw courage, about Joe's decision to volunteer for it. Certainly he was well aware that over recent years the public spotlight had increasingly fallen on "the kid," as he called Jack, who had become first a bestselling author and then a war hero. According to Angela Laycock, whose husband Robert led Britain's commandos, Joe Jr. had "confided to [her] that he was sure it was his brother Jack who would ultimately be President." She "had the feeling Joe was in awe of Jack's intelligence and believed that his own was no match for it, particularly since his younger brother's recent triumphs."[101] As even Rose Kennedy recalled of the *PT 109* incident, "In their long brotherly, friendly rivalry, I expect this was the first time Jack had won such an 'advantage' by such a clear margin. And I daresay it cheered Jack and must have rankled Joe Jr."[102]

It was an almost biblical drama, the two brothers who were ardent admirers as well as closet rivals. Reporters later noted how little Joe's name came up in conversation with President Kennedy. But that was not the case at the time. "Joe seemed like someone in love asking news about the object of his affection," a

Cavendish family member recalled. "It was a mutual obsession. Whatever Jack said to Billings, Joe had to know. Whatever Joe said to [a girlfriend], Jack had to know."[103] A visitor to Hyannis Port likened the core atmosphere to being "either in Joe's gang or Jack's gang at a dysfunctional boarding school." It only remains to add that Joe's death came as a terrible fulfillment of Ambassador Kennedy's worst fears about the human cost of the war, and that from then on the ambassador threw himself into the promotion of Jack's career to an even greater extent, if possible, than before. His sorrow turned to fixation.

As a family, the Kennedys came through long and bitter experience to prefer a process of private grieving to one of public anguish in the face of tragedy. If Jack now had occasion to brood on fate's implacable malice, he kept it from even his closest friends. Like the "debonair and brilliant and brave" gentleman-soldier Raymond Asquith (a casualty of the Somme in September 1916) whom he so admired, the young Kennedy strove to maintain an air of wry detachment to events that might have driven other men to self-pity or paranoia. In February 1945, the widowed Kick wrote from England to mourn the loss of two more of her brother's close friends. "The news of Bill Coleman really upset me because I know how much he meant to Jack and how Jack always said that he would do better than anyone else he knew, and then Bob MacDonald lost in a submarine. Where will it all end?"[104] In later years, Jack himself frequently spoke of the character-building aspects inherent in suffering. "His sense of the human tragedy fortified him against self-deception and easy consolation," he noted of Robert Frost, following the poet's death in January 1963.[105]

Meanwhile, Kennedy had separated from the navy and continued his latest convalescence at what he called a "geriatrics' hotel" set among the foothills of the Hieroglyphic Mountains at Castle Hot Springs in Arizona. Jack's first impression as he entered – a man of twenty-seven – was that by doing so he had lowered the average age in the place to around seventy. His time there was not all to be bingo and afternoons lounging by the pool, however. Bashing it out on his vast Underwood typewriter, Jack wrote a new article, "Let's Try an Experiment for Peace," which argued for some form of arms control in the postwar world. "We will soon have only three countries – the USSR, Britain, and the United States – in a position to wage total war," he predicted. "There will, of course, have to be a strong growth of mutual trust between these countries before any comprehensive [disarmament] plan can be worked out. There are many people who feel that Russia's unilateral settlement of the problems of Eastern Europe precludes any workable postwar agreements being made with them."[106]

Having pressed the case in *Why England Slept* for a military buildup by the Atlantic allies, now Kennedy warned against an arms race that could prove mutually ruinous in the years ahead.

In time, Ambassador Kennedy recruited his old ghostwriter Arthur Krock to help Jack with stylistic revisions and matters of basic spelling, which the professional journalist thought "dizzy" and compounded by the many "fussily annotated and semi-legible manuscript revisions" to the text. Krock sent back his changes in early February 1945, telling the ambassador that the piece "seems publishable." Jack's article subsequently did the rounds of the New York magazines, all of which rejected it. The *Atlantic* editor added the scathing comment that it was an "oversimplification" and in need of "thinking ... and conclusions not based on clichés."[107] John Kennedy's first known reflection on postwar arms control and the urgent need for East-West détente remains commercially unpublished today.

In his remaining time in Arizona, Jack went on to compile a memorial album to his brother, *As We Remember Joe*, which came off the press in a privately printed edition of 350 copies. Curiously, Ambassador Kennedy once confided that he was never able to finish reading the book, although it's not clear if this was because he was overcome with emotion or because he now preferred to devote his energies to promoting his second son's career rather than dwell on the past.

In November 1944, Joseph Kennedy had learned of the various legal and financial problems of seventy-year-old US representative James Michael Curley of Massachusetts, who was then struggling to repay some $45,000 in penalties and interest following a pre-war fraud conviction. The details of what followed are unclear, due to the ambassador's preference for doing such business in cash (often disbursed in pay toilets, to ensure added privacy), but it seems fairly certain that a deal was struck whereby Curley's debts would be cleared in exchange for his promise to resign his congressional seat in the eleventh district and instead run for an unprecedented fourth term as mayor of Boston. The significance of this was that it created a job opening that a young, well-connected, personable Irish–American war hero like Jack Kennedy might fill. On December 26, 1944, Representative Curley announced that after six years of failing to do so, he had now "squared things away with the courts," and having made restitution he would be "devoting [him]self anew to the people of Boston." "Curley knew that he was in trouble with the feds over the mail fraud rap," Joseph Kennedy's cousin and political fixer Joe Kane later told an interviewer. "The ambassador paid him to get out of the congressional seat, and Curley figured he might need the money."[108] In February 1945, Jack wrote to tell Lem Billings that he was "returning to Law School at Harvard … and then if something good turns up while I am there I will run for it. *I have my eye on something pretty good now if it comes through.*"[109] Twelve years later, Joseph Kennedy told a reporter, "I got Jack into politics. I was the one. I told him Joe was dead and that it was therefore his responsibility to run for Congress." Even as the war continued, the ambassador seems both to have relinquished his own remaining ambitions of elected office and to have critically reviewed his former air of guarded respect for President Roosevelt. "Harry, what are you doing campaigning for that crippled son of a bitch that killed my son Joe?" Kennedy demanded of Roosevelt's new vice president, Harry Truman, over dinner in Boston.[110]

★ ★ ★

THE WAR MADE the presidency of John Kennedy possible. Before he wrote *Why England Slept*, Jack could be (and was) dismissed as a dilettante millionaire's boy, whose undoubted charm and impressive conversational repertoire largely cloaked the physical afflictions and moral immaturity expressed in his lingering penchant for schoolboyish sexual crudity known only to a few intimates such as Lem Billings. After the book's success, Jack was clearly a man to be watched in the future. As if to demonstrate that destiny had summoned him to higher planes, he soon went on to favor even seasoned political figures like Lord Halifax or Secretary Forrestal with his views on world affairs. These hardened diplomats listened to the young navy veteran as an equal. From this point on, Jack began intellectually asserting himself. It's striking to see the way in which he came to write of the still largely unforeseen challenges of the postwar world. The evidence of his unpublished article and conversations with men like Halifax suggest that he was well aware that the post-1945 division of Europe would be the burning ideological issue of its day, a fact of life all US presidents from Harry Truman onward would need to recognize when dealing with successive leaders of a Soviet Union who clearly saw their national security bound up with the conquest and occupation of their contiguous states. Clichés now, Kennedy's attention to such matters as the troubled US–Soviet relationship showed his originality in early 1945.

"We will have to demonstrate to the Soviet our willingness to try to work out European problems on equitable lines," he wrote, "before the Russians will put any real confidence in our protestations of friendship. The Russian memory is long."

What was more, "Science will always overtake caution with new terrors against which defense cannot be anticipated," Jack predicted. "It is not an exaggeration to expect that missiles will be developed to a point where theoretically any spot on the globe can send to any community in the world, with pinpoint accuracy, a silent but frightful message of death and destruction."[111]

Clearly, there was much of the future President Kennedy in this summation. By 1945, he had deepened his temperamental affinity for the sort of patrician English outlook on life personified by Raymond Asquith or Billy Cavendish – droll, poised, phlegmatic, and with what seemed to Jack the "priceless ability to talk lightly of weighty things" – first with personal observation of wartime London and then by direct combat experience of his own. He had come to intellectual maturity after a lengthy consideration of how far a peace-loving democracy like Britain should prepare itself for war and how those same precautionary measures, if unchecked, might ultimately lead to a rapid proliferation of weapons of such terrible power that the human race itself stood to be erased at the touch of a button. They were the same basic concerns about the precariousness of man's continued existence on the planet that Kennedy brought with him when he entered the White House sixteen years later.

4

A VERY BROAD-MINDED
APPROACH TO EVERYTHING

IF 1940 CAN BE SEEN as the year John Kennedy left childhood, 1945 was the year he found his place in the adult world. In the period from late April to early August, he was on hand to see the great postwar powers in action at the United Nations conference in San Francisco; witnessed the watershed British general election that saw the nation's wartime savior Winston Churchill unceremoniously evicted from office and replaced by a socialist government that then imposed much of the apparatus of the modern welfare state; wandered among the ruins of Berlin, where he came in contact with current and future international leaders, including his two immediate predecessors as president; and watched at firsthand as Russian soldiers brutalized their defenseless German civilian former adversaries, an experience that contributed to his lifelong distaste for the practice of communism. On the day Kennedy flew home after his summer in Europe, the United States dropped the atomic bomb on Hiroshima – surely the realization of the "silent but frightful message of death and destruction" he foresaw in his unpublished article six months earlier. Writing to Harold Tinker, his old prep school English teacher, Kennedy said, "The war makes less sense to me now than it ever made, and that was little enough – and I should really like – as my life's goal – in some way and at some time to do something to help prevent another."[1]

Many who knew Kennedy have described him as keeping a certain remove between himself and others, as though he had his guard up, or as though he moved among them as an unusually self-effacing and literate news reporter rather than an active participant in events. He had the rare journalist's gift for the small but telling detail. Years later, *Time* magazine's veteran Washington correspondent Hugh Sidey asked President Kennedy for his impressions of Nikita Khrushchev following a fiery encounter with the Soviet leader in Vienna. Instead of speaking in platitudinous terms about East-West relations, Kennedy noted the Russian's "bright, shifting eyes, the quick wit, the clunky gray suit that seemed made in a factory, the peasant vitality in his hand gestures, the peace medal that swung from his lapel."[2] Kennedy could invariably find the human side to a complex situation. He rarely took politicians entirely seriously, even if they did so themselves. Aside from his skills of direct observation, Kennedy's voracious reading on history and government, along with personal experience of British life, now brought him unique insights into the country where his sister Kick continued to live as Lady Hartington. "The Conservative Party, fat and happy with years of victory, let their political ace, Mr. Churchill, carry the ball," Kennedy wrote of Britain's first post war election, having defied conventional wisdom and predicted Churchill's defeat. "Instead of a vigorous campaign on the virtues of private enterprise, they offered a watered down version of blood, sweat, and tears for the years of peace. Blood, sweat and tears was fitted to the desperate days of 1940, but not to 1945 to a people whose chronic fatigue and exhaustion had brought them to a sharp-tempered dissatisfaction with life in England."[3]

★ ★ ★

ON FEBRUARY 27, 1945, Kathleen Kennedy wrote from London to her brother Jack, then languishing in his Arizona sanitarium. "You sound like you are getting a good rest but somehow I can't see you staying there for long. Am sure you'll get the wanderlust and other kinds of lust before the passing of many moons."[4]

Kick was right to predict that Jack would soon tire of life in the arid Phoenix suburbs. His old friend Inga Arvad had Hollywood connections, and as a result of these he enjoyed some time there mingling with the stars, even if the famously taciturn Gary Cooper, a Kennedy favorite, proved to be that rare actor whose screen image was the real man. "Gee, Charlie," Jack ruefully told a friend, "that was about a three-word dinner we had. Nobody said anything, and if they did, Gary said zero!"[5]

Jack had also started to read Thomas Macaulay and was very impressed by his ideas about the progressive model of British politics, the will to power, and the way certain strong-minded individuals could single-handedly change society. He took as his personal motto the nineteenth-century historian's words, "We must judge a government by its general tendencies and not by its happy accidents." Clearly, Jack wasn't about to make a career in Hollywood. In late April 1945, following some discreet lobbying by his father, he set off up the coast to San Francisco, where he would cover the inaugural United Nations assembly for the *Herald-American*. Over the next month he filed seventeen three-hundred-word stories at $250 apiece, most of them concerned with the problem of Soviet intransigence. "We have a long way to go before Russia will entrust her safety to any organization other than the Red Army," Jack noted, after enduring "endless hours" of Andrei Gromyko in action, if that was the word for it. "There is a heritage of 25 years of distrust between Russia and the rest of the world that cannot be overcome completely for a good many years."[6]

In another report, which owed something to Macaulay's gift for distilling complex diplomatic issues down to the essence,

Jack compared the high-stakes negotiations taking place at San Francisco to "an international football game," with the Soviet representative "carrying the ball" while the Anglo-American team "tried to tackle him all over the field."[7] It was a prescient glimpse of the brave new postwar world: even as their armies continued to fight side by side in Germany, the "big three" leaders were squabbling over the future of Europe, and Winston Churchill was soon warning about an iron curtain being drawn down over the continent.

During the conference, Kathleen Kennedy wrote frequently to Jack to share her hopes, her plans, and sometimes her slightly morose thoughts about her life in England. "I feel like a small cork that is tossing around," she confided in one letter home. "I know that there are hundreds like me, and lots more unfortunate, but it doesn't help heal the wound."[8] Like others, Kick would come to see her brother as intelligent and capable but with a peculiar hollowness in his emotional life, a detachment that extended to his own family members. "I write you every minute for advice but none seems to come through," she complained at one point.[9]

Invoking her conviction that "Britain today is the world's most fickle country," Kick's letters also frequently included reports of national political unrest. "All the Conservatives have been very shocked by the result of the by-election held at Chelmsford on April [26]," she told Jack, an augury of Churchill's stunning defeat in the general election three months later.[10] "Nearly all the boys that you knew here have been adopted by various constituencies," Kick noted in another letter. "Of course they will stand as Conservatives … What about you? What are your plans?"[11]

To an ambitious young anglophile, entranced by the atmosphere of Westminster politics, there could be only one answer to this question. In late May, following an approach from Ambassador Kennedy, the Hearst Newspaper group invited Jack to go to London to cover the July 5 election and then to travel on to the Allied summit in Potsdam.★ While overseas, he would also be the guest of Secretary of the Navy James Forrestal, another friend of the family. Jack's last report from San Francisco anticipated his new assignment. "The British Labor Party is out for blood," he informed his readers on May 28, 1945. "They are going all the way: Public ownership of the Bank of England, Government control of rents and prices, gradual Government ownership of mines, transportation, planned farming – the works."[12] Most Americans, to the extent that they thought about British politics at all, then assumed that seventy-year-old Winston Churchill enjoyed almost a divine right to power. As recently as May 8, the wartime premier had joined the royal family on the balcony of Buckingham Palace to bask in the adulation of a hundred-thousand-strong crowd, including Kick Kennedy, massed in the street below to celebrate victory in Europe. As the king and queen saluted the sea of cheering faces, Churchill "stared [down] and beamed paternally."[13] It was a heady scene. "Short of being named dictator for life, it [was] hard to see what more the adoring public could do to signify their love of their cigar-smoking PM," one American correspondent wrote. Even in the British press, the betting was on Churchill being returned to power. "If ever there existed any doubt about the continuing popularity of the Prime Minister among all classes in the country, it was completely dissipated today," the London *Times* wrote of an election stop on June 25. "His reception was so tumultuous and overwhelming that his programme was seriously delayed." Traveling about by open car, languidly raising his two fingers in a *V* symbol to repeated cheers of "Good old Winnie!" Churchill himself told an eve-of-poll rally, "I feel it in my bones that you are going to send me back to power with a great majority … The eyes of the world will be on us tomorrow. If we go down, then all the ninepins

★ In order to count the votes of serving British troops, it would be July 26 before the election result was made known.

of Europe will go down with us."[14] Churchill's private secretary noted in his diary that night that even the Labour leader Clement Attlee "expected a Tory majority of 30."[15]

Twenty-eight-year-old Jack Kennedy would see something that most of the world's seasoned political observers missed, however; the proverbial wind of change was blowing through Britain, and as a result the nation would prove receptive to Attlee's brand of austere socialism.

Jack's first campaign dispatch from London proved something of an eye-opener to American audiences. Under the headline "Churchill May Lose Election," he told readers of the New York *Journal-American* on June 24, 1945:

> Britishers will go to the polls on July 5 in the first general election in almost ten years, and there is a definite possibility that Prime Minister Winston Churchill and his Conservative party may be defeated. This may come as a surprise to most Americans, who feel Churchill is as indomitable at the polls as he was in war. However, Churchill is fighting a tide that is surging through Europe, washing away monarchies and conservative governments everywhere ... England is moving irresistibly toward some form of socialism, if not in this election then surely at the next.[16]

In the continuing grip of food and clothing rationing, its bombed-out houses caked in soot and dust, great sprays of weed flowering through cracked pavements, pervaded by a smell of damp coal smoke and human decay, London that wet summer of 1945 was a grim place. The transport system was in disarray due to fuel shortages, and streetlights extinguished during the war only gradually returned to provide soupy, "dim-out" conditions on most nighttime roads. Prostitutes – one commodity of which there was now a surplus – continued to shine a torch on themselves as a means of soliciting. Once-elegant public squares and gardens lay converted to cabbage patches. Blast damage had destroyed windows and torn the leaves off the trees. The chamber of the House of Commons itself, a symbol of the way of life Britain had been fighting for, had been leveled by an incendiary bomb in May 1941 and now stood as a derelict, weed-filled grotto, a blue tarpaulin stretched overhead keeping a kind of demented beat as it flapped wildly in the apparently incessant rain.

The experience of living in London again after six years' absence left a permanent mark on Jack Kennedy. The political result was to give him a healthy awareness of the way in which even an essentially conservative society like Britain would periodically vent its dissatisfaction with the old order. Under the prevailing social and economic conditions of 1945, any residual public affection for a national icon like Churchill would simply be "swept away in a populist earthquake," Kennedy noted.[17] Once again, it was a case where the British political experience would fill out Jack's youthful education with a hard, practical lesson on the realities of power.

In London, Kennedy became increasingly convinced of the dislocating possibilities of war and of one particular core truth offered by the British model: that real social change followed victory, not defeat. His own gesture to the hard times included carrying a Ministry of Food ration book – printed in suitably dreary brown – and driving around in Kick's tiny, two-door Austin Seven, officially restricted to a fuel ration allowing it to travel just 150 miles a month. Jack leavened the austerity when it came to his social life, however. Installing himself in a suite at the Grosvenor House Hotel, he played host there most evenings to a group including David Ormsby-Gore, William Douglas-Home, and Hugh Fraser, often taking them on to dinner at the American Red Cross Club on Shaftesbury Avenue, where somewhat incongruously there were unlimited supplies of hamburgers and Coca-Cola, neon lighting, and a large, red-carpeted lounge that featured a radiogram, a jukebox, and a nightly free movie. Kick had previously written to advise Jack that she had "a few girls lined up for you here," and characteristically he seems not to have restrained himself in that area.[18] Among his close London companions was the English tennis star Kay Stammers, who was thirty-one, separated, and known for her on-court habit of wearing white linen shorts cut to a sensational four inches above the knee.

"Jack was spoilt by women," Stammers later remarked. "I think he could snap his fingers and they'd come running. And of course he was terribly attractive and rich and unmarried … I thought he was divine."[19] Kennedy's other London dates included his late brother's mistress Pat Wilson and Hugh Fraser's widowed sister Veronica, who in time wrote to thank him for the "*lovely* stockings – it was sweet of you and they are a *great* joy."[20] An elderly English lady adds that "the young American struck me as a kind of blessing conferred on our condition," which might translate as "he was a breath of fresh air."

At the end of June, Jack and his latest partner squeezed into the back seat of Kick's Austin and, exhausting their notional monthly petrol allowance, drove all day and part of the night ("the highways like some Kansas farm-track") to join Fraser as he campaigned as the Conservative candidate in the Stafford and Stone constituency, 150 miles northwest of London. Kennedy was intrigued by this glimpse of a "real England … quite different to the incestuous bartering-house of Westminster."[21] Then still a quaint market town at heart, Stafford's outlying industrial works had attracted Hitler's bombers at regular intervals since 1940, with the result that "columns of cars crowded with refugees and luggage in bags and sacks roll[ed] through to the north," the *Birmingham Gazette* had written. "Houses had their windows blown out, the public baths lost their ceiling … intensified restrictions and controls, transport difficulties, worsening food supplies, and worries about the future all magnified the material damage." Stafford's postwar civic planners soon finished the job the Luftwaffe had begun, throwing up entire prefabricated neighborhoods on old bomb sites or green fields.

"Clearance" was the word, the result a gaudily modern facelift whose chief physical characteristics were endless one-way traffic systems, roundabouts, and mortuaries. When Jack Kennedy and his party arrived there, Stafford offered a "stark contrast in styles … you saw new construction – cranes and scaffolds – wedged up against a thatched roof or an ancient stone church."[22]

This "incredible visual patisserie" of prim, timbered cottages and squat, concrete apartment blocks offered a snapshot of a "chang[ing] Britain … one [in] which the Conservatives can no longer assume a right to govern. The old allegiances are shifting." Jack thought he knew the reasons why. He told Fraser that the Tories were doomed if they continued to be seen as defenders of the rich and, particularly, the privileged. Churchill's party needed to capitalize on victory over Hitler by erecting a "really durable system to help all classes of society to stand on their feet."[23] Writing in the *Journal-American*, Jack predicted that Britain would sooner or later elect an "unapologetically socialist" government, and that the Conservatives had only themselves to blame for it. "Instead of indulging in a broad program of public spending in the 1930s as we did," he told his readers, they had "tightened the country's belt and advanced its budget with consequent hardship for the people and political unpopularity for themselves."[24] It was the social counterpart to the failure of successive British governments to rearm their nation's military during the same period. As a result of the Tories' lassitude, power would inevitably pass to a left-wing regime that would "impose further controls [on a people who] have already endured a long and savage war." The British model, Jack concluded, would stand as a warning to other nations of the need to organize government around the interests of all the people. "This country will carry through in the next few years some economic changes that many in America and England feel cannot be made without an important limitation on democratic government," he wrote. "By watching England, we still have much to learn."[25]

After leaving Fraser, Kennedy again drove through the night to cover his friend Alastair Forbes's campaign as the Liberal candidate in Hendon, north London. Kick had first introduced the two men, who shared a taste for high-minded political table talk occasionally leavened by sexual gossip. Born in 1918, Forbes held a British passport although he sprang from an American family distantly related to the Roosevelts. During the war he had served for a time with the Royal Marines but was invalided out, suffering from lung problems. Forbes was intimate with many female representatives of a vanishing world of European café society and was said by his obituarist to have had "an enormous capacity to entertain, amuse or offend according to whim."[26] He never wavered in his affection for Jack Kennedy, who was one of the few public figures to escape his often "castratingly rude," if engagingly gossipy, articles in the likes of the *Daily Mail*. Of Margaret, duchess of Argyll's memoirs, Forbes ventured, "Her father may have been able to give her some beautiful earrings, but nothing to put between them." Brilliant, libidinous, and shamelessly indiscreet, he was like Jack Kennedy without the latter's carefully maintained internal gyroscope. The contradiction in Forbes's character is illustrated by the fact that, while standing for the Liberal Party in his Hendon constituency, he actually voted Labour.[27]

"Jack came up to listen to speeches," Forbes recalled. "That was the first time we really seriously began talking about politics together. What struck me then was that he was more intellectual than any other member of the family," by which he chiefly meant Joe Jr. and Kick. In some ways, the youthful and svelte American reporter reminded Forbes of the elderly and increasingly portly British premier. "He had a detachment [like] Winston Churchill in the sense that his life had been protected by money. Money was a great insulator. If you don't sort of make your bed and get your own breakfast and have a certain amount of conversation with people who are doing all sorts of ordinary, simple jobs, it does rob you a great deal of empathy." To Forbes, Jack was a "made" politician, tempering his isolating, privileged status in life by a "fantastically good instinct," fuelled by an "insatiable quest for knowledge – for every question you asked, he'd ask you ten in return."[28]

Not all Kennedy's British friends shared what Forbes called his "textbook New World optimism" about life. But a visit to Jack's London hotel suite was nevertheless invariably an antidote to any fleeting moments of depression. The atmosphere there, characterized by "constantly ringing phones, clothes flung around the floor, pretty girls reclining in armchairs," struck twenty-seven-year-old David Ormsby-Gore – seemingly one of the few of their circle not yet standing for parliament – as "a tonic ... I hadn't got a clue what I wanted to do in life, but in the interim you felt yourself energized by [Kennedy's] presence."[29]

William Douglas-Home, thirty-three, had already stood unsuccessfully as a Liberal candidate in three by-elections and was making a name for himself as a comic playwright. In September 1944, while serving as an officer in the Normandy campaign, Home was cashiered by the army for refusing to participate in an attack on the enemy-held port of Le Havre without first allowing its civilian population to be safely evacuated. He served eight months' imprisonment with hard labor. Although Ambassador Kennedy warned him against it "for the sake of your future career," Jack proved to be a loyal friend. "I'd been in trouble," Home remembered, in something of an understatement, "but when [Kennedy] came over in 1945 to stay with his sister, we used to have lunch together and discuss politics again. He had a very broad minded approach to everything. I mean he saw everybody's point of view. Although he had a strong one himself."[30] Kennedy in turn thought "William quite confident that his day will come after his disgrace has passed, [and] some say he will be Prime Minister ... I doubt that he will ever meet with such success because people distrust those who go against convention," he added. In Lanark, Scotland, William's older brother Alec, the future fourteenth earl of Home and a

Conservative MP, duly lost his seat to the Labour candidate, who was a former train driver. Alec Douglas-Home had been an aide to Neville Chamberlain at the time of Munich; eighteen years later, as prime minister, he was briefly President Kennedy's partner in the Atlantic alliance.

On June 29, Jack, dressed incongruously in white tie and tails, again took to the passenger seat of Kathleen's "boxlike" car on their way to dinner at Compton Place, the Devonshires' magnificently baroque estate at Eastbourne on England's south coast. For all the religious difficulties raised at the time of Kick's marriage to Billy Cavendish, she had been "completely amalgamated into [the] family – it had become hers."[31] On arrival, Jack found the fifty-year-old duchess, the former Lady Mary Gascoyne-Cecil, "looming up at us like a galleon in full sail," to quote another guest present. Kennedy himself called his hostess "a woman of intense personal charm and complete selflessness."[32] Had Kick's brief marriage been blessed with issue, this emblematic figure of the English landed class would have been the grandmother to Jack's nephews and nieces. "Just looking at her made you feel that at any moment the strains of 'Pomp and Circumstance' would suddenly burst forth," he joked. Jack was less immediately drawn to the duke, whom he thought "an eighteenth-century story book" character, and "an anachronism [with] hardly the adaptability to meet the changing tides of the present day." This was mild compared to his subsequent private diary comment. The duke was "fully conscious of his obligations," Kennedy wrote, "most of which consist of furnishing the people of England with a statesman of mediocre ability but outstanding integrity."[33] Also present at dinner that night was twenty-five-year-old Andrew Cavendish, the marquess of Hartington since his older brother's battlefield death and another of the returning young British army officers to stand as a National Liberal (or de facto Conservative) candidate in the 1945 general election, only to lose to the Labour candidate by a crushing twelve thousand votes in a Midlands constituency dominated by the coal mining industry.

On July 1, Jack was back in London, his ever-present notebook in hand, to record the final rites of the campaign: Churchill's indomitable optimism; the slow, backfiring procession of loudspeaker vans spluttering up and down Oxford Street; and the stinging indignation of Harold Laski, Jack's old college tutor and now the Labour chairman, whom the premier suggested could be the director of a "socialist Gestapo" if his party was elected. A born reporter, Jack never lost the art of gathering information, nor of seeing the essential absurdity of at least a part of the modern ritual of political campaigning. Whereas the Conservative government had let the country drift perilously close to the economic rocks, he wrote in his final dispatch to the *Journal-American*, the Labour Party "have been free to promise everything to everyone, which they have. The farmer, agricultural worker, shopkeeper, small business man and worker have all been promised better days. [Actual government] may be Labour's great crisis," Kennedy predicted.[34]

Just as Jack was affectionately cynical about the sort of "story book" Tory grandee personified by the duke of Devonshire, so too he long remained wary of those on the left, like Harold Laski, who "proposed the idea of the proletariat being the only group of people that mattered." After attending an election rally at which Laski gave the keynote address, Jack wrote in his diary, "He spoke with great venom and bitterness, and at the conclusion when asked if it were true that he wrote a letter to Mr. Attlee requesting him to resign as head of the Labour Party, he replied with asperity that it was 'none of their business.' ... Odd this strain that runs through these radicals of the Left," Jack mused. "It is that spirit which builds dictatorships, as has been shown in Russia ... These Leftists are filled with bitterness, and I am not sure how deeply the tradition of tolerance in England is ingrained in these bitter and discontented spirits. I think unquestionably, from my talk with Laski, that he and others like him smart not so much from the economic inequality but from the social."[35]

Here was the essential Kennedy balancing act he would take with him all the way to the White House. The sort of conservatism that existed for the benefit of an "unproductive few, quaffing port and oppressing the peasantry" was "out – the way of the last century, not of this one," he told David Ormsby-Gore.[36] But elitism, inefficiency, and corruption were no more acceptable when they were perpetrated by institutions with noble goals. One of the intriguing things about Kennedy's strangely detached personality is the contrast between his obvious love of the good life as represented by well-heeled British friends such as the Homes and the Devonshires and his penetration of the logic of the more reactionary wing of the Tory party, which he answered with exceptional insight. Similarly, he was all for the sort of social mobility his own family story exemplified, provided this followed on from individual graft and not "spurious government programs and subsidies."[37] Any time a politician inserted himself into the workings of the free market, Jack privately noted, "a bureaucracy ends up strangling the very progress it purports to foster." Surveying the British political landscape as a whole, Kennedy distilled his credo in a diary entry dated June 21: "Socialism is inefficient," he wrote. "I will never believe differently. But you can feed people in a socialistic state, and that may be what will ensure its eventual success."[38]

Perhaps what's most interesting about the tone of Kennedy's 1945 British diary is the note of scholarly restraint largely absent in his accounts of earlier travels. Before the war, political aperçus on his part about the English or continental systems of government still vied for space with lingering appreciations of well-endowed blondes or unusually attentive night nurses. But now it was suddenly as though he were writing for posterity and not just his own amusement. "The Kennedy diary is far from a reporter's notebook," Hugh Sidey perceptively wrote. "For one thing there are too many polished and completed sentences …

He may have had the notion that he might gather his material and expand it into a book once he was done with his journey and could collect all his thoughts ... I suspect the example of the young Churchill may have lurked somewhere in the back of his mind."[39]

★ ★ ★

ON WEDNESDAY, JULY 25, Kennedy ended a brief visit to Ireland – showing his customary tact in refusing to be drawn into whether or not the two halves of the country should be unified into a single, Catholic republic – to fly first to Paris and then Berlin. Meanwhile, his great British political hero was traveling in the opposite direction. Winston Churchill left the Allied conference at the Cecilienhof Palace in Potsdam that same afternoon in order to be on hand for the election result in London, contentedly going to bed "in the belief that the British people would wish me to continue my work."[40] Shortly before leaving Potsdam, the premier had appeared for a group photograph with his political counterparts, Truman and Stalin. Three wicker chairs had been arranged for the event so that they were exactly one foot away from each other on the palace lawn. Seconds before the pictures were taken, however, Churchill seized the arms of his chair and shunted it sideways so that it was touching Truman's. As a result, the leaders of the two Western democracies appeared to be as one, while the Soviet dictator, resplendent in a white military tunic, stared serenely ahead, isolated from his former allies. To Churchill's doctor and confidant Charles Moran, it was a "curiously fitting" alignment.[41]

By noon the following day, it was all over. Clement Attlee's Labour Party won 393 parliamentary seats to 197 for Churchill's Conservatives. Labour gained a majority of 145 over all other opposition groups combined. Amid the landslide, there were a few individual Tory success stories, such as Kennedy's friend Hugh Fraser at Stafford, while Alastair Forbes, a Liberal, managed to lose at Hendon to an Eton- and Oxford-educated Conservative candidate by the name of Sir Hugh Vere Huntley Duff Munro-Lucas-Tooth of Teanich (or Hugh Tooth, as he understandably later preferred to call himself). It's agreed to have been one of the great electoral shocks of the twentieth century, marking the supposed arrival of an energetic, confident, populist Labour administration, bent upon social action, and the humiliation of their Conservative rivals, whom they derided as reactionary, hidebound, senile, discredited, divided, and defective. When leaving his official country home that weekend, apparently for the last time, Churchill signed his name in the visitor's book before adding the single word, "*Finis.*"

"The overwhelming victory of the Left was a surprise to everyone," Kennedy modestly noted the following morning. "My own opinion is that [the result] was about 40 per cent due to dissatisfaction with conditions over which the government had no great control – 20 per cent due to a belief in Socialism as the only solution to the multifarious problems England must face – and the remaining 40 per cent due to a class feeling – i.e., that it was time 'the working man' had a chance."[42] Once again suggesting that he saw himself as writing for posterity (who else uses a word like 'multifarious' in his private diary?), and showing his pragmatic affinity for the middle ground, in the process recording an impressive prediction about the course of internal Labour politics for the next seventy years, Kennedy added, "The Socialists will stay in for a long time if the conservative wing of that party – men like Attlee and Bevin – remain in office. But," he warned, "if the radical group like Laski, Shinwell, and Cripps become the dominating influence, there will be a reaction ... Labor is under the great disadvantage of having made promises to numerous groups whose aims are completely incompatible. The Conservatives may pick up some of these votes, at least those of the middle class, when conditions make it impossible for Labor to implement many of its promises." Kennedy's summation of the essential state of British party politics is still valid today, and it looks likely to retain its potency for some years to come.[43]

After several close misses – including a misty glimpse of his ancestral land from the deck of the SS *Washington* in July 1937, and a brief airport layover two years later – Jack now finally set foot in Ireland. The country's impact on him was certainly deep, but not perhaps in the way that might have been expected. For example, he rarely referred to his family heritage or interpreted his later career as an outstanding Irish–American success story. Nor did it leave him with a visceral dislike of the British. Rather than parading his immigrant roots or his religion, Jack took the view that these were private matters – although it's true that his reserve on the subject could sometimes fail him when there was a perceived electoral advantage to be gained from presenting himself as having struggled to emerge from a minority group. Kennedy was not, in truth, very interested in the content of religious doctrine at all. The record shows both that he regularly attended Mass (sometimes arriving there fresh from a lover's bed) and was known to break into a vocally resonant, if not musical, rendition of "Danny Boy" or some other popular tearjerker when surrounded by his late-night cronies in the White House. But Kennedy was not an obviously nostalgic or a pious (as opposed to principled) person. He could always enjoy a good joke about Ireland and, for that matter, about the Church. Taking her leave after a White House cocktail party, David Ormsby-Gore's wife Sissy once remarked to her host, "I don't know whether to kiss you or say 'Good-bye, Mr. President.'" Kennedy replied instantly, "You're a good Catholic, Sissy – you can kiss my ring."

It was as if Jack had been endowed by nature with a double charge of irony and detachment in almost every area of life, while other members of his clan had avoided these qualities altogether. "John was the more secure, the freer, of the two – freer of his father, freer of his family, of his faith, of the entire Irish–American predicament," Arthur Schlesinger wrote in his otherwise warmly admiring biography of Robert Kennedy.[44] Bobby, for his part, never quite got over what he saw as the injustice of the London government's continuing oppression of the Irish, and he once brought a formal embassy dinner to a stop by loudly berating a senior British official on the subject. Jack, by contrast, simply treated people as individuals and tried to judge them by their actions rather than their tribal affiliations. Refreshingly, he wasn't the sort of politician who defined himself by his formative experiences in life. "It's what you make of circumstances, not what they make of you," he once informed David Ormsby-Gore.[45]

For Britons of a certain age, it must sometimes feel that their entire life has been spent in the wake of sterile, unresolved arguments about their country's relations with Ireland. The whole checkered saga – from the Cromwellian suppression of 1649–1653, followed by the island's eventual partition, through to the recurrence of the "Troubles" in the 1970s and 1980s, to today's fitful peace – has provided one of the longest-running and, at times, circular debates in European history. When Kennedy arrived in Dublin in July 1945, the most pressing domestic political issue was the campaign by sixty-two-year-old Éamon de Valera, southern Ireland's head of government for the past thirteen years, to reunite the twenty-six counties of the South with the six of the North. Jack's report to the *Journal-American* rightly began, "The fundamental motivating force behind Irish politics [is] the age-old quarrel with England," although in the next sentence he wryly agreed with the verdict of the eighteenth-century poet-politician Richard Sheridan: "A quarrel is a very pretty quarrel as it stands. We should only spoil it by trying to explain it."[46]

In the same vein, Kennedy seems to have been simultaneously impressed and amused by the "brilliant, austere figure" of de Valera when he interviewed him on July 25. He and his men "have not forgotten, nor have they forgiven," Jack wrote. "The only settlement they will accept is a free and independent Ireland, free to go where it will be the master of its own destiny."[47] But what did that mean in practice? De Valera's recent attempt to define his country both as a republic and, at the same time, a member of the British commonwealth, owing allegiance to the king, "left the situation to many observers as misty as the island on an early winter's morning," Kennedy admitted. Ireland had remained neutral during "the Emergency" (as the Dublin government referred to World War II), and just weeks earlier de Valera had seen fit to offer his condolences to the German minister-in-residence on the death of Adolf Hitler, a courtesy denied the US representative on the passing that month of President Roosevelt. No wonder, perhaps, Jack was unable to see a solution to the problem in sight. Referring to a recent parliamentary debate on Irish unification, he wrote:

> In the north, Sir Basil Brooke, head of the government of Ulster, listened to the debate and roared down to the gentlemen in Dublin that "not an inch" will he give up of the six counties.
>
> And in the south, de Valera hurled back the challenge that from his present position he will retreat "not an inch."

"At this weekend," Kennedy was left to conclude, "the problem of partition seems very far from being solved."[48]

★   ★   ★

JOSEF STALIN retained his usual sphinx-like poise when, on July 28, he looked across the Potsdam conference table to see Churchill's place there taken by the unassuming figure of sixty-two-year-old Clement Attlee, hunched deep down in his chair ("a bank clerk in both appearance and manner," Kennedy privately felt), characteristically blinking rapidly and fiddling with his pipe. The new British premier's opening remark to his fellow heads of government was to make a rather strained analogy between choosing a cabinet and selecting a cricket team, neither one of them a task the Soviet dictator was personally familiar with. Perhaps Stalin allowed himself a brief reflection on the curious ways of democracy. His only previous comment on his new Allied colleague had been to note, "Mr. Attlee does not look to me like a man hungry for power."[49]

Jack Kennedy also arrived in Berlin that day. At this point the twenty-eight-year-old roving newspaper correspondent was arguably better informed on crucial world events than were the heads of either the British or American delegations. After some three months in office, President Truman, to quote his biographer David McCullough:

> had no experience in [international] relations ... He didn't
> know his own Secretary of State, more than to say hello. He
> had no background in foreign policy, no expert or experi-
> enced advisers of his own to call upon for help ... President
> Roosevelt had done nothing to keep him informed or pro-
> vide background on decisions and plans at the highest levels.
> Roosevelt, Truman would [complain] privately, "never did
> talk to me confidentially about the war, or about foreign
> affairs, or what he had in mind for peace after the war."

After dining with Truman in Berlin, Kennedy's patron James Forrestal wrote in his diary that, like most outsiders, the new president had had "no idea in advance what the outcome of the [British] election might be."[50] Compared to this, the young reporter for the *Journal-American* was a skilled and experienced observer of world affairs, having covered recent critical events in San Francisco and London and come to know most of the key players now assembled in Potsdam.

Drafted in an ironic style unusual in the mainstream press of the day, Kennedy's dispatches, if not always brilliantly concise, were humorous, literate, and intelligent, and showed rare insight into and sympathy for the British position. Concomitant with this was a growing distaste for Soviet excesses that can only have fuelled his deep and, as it turned out, lifelong anticommunism. "The Russian treatment of the Germans [has been] bad," Kennedy noted with some restraint in his diary. "Raping was general. The Russians stole watches in payment and cameras were second choice ... If a split among the Big Four [France included] develops as far as long-time administrative procedure," Jack added presciently, "it will be serious ... Germany will be unable to build and maintain communications, roads, canals, trade, coal, and food. If we don't withdraw and allow them to administer their own affairs, we will be confronted with an extremely difficult administrative problem. Yet, if we pull out," Kennedy concluded, "we may leave a political vacuum that the Russians will be only too glad to fill."[51]

In Berlin, Jack witnessed for himself the ruins of the city where he had happily strolled with his new color movie camera just a week before the outbreak of the war. The Excelsior Hotel, his home then, had been blown to pieces. Picking his way through the rubble – notebook, as ever, in hand – he encountered a population of gaunt, gray-faced men and women shambling through a barren, bombed-out landscape, as often as not clutching their pitiable worldly possessions in their arms. A German girl Kennedy interviewed told him that she and her two sisters had been stripped naked and robbed by Russian soldiers, although the ordeal for once had fallen short of rape. "Her brother was killed on the Eastern front and her fiancé is in an Italian prisoner-of-war camp," Jack recorded. "She feels that Russia and the United States will fight when Russia is ready. They now know that our equipment is far superior. She feels that that war would be the ruination of Germany which would be the common battleground."[52]

On July 30, General Eisenhower, supreme commander of the Allied forces, flew in for a working breakfast with Truman and his aides. Fifteen years later, in the heat of an election campaign, John Kennedy would go on to portray Ike as an old man asleep at the wheel, under whose watch the communists had opened up an ominous "missile gap" over the United States. In 1945, however, he had nothing but praise for the victorious Allied commander. "He has an easy personality, immense self-assurance, and gave an excellent presentation of the situation in Germany," Jack wrote on August 1. A young British army officer named John Roland Riley also witnessed the meeting of America's thirty-fourth and thirty-fifth presidents. Ike, he wrote in a letter, had fixed Kennedy with his "sharp little eyes, as if reviewing a subordinate's turn-out," while "offering a thin smile, [but] neither man had prejudiced the frontiers of discipline and rank" by any greater show of friendliness. "There was a stiff nod and a handshake, and [Eisenhower] moved on down the line."[53]

Back in Berlin, Kennedy toured the remains of Hitler's Reich chancellery – "the walls chipped and scarred by bullets, showing the terrific fight which took place at the time of its fall … His air-raid shelter was about 120 feet down into the ground – well furnished but completely devastated. The room where Hitler was supposed to have met his death showed scorched walls and traces of fire. There is no complete evidence, however, [about Hitler's] body. The Russians doubt that he is dead."[54]

Fifteen miles away, in Potsdam, there were still peaceful, lakeside villas to be seen, untouched by the war. Lush vineyards dropped gently down to the water, which was covered by a dove-blue summer haze. Pulling up in a jeep to the official American residence, or so-called Little White House, Kennedy was asked to wait outside while Secretary Forrestal went in to confer with President Truman. Later, at the Cecilienhof Palace, Jack noted fastidiously that he had inhaled "the powerful fog of tobacco smoke" lingering from that morning's session of the Big Three, "hanging like a pall" over the dark, oak-paneled room."[55] There was not a shred of evidence pointing to the specific source of this reek – Attlee and Stalin were both confirmed pipe-smokers – although John Riley, briefly present in the hall, recalled that the Soviet dictator, like most of his entourage, "tended not to over-do it when it came to personal hygiene."[56] Earlier that week, Truman had mentioned to Stalin in a corner of that same room that the United States had "recently tested a new weapon of unusual destructive force." Stalin had asked no questions about the weapon, replying merely that he hoped the Americans would make good use of it against the Japanese. The subsequent rapid Soviet development of their own nuclear technology and the somehow inevitable process of "brinkmanship," or the art of moving up to the verge of mutually assured destruction, became the single greatest foreign policy preoccupation of the Kennedy administration. It's possible almost to see Stalin and his puff of pipe smoke when coming to analyze the course of the 1960s arms race, like a ghastly phantom limb after an amputation.

In one way or another, Jack Kennedy was now coming to adopt a personal and political aversion to communism and communists – almost a physical disgust – that prefigured the "Red Scare" widely observable in the United States only a year or so later. By the following October, Kennedy was telling a Boston radio audience, "The time has come when we must speak plainly on the great issue facing the world today. The issue is Soviet Russia," which he depicted as "a slave state of the worst sort," one "embarked upon a program of world aggression ... The freedom-loving countries of the world must stop Russia now, or themselves be destroyed," he continued, soaring into Churchillian rhetoric. "The crisis is both moral and political. The years ahead will be difficult and strained" – another touch of Churchill – "the sacrifices great, but ... only by supporting with all our hearts the cause we believe to be right can we prove that cause is not only right but that it has strength and vigor."[57]

It's long been argued that neither instinct nor training had conspicuously cut the Kennedy family out as liberals, but even so, after August 1945 Jack's antisocialist convictions would come to assume some of the qualities of a moral crusade.

Meanwhile, Kennedy flew down to Salzburg, where he enjoyed a leisurely dinner fortified by champagne and cigars allegedly liberated from Reichsmarschall Goering's car, though this last detail remains in historical dispute.[58] The next morning he inspected Hitler's mountain retreat at Berchtesgaden. Although the residence itself had been completely gutted by RAF bombs, it was still an impressive setting. "The elevator was a double-decker, a space being left on the lower deck for the ss guard," he wrote. "The lair itself had been stripped of its rugs, pictures, and tapestries, but the view was beautiful – the living room being round and facing out on every side on the valley below."[59]

Many of Jack Kennedy's recurring bouts of ill health seemed to start in London, and no sooner was he back in his suite at the Grosvenor House Hotel than he was stricken with what the attending US Navy doctor called "general unease ... Was well until yesterday afternoon when he had a chill, became nauseated, vomited several times, had vague abdominal discomfort – slept fitfully during the night."[60] This was perhaps to understate the true gravity of the situation. Kennedy "was in his bed, pale and drowsy, apparently oblivious to the world," David Ormsby-Gore remembered of a visit to the man now resident at the US Naval Clinic, a low, redbrick building set among the docks of Deptford in southeast London. "The doctor apprised him of our presence ... With a visible wrench, he'd start up and engage his visitors, smiling and assuring us all was well ... Then minutes later the whole exercise would begin again, and confronted with this distressing scene [all] we could do was quietly withdraw."[61]

"He was sick, really sick," Jack's friend Patrick Lannan, a former fellow patient at the "geriatrics' hotel" in Arizona, confirmed. "He scared the hell out of me. I must admit I'd never seen anybody go through the throes of fever before – you know, when I saw the bedclothes wringing wet and this guy burning up. It went on for several days. It kept going on, and then it finally came to pass."[62]

On the Monday morning of August 6, Kennedy was thought well enough to fly back to Washington with Secretary Forrestal. After a refueling stop en route, they touched down at the newly

opened Andrews Field Air Base just before dawn the following day. The secretary went off in one car, and Jack went off in
another. As they settled in for the eight-hour drive up the coast
to Boston, Kennedy's chauffeur handed his passenger a copy of
that morning's *New York Times*. The headline read, "FIRST ATOMIC
BOMB DROPPED ON JAPAN; MISSILE IS EQUAL TO 20,000 TONS OF TNT;
TRUMAN WARNS FOE OF A 'RAIN OF RUIN.'"[63] Here were the "new
terrors [of] death and destruction" Jack himself had predicted.
Their daily consequences would preoccupy him as his nation's
commander-in-chief a generation later.

★   ★   ★

WHEN JOHN KENNEDY threw the switch of his political career,
turned on with such dazzling voltage that winter of 1945–1946,
his early public speeches concentrated less on narrowly domestic
affairs than on the great tides of British and European history.
"Responsibility is a very sobering thing," he told an American
Legion audience in Boston. "Although Mr. Laski may talk about
the new foreign policy of socialism, Britain stands today as she
has always stood – for the Empire. Britain's relations with the
countries of Europe and Asia will not be substantially different
than they have ever been," he added with apparent approval.[64]

A key theme in almost all Kennedy's speeches was the need
for ever-closer Anglo-American cooperation in the uncertain
postwar world. Jack's remarks to an audience of veterans at
Boston's Statler Hotel on what would become known as the
Atlantic "special relationship" earned admiring reviews from
the press. "Any doubt that this is fast becoming a young man's
world was dispelled ... when 28-year-old 'Jack' Kennedy held
the attention and then won the applause of several hundred persons, many nearly twice his age," the *Boston Herald* reported.[65]
Speaking to a local radio audience, Kennedy managed to combine a scholarly tour d'horizon of recent British history with a
rousing tribute to American values:

I came away [from London] with one great impression – the greatness of my own country. Unless he has been abroad since the war ended, no American can possibly realize what a tremendous place America occupies in the world today. In England, before the war, an American was just a tourist and America the land where the tourist came from … But now a change has come about. All of our millions of young men who swarmed over Europe, all the millions and millions of tons of equipment that were poured by us into the war has [*sic*] made Europeans realize that here, indeed, is the great productive giant of our time. We occupy a great position in the world today … We must measure up to our responsibility.

A day or two later, Jack wrote to his friend Pat Lannan: "I'm sending you my speech, which went over pretty well." Toning down the rhetoric of his formal remarks, he added, "It's the old bull-shit with a new twist."[66]

As Lannan soon discovered, Ambassador Kennedy, as he still liked to be known, took a radically different view of Anglo-American affairs than his son. Perhaps according too much weight to historical precedent, Joe now thought that Britain was a dangerous mixture of imperial aggression and socialist domestic policies. The most important task in refashioning postwar security arrangements was not to check the rampant territorial ambitions of the Soviet Union, he privately remarked, but to ensure that the British "keep their pants zipped up" in their foreign relations and not revert to "storm[ing] around the globe acquiring new slave colonies."[67]

Speaking of a visit to the Kennedy compound at Hyannis Port, Lannan remembered:

I guess I made a terrific faux pas. We were all sitting down, and Joe came down with the goddamnest outfit on, your eyes would come right out of their sockets: it was kind of a red silk coat and shawl collar on and silk pants – the strangest getup.

We finally sat down for dinner and Joe got on into a big argument about the British parliament, and at that time he had
turned very anti-English. God, he went on and on about the
British parliament.

I took the position just directly opposite to the old man,
and I could hear every fork and knife at the table suspended
in midair, because you know, this was something you
didn't do.[68]

On January 31, 1946, the ambassador and his family were
enjoying an afternoon's sport from the comfort of their box
at the palm-fringed Hialeah Park racetrack a few miles outside
Miami. The backdrop reminded Joe (who could seldom resist
resorting to Hollywood for a good analogy) of "some dusty
biblical epic, except we were watching horses run around, and
not Christians being eaten by lions." Somewhere between the
fourth and fifth races a man incongruously dressed in a heavy
woolen suit and a brigade tie knocked on the door and said,
"Mr. Winston Churchill is seated in the grandstand, and won-
ders if he might have the honour of your company for light
refreshments there?"

Joe gave it a moment, and then said, "I'll be down later,"
before muttering as the door closed, "But I'll be damned if I
share a drink with the old buzzard."[69]

It was the first meeting between the defeated prime minister
and the retired ambassador since the night in August 1940 when
they had sat down at the Cabinet Room table in London to discuss the state of the war and review the Tyler Kent affair, while
the air-raid sirens had howled in the street outside. Kennedy had
refused a drink on that occasion, too. Now Churchill was on a
working holiday in the United States, where he would receive
honorary degrees, deliver speeches, and eventually address
an audience in Fulton, Missouri, on the subject of Stalin's
global designs. For the present, the former PM was content to
sit puffing his cigar, affably waving his fedora at the occasional

good-natured repartee of the crowd. He seemed genuinely pleased when Kennedy finally joined him.

"I remember that one of the last times we met we were having dinner during a Nazi raid," Churchill remarked. "It didn't bother us much, though, did it?"

According to Kennedy's notes of the reunion, he said nothing in reply.

Undaunted, Churchill changed tactics. "You had a terrible time during the war," he allowed, nodding his "great jowly red face" several times in emphasis. "Your losses were very great. I felt so sad for you and hope you received my messages."

Another silence ensued. "The world seems to be in a frightful condition," Churchill added.

At last Kennedy spoke. "Yes," he agreed. "After all, what did we accomplish by this war?"

"Well, at least we have our lives," Churchill offered.

"Not all of us," the ambassador replied, speaking with some bitterness.[70]

On April 9, 1946, John Kennedy "authorized the circulation of papers in his behalf for the Democratic nomination in the 11th Congressional District now represented by Mayor James Michael Curley," the *Boston Globe* reported.[71] His formal announcement, made over a local radio station, offered a panoramic view of world affairs. Delivered in uncharacteristically shrill tones, it was not one of those speeches that dwelt unduly on parochial issues such as the state of the municipal sewers. "Voters of the 11th Congressional District!" Kennedy began, sounding like an eighteenth-century French revolutionary calling for the tumbrels. "The people of the United States and the world stand at the crossroads! What we do now will shape the history of civilization for many years to come! We have a weary world trying to bind up the wounds of a fierce struggle," Jack continued, lowering the volume somewhat. "That is bad enough. What is infinitely worse is that we have a world which has unleashed the terrible powers of atomic energy. We have a world capable of destroying itself. The days which lie ahead are most difficult ones. Above all, day and night, with every ounce of ingenuity and industry we possess, we must work for peace," Jack went on. "We must not have another war."

But where Ambassador Kennedy had come to believe that war was never the answer, his son sided with Churchill in declaring that the Anglo-American alliance had saved the world from tyranny – and might do so again.

"It is no answer to the problem to say that we shall not go to war in the future, no matter what the cost, and leave it at that," Jack told the listening voters of the eleventh district. "If another Hitler were to appear on the world scene, if totalitarianism were to threaten once more to engulf the world, then we would face the same situation which we faced before, and the only course would be war." After regretting the recent decision to give Stalin the power of veto in the United Nations Security Council and berating Soviet foreign policy generally, Jack continued:

> If we in America disclaim any claims to territory, then we can stand forth as the leader of the conscience of the world. China and France will stand by us. The Labor government of Britain will stand by us. The small nations of the world will stand by us. Then we can appear before the United Nations and make our stand clear to Russia that we will not permit her to spread her totalitarianism throughout the world. It will be Russia against the conscience and power of the world, and Russia will be forced to yield.[72]

With the exception of Chinese support, this was a remarkably accurate preview of the main trends of American foreign policy as they emerged under President Kennedy beginning in 1961.

Long before then, Jack had begun to feel toward Britain an affinity – a personal and political closeness – that he would enjoy with no other country; it literally was his second home. Kick Kennedy had stayed on in London, where she rapidly cultivated

the same sort of raffish, upper-class set – the likes of Michael
Astor, Hugh Fraser, Tony Rosslyn, Freddie Birkenhead, and
David Ormsby-Gore – who proved so congenial to her favorite
brother. Frequently seen haunting the dining rooms and bars of
the House of Commons, Kick, some thought, might even have
parliamentary ambitions of her own. She seems to have been
somewhat torn by whether to range herself with the Tories or
the Liberals, but like Jack she had no time for "the Bolsheviks in
power now." A generation earlier, Nancy Astor had shown the
feasibility of an American-born woman becoming a British MP,
and it was thought that, like her, Kick would have had little difficulty in raising the necessary £150 candidates' deposit.

For now she lived in a £40,000 mews house a few minutes'
walk away from parliament (a "great gloomy barrack" according to Evelyn Waugh, with the "most God-awful sentimental oil
paintings of her late husband on the wall"), hosting innumerable
tea parties, "talking loudly, shrieking with laughter, and trading
outrageous gossip about aristocratic infidelities." At the weekends it was the same routine, only transferred to "some huge,
draughty house where she would stride around in jodhpurs,
drinking sherry and telling one, 'My dear man, do light me a
gasper.'"[73] Kick, in short, had gone native.

One of her closest British friends was Pamela Churchill,
a twenty-five-year-old socialite who was then in the throes
of divorcing the former prime minister's son Randolph and
already well on her way to becoming the "twentieth century's
greatest courtesan," as several newspapers would later call her.[74]
Early in 1946, Pamela accepted Kick's invitation to join her on
an extended winter vacation at the Kennedy family's home in
Palm Beach. On the whole, this was not distinguished by its air
of monastic restraint. While in Florida, Pam's principal activities
included horseback riding, mixing "industrial-strength" cocktails, and "flirting outrageously" with Kick's "superbly dishy"
big brother. (When the moment came, however, it was thought
wise that the Kennedys' houseguest not be presented to her

soon-to-be ex-father-in-law when he appeared unexpectedly at the local racetrack.) Jack had not only ideological but family connections to Britain, therefore. No one could ever accuse him of lacking an appreciation of that country's impressively rigid social structure, or for that matter its equally pervasive gift for the humor of irony and understatement, which he took as his own in public discourse and private conversation alike. "Well, he's not exactly David Niven, is he?" Jack would later remark of the crudely attired Nikita Khrushchev. In Kick, he had someone who regularly provided him with insightful and salacious tidbits about political life in Westminster and who delighted in passing on the comment of Lady Eva Anderson, the wife of Churchill's wartime chancellor of the exchequer, that the young Kennedy was someone well suited to "straighten out Anglo-American relations in years ahead."[75]

The practical consequences of all this personal empathy, real as it was, can, however, be exaggerated. Jack Kennedy may well have been both enthralled and amused by the kind of effortlessly superior British aristocrat epitomized by a Michael Astor or Hugh Fraser, but he was already too good a politician to present himself to the voters of Boston, with its lively Irish subculture, as anything that could be confused for a caricature of an English gentleman. A speech Kennedy delivered on July 4, 1946, entitled "Some Elements of the American Character," made it clear which side of the Atlantic he most truly represented.[76] "Considerations of mutual strategic interest" should – and would – remain the guiding principle of future Anglo-American relations, Jack told his audience. "Our national idealism finds itself faced by the old-world doctrine of power politics," he added, setting American magnanimity in contrast to those of her wartime allies primarily guided by economic or military concerns. There would be "challenges ahead" in the nation's dealings with European friend and foe alike, he admitted. For Jack, however, that challenge could best be met by his country rising up to meet its moral destiny. "For if we remain faithful to the American tradition, our idealism will be a stead-fast thing, a constant flame, a torch held aloft for the guidance of other nations," he told the electors of the 11th district.[77]

From London, meanwhile, Jack's sister reported that he now commanded a numerically small "but very well positioned" British fan club. Of a visit to her twenty-six-year-old friend Richard Wood, son of Lord Halifax, at his family's 13,500-acre estate in north England, Kick wrote, "There's nothing they don't know about the Eleventh Congressional District."[78] Along with the likes of David Ormsby-Gore, Andrew Cavendish, and Hugh Fraser, Wood was one of the generation of well-heeled young Conservative politicians who went on to win government office when Harold Macmillan came to power a decade later. They were, broadly speaking, the peer group to America's own 1960s' crop of "the best and the brightest" of public officials, if nec-essarily lacking their ultimate responsibility for the escalation of the Vietnam War. Having lost his legs to a German mine in 1943, Wood himself successively became a Tory MP, took on the thankless job of managing Britain's domestic labor relations at the time of the Kennedy administration, and eventually retired as Baron Holderness, dying in 2002.

"Everyone says you were so good in the election," Kick Kennedy wrote her brother, speaking of the Boston primary in which he beat his nearest Democratic rival by 19,426 votes to 10,875, although oddly enough, Kick admitted, London's *Daily Telegraph* had failed to report the fact. Even so, "the outcome must have been a source of great satisfaction … The folks here think you are madly pro-British so don't start destroying that illusion until I get my house fixed. The painters might just not like your attitude!"[79]

Two weeks later, Jack's Independence Day speech confirmed that a judicious degree of anti-British rhetoric would rarely go amiss at a Boston political rally. The question then arose whether he should go on to give a full-scale oration denounc-ing the whole history of England's supposed mistreatment of

Ireland over the centuries. Ambassador Kennedy's instincts were all for it – "It touches your pride to be an Irish Catholic ... that's the stuff to give them," he told his son.[80] But Jack was more cautious. Speaking at a charity dinner on October 14, 1946, he attacked not Britain's foreign or colonial policy but her culture of "social and welfare dependence" under the Attlee government. Kennedy announced:

> A year ago, I had the opportunity of observing the British elections. There were a number of reasons why the Socialist Party won, but there was one great reason that outweighed all others, and that was a growing and complete dependence on the government to do everything. That feeling was strong, not only in Britain, but in all of Europe. Here in America we could let the government do this job. Perhaps some day we will have to, but I think it is far better if the people in this community do the job, if they willingly accept the obligation to help each other.[81]

This was both a progressive and time-honored position. In later suggesting that able-bodied welfare recipients be required to work as a condition of receiving aid, Kennedy could be said to have anticipated the spirit of the Reagan and Thatcher reforms of the 1980s. Conversely, his emphasis on the role of the Church and voluntary sector in providing basic social services followed the pattern of several major British political thinkers on the theme of individual responsibility and self-help, most notably John Stuart Mill in his 1859 classic *On Liberty*, which Jack had read.[82]

★ ★ ★

LIKE OTHERS, then, Kennedy had doubts both about the practicalities of the modern European welfare state and the socialist "project" in general, feeling there was an impelling need for

"Churchillian values of independence and self-reliance" throughout the continent. The whole thing simply involved too many "false moral equivalents, double standards, and wishful thoughts when it [came] to paying bills," Jack remarked drily. In contrast to his old tutor Harold Laski, he never described communist Russia as a "utopia" that it was immoral as well as dangerous to oppose. Nor had Jack seen "Peace, Love, and Brotherhood" bursting forth in any meaningful sense on the streets of postwar France or Germany. These countries represented "the most searing" of modern political failures. To Jack, even the more cautious social-democratic initiatives of the Attlee regime in London would ultimately have to be judged "on their delivery, and not their promise."[83]

But if Kennedy reserved judgment on the current British government, clearly he still personally identified with those twinned virtues of rigorous intellectual inquiry and loose morality that seemed to characterize many of his oldest English friends. "I was in a nightclub in London," Kay Stammers recalled of his tour of duty there in July 1945, "and Jack came in … I found him terribly attractive. Wonderful sense of humour … British men treat women differently from the way American men do. American men idolize women, but to an Englishman, his clubs and sports are likely to come before his women … Jack had much more of an Englishman's attitude toward women. He really didn't give a damn. He liked to have them around and he liked to enjoy himself, but he was quite unreliable. He did as he pleased."[84]

A practical demonstration of this apparently blasé old-world approach to affairs of the heart came early on in Kennedy's bid for Congress.

"The first thing he did," one of his campaign aides recalled to the author Nigel Hamilton, "was to get one of [the] staff pregnant. I went in one day – I was taking a law degree after leaving the navy – and I found him humping this girl on one of the desks in his office. I said, 'Sorry,' and left! Later, the girl told my wife she had missed her period, then learned she was expecting. I told

Jack. 'Oh, shit!' was all he said! He didn't care a damn about the girl – it was just the inconvenience that bothered him! In that sense he was a pretty selfish guy."[85]

This was an unconventional moral approach to life for an aspiring young public officeholder in 1940s Boston, let alone one who happened to be Roman Catholic. But Kennedy nonetheless enjoyed two great assets his political rivals could at best only feebly approximate. He had his father's wealth, which among other things allowed him to hire a professional staff, take out extensive print and radio advertising, and plaster Boston with "Kennedy for Congress" posters. It's been estimated that the ambassador lavished between $250,000 and $300,000 on his son's campaign, which was more than that of Jack's ten Democratic primary challengers and his eventual Republican opponent combined. Joe himself is said to have remarked, "With what I'm spending I could elect my chauffeur."[86]

Kennedy's other great advantage over his opponents came from his status as a war hero who had gone on to personally witness some of the critical events of recent European politics. Unusually for a first-time congressional candidate, his speeches dwelt on affairs in London, Paris, and Moscow as much as they did on parochial or hometown issues. Here Jack was in his element. At a convention of young Democrats, addressing "The stake of the veterans in the national elections," he quoted Rousseau and insisted that Americans had a moral obligation to set a lead for the rest of the world. A week later, he was citing Plato and Aristotle in support of his theme that "We should [take] an active interest" in affairs both at home and overseas. Speaking to the Boston Boot and Shoe Club, he announced, "Soviet Russia [is] a slave state run by a small clique of ruthless, powerful and selfish men." This was still something of a pioneering view of a nation that had been America's comrade-in-arms only a year earlier. The ordinary citizens of Russia were "literally chained to the Hammer and Sickle," Jack added. "They cannot even [travel] without special permission from the government. The Russian cannot leave his home for more than 24 hours without reporting the fact to the police."[87] Even when the Soviet Union officially renounced much of its Stalinist past later in the 1960s, Kennedy refused to relax his own deep-held opinion that Moscow was "waging a relentless struggle to gain control" around the globe. The seeds of that view were sown in 1945–1946.[88]

When the voters of Massachusetts's eleventh district went to the polls later in November, they elected Jack Kennedy by an almost threefold margin over his Republican opponent. One of the new representative's first acts on arrival in Washington was to support President Truman's proposal for a $400 million aid package designed to contain Soviet aggression in southeastern Europe. The vote again showed just how far Jack had come from his father's position, because in March 1947 the ambassador publicly called on Truman to refrain from any such subsidies in the future and thus to leave "Marshal Stalin free to proceed" as he saw fit. "The wise step is to keep the American way of life as strong as our resources can make it, and permit communism to have its trial outside the Soviet Union," he concluded.[89] Reflecting bitterly that this policy put him sharply at odds with his own son, Joe turned to a dinner guest at Palm Beach one night and asked him, "What's wrong with me?"[90]

5

EUROPE'S NEW ORDER

WHEN THE EIGHTIETH United States Congress convened on January 3, 1947, the eleventh district of Massachusetts gained an unusually well informed and cosmopolitan representative. Unfortunately, John Kennedy's primary area of expertise – British and European reconstruction and the threat of global communist subversion – offered few immediate career opportunities for a twenty-nine-year-old Washington freshman. Operating from a spartan third-floor room in the old House Office Building, Jack found himself assigned not to the choice Foreign Affairs Committee but to those concerned with administrative arrangements for the District of Columbia and the regulation of unions and organized labor. In the Cold War atmosphere of 1947, the prospect of Soviet expansionism overseas and communist agitation at home now seemed to offer a dual challenge to the traditional American way of life. As a US representative, Kennedy consistently supported interventionist measures that included aid to Greece and Turkey, the Marshall Plan, and the further dispatch of US ground forces to Western Europe. To do otherwise would have "tremendous strategic and ideological repercussions throughout the world," he argued, in an early expression of what became known as the "domino theory." "The barriers would be down, and the Red tide would flow across the face of [Europe] with new power and vigor," Jack added.[1]

Nevertheless, Kennedy spent significantly less of his time in helping shape the contours of postwar American foreign policy than he did in the world of arcane legislative procedures. Lem Billings recalled that Jack "found most of his fellow congressmen boring, preoccupied as they all seemed to be with their narrow political concerns. And then, too, he had terrible problems with all the rules and customs that prevented you from moving legislation quickly and forced you to jump a thousand hurdles before you could accomplish anything. All his life he had had troubles with rules externally imposed and now here he was, back once again in an institutional setting."[2] Kennedy himself alluded to this issue when he later remarked, "We were just worms in the House – nobody paid much attention to us nationally ... Most other congressmen and most other people outside the district didn't know us."[3]

Jack Kennedy's arrival in Washington hadn't gone entirely unnoticed in the wider world, however. In Britain, twenty-eight-year-old David Ormsby-Gore then divided his time between farming his family's 1,500-acre estate in Oswestry, Shropshire, and a brief commission in his county's yeomanry. Still undecided whether to embark on a political career of his own, Gore thought his friend Jack's election "fairly remarkable." Merely connecting the aspiring American statesman with the playboy tourist of a short time earlier "required an imaginative leap," Gore admitted. Kennedy's new-found respectability was both "impressive and somehow a little difficult to take seriously."[4]

For his part, Harold Macmillan was then an obscure fifty-three-year-old Conservative MP with limited ministerial experience. Through an improbable sequence of events, most notably the fiasco of the 1956 Anglo-French invasion of Suez, within a decade he would emerge as one of the most influential statesmen of the century. When Macmillan first heard of Jack Kennedy, he thought of him primarily in terms of his father. Through Winston Churchill, he knew a great deal about the former us ambassador, "and we regarded him with some contempt," Macmillan told his official biographer.[5] His private comments were even less enthusiastic. Joe was "a pariah ... a man of low character," Macmillan said.

To many Britons, then, the Kennedy name was not one that seemed to herald the promise of a new golden era in Anglo-American relations. Writing to an army friend, David Ormsby-Gore later observed, "It was hardly a promising backdrop that greeted us [Atlanticists] in 1961." Set against these historical concerns, however, there were those of a more sentimental or warmly human variety. In September 1956, the sixty-two-year-old Macmillan, then the British chancellor of the exchequer, traveled to the hamlet of Spencer, Indiana, to read the lesson at his late mother Nellie's hometown church. "I owe her everything," he said, in a stirring speech that was full of family pathos. "I found it rather difficult to get through, without breaking down," the normally unflappable Briton wrote in his diary. "I really felt that my mother was there watching us and enjoying the satisfaction of so many of her hopes and ambitions for me."[6] Just as Kennedy identified with a certain strata of upper-class English life, so Macmillan felt a "deep, profound and abiding" affinity for the American heartland. The connection between the two future principal leaders of the Western alliance could even be said to "run in their blood." Since Macmillan's wife Dorothy was the daughter of the ninth duke of Devonshire, this made him Kick Kennedy's uncle by marriage. In another twist, David Ormsby-Gore's sister Katharine would go on to marry Macmillan's son Maurice. The three leading architects of the Atlantic "special relationship" of the early 1960s – Kennedy, Macmillan, and Gore – were thus not only ideological soul mates but friends and family.

Lem Billings was another of Kennedy's old circle who briefly struggled to reconcile Jack's priapic-swinger image with that of the idealistic public servant. Like others, Lem, while acknowledging the "tremendous feat" of his friend's election, initially wondered if he were entirely serious about his new role. "Dear Jack," he wrote in a teasing letter of January 1947:

> Just a note to give you a few pertinent remarks on your latest write-up in the Choate Alumni News ... Between you and me, Jack, don't you think [their old English teacher] Tinker is going overboard? I never seriously objected when he put your picture (well in the background) in the front piece, [but I] draw the line when "Jack Kennedy's challenge" is announced in large letters on the cover, followed by a long and boring article on the content of that challenge ... Some of us other graduates felt just a little bit put out.[7]

Behind the public persona, the private Kennedy was difficult to locate. Jack remained temperamentally closer to Kathleen than to any of his other six surviving siblings. Their letters to each other are a mixture of social and personal gossip, usually involving the foibles of the British aristocracy, and often read like something out of the diary pages of the lifestyle magazine *Tatler*. "Dined with Margaret Biddle," Kick reported on May 16, 1947. "She has now decided to sell her house in the country ... Tony B's wife is having a baby. I found her absolutely miserable ... Spent the weekend at Eastbourne. The Duchess, Elizabeth and Anne are off to Italy ... I watched the royal family arrive in coaches from the station. [David Ormsby-Gore's mother] Lady Harlech, who went as lady-in-waiting, said they had all got terribly thin."[8]

Kick herself, now twenty-seven, was chatty, intelligent, frivolous, hedonistic, charming, and by all accounts something of a snob. Though good-looking, she was afflicted by the Kennedy teeth and a generally unkempt bouffant hairdo. A visitor to her house in London's Smith Square found clothes "flung over sofas, half-eaten meals shoved around the floor, and a touch of the slapdash to the sleeping arrangements."[9]

At some stage over the hot English summer of 1947, Kick took up with thirty-six-year-old Peter Wentworth-Fitzwilliam, a much-decorated war hero who had served alongside the author Evelyn Waugh in the newly formed British commandos. Waugh thought his brother officer a "king dandy and scum," although, writing to his wife after the war, he reported, "I think I have just bought a castle. It has about fifteen bedrooms, five reception, 80 acres of park, with as much farm land as you want. It belongs to Peter Fitzwilliam who wants a friendly neighbour."[10] As the eighth earl Fitzwilliam, Kick's new suitor enjoyed an estimated fortune of £45 million (£1,150 million or $1,725 million today) and ownership of the family's seat of Wentworth Woodhouse, a 365-room Jacobean palace near Rotheram in Yorkshire. The main house was said to cover some 250,000 square feet of floor space and be surrounded by eighteen thousand acres of land, although experts weren't unanimous as to the exact figures. It was agreed to be the largest private home in the United Kingdom. Imposing as it was, this was only one of several Fitzwilliam family estates spread throughout England and Ireland. There was also an extensive art collection, dozens of thoroughbred racehorses, a private coal mine, and "about 1,000 indoor servants and gardeners," although again no one seemed to know the precise number.

As a young man in pre-war London, Fitzwilliam had become hooked on high-stakes poker, at which he won and lost enormous sums of money, and champagne, which he drank "in wholesale quantities."[11] Like Billy Hartington before him, he was fabulously privileged, Protestant, and "something of a bounder."[12] More pertinently, Fitzwilliam was also married. His wife Olive, or "Obby," was both an Irish bishop's daughter and an heiress to the Guinness brewery fortune, and she and her husband had a twelve-year-old child. Obby was an alcoholic and the marriage was unhappy, but lawyers had advised the couple that at least for the present any divorce or public separation was out of the question.

Several of Kathleen's British friends, like Elizabeth Cavendish, thought she seemed "terrified" of her parents' likely reaction when they came to learn of her relationship with Fitzwilliam. "It was a terrific scandal."[13] Kick's fears were realized when Rose Kennedy promised to disown her daughter if she married a divorced man. Jack, by contrast, seems to have regarded the whole affair with detached amusement, perhaps enjoying its air of intrigue and rebellion, as well as its connection for him to another high-born British roué. Right to the end, he wrote to his sister as if they were intimate, witty friends, each recording the foibles of their rarefied but faintly ludicrous social circle, eagerly soliciting every detail of her life in London.

With his new-found political status, Jack had moved beyond merely questioning his father's values and come to treat the "old man" with a certain degree of qualified respect that took the place of his former hero worship. Their differences existed on both the personal and political level. Just as the United States had had no business going to war with Germany, the ambassador stubbornly maintained, so she should now try to accommodate Soviet Russia. Washington could not "possibly finance resistance to other systems of government [without] impoverishing this nation," Joe told Arthur Krock, with the request that he publish his views.[14] The sensible option, instead, was to negotiate with Stalin, whose program of global expansion and conquest was "drive[n] by economic rather than ideological" factors. To Joe, apparently on his way to becoming an international pariah for a second time, it was all strictly a matter of business.

By contrast, from his earliest days in Congress, Jack Kennedy seems to have been passionate, even obsessed, about the postwar communist terror in Europe. The young representative did not trust Moscow, and he did not trust those Americans who imagined they could ignore the problem. Jack interpreted anything that happened in that sphere of the world through the prism of what he had personally witnessed in Britain during the years 1938–1939: appeasement and isolationism in the face of a dictatorial bully would not prevent a war but could actually encourage one. "We have only to look at the map to see what might happen if Greece and Turkey fall into the Communist orbit," Jack told an audience at the University of North Carolina in March 1947. He proceeded to again lay out his version of the domino theory of world affairs, arguing that the collapse of even one relatively small, friendly nation might lead to a succession of neighboring losses. Kennedy went on to announce on the floor of the House, "If Italy is to be saved, we must act immediately. If not, she may soon fall before the onslaught of communism ... [Italy] has met with cold contempt on the part of the Soviet Foreign Minister. This cold contempt has continued to be the attitude of the Soviet Union, which seeks to destroy the freedoms of peoples everywhere."[15] Earlier that year, Jack had had his staff cut out the newspaper reports of Winston Churchill's latest tour of the United States and underlined one in which Churchill wondered if the "great English-speaking allies of 1941–45" had merely replaced one omnivorous European evil with another.

★ ★ ★

ON JULY 28, 1947, the 80th Congress adjourned for the summer. A month later, Jack Kennedy boarded a Pan Am DC-4 for one of the first regularly scheduled passenger flights from New York to Shannon Airport in western Ireland. Officially, he was to spend four weeks in Europe as part of a US delegation to study postwar reconstruction and the possible future impact of the Marshall Plan. In practice, this meant his traveling about diligently taking a great deal of notes while also indulging his taste for the gentlemanly life of the continent's upper classes. Early in September, Jack joined his sister Kick for an extended house party at the twelfth-century Lismore Castle in County Waterford.

Originally a monastery, the estate had passed into the Cavendish family's hands in 1753, making it a relatively recent addition to their property portfolio. It had some twenty bedrooms, several of them said to be haunted by the headless ghost of Sir Walter Raleigh, a former resident, seven acres of formal gardens, and its own railway stop. "Up the winding road above the River Blackwater," Jack wrote, recalling his first glimpse of the place, "and the house itself … a gray, mysterious hulk towering out of the haze."[16] It was the setting for a Hollywood fairy tale – "like a castle out of *Le Morte d'Arthur*," another visitor felt.[17]

Kennedy could (and did) make a reasonable claim that his stay at Lismore, redolent as it was of something out of a comic opera, still qualified as a "working" holiday. The castle's guest list included Jack's MP friend Hugh Fraser; Tony Rosslyn, who sat in the House of Lords; Sir Shane Leslie, an Anglo-Irish diplomat and writer, who happened to be Winston Churchill's first cousin; and fifty-year-old Anthony Eden, Britain's wartime foreign secretary and a future prime minister, who like his fellow Conservatives was then sitting in the political wilderness. To add an air of country-house intrigue to the gathering, the generally cool and aloof Eden, who was separated from his wife, showed a distinct romantic interest in Lady Hartington, as he referred to Kathleen. "I long to see you," he wrote to Kick a short time later. "I love your letters, especially when you write as you talk, for then I can imagine you are here. How I wish that you were, and I do believe that you would enjoy it too."[18] As suave and dapper as a tailor's dummy, Eden was nonetheless tortured by bouts of depression, deepened by the loss of his eldest son in the war, and afflicted with a clipped, hesitant speaking style that often failed to carry his audience. He was also nearly twice Kick's age. It was widely believed at Lismore that they had had an affair, or at least an understanding of some sort, but that Kathleen's heart belonged to Peter Fitzwilliam.[19] It's possible that Eden – who was also conducting an affair with Dorothy, Lady Beatty, estranged wife of his political colleague David Beatty – simply mistook friendliness for friendship on Kick's part. If so, it would not be his last misjudgment of American intentions. "She [Mrs. Eden] is in New York and refuses to return, so Anthony lives in a rather squalid house with very few comforts," Kick reported in a letter home to Boston. "He is a nice man and fascinating to talk to for me," she added.[20]

While at Lismore, Jack Kennedy was regarded by his fellow guests as an astute young politician who talked persuasively and at length about the communist threat. "It was like an obsession with him," Hugh Fraser recalled. He was also heralded as an apostle of modernity, in terms of both style and substance. Fraser remembered him "never wearing a hat, which was then the height of nonconformity, and speak[ing] effusively and compassionately about the 'humble Irish folk' we sometimes passed in the car."[21]

At night, Kennedy slept in the castle's Queen's Room, where a blazing log fire illuminated walls hung with gilt-framed ancestral portraits. He also enjoyed an en suite library, a four-poster bed, and a rather primitive bathtub. There is not a shred of evidence pointing to any romantic activity during his two-week stay, although one of his fellow guests at Lismore was twenty-seven-year-old Pamela Churchill, whose long life of amorous adventure would include affairs with several wealthy Americans. Ebullient almost to a fault, Pam was pretty, auburn-haired, and sexy, with "kitten eyes full of innocent fun," in Evelyn Waugh's phrase. In later days she was sometimes known to spice up the proceedings at an otherwise stuffy diplomatic cocktail party by approaching a favored male friend and inviting him to guess the color of her underwear. (She eventually became an American citizen and the United States ambassador to France.) At eight each evening, twenty or so guests sat down in Lismore's formal dining room, under cathedral-like stained glass windows embellished with the Devonshire family motto *Cavendo tutus* ("safe through caution"), where waiters in black livery served them from silver dishes.

Mysterious but well connected, sixty-year-old Shane Leslie was a globe-trotting exotic whose wife Marjorie was the daughter of a retired US ambassador. Leslie himself was said to have played some small role behind the scenes in persuading President Woodrow Wilson to declare war on Germany in 1917. In later years, he had acted as a point man between Churchill and Roosevelt. Having lost most of his family fortune in the Wall Street crash, Leslie turned his hand to writing novels and poetry, if with limited commercial success. A Catholic convert and latterly a supporter of Irish unification, he often engaged Jack Kennedy on subjects of mutual interest at Lisborne. Leslie found the young congressman socially charming – "he acted as if he was lucky to be with you" – but also someone who "kept a kind of barrier up between himself and the rest of the world." It was the same thing when they came to discuss the great political issues of the day. According to Leslie, Jack was happy to make a "symbolic" gesture such as accepting his invitation to join the Ancient Order of Hibernians, an Irish-Catholic fraternal society that raised money for charity and thus an uncontroversial affiliation. Kennedy could also be called upon to "rescue an otherwise bog-standard speech with some nicely evocative phrases" each St. Patrick's Day. But Leslie drew a blank when attempting to bring the younger man around to actively support the cause of Irish nationalism, if necessary by direct action against the Westminster government. "The Congressman was not persuaded of the case," he was left to admit. What was on display those nights in Lismore, as in the Kennedy White House, was a kind of "friendly detachment" that also had a physical counterpart. "Jack recoiled if you so much as patted him on the shoulder," Leslie wrote."[22]

Characteristically, Kennedy also wanted to get out and see the "real Ireland." There is an enduring story, possibly apocryphal, of his having strolled one night into Mulligan's pub in Dublin, where he's supposed to have "shared a pint of Guinness with locals before driving home to the castle for dinner." In assessing this account, we should perhaps remember that Jack would have faced a round trip of some 260 miles over country roads in order to travel from Lismore to the Irish capital and back, and also that he rarely if ever touched a glass of beer. If the evidence is fragile, the story was sturdy and later found its way into several early Kennedy biographies.[23]

We know that on or around September 11, Jack and Pam Churchill requisitioned Kick's new "boat-like" American station wagon and drove for some four hours over rough rural lanes to New Ross, a small market town and semiderelict port on the banks of the river Barrow. For all its air of bucolic charm, it must have seemed to possess a certain raw energy and racy promise compared to their final destination, the southern outpost of Dunganstown. For the last mile or two of their journey, the station wagon bumped down a winding, rutted lane populated by chickens and geese. At one point the congressman rolled down the window to ask directions of a passing bicyclist to the "Kennedy house." "Which Kennedys will it be that you'll be wanting?" the cyclist replied.[24] At length the travelers pulled up at a small, weather-beaten farmhouse where a young woman appeared, surrounded by crying children and barking dogs. "I'm your cousin John from Massachusetts," a beaming Jack announced, extending a hand. "This" – he indicated his companion, dressed for the occasion in an emerald-green coat and a yellow motoring bonnet, trimmed with a froth of pink veil – "is Lady Pamela Churchill, of Winston Churchill's family." "Will you be wanting tea, then?" his hostess inquired. Kennedy had finally returned to his ancestral roots, where a century earlier his great-grandfather Patrick had eked out a living as a cooper, hammering together whisky barrels, and harvesting an increasingly meager potato crop.

By all accounts, Jack was genuinely moved and charmed by the subsequent warmth of his welcome. For the next hour or so, his cousin, Mary Ryan, served tea and told stories at her modest kitchen table. The home itself, which had no pretension to elegance, boasted a rough stone floor and an imperfectly thatched roof. There was also an outdoor lavatory. At the door of this retreat, Pamela would later recall, "some sort of pig, or hideously tusked dog" had lain sunning itself, "emitting gastric noises, and indifferent to the flies which settled on the corners of its eyes and crawled across its mouth." Despite or because of the ramshackle atmosphere, Jack thought the whole experience "wonderful" and claimed later that he "left in a flow of nostalgia and sentiment." Mary Ryan, for her part, commented of the frail young American, "He didn't look well at all." James Kennedy, another cousin, added, "Begod, he was shook looking."[25]

The family's simple hospitality touched Jack deeply. Before leaving Dunganstown, he asked Mary Ryan if he could do anything for her, and she suggested that he give some of the older children a treat by driving them around the village in the station wagon. He did so, to their mutual delight. Later, Jack produced a camera and took several photographs, in which goats, dogs, sheep, livestock, and poultry of all kinds jostled for prominence with the family group. Sixteen years later, while flying toward the same location on *Air Force One*, President Kennedy would still clearly recall the emotion of the moment. "For me, the visit to that cottage was filled with magic sentiment," he remarked to aides. "That night at the castle ... I looked around the table and thought about the cottage where my cousins lived, and I said to myself, 'What a contrast!'"[26]

Pamela Churchill evidently failed to share the "magic sentiment" of the congressman's homecoming. When on the return drive to Lismore Kennedy asked for her thoughts on the visit, she remarked archly, "It was just like *Tobacco Road*" – a reference to Erskine Caldwell's novel about depression-era Southern sharecroppers. The ferocity of Jack's rebuke gives some backing to the view that the two of them had become intimate. A "furious exchange" had ensued. Jack later remarked, "I felt like kicking the English lady out of the car." To be fair to Pam, her friend Kick Kennedy also stood aloof from the prevailing family nostalgia. Angry that Jack had returned from Dunganstown late for dinner, she asked him only, "Did they have a bathroom?"[27]

On September 21, Jack was back in London. Operating from a £90 a night (£2,000, or $3,000, today) suite at Claridge's Hotel, he soon sought out his old double-barreled friends Robert Gascoyne-Cecil and David Ormsby-Gore, both of whom went on to become Conservative MPs at the next election, and to arrange an interview with their senior colleague Selwyn Lloyd, a future foreign secretary and chancellor of the exchequer. Twenty-five years later, Lloyd remembered that his visitor had been "very gracious and fair" about recent British foreign and colonial policy and "positively effusive" about the contribution of the former premier. "He idolised Churchill, and bombarded me with questions about the old man. Was he in good health? Where was he living? Would he ever return as PM? There was a cordial political respect there, but also a kind of hero-worship." Lloyd came to believe that Jack was in part "seek[ing] to atone for his father's performance" as US ambassador during the dark days of 1938–1939. Unfortunately, an attempt to meet Churchill himself again had to be abandoned because of illness – that of the thirty-year-old congressman, not of the wartime leader more than twice his age. Jack's cyclical poor health when in England now returned with a vengeance. Confined to the London Clinic with what his office called a "recurrence of malaria" contracted while serving with the navy, he was in fact suffering from Addison's disease, a fatal adrenal condition that so weakens the body's immune system that the victim can often be killed by a common cold. A nurse was hurriedly summoned from New York, and she accompanied Jack home on the *Queen Mary* early in October. Her patient was so infirm on his arrival that a priest gave him the last rites before a private ambulance took him to the Lahey Clinic in Boston.[28]

There has been a good deal of fevered prose over the years on the subject of whether or not Kennedy felt himself to be fated to an early death. A heightened sense of his mortality,

the theory goes, must have contributed to his gladiatorial sex
drive – a case of "So many women, so little time." It's true that
the congressman's Washington home at 1528 31st Street in the
upscale Georgetown neighborhood would in time assume some
of the properties of a particularly louche underground jazz club,
where his fellow us representative, Frank Thompson of New
Jersey, remembered "the girls just went crazy" and "he had a
smorgasbord of women to choose from."[29] Shortly after returning from his trip to Europe, Jack, echoing his doctors' prognosis,
calmly told the journalist Joseph Alsop that he didn't expect to
live beyond forty-five, "but there was no use thinking about it
… and he was going to do the best he could and enjoy himself as
much as he could in the time that was given him." It's possible to
agree with Alsop that there was something a bit self-consciously
Byronesque to Jack's repeated assertions about the need to live
for the day. But it's also true that the diagnosis he received
in September 1947 would have encouraged a degree of short-
termism in most people. Jack's London doctor, Sir Daniel Davis,
told Pam Churchill, "That American friend of yours hasn't got
a year to live."[30]

Kennedy's incessant womanizing, his compulsive need for
noise and company, his boisterous pleasure in driving a car
too fast, or taking a plane trip in dangerously stormy weather
all bespoke more than youthful high spirits. "The [Addison's]
crisis really came about because Jack somehow forgot to take
his medication with him when he crossed the Atlantic," David
Ormsby-Gore recalled. "As I understand it he then fell ill, and it
was only at that point that he casually enquired if someone could
please fill his prescriptions and send them over on the boat from
New York."[31] Perhaps it's more accurate to speak not so much
about an actual death wish on Kennedy's part as it is his simple
refusal to take his health seriously. "Sublimely indifferent" was
Ormsby-Gore's assessment of his friend's attitude. However, it
wasn't all Dionysian revelry and suicidal excess at the young congressman's home. An Englishwoman named Dinah Bridge – one

of the extended Astor family – found herself living next door to Kennedy in the winter of 1947–1948. She remembered him as "a mixture of gaiety and thought … He seemed quite serious, and then suddenly, he'd break away from reading to make jokes, and sing a song. But I think he did appear to be quite a serious thinker and always probing into things – literature, politics, etc." Summarizing the atmosphere at the 31st Street house in general, she added, "[He] was always in a hurry."[32]

Kennedy's latest health crisis having passed, he returned to plunge with almost frenetic energy into a special session of Congress beginning on November 17, 1947. It may be that he had a "sentimental attachment to England, and her whole island story," as Dinah Bridge later recalled. But that affinity fell short of unwavering political support on Jack's part for current British foreign policy. His eventual line, like that of many American politicians of both parties, was that it was high time that most if not all the United Kingdom's overseas possessions be given a greater say in the conduct of their own affairs. "The paladins of the old Empire are anachronistic [and] should realize that we live in the twentieth century," he remarked to a group of British friends, including Bridge, in one of those sudden shifts from the frivolous to the intense – and perhaps also the slightly pompous – that constitute the basic fabric of his public career.

Kennedy continued to put a good deal of faith in the United Nations as the best-positioned body to prevent the Soviets from exploiting the world's newly independent states. "The whole concept of the UN is that of the evolution of law, backed up by force utilized under the guidance and restraint of the Security Council," he informed Congress. Like many other observers, Jack applauded the British postwar decision to leave India, while expressing concern that "the amputation of that continent along religious lines" (with the creation of the predominantly Muslim states of West and East Pakistan and Hindu-majority India wedged in between) would result in "wholesale administrative chaos."[33] It did. What ensued in the winter of 1947–1948 was some way short of a textbook example of smooth decolonization. An estimated 700,000–800,000 people died in the riots that followed partition, which also created some 14 million long-term refugees.

Kennedy also took an objective view of the events surrounding the British departure from Palestine and the subsequent foundation of the state of Israel in May 1948. Nine years earlier, Jack had visited the Middle East in the course of an extended trip that had been part sex tour, part fact-finding mission on behalf of his father. "Dear Dad," he began a four-page letter from Jerusalem, "I thought I would give you my impressions on Palestine while they were still fresh in my mind, though you undoubtedly, if I know the Jews, know the 'whole' story," the twenty-two-year-old wrote. There followed a chronological list of the various mandates and initiatives proposed by London over the years, with a short and incisive commentary on each. "I see no hope for the working out of the British policy as laid down by the White Paper," Jack admitted. A binational Palestinian state was doomed, he added, for the simple reason that "all ... sides have such great interests, all in a great measure conflicting, and all having great means of putting on pressure." Thus the "only thing to do will be to break the country up into two autonomous districts, giving them both self-government to the extent that they do not interfere with each other, and that British interest is safeguarded. Jerusalem, having the background that it has, should be an independent unit. Though this is a difficult solution yet, it is the only one that I think can work." Before closing the letter, Jack characteristically made the distinction between his disapproval of the general trend of British colonial policy and his admiration for the individuals expected to enforce it. "Incidentally, I have become more pro-British down here than I have been in my other visits to England as I think that the men on the spot are doing a good job," he told his father.[34]

It was the same story when Kennedy came to visit David Ormsby-Gore in September 1947, during the brief interval

between his leaving Lismore Castle, falling ill, and being invalided home. "I remember him coming to lunch with us in
London," Gore recalled, "and the whole of lunch we did nothing except discuss the Palestine situation and what might be
done about it and whether [British foreign secretary] Balfour
had been right to make his declaration in 1917 offering a home
for the Jews in Palestine and so on. It was immediately apparent on that occasion when he came to London, that his mind
was turning very much towards world affairs and political
problems."[35] Indeed, to one of the young women present at
Gore's home that day, Kennedy now appeared "exceptionally zealous to talk business – quite unlike the Jack of old who
once rested his hand on my knee under the dinner table."[36]

For her part, Kick Kennedy, now four years into her wid-
owhood, seemed to lack nothing that would make for earthly
happiness: good health, a circle of well-connected friends, a
large personal fortune – and the ultimate prospect of becoming mistress of Britain's largest private house, along with
half-a-dozen other Fitzwilliam family estates that made the
various Kennedy homes seem almost modest by comparison.
A flavor of her life in England bubbles through in a letter she
wrote Lem Billings: "Spent Easter weekend at Lady Astor's,
and it was really wonderful … All of the guests turned out
to be very nice and the other four girls were really the best
English girls I've met. The Duke and Duchess of Kent came
for dinner one night. She is lovely but he is very disappointing.
We all played musical chairs and charades. Very chummy and
much gaiety. Dukes running around like mad freshmen …"[37]

Twenty years earlier, Kick had written her father a childishly
formed letter one wet Sunday afternoon in Bronxville. "Dear
Daddy: I hope you are having a nice time in Florida. Do you
go in swimming? Is the water cold? I am getting along fine in
school. The drug store man gave pat [*sic*] and Eunice and me a
little box of powder for my doll and I went to open it and it
spilled all over me. Your loving daughter, Kathleen."[38] Any

parent will see the charm and poignancy of this little note. The ambassador carefully preserved it among his personal effects for the rest of his life. Kick adored her father, and at the age of twenty-eight, she admitted to friends, she was still struggling to impress the "old man" and win his approval. In the spring of 1948, Joe agreed to meet with her and Fitzwilliam in Paris, apparently distraught that his favorite daughter would consider marrying a divorced Protestant playboy and intent on stopping it, although possibly also impressed that the high-spirited granddaughter of a first-generation Boston-Irish innkeeper was apparently able to capture the hearts of a succession of Britain's most eligible young aristocrats.

On May 13, Fitzwilliam and Kick boarded a flight to the French Riviera, where they planned to relax for the weekend before returning north to meet the ambassador. They never arrived. Their twin-engine plane stopped to refuel at Le Bourget outside Paris, and by the time the two passengers returned from lunch a thunderstorm had grounded all commercial air traffic in the area. The pilot urged them to wait, but Fitzwilliam characteristically insisted they press ahead. The plane smashed into the hills of the Rhône Valley, killing everyone aboard. Kathleen's body was found beside the wreckage, a string of rosary beads on the ground nearby. For some thirty years, the newspapers would routinely refer to Fitzwilliam as merely a Kennedy family friend, the ambassador having kept the couple's relationship as secret as possible from reporters.

★ ★ ★

ON MAY 17, 1948, John Kennedy's secretary wrote to the State Department, "The Congressman, in order to attend his sister's funeral services in London, is flying from New York this evening at 5:30PM. The passport he obtained last summer to go abroad we have been unable to locate, and would more than appreciate the issuance of a special duplicate this afternoon."[39] When the phone call came telling him that Kick's plane was missing, Jack had been at home in Georgetown. After hearing the worst confirmed, he repeatedly put on his sister's favorite record of Ella Logan singing the Irish nostalgic air, "How are Things in Glocca Morra?" from the musical *Finian's Rainbow*. Then he turned away and wept. In the end, apparently overcome by grief, Jack didn't travel to Britain. On May 20, Ambassador Kennedy was the only family member in attendance at Kathleen's requiem mass at Farm Street Church in central London. After the service, her body was borne away for burial next to her husband in the family plot at Edensor, near Chatsworth. In a significant break from tradition, the Duke of Devonshire permitted a Roman Catholic priest to officiate. David Ormsby-Gore, Hugh Fraser, and Randolph Churchill were among the mourners, and there was a wreath from Churchill's father. The ambassador "wore a crumpled blue suit," Debo Devonshire, Kick's sister-in-law, wrote, "and he was crumpled just like the suit. I never saw anything like it."[40] Even at this wrenching time, there were those who found themselves unable to forgive Joe's performance as his nation's ambassador to Britain. "He stood there alone, unloved and despised," Alastair Forbes recalled. In Boston, Rose Kennedy somehow managed to find the strength to carry on in the face of the loss of a second child in tragically similar circumstances to that of Joe Jr. four years earlier. "That airplane crash was God pointing his finger at Kick and saying 'No!'" Rose later said.

Kathleen's death undoubtedly contributed to Jack Kennedy's conviction that life should be lived as if every day might be the last. His friend Charles Spalding remembered, "He always heard the footsteps ... Death was there. It had taken Joe and Kick and it was waiting for him. So, whenever he was in a situation, he tried to burn bright; he tried to wring as much out of things as he could."[41] That June, speaking about Kick, Jack spoke of destiny as well when he told David Ormsby-Gore, "True freedom means pushing oneself to the full all the time, always knowing of one's approaching end."[42]

Perhaps marrying resignation to man's indefeasible fate in life with a healthy dose of political ambition, Kennedy traveled to London for another fact-finding tour beginning on June 29, 1948. Officially delegated to study the "labor situation" in Britain and France, Jack quickly arranged to visit West Berlin, an area the Soviets were then attempting to bring into closer compliance to the communist ideal by severing all its road and rail links to the rest of the world. A tenacious British and American airlift just barely managed to supply the city's 2.5 million civilian population for the next twelve months. Kennedy was personally briefed by General Lucius Clay, the military governor of Allied-occupied Germany, as well as other senior commanders on the ground. The overall picture cannot have improved the congressman's feelings toward the Soviet regime. Following that, Kennedy spent several days at the Hotel Georges V in Paris and at Claridge's in London, although he seems not to have found the time to visit his sister's freshly dug grave 150 miles away at Chatsworth.

Easily returned to the House in November 1948, Kennedy was now beginning to forge a distinctive political philosophy: optimistic about the future, exalting "Americanism" at every turn, his basic message, as he put it in a later radio address, was nonetheless that "expenditures, taxation, domestic prosperity, the extent of social services" all hinged on the basic issue of stemming the communist tide at home and abroad.[43] He consistently voted against any cuts in us aid to Britain or Western Europe. His main policy concern was the undeclared war now underway between the former allies in the struggle against fascism, and his intellectual guiding light was seventy-four-year-old Winston Churchill, who not for the first time stood on the brink of an unlikely comeback. Among the young congressman's office files are pages of heavily annotated newspaper reports describing the British Conservative Party's sixty-ninth annual conference in October 1948. Rampaging Soviet forces on the ground "now exceed those of all the Western countries put together," Churchill told his audience in Llandudno, North Wales, before adding, "We support the foreign policy of His Majesty's Government in taking a firm stand against the encroachments and aggressions of Soviet Russia, and in not being bullied, bulldozed and blackmailed out of Berlin, whatever the consequences may be ... I hope you will give full consideration to my words," Britain's wartime premier continued. "I have not always been wrong. Nothing stands between Europe today and complete subjugation to Communist tyranny but the atomic bomb in American possession." Churchill concluded with a dramatic passage from Luke 23:31, in which Christ, while on his way to his crucifixion, inquires metaphorically, "If they do this when the wood is green, what will happen when it is dry?"[44] Kennedy underlined the quote, which he would later use himself when campaigning for higher office. It was another example of the way in which Britain's former and future prime minister contributed to the intellectual formation of America's thirty-fifth president.

Churchill embarked on another American tour in March 1949, a visit that was half democratic political rally and half personal fundraising drive. The latter took the form of what he called the "great contract." Churchill would supply the Time-Life publishing empire with advance book excerpts and essays in exchange for a guaranteed sum and "reasonably elastic" expenses. According to the author Thomas Maier, Time-Life's owner Henry Luce "did everything to keep his correspondent happy. He paid for vacations and hosted gala events in his honor, reminding the public of his greatness." "It can be worth the space plus the money if, in some sense, Churchill becomes 'our author,'" Luce explained to a skeptical colleague.[45]

A representative example of Time-Life's hospitality came on March 25, 1949, when Luce hosted a gala dinner for Churchill at the Ritz-Carlton Hotel in New York. The British guest of honor laid it on thick when it came time for him to speak. "Gentlemen," Churchill told his black-tie audience, "many nations have arrived at the summit of the world but none, before the United States, on this occasion, has chosen that moment of triumph, not for aggrandisement, but for further self-sacrifice – sacrifice for the causes by which the life and strength of mankind is refreshed. The United States has shown itself more worthy of trust and honour than any government of men or associations of nations that has ever reached pre-eminence by their action on the morrow of the common victory won by all. I wish to express the thanks of my own dear island and of its Empire, Commonwealth and also of the many countries in Western Europe who are drawing together on the broad ideals of Anglo-Saxon, British-American, call it what you will, unity, which alone gives an opportunity for the further advance of the human race."[46]

This is a statement easily misunderstood, as Churchill combined a profound sentimental attachment to the United States with an equally striking independent streak when it came to defending British interests. The same could be said in reverse of Jack Kennedy. So badly was the congressman afflicted by anglophilia, at least on a social level, he could almost have stepped from the pages of a Henry James novel. In stark contrast to his father, Kennedy remained a vocal champion of the "world's greatest living freedom-fighter," as he called the visiting Englishman. It may not be going too far to speak of a pathological hero worship on the younger man's part. When Churchill sat down following his speech at the Ritz-Carlton, the thirty-one-year-old congressman was at the forefront of those who leapt to their feet in sustained applause. A day or so later, Jack was again on hand at an impromptu press conference held shortly before the distinguished British visitor boarded his homeward ship. Sporting his utilitarian wartime boilersuit, Churchill told the assembled well-wishers, "I wore this once to the Kremlin. It didn't go down so well: pushing democracy too far." The *New York Times* headline read simply, "MAY HE COME AGAIN SOON."

Kennedy, always sensitive to changes in the public mood, was well aware of the findings of a January 1949 opinion poll that 72 per cent of Americans "do not believe that Soviet Russia genuinely wants peace" and a similar number convinced that "Reds wish to rule the world." Reflecting that same month on the defeat of Chiang Kai-shek's nationalists at the hands of Mao Tse-tung's communists in the civil war in China, the Massachusetts congressman announced on the House floor, "The failure of our foreign policy in the Far East rests squarely with the White House and the Department of State."[47] This showed a significant departure by the sophomore Democrat from the views not only of his de facto party leader and chief executive but of his own father. It was the same story when President Truman came to commit ground forces to Korea in hopes of unifying the peninsula under a pro-Western government. Joe Kennedy told a college audience not only that the United States should "pull out both there and any other place in Asia where we cannot hold our defense in the face of Soviet [interference]," but also that she should disengage from Europe. Nor did the former ambassador shy from inviting the obvious comparison to Munich. In fact, he welcomed it. "If it is wise in our interest not to make commitments that endanger our security, and this is appeasement, then I am for it," he announced, adding specifically of Berlin, "Everyone knows we can be pushed out the moment the Russians choose ... Isn't it better to get out now?"[48]

Jack Kennedy also saw the historical parallel to 1938–1939 but drew a very different conclusion from it. Initial American reverses in Korea painfully demonstrated "the inadequate state of our defense preparations," he said. "Our military arms and our military manpower have been proven by [the campaign] to have been dangerously below par."[49]

The younger Kennedy was already an extraordinary amalgam of idealism and cynicism, passion and detachment. An astute analyst of other men's character, he refused to indulge in introspection or self-pity when it came to his own. It was sometimes difficult to distinguish between what Jack truly believed and what he affected to believe for public consumption. David Ormsby-Gore spoke for many when he said later that his friend had seemed to him to incorporate "several different personalities, rarely predictable or entirely uniform in their views." But there was one area in which John Kennedy would prove remarkably consistent over the course of the last fifteen years of his life. Like his late sister before him, he remained the embodiment of the special Anglo-American relationship.

6

JOHN F. KENNEDY SLEPT HERE

IN 1951, BRITAIN WAS still suffering from the lingering effects of victory over Hitler. The cumulative blows of the last dozen years had left the nation permanently verged on the brink of bankruptcy. In August, Hugh Gaitskell, the new Labour chancellor, revealed that the United Kingdom had incurred a gold and dollar deficit of $638 million, and that as a result "We may shortly face the grave choice of deciding whether to mobilise all our financial assets and overseas infusions in order to preserve our currency, [or] let it find its own level." Britain's participation in the Korean War and the resulting increase in defense spending placed further strain on a budget already sorely tested by the National Health Service and the other accompanying apparatus of the modern welfare state. Although President Truman went on to sign the Foreign Aid Bill, guaranteeing the UK $7,329 million in loans and credit, even then the government would find it hard to hold the country together. Economic hardship made life grim for many ordinary Britons, for whom the accent was on "making do." Clothing coupons and food queues remained a way of life throughout the postwar decade. The Fuel Order meant that shopkeepers kept their lights dimmed even in winter months, and goods such as televisions, fridges, and radiators were still unimaginable luxuries to all but a privileged minority. Having called an election in October in hopes of increasing their parliamentary majority, Labour instead found themselves rejected in favor of Winston Churchill's Conservatives. Politically, the country was split down the center. The slimness of their victory, with a majority of only twenty-six seats over Labour and seventeen over all parties combined, would constrain Tory policy making for years to come. "God help me conduct my arduous task," the returning seventy-six-year-old premier drily remarked.[1]

When Jack Kennedy arrived in London on January 9, 1951, therefore, he brought with him not just a briefcase full of official papers on British armaments and defense expenditures but also a brown-paper parcel stuffed with nylon stockings, chocolates, tea, and other hard-to-obtain consumer goods, which he duly distributed to suitably grateful friends. It was left to David Ormsby-Gore to act as a link between the two distinct parts of Kennedy's tour. Now elected to parliament, Gore was beginning to interest himself in the cause of a unified Europe that would be part of a grander, global coalition against the perils of communism. The Conservative MP and his friend the Democratic congressman were soon involved in a lively exchange of ideas. According to Gore, their eventual consensus was on "the need to promote the concept and the reality of an Anglo-American united front to resist the transgressions of the Soviet Union."[2] This same high-minded resolve on the priorities of Western strategy was echoed in an eve-of-departure news bulletin carried by the Mutual-Yankee radio network. "Congressman Kennedy explained that any decision by Congress to send troops to Europe will depend in large measure on what effort Europe makes to rearm itself," the station reported. "And to discover just how far these various nations plan to go, Kennedy plans to have clear-cut personal observations which he will secure by personal dialog with the heads of countries involved."[3]

In practice, this meant that Kennedy went around with an old-school reporter's pad and pencil and interviewed as many British politicians as time allowed, dutifully recording their often crusading views about the spread of communism and Soviet subversion in general without ever seeking to impose his own. This dispassionate research process, in which Jack let his subject do most of the talking, was essentially the same approach he took with him into the White House. Harold Wilson, then newly elected leader of Britain's opposition Labour Party, would encounter the technique on a visit to the Oval Office in April 1963. "One immediately saw that [the president] was a journalist as much as he was a politician, and that he was constantly probing and marshaling all his facts before ever uttering a word for the record. I must say, I warmed to the man ... I mean, John Kennedy looking you in the eye and asking you, 'What's good and what's bad about the current NATO setup?' as if he valued your opinion. It's very flattering."[4] We have pages of Kennedy's handwritten notes from his British and European travels of 1951; fussily detailed, annotated with facts and figures such as a particular country's annual steel output, or corn yield, or her precise individual expenditures as a percentage of gross national product, they bear the imprint of the true reporter.[5] Impressive in itself, this same inquisitive discipline would one day make President Kennedy uniquely well attuned to the needs of the working press, who took to him as one of their own as a result.

Characteristically, Kennedy's latest British tour also embraced a variety of leisure activities, many of them consonant with those of today's rock star – such as his taking the short-term lease on a furnished flat in London's Mayfair, a home remembered as "painted red and gold, with a big bearskin rug on the floor of the bedroom, where Jack was fond of entertaining his female guests."[6] Much of the more formally social component of the visit again took place in the company of well-heeled friends such as David Ormsby-Gore and Andrew Cavendish and involved a good deal of time spent in drafty British country houses. Jack stood out from most of his fellow guests in never quite taking to shooting or fishing as a recreation, but he was also not averse to the grouse-moor image, lending as it did a certain old-world respectability to the son of an Irish–American former liquor importer and alleged bootlegger.[7] Perhaps Jack didn't dress up in tweed plus-fours, as Gore or Cavendish sometimes did, but shuffling into the Ritz Grill in London one evening wearing a somewhat distressed black tail-coat, with a white handkerchief flopping from his pocket, stooped as a result of his bad back, he seemed, at age thirty-three, to be "play[ing] the Grand Old Man, someone who looked like a slightly decrepit upper-crust English fogey more than a dynamic young American."[8]

Kennedy's friend Alastair Forbes thought that at this time "he was not a decisive man ... He would prefer to postpone matters. He would prefer the matters to settle themselves by the interplay of conflicting forces."[9] It was as if the sheer mass of detail he carried around with him precluded his taking a quick or fixed position on the issues. When pressed by Senator Tom Connally, chairman of the Joint Congressional Foreign Relations Committee, for his views on whether to maintain existing us troop levels overseas through 1951–1952, apparently in hopes of a yes or no answer, Kennedy replied:

> I would want the Congress to basically set the policy of six European divisions for every one American division. I would put no particular limit upon the number of our divisions we send to Europe so long as this ratio system was in effect. I am not trying to limit the American effort in Europe. I am trying to bring the European effort up to match it, considering that we have responsibilities elsewhere, and that much or most of their equipment is going to come from the United States. I do not think that is unreasonable.[10]

Kennedy's stance on the defense of Western Europe in general and of Britain specifically again placed him at odds with his father. Speaking on the floor of the House, Jack noted that, budgetary constraints aside, "We must be able to put sufficient American forces in the field in that area to demonstrate to the Europeans that we believe [the continent] can be held ... We must mobilize our manpower to a far greater degree than we have as yet planned."[11] Just three months later, Ambassador Kennedy told his audience at the University of Virginia that he opposed increased American troop deployments abroad, Marshall Plan aid to Europe, the "whole concept and organiza- tion" of NATO, and most other US overseas commitments in the fight against communism. "A first step ... is to get out of Korea," Joe announced. "The next step ... is to apply the same principle in Europe." Such isolationism was "very much in accord with our historic traditions," he noted. "We have never wanted a part of other peoples' scrapes."[12]

Ambassador Kennedy fiercely opposed continuing US subsidies to Britain, particularly once that "old drunk and war- monger" Churchill was back as prime minister. From Yugoslavia to Greece and on to Berlin, it seemed to Joe that the way led inexorably to "another world cataclysm." In the older Kennedy's view, to resist the Soviet Union was a strategic error that could only further waste American lives and treasure. "Let Communism spread, meanwhile keep the US fat," *Time* magazine quoted him as saying.[13] Joe was incensed by Churchill's World War II memoir, *The Gathering Storm*, and the several volumes that followed it. "They should be handled with great care," he wrote in an open letter to the *New York Times*. "They are replete with serious inaccuracies on the basis of which judgments are made that are unfair to individuals and events ... Churchill's misquotations of documents that are public make it difficult for one to rely on his quotations from documents that are not generally available," Kennedy concluded. "Other facts not yet made public may further bring into question Mr. Churchill's position as a raconteur of history."[14] There's some anecdotal evidence to suggest that Joe directed one of the gardeners at his Hyannis Port estate to throw his presentational copy of *The Gathering Storm* onto a bonfire. Whatever the truth or otherwise of this story, some discrepancy can be said to exist between the ambassador's opinion of Churchill as historian and that of his son, who thought the collected work "magnificent." Jack later kept Churchill's four-volume biography of his ancestor the duke of Marlborough prominently displayed on his desk in the White House.[15]

Henry Brandon was one of those cosmopolitan, highly literate, and sexually wolfish Britons whom Jack gravitated to, perhaps particularly admiring Brandon's inexhaustible intellectual curiosity and vibrant libido. The two men became close friends in the early 1950s. Born in Slovakia in 1916, Brandon had been educated in Prague, Lausanne, and Paris before settling in England and becoming a foreign correspondent of the *Sunday Times*. After reporting on the fall of Germany and the San Francisco conference establishing the United Nations, he took up what proved to be a thirty-five-year-long assignment in Washington, D.C. In some ways Brandon would seem to represent the sort of idealized, morally liberated transatlantic jet-setter Jack himself might have become had he ultimately chosen journalism over politics. As he nearly did so, it's not an entirely idle conjecture. In time, Brandon's own affection for Kennedy blended with the satisfaction of having a well-placed source in the US government who actually understood the ways of the media.

"Jack was the easiest person to talk to from a newspaperman's point of view," Brandon recalled. "I think he had this marvelous gift of being absolutely frank, giving you the impression that he's telling you more than he should – and he very often did – and that you sometimes sort of looked over your shoulder whether anybody's listening and you said to yourself, 'My God, I can't tell anybody about this.' He never said, 'This is for background only,' or 'This is off the record.' He left it entirely up to you."[16]

Like others, Brandon thought Kennedy "a British squire" in his essential outlook on life. "He had these two sides to him. He could be gay and light-hearted and social and flippant, and then in the next minute he could be very serious, discuss very serious problems, ask very serious questions ... 'How would the English react to this? How would Europe react to that?'"[17]

By late 1951, Kennedy was already a third-term congressman with his eye on higher things. His efforts to carve out a position distinct from that of his father on the major foreign policy issues of the day sometimes engendered a certain amount of friction with other members of his family. One of the former ambassador's friends, Kay Halle, remembered visiting Jack when he was a seventeen-year-old laid up in a hospital and finding him propped up in bed reading Winston Churchill's *The World Crisis*.[18] Although Jack was then "completely dominated" by his father, clearly this was no longer the case. "Kay, I wish you would tell Jack that he's going to vote the wrong way," the elder Kennedy now told Halle at a Washington cocktail party. "Dad, you have your political views and I have mine," the congressman replied. "I'm going to vote exactly the way I feel I must vote on this. I've great respect for you, but when it comes to voting, I'm voting my way."[19] Henry Brandon wasn't alone in thinking that John Kennedy's career seemed in some ways to offer atonement for his father's unhappy term as US ambassador to Britain. "He was very much influenced by what happened in England in 1940, and somehow he tried to live down the reputation of his father. Joe had not much faith in Britain in those days. The dispatches issued by the State Department, the official ones, bear that out. I think in a curious way Jack tried to compensate for all that."[20]

With Churchill's return to power, John Kennedy's support for Great Britain intensified. He voted consistently for greater American subsidies to London and for the stationing of more US troops alongside British forces on the ground in Western Europe. Only a decade later, as president, he boldly outlined his vision of a "full and equal" Atlantic Partnership with a continent still (if just barely) dominated by Britain. "I will say here and now on this day of independence," Kennedy told an audience on July 4, 1962, "that the United States will be ready for a 'Declaration of Interdependence.'"[21] Such lofty goals of economic and military unity did not, however, blind him to "certain longstanding ills [and] excesses" of British foreign policy. With one or two notable exceptions, such as Guiana, Kennedy would increasingly come to "ally the United States with the rising tide of nationalism around the world," as he put it, convinced that "previously subordinated states [should be] liberated from their historic past," if simultaneously that helped to bolster the Western side in the global war against communism. "My nation was once a colony," President Kennedy would remind the UN in 1961, "and we know what colonialism means."[22]

By the middle of 1951, Kennedy was a critical and sometimes vocal admirer of maverick Republican senator Joseph McCarthy of Wisconsin, the chief protagonist of a heated debate about widespread communist subversion within the US government. The senator's almost religious stance against communism initially struck a chord with many ordinary Americans, if not always their elected officials. In time, Jack would become the only seated Democrat to vote not to censure McCarthy, partly, he later rationalized, because "my brother [Bobby] was working for Joe ... It wasn't so much a thing of political liability as it was a personal problem."[23] This was not a position that conspicuously endeared him to the liberal community.

In 1954, Kennedy's friend Alastair Forbes witnessed an odd and touching incident that seemed briefly to unite two disparate sides of Jack's social circle:

> I was having a conversation with [Kennedy] and [the premier's son] Randolph Churchill ... Churchill had joined in the conversation and said something, and Mrs. [Lorraine S.] Cooper turned on him and said, "Well, that's an extraordinary thing for you to say, coming from Wisconsin."

Randolph said, "What the hell do you mean? I don't come from Wisconsin. Who the hell do you think you're talking to?" She said, "Why, I'm talking to Joe McCarthy, aren't I?" And he said, "The hell, Madam, you're talking to Randolph Churchill."[24]

As Forbes later explained, the confusion was "to do with the brash personalities of both men, as well as their similar political convictions." In time Churchill's private epithets, such as the one comparing the Soviet hierarchy to "coprolites" and "fecal debris," would be echoed in the senator's table talk.

It's worth repeating that John Kennedy's personal affinity for a certain kind of aristocratic British life didn't invariably mean that he endorsed British overseas policy or that he necessarily looked to Britain for his broader political theories. The Soviet Union was the primary menace in the world, and Kennedy took as his watchword Winston Churchill's warning of May 1945: "The way is now open to the Russians to advance if they choose to the waters of the North Sea and the Atlantic."[25] Churchill and Kennedy, both hard-headed pragmatists, came up with essentially the same solution to the challenge of Soviet aggression: standing united and firm until such time as Moscow overreached itself and was forced to retrench. With that major exception, Jack was not the least concerned with bolstering British foreign policy as it developed in the early 1950s. He viewed Anglo-American relations from a big-picture perspective, as an ideological partnership in the worldwide struggle against communism, not as a prop for the individual vagaries of British colonial rule.

It's also worth repeating in what direction Jack Kennedy's social tastes continued to swing. By 1951, he'd already reached the conclusion that while "as a mass" the British could be difficult, "man by man" they were the second finest race on earth. Looking back fondly on his early days in the United Kingdom, he thought of Talleyrand's remark that anyone who had not known France before 1789 had never known "the sweetness of life." Alastair Forbes remembered that on many of the nights he was in London, Jack would go straight from conducting some high-powered interview to a sparkling Mayfair or Chelsea dinner party, where he found "a much-needed escape [from] some of the frustrations and tensions of full-time politics." As a general rule, such relief tended to come in the company of various sleek young women. A striking example was his friendship with the blonde, Polish-born Alicja Kopzynska, an aspiring actress who was aged somewhere between fifteen and seventeen when Jack met her in 1951. Some years later, the Italian weekly magazine *Le Ore* reported that the couple had gone on to get engaged, but that Ambassador Kennedy had disapproved of the match "because of the intending bride's status as a Jewish refugee." Little is known of Kopzynska's future career, beyond the fact that she later moved to New York, changed her name to Alicia Darr, and stepped out with the likes of Gary Cooper and Tyrone Power before in 1957 marrying the English swords-and-sandals actor Edmund Purdom. A year or two later, in Rome, she sued her husband for "concubinage, insult and assault" following an incident outside a local nightclub. After that, Darr moved around Italy and various hotels on the French Riviera, often leaving no forwarding address, continuing to reminisce about her affair with Kennedy to anyone who might be interested. A memo alleging that she had at one time become pregnant with the future American president's child reached the desk of FBI director J. Edgar Hoover in January 1961. Hoover's handwritten instruction read, "Send this to A.G." (or Attorney General, who happened to be Jack's younger brother Bobby).[26] Later married for a few days to the Singer Sewing Machine heir Alfred Corning Clark, Alicia Darr was survived only by her memoirs, interviews, and debts.

Kennedy's British connections during his early thirties were as varied as they were plentiful. During the day, he sought out men like David Ormsby-Gore and Hugh Fraser, with whom he continued to discuss the great tides of "history, culture, political and economic theory and core moral values" shared by the two Western superpowers; and by night he turned his attention to the young and female members of society.[27] Kennedy's policy with women wasn't all that different from that with men whom he wanted to charm. He flattered them, listened to them, teased them, and generally threw in some self-deprecating wit. Added to his looks, intellect, and "Harvard gloss," as *Today* put it, it was a potent formula. Kennedy's impressive train of English girl-friends "may well have run into the dozens," one well-placed source estimates. Speaking of the blue plaques that commemorate a link between a location in Britain and a famous person or event, the same individual adds, "There would be more than one building in London that could truthfully say, 'John F. Kennedy Slept Here.'"[28]

Of course, Kennedy still knew relatively little of the harsh reality of many ordinary Britons' lives. "Conditions in England have always been difficult for the working man," he'd noted of the election result that swept Churchill from office in July 1945. "Long ago, Disraeli wrote of two nations in England, rich and poor, and in the last five years things have been particularly difficult."[29] True as this was, Jack formed his opinions largely as a result of his exchanges around the dinner table with a succession of like-minded, privileged young men and women, rather than by immersing himself in the lower strata of British society. Other than what he may have read in the papers, he knew nothing of the country where shortages and rationing remained a daily fact of life for millions of people, strike action frequently brought the nation's rail networks or coal supplies to a halt, and the winter cold caused milk – still delivered to many doorsteps by a horse and cart – to explode spontaneously in its bottles. Kennedy may have been an exceptionally shrewd observer of the British political scene, but he knew as little of life in the working-class areas of Glasgow, Liverpool, or Manchester as he did of the dark side of the moon.

In October 1951, Kennedy went back to Europe as part of a thirty-thousand-mile, ten-nation fact-finding mission, an opportunity not only to further educate himself about those regions but to burnish his foreign policy credentials for the home electorate. Following stops in London, Paris, and Rome, there was a lengthy tour of the Middle East and Asia. In Tehran, Jack noted in his diary that 'the British [had] been extraordinarily short-sighted, almost stupid" in their policy. As a result, "the US is now concerned, on the one side, with preventing the Russians from gaining control of the country and, on the other, do not want to strain the British-American partnership in Western Europe ... London [has] repeatedly warned if we now move in with economic assistance it would finish that alliance."[30] In general terms, Kennedy saw the merits of British colonialism as a means of bringing progress to backward countries. But it had also produced significant local resentment. "The British act as if they did us a favor," he scribbled in his journal while in Tehran. "They do not seem to have learned the facts of life in 1951 that the Iranians are willing to go down in a mass of nationalist hysteria regardless of any economic arguments."[31]

Considering that they were never intended for public consumption, Kennedy's travel notes prove once again that he would have made a brilliant popular journalist. Most of his observations are a mixture of sweeping geopolitical overviews, character sketches, and local color. In Tel Aviv, he wrote, "The soldiers appear tough, rugged, and cocky. Jews very aggressive, confident ... British ambassador says important for Arabs to recognize that Israel is here to stay. Says that 500,000 people were here in 1948 at end of British mandate. 700,000 have since come in. But about 600,000 have left [the] country. Says less land under cultivation now than in '48 – Jews not an agricultural people."[32] In New Delhi, Kennedy reported that Baj Pai, head of the Indian foreign office, had spoken of the mixed legacy of British rule: on one hand, a civilized system of government and all that entailed; on the other, the medieval living conditions endured by millions of ordinary citizens. "Interested now in relieving poverty, or communism will develop," was Jack's terse summary of the situation.[33]

After New Delhi, Kennedy went on to Jakarta, Singapore, Kuala Lumpur, Saigon, and Seoul. On October 16, he was in Rawalpindi to meet Liaquat Ali Khan, the prime minister of Pakistan, just hours before he was assassinated – either by a Pathan extremist or a CIA hit man, according to which account you read.[34] The British Royal Air Force was flying Jack around, which meant that he was spending up to ten hours a day in an unheated World War II prop plane before plunging into another exhausting round of interviews and talks. Although Kennedy bore a note from the State Department confirming that he had been vaccinated for "Cholera, Typhoid, Smallpox, and Plague" he was taken seriously ill in Korea and airlifted to the American base at Okinawa with a temperature of 105 degrees. That concluded his forty-two-day tour.

In the context of most Americans' experience of the world, Kennedy's travels were heady stuff, qualifying him as an expert on foreign affairs. Once back in New York, he told a nationwide radio audience that his trip had convinced him of the need for greater understanding toward those races emerging from British colonial rule. "If one thing was bored into me," he said, "it is that Communism cannot be met effectively by merely the force of arms," and that what was needed was the "rebirth of our traditional empathy for the desires of men to be free." More specifically, Kennedy noted that US support of British interests in Iran and elsewhere in the Middle East had "intensified the feeling of hostility towards us until today we are definitely classed with the imperialist powers of Western Europe."[35]

That same winter, Kennedy told friends that he would both be running for the US Senate and getting married. There may conceivably have been a link between these two life-changing decisions. Jack knew that he had to present himself to voters as a family man in order to pursue his career to its ultimate destination. Adlai Stevenson, the 1952 Democratic presidential nominee, was divorced, and this would not help him with the still-significant number of Americans who identified themselves as traditionally minded Christians. Kennedy was clearly a man in a hurry in both his public and private life. He announced his intention to marry the attractive, baby-voiced Jacqueline Bouvier, twelve years his junior, after he met her at a dinner party in the fall of 1951. Even so, the prospective bride was to remark on the "spasmodic courtship" that intervened before their eventual wedding two years later.[36]

Jackie was the perfect Washington wife as that role was then defined, someone who appeared at once to be regally aloof and girlishly naïve, often punctuating her speech with words like "gosh" and "golly," gasped out in a tiny whisper while she fixed her listener with her fluttering brown eyes and an adoring smile. Yet she was nobody's fool. A *Look* magazine reporter who knew the future First Lady well described her as "very strong-minded and very tough ... I think this is one thing that old Joe Kennedy liked about her, that she was a tough babe."[37] Others have speculated that she may have found her marriage and its prevailing atmosphere oddly like returning to childhood. It's argued that Jackie's heroic discretion on the subject of Kennedy's continuing infidelities broadly followed the pattern of her mother Janet and her mother-in-law Rose, both of whom had married philandering husbands.

Like Jack, Jackie was feisty, vivacious, an anglophile, feline, gossipy, and an inveterate lover of show tunes such as "Kiss Me, Kate," which would eventually serve as a sort of soundtrack in the White House living quarters. "[Kennedy] saw her as a kindred spirit," Lem Billings noted. "I think he understood that the two of them were alike. They had both taken circumstances that weren't the best in the world when they were younger, and learned to make themselves up as they went along ... They were so much alike. Even the names – Jack and Jackie: two halves of a single whole. They were both actors, and I think they appreciated each other's performances."[38] Better — or inner — reasons for the Kennedys' durable love affair aren't available to an author, and they may not have been to the parties themselves. He was always true to her in his fashion.

In the November 1952 elections, Jack Kennedy defeated popular three-time Republican senator Henry Cabot Lodge of Massachusetts by 70,737 votes out of some 2.4 million cast. John Fox, the owner of the *Boston Post*, would recall that on the day before his paper endorsed the Democratic challenger, he had "talked to Ambassador Joseph Kennedy ... who agreed to lend" him $500,000.[39] Jack was sworn in to his new office when the eighty-third Congress convened on January 3, 1953. It happened to be ten years to the day since he first received orders to report for overseas combat duty, an event marking the effective beginning of the Kennedy myth. Seventeen days later, he and Jackie attended the three-hour inaugural ceremony and parade investing Dwight Eisenhower as the nation's thirty-fourth president. Incredibly, Jack himself would succeed him.

In May, Jackie traveled to London for the coronation of Britain's Queen Elizabeth. Her dispatches home for the *Washington Times-Herald*, the newspaper where Kick Kennedy had worked during the war, were smart but homespun, with an emphasis on matters such as whether top hats were still required dress for English gentlemen or the precise shade of pink currently fashionable for ladies attending the races at Royal Ascot. Senator Kennedy was unable to be on hand, preoccupied as he was debating legislation that would ultimately establish the US Small Business Administration and arguing the merits of a proposed canal transit system between eastern Canada and the Great Lakes.[40]

★   ★   ★

AS SOON AS the Senate recessed, Kennedy announced that he would again be visiting Europe. Officially, he wanted to study "the ramifications … of Great Britain's dissolution of her empire and other world events," although this time around his reportorial quest also allowed for a significant recreational element. It was Jack's last summer of bachelorhood, and he would be traveling with his old Harvard roommate Torb Macdonald. Both Joe and Rose Kennedy were strongly opposed to the trip, apparently fearing it would damage their son's health, if not his political prospects. "I am hoping that he will take a rest and not jump from place to place, and be especially mindful of whom he sees," the ambassador wrote to Macdonald. "Certainly one can't take anything for granted since he has become a United States Senator. That is a price he should be willing to pay and gladly."[41]

Jack dutifully conserved his energies in Britain, restricting himself to a few dinners with the likes of David Ormsby-Gore and his patron Selwyn Lloyd, the undersecretary of state at the Foreign Office. Lloyd's diary records his view of his visitor as "sympathetic impression, modest, decent fellow … *Very* American. Believes he can find out what he needs to know by direct questioning. Mixture of a bright undergraduate and hardened interrogator."[42] Ambassador Kennedy's fears for his son would be realized only when Jack moved on to the French Riviera, where he met a blonde, twenty-one-year-old Swedish model named Gunilla von Post. During the course of their beachfront evening together, she later recalled, "He turned and kissed me tenderly, and my breath was taken away. The brightness of the moon and stars made his eyes appear bluer than the ocean beneath us."[43] At that stage, Kennedy had mentioned that he was going to be married shortly. He and von Post nonetheless stayed in touch and allegedly consummated their relationship when finding themselves together in a Swedish castle in August 1955. "I was relatively inexperienced," she wrote, "and Jack's tenderness was a revelation. He said, 'Gunilla, we've waited two years for this. It seems almost too good to be true, and I want to make you happy.'"[44] In between these two encounters, John Kennedy married Jacqueline Bouvier on September 12, 1953, in Newport, Rhode Island, where the bride's mother and stepfather lived. Although one Republican critic quipped that it was more like a "merger than a marriage," the better-placed observer David Ormsby-Gore came to believe that it was "only with his wife and children that Jack's restless spirit ever found peace."[45]

* * *

GIVEN HIS family ancestry, John Kennedy would rarely be inhibited when it came to commenting on Ireland's historic feud with England. But, unlike his father, he took no side on the issue. "Racial ties and past bitterness should not influence our [policy] there," he'd written as long ago as 1941 in an article in the *Journal-American*. Thirteen years later, Kennedy was similarly neutral when he came to address a rowdy St. Patrick's Day audience at a dinner in New York. Although the Irish had "genuine grievances," he allowed, these were mild compared to the sufferings of those living under communist rule. "Neither St. Patrick's Day nor any other day is a time of rejoicing for 800 million people in the world today," he said, in tones that might have been adopted from Winston Churchill. "[They] live out their lives in despair and deprivation behind the Iron Curtain. For them totalitarian power has been substituted for individual rights and human decency. Unalterable adherence to a pagan party line has replaced free expression of opinion … For the 19 million people of East Germany to the ten million persons in Red-controlled VietMinh, there is no rejoicing in the name of religion and independence on this St. Patrick's night."[46] As each audience member later stepped out of the hall to go home, a Kennedy staffer handed him or her a printed sheet full of further, minutely detailed statistics about communist oppression around the globe. "Worthy as this was," one attendee remembered, "it wasn't quite what we had in mind for a night more associated with community singing and Guinness." He characterized Kennedy himself as a "genial fellow, who listened politely but wouldn't be tied down on the issue of a free Ireland. He'd say, 'What do you think about "X" as a position?' and you'd say, 'Well, what about "Y"?,' and then in a few minutes it would be back to 'X' again ... You might as well have been eating your soup with a fork."[47]

The thirty-four-year-old Irish foreign minister, Liam Cosgrave, invited the Kennedys to lunch when they later appeared in Dublin for what would be an extended European shopping junket combined with another of Jack's fact-finding tours. Although his enthusiasm for the United States had slightly waned over Joseph McCarthy's continuing anticommunist crusade, Cosgrave would remember the visiting Massachusetts senator in the warmest terms: "He was very friendly, matter of fact, devoid of pretense of any sort, good sense of humour, clear grasp of the essentials, the current international political situation, was reasonably familiar with conditions here."[48] Kennedy was then in such pain from his back that he found it difficult to walk even with crutches, and to climb or descend stairs was a protracted agony. As Cosgrave recalled, "Those who didn't know [him] were always struck by his boyish appearance, but when you were nearer to him he didn't look quite so young. In fact his face showed certain signs of the suffering he'd undergone." When a member of Cosgrave's Fine Gael Party subsequently went to Washington, he too found Jack "extremely affable, or at least with a sort of professional charm that carried him through. He accepted the flag and the other gifts we brought him with a great show of enthusiasm, promising to stay closely in touch. Somehow you still wondered whether in fact he would remember you thirty minutes later."[49]

In September 1954, David Ormsby-Gore was in New York as part of a British Foreign Office delegation to the United Nations. Like so many others, he found the atmosphere in the General Assembly, with its interminable discussions about whether to "note" or to "affirm" a past motion or to "review" or "assess" a developing issue "remarkably like being in the grip of a vast and exceptionally obtuse civil service, relocated to a madhouse." So it was something of a tonic for Gore to be invited to Hyannis Port to discuss world affairs with his old friend Jack Kennedy. It was the latest in a series of incremental steps that led them from the intoxicating if rather incestuous world of pre-war London society dinner parties into the rarefied heights of the White House. Over the course of the weekend, Gore spoke of his recent experience of conducting arms-control negotiations with the Soviet representatives at the UN, an ordeal he likened to undergoing extensive dental work without prior anesthetic. Kennedy himself lay on a couch, barely able to move, leaving Jackie to take notes on matters such as the recently concluded Indochina War or the prospects for the Southeast Asia ("SEATO") alliance in resisting regional Soviet aggression. Gore later accompanied the couple back to New York, where on October 21 Jack underwent a three-hour spinal-fusion procedure. Told that he had a fifty-fifty chance of surviving, he'd remarked merely, "I'd rather be dead than spend the rest of [my] life hobbling on crutches and paralyzed by pain."[50] Among Jack's last words as he was wheeled into the operating theater were: "Well, David, do they really mean to imprison Berlin?"[51]

Kennedy's surgery was a mixed success. After falling into a coma and again receiving the last rites, he rallied sufficiently to be moved to the family's Palm Beach home in time for Christmas. Following a second operation, he was able to resume his Senate duties and in turn to make yet another trip to Britain. The back-bench MP Hugh Fraser would later remember Kennedy's arrival in London with a mixture of amusement and exasperation. "Jack said, 'I want to see these people like Eden and so forth,' so I laid it all on ... They were all lined up, these Cabinet ministers. I was anxious, of course, and Jack was three-quarters of an hour late. I had to ring up ... I don't know what happened to [him]. Then [he] turned up and it all went off very well. He had enormous charm. He could charm a bird off a tree if he wanted to."[52]

In another sense, Kennedy's timing in Britain was impeccable. Winston Churchill, approaching eighty and in failing health, had remarked to a colleague in April 1954, "I feel like an aeroplane at the end of a flight, in the dusk, with petrol running out, in search of a safe landing."[53] By then bordering on senile, he finally retired as prime minister a year later. His successor was Anthony Eden, the man Kennedy had met at Lismore Castle (at that time his prospective brother-in-law) and the first point of contact on his most recent trip to London. From the days of shared euphoria and hope in 1945, the Anglo-American relationship had increasingly become one of a giant industrial complex and its loss-making overseas affiliate. Jack at least had the advantage of personally knowing the principals involved at both ends of the operation. His early affection for Churchill would be matched by a growing respect for Eden, the man, apparently, for a new and more progressive era. "Great Britain," Kennedy privately remarked, "hav[ing] exercised its muscles, must now exercise its brains," a hope cruelly dashed only a year or so later by the debacle at Suez.

Kennedy gained more attention with the January 1956 publication of a series of inspirational essays he collected into a book called *Profiles in Courage*. Like *Why England Slept* before it, it owed an unspoken debt to its researchers and ghostwriters, with Jack perhaps more in the role of an executive editor than a traditional author. The book quickly became a bestseller and won a Pulitzer Prize in April 1957: another significant milestone in positioning Kennedy as a deep thinker, a scholar of the Western political tradition, and a man to watch for the future.

★   ★   ★

KENNEDY SAILED FOR EUROPE again in August 1955, a visit that included both a meeting with Eden in Downing Street and a reunion with Gunilla von Post at her Swedish castle. From there he joined Jackie on the French Riviera, before traveling back

through Paris, Warsaw, and London and finally taking up residence at the Shelbourne Hotel in Dublin. A sign of Kennedy's
still relatively modest foreign reputation came when Jackie
called the offices of the *Irish Independent* one Sunday morning and told them that her husband, the junior senator from
Massachusetts, was in town and available for interviews. The
paper's chief reporter, a man by the striking name of Mickey
Rooney, declined the offer, choosing to play golf instead.[54]

Kennedy told *The Times*, on the other hand, he thought
Anglo-American relations "absolutely the great thing in the
world today," a bulwark against Soviet expansionism. He
broached the same theme in a series of speeches over the winter
of 1955–1956. As prepared by his staff, Jack's remarks at the
annual review of the New England Air Reserve in suburban
Boston at one point read, "Great Britain, with only 800,000 in
service, is cutting its force by at least 100,000 men." Moments
before he took to the podium, Kennedy changed this line to
say, "Great Britain, *our strongest partner in NATO*, with only
800,000 ..." [emphasis added]. It was a small but telling example of his true feelings about America's historic alliance, one he
evidently thought transcended the mere accountancy of troop
levels, ships, and planes.[55]

Lyndon Johnson's appointment as Senate majority leader in
January 1955 provided another opportunity for Kennedy to
present himself as a leading authority of overseas affairs. During
the previous two years, Jack had consistently spoken out on
the need to confront communism, either by peaceful debate
or more direct means. One congressional ally remembered the
obvious passion of a speech extolling the Atlantic partnership,
"his eyes flashing [and] his hands waving up and down like an
orchestra conductor." In January 1957, Johnson named the
Massachusetts freshman to the fifteen-strong Senate Foreign
Relations Committee, despite the rival claims of several senior
colleagues. It may be that this choice assignment reflected Jack's
long experience, ceaseless globe-trotting, and undoubted grasp

of the underlying trends of postwar international affairs. But it also owed something to old-fashioned political horse-trading. According to Johnson, Ambassador Kennedy "bombarded me with phone calls, presents, and little notes telling me what a great guy I was … One day he came right out and pleaded with me to put Jack on the foreign relations committee, telling me that if I did, he'd never forget the favor for the rest of his life … I kept picturing old Joe Kennedy sitting there with all that power and wealth feeling indebted to me [and] I sure liked that picture."[56]

On March 17, 1956, John Kennedy gave his traditional St. Patrick's Day speech in Chicago, the ritual moment when he allowed himself to portray Britain as a land of uptight class oppression and Ireland, by contrast, as one of universal knowledge, individual freedom, and compassion. First, there was his now familiar joke about the weather. "I have not heard a report from the Emerald Isle tonight," Jack quipped, "but I am certain that no rain fell – at least officially." Following that icebreaker, he referred again to the "billion people [who] are held today in an iron captivity stretching in a great half circle from the plains beyond the captive city of Warsaw in the West to the Red River Delta beyond the trampled city of Hanoi in the East." It was another distinctly Churchillian touch. "Today," he continued, "while free Irishmen everywhere marched to the tune of 'O'Donnell Abu' and 'The Wearing of the Green,' only hobnail boots clattering on darkened streets rang out in these enslaved nations." From there Kennedy went on to compare the privations suffered by the Soviet Union's client states to the historic struggles of the Irish against the "infamous tyranny" imposed by Westminster. He ended by quoting the words of Sir Roger Casement, the Irish-born diplomat whom the British had hung at the height of the Great War in 1916 following his attempt to raise a somewhat ramshackle pro-German insurrection. It was a masterstroke of political theater.

"'When all your rights,'" Kennedy declaimed in Casement's voice, "'become only an accumulated wrong; when men must beg with bated breath for leave to subsist in their own land, to think their own thoughts, to sing their own songs – then surely it is a braver, a saner, and a truer thing to be a rebel in act and deed.'" The roar of approval that greeted Kennedy's oration was "truly deafening," it was reported. Clearly he had struck the most responsive possible chord with his audience.[57]

During 1956, with his eye now on the White House, Kennedy set out a nuanced series of foreign policy positions that sought to curb the "odious and malign" influence of the Kremlin while still scolding Britain and any other Western powers who chose to maintain overseas colonies for their own enrichment. "The most potent single force in the world today," Jack announced in a speech on the Senate floor, "is neither communism, nor capitalism, neither the H-bomb nor the guided missile – it is man's eternal desire to be free and independent." He added: "The single most important test of American foreign policy today is how we meet the challenge of imperialism."[58]

In private, Jack continued to seek the advice of the practical and nonideological David Ormsby-Gore, one of those British officials sensitive to the need for further decolonization but also to the "desirability of newly independent governments which will work satisfactorily with the Americans and ourselves." This was essentially Kennedy's own guiding principle over the next seven years. It coexisted with his continuing affinity for the more literate and morally relaxed members of the British establishment. In early October 1956, Jack was in the process of traveling some twenty-five thousand miles around the country on behalf of the Stevenson–Kefauver Democratic presidential ticket, while also coming to address the developing crisis wrought by the Anglo-French "lunatic action" in Suez. In the midst of this, he showed his remarkable capacity to simply switch off from events when he joined his friend William Douglas-Home for the opening night of his play, *The Reluctant Debutante*, on Broadway.

"He came into the St. Regis Hotel," Home recalled, "where I was sitting with my wife and Wilfrid Hyde-White, the actor. Hyde-White was in a very highly nervous state, as all actors are. And I said, 'You know Jack Kennedy. This is Wilfrid Hyde-White, my leading actor.' And he said, 'Is he up to it?' That reduced Mr. Hyde-White to a pulp from that point on, and then when he came on stage that night, he found Kennedy sitting in the second row watching him. Everything went well. But that was the way Jack talked to people, so vital the whole time."[59]

Of this "congenial young Yank" who seemed to flit between the impish and the intense, Douglas-Home recalled, "Jack used to talk about politics a lot. And I used to talk about plays. And he always used to say, 'Let's get it straight. What are we talking about now, my politics or your plays?'" Despite his own family connections at the heart of the British government, Home was sufficiently impressed by the "Yank's" acumen to later urge him: "Write to me, if you have time, placing your views on the political future of this country before me, for my education and my future action."[60]

Now approaching forty, Kennedy had at last parted company with his father on almost every strand of current American foreign policy, not least the necessity of an ever-closer engagement with the British. In time, their disagreement extended to the political calculation of whether Jack should allow his name to go forward as a possible running mate to Adlai Stevenson at the 1956 Democratic convention. The ambassador was not in favor. At the critical moment, Jack "turned to Bobby [Kennedy] and said, 'Call Dad and tell him I'm going for it.'" Bobby, according to family friend Kenneth O'Donnell, placed the call, "by no means an enviable assignment ... Jack disappeared from the room, leaving me alone with Bobby when the call went through. [Joe's] blue language flashed all over the room. The connection was broken before he was finished denouncing Jack as an idiot who was ruining his political career."[61]

It was the same story when Jack came to set out his foreign policy agenda, to which there were three core principles: "The need for America's global involvement, for the closest possible partnership with Great Britain, and the containment of the Soviet Union."[62] This was in sharp contrast to his father's belief in the paramount importance of international financial relationships, where, if problems arose, he was prepared to be flexible, trusting that he could use his negotiating skills to smooth his way through. During a father and son meeting with Hearst newspaper editors at around this time, Jack abruptly got up and left the room after listening to Joe hold forth on the current world situation. "Jesus, what's happening?" his friend Paul Fay, who followed him out, asked. "Why did you do that?" Jack replied, "Listen, I've only got three choices. I can sit there and keep my mouth shut, which will be taken as a sign that I agree with him. I can have a fight with him in front of the press. Or I can get up and leave."[63]

Jack later told the journalist John Martin, "My father is a conservative. We disagree on many things. He's an isolationist and I'm an internationalist … I've given up arguing with him. But I make up my own mind and my own decisions."[64]

The Kennedy family strides out in London, where they arrived to some fanfare in 1938 and left again in 1940 amidst growing mutual acrimony with the British press. Courtesy John F. Kennedy Presidential Library and Museum.

Twenty-year-old Jack Kennedy with "Offie" (so named for the dog's resemblance to a US Embassy secretary) during the Harvard undergraduate's European "adventure of a lifetime." Courtesy John F. Kennedy Presidential Library and Museum.

Joe Junior, Ambassador Joseph Kennedy, and Jack arrive in England, July 4, 1938. The ambassador's friend Arthur Krock was told to ensure that Jack was in bed, alone, by midnight on each day of the Atlantic crossing. "The curfew was not maintained," Krock later admitted. Courtesy John F. Kennedy Presidential Library and Museum.

September 3, 1939: Kathleen, Joe, and Jack Kennedy on their way to the House of Commons to hear Neville Chamberlain's declaration of war against Germany. Later that afternoon, the Kennedys found themselves crouching among several terrified English families in the basement of a London dress shop. Courtesy John F. Kennedy Presidential Library and Museum.

Kathleen Kennedy and her husband Billy Cavendish, marquess of Hartington, on their wedding day in May 1944. On hearing the news of her engagement, the bride-to-be's mother wrote to her: "Heartbroken — Feel you have been wrongly influenced." Kathleen was widowed just four months later. Courtesy John F. Kennedy Presidential Library and Museum.

Talbot Square, London, where Jack and his traveling companion Lem Billings put up on a prewar visit. Author's collection.

A view of 14 Prince's Gate, London. Once the home of the American banker J. P. Morgan, Ambassador Kennedy and family were periodically in residence here from 1938 to 1940. Author's collection.

Joe and Rose Kennedy in November 1940, at about the time the ambassador was busy telling the press that Hitler would win the war. "Democracy is all done," Joe added.

"Debo" Cavendish, Evelyn, dowager duchess of Devonshire, and Kathleen "Kick" Kennedy — by then marchioness of Hartington — seen in August 1944, a month before Kathleen's husband fell in action.

September 21, 44

*HYANNISPORT
MASSACHUSETTS*

*Dear Duchess:
The news of Billy's death was about the saddest I have ever had. I have always been so fond of Kick that I couldn't help but feel some of her great sorrow. Her great happiness when she came home, which even shone through her sadness over Joe's*

Jack Kennedy's condolence letter to "Moucher" Devonshire following the battlefield death of her son Billy, in which he quoted John Buchan: "Debonair and brilliant and brave, he is now part of that immortal England which knows not age or weariness or defeat." Courtesy John F. Kennedy Presidential Library and Museum.

The young author of *Why England Slept* signs a copy of the book for actor Spencer Tracy.
Courtesy John F. Kennedy Presidential Library and Museum.

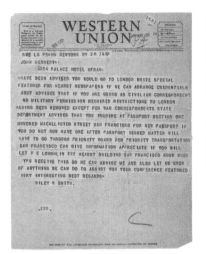

Kennedy's summons from Hearst Newspapers to cover the first postwar British general election proved him to be an acute observer of Westminster politics. "There is a distinct possibility that Prime Minister Churchill and his Conservative party will be defeated," he wrote in a dispatch of June 24, 1945, a feat of prediction beyond most of the more seasoned correspondents. Courtesy John F. Kennedy Presidential Library and Museum.

Lismore Castle in County Waterford, "the setting for a Hollywood fairy-tale," where the thirty-year-old Kennedy rediscovered his Irish roots in the summer of 1947. By Dermot (Own work) [CC BY-SA 2.5 (http://creativecommons.org/licenses/by-sa/2.5)], via Wikimedia Commons.

Winston Churchill in characteristic pose.

Kennedy and Harold Macmillan at their first meeting, Key West, March 1961.
"On the one side," Macmillan wrote, "was the President of the United States and
Commander in Chief of all American forces, surrounded by officers of every rank and
degree in a great naval fortress, and receiving all the honour due to a head of state; on
the other, [his secretary] Tim Bligh and I, with Harold Caccia in support."

The Kennedys with the queen and Prince Philip at Buckingham Palace, June 1961. The queen later wrote to the president, "It is a great comfort to me to know that you and my prime minister are so close, and that you have confidence in each other's judgement and advice. I am sure that these meetings and this personal trust and understanding are of the greatest importance to both our peoples."

Forty-three-year-old David Ormsby-Gore presents his credentials as Britain's ambassador to Washington at a White House ceremony in October 1961. Gore signaled that a new era in Atlantic relations had begun when he sent the president a five-page hand-written letter beginning "Dear Jack," symbolizing a warm friendship that had begun twenty-three years earlier in England. At the height of the Cuban missile crisis, Lyndon Johnson was heard to observe that "the limey" was seated front and center at a meeting of a steering group in the White House Cabinet Room, while he, the vice president, was "down in a chair at the end, with the goddamned door banging into my back." Courtesy John F. Kennedy Presidential Library and Museum.

opposite, bottom
British and American officials pose for a group photograph on the White House lawn. Front row, left to right: US representative to the United Nations Adlai Stevenson, Secretary of State Dean Rusk, Kennedy, Macmillan, British foreign secretary Alec (Lord) Home, and British ambassador Harold Caccia. Averell Harriman and David Bruce, dark and light tie, respectively, stand behind Stevenson and Rusk. Courtesy John F. Kennedy Presidential Library and Museum.

Kennedy and Macmillan prior to their talks at Bermuda in December 1961. The president, who was suffering from an acutely painful back, was thought by some to have taken the opportunity of the PM's lengthy recitation on global monetary reform to discreetly take a nap. Courtesy John F. Kennedy Presidential Library and Museum.

Kennedy and the American actor Elliot Reed next to Macmillan and the British actor Peter Sellers at the White House Correspondents Dinner in Washington, April 1962. Both actors were accomplished impersonators of their respective national leaders. Life imitated art on this occasion: Reed had starred opposite Marilyn Monroe in *Gentlemen Prefer Blondes*, while Sellers was then preparing to shoot *Dr. Strangelove*, a film that showed the almost absurd ease with which a nuclear war could be triggered. Courtesy John F. Kennedy Presidential Library and Museum.

The special relationship at work — Kennedy and Macmillan meet in the White House Cabinet Room. David Ormsby-Gore, holding a paper, sits on the left of the prime minister. Courtesy John F. Kennedy Presidential Library and Museum.

Kennedy in New Ross, Ireland, where he charmed the crowds but made only a few hazy allusions to the country's historic difficulties with the English.

When President Kennedy went on to visit Harold Macmillan at Birch Grove, his home in the English countryside, the prime minister thought it all "more like a play, or rather the mad rehearsal for a play, than a grave international conference." Here the presidential motorcade makes its way through the narrow rural English streets. Courtesy Harold Waters.

Birch Grove, where Kennedy came to discuss nuclear arms and apparently also to give renditions of his favorite Irish sea shanties. Courtesy Andrew Baird.

Kennedy and entourage with Dorothy Macmillan, with whom he shared a wisecracking sense of humor, a love of gossip, and a tendency to stray from their wedding vows. They were also related by marriage. Courtesy Antony Lewis.

Kennedy strides from *Air Force One* at England's Gatwick Airport in June 1963, while Harold Macmillan brings up the rear. Courtesy John F. Kennedy Presidential Library and Museum.

President Kennedy after attending mass at Our Lady of the Forest Church, near Macmillan's country home, on June 30, 1963. He left Britain for the last time later that afternoon. Courtesy John F. Kennedy Presidential Library and Museum.

The president's thank-you cable to Macmillan for his overnight hospitality in June 1963, a typical mixture of the personal and the political. Courtesy UK National Archives.

Kennedy relaxes on board the presidential yacht *Honey Fitz* off Cape Cod, July 28, 1963. The bare-chested Ambassador Ormsby-Gore is to the right, partly hidden, speaking to the president's sister Jean. Jacqueline Kennedy sits under a straw hat.

Kennedy signs the bill conferring honorary US citizenship on his political hero, Winston Churchill. Just six months later, the eighty-eight-year-old Churchill sat "mute with sadness . . . tears streaming down his face," while listening to news reports of the president's assassination. Courtesy John F. Kennedy Presidential Library and Museum.

The bust of President Kennedy on Marylebone Road in central London, subscribed for by fifty thousand British citizens.

A more official tribute, the memorial stone at Runnymede, which Queen Elizabeth dedicated in May 1965 "in memory of John F. Kennedy, whom in death my people mourn, and whom in life they loved and admired."

7

FAMILY FEUD

ON MONDAY, JULY 30, 1956, President Eisenhower's special ambassador, Robert Murphy, a sixty-two-year-old Irish–American whose State Department desk bore the sign "Quiet reflection disentangles every knot," arrived in London to discuss what were called "matters of mutual interest" to the Anglo-American allies. Murphy dined that night with his old wartime colleague Harold Macmillan, also sixty-two, until recently Britain's foreign secretary but now in the thankless role of chancellor of the exchequer. After six months of nearly permanent crisis management, Macmillan told a colleague that he looked forward to discussing "greater things than the current price of eggs" with his American visitor.[1] Murphy, for his part, had little reason to expect anything but "a convivial meal, punctuat[ed] by a gentle tour of the common ends and mutual objectives" of the Atlantic alliance.

This was not quite what happened. According to Murphy, Macmillan had soon moved on from the pleasantries about shared values and the indissoluble spirit of 1945 to discuss a crisis of more tangible concern to the British. Were his country not to take proper action in the matter, he added, "We will become another Netherlands."[2] There were "fundamental points of principle [and] national prestige" involved. Macmillan subsequently wrote with some satisfaction in his diary, "It is clear that the Americans are going to 'restrain' us all they can," and that he had "done [my] best to frighten my dinner guest out of his life." Macmillan concluded, "We have succeeded in thoroughly alarming Murphy. He must have reported in the sense which we wanted, and [US secretary of state] Foster Dulles is now coming over post-haste. [It] is a very good development."[3]

Again, this was not quite how events unfolded. In fact, within only a few more weeks, Britain, like a spurned lover, would effectively have to beg the United States for her forgiveness, having in the meantime put what Dulles called "intolerable strain" on the special relationship. As a result, there would be no more unilateral colonial adventures or furtive tactical deals struck behind Washington's back. There may have been periods of coolness along the way, but as a direct consequence of the Macmillan-Murphy dinner and all that followed, the essential working premise of the Atlantic alliance for the last sixty years has been that Britain will adhere to US policy, even at its most exasperating.

The crisis in question was Suez. Since some eighty-five books – not to mention the wealth of scholarly articles, self-serving memoirs and interviews, and a continuing lively Internet exchange – are all available on the subject, it's perhaps best to be brief on the event often said to have marked the point when the British political establishment fatally overreached itself.

The crucial issue at stake was what action to take against Egyptian president Colonel Gamal Nasser following his nationalization on July 26, 1956, of the Suez Canal Company. As at Munich, if on a smaller scale, it was a case of whether Britain should make a foreign dictator's transgressions a *casus belli* or seek to negotiate instead. Nasser's "grab," Macmillan argued, was not only in flagrant breach of the 1888 Treaty of Constantinople, but also, of more practical concern, a serious threat to Britain's oil supplies. The British government or private British firms owned more than a third of the ships that passed through Suez in 1955. "This was intolerable," Macmillan noted. The canal was, as he loved to say, "our lifeline of Empire," the historical link with imperial possessions in India and the east. The British chancellor, who took a leading role in events, flew to Washington in September 1956 in order to personally brief President Eisenhower on the fast-developing situation in the region. He later wrote that "Ike's manner could not have been more cordial," and the Englishman came away convinced that the United States would not oppose – in fact, would discreetly support – the use of force against Nasser. This, too, was a serious misapprehension.

Five weeks later, when Anglo-French bombing raids had all but destroyed the Egyptian air force, Eisenhower's anger was sufficient for either Prime Minister Eden or, in some versions, Eden's press secretary, to have picked up the transatlantic phone and heard a flow of military language at the other end so furious that the receiving party had felt it best to hold the instrument away from his ear. Nor was this just personal rancor on Ike's part: the US administration was soon moved to join with the Soviet Union in tabling a UN Security Council resolution calling on all fellow members to refrain from the use of force in Egypt. Following that, the Americans convened an emergency meeting of the UN General Assembly to secure an immediate ceasefire in the area. The motion was passed by sixty-four votes to five. Only Britain, France, Israel, Australia, and New Zealand opposed it. Somewhat disarmingly, Macmillan was later to acknowledge, "We certainly made a profound miscalculation as to the likely reaction in Washington to our intervention … We altogether failed to appreciate the force of the resentment … For this I carry a heavy responsibility."[4]

It was a "regrettable lapse," Macmillan was forced to admit, as the roof fell in on the Atlantic alliance, and the Soviets threatened to launch retaliatory attacks on Western Europe.

Diplomatic pressure on Britain was soon followed by economic sanctions. Macmillan wrote bitterly of the United States resorting to a form of "financial blackmail [by] selling of sterling by the Federal Reserve Bank." Later attempting to draw on British gold reserves with the International Monetary Fund, the chancellor "received only the reply that the American Government would not agree to the technical procedure until we had consented to a ceasefire [in Suez]."[5] One large nation had thus effectively frozen the bank account of a friendly smaller nation. At that stage, Anthony Eden, who had been running a fever of 105 degrees and living on a diet of stimulants and tranquillizers, took his doctor's advice and left London for a rest cure in the Caribbean. The British gold reserves continued to plummet. Fuel rationing returned to the United Kingdom. Shortly after Eden's departure, George Humphrey, the us secretary of the treasury, placed a Saturday night phone call to the caretaker prime minister, "Rab" Butler. To do so, he "had shut [himself] with the telephone in the meat safe so as to avoid the intrusions of my family." Humphrey's essential message was that Washington was now prepared to support the pound and "'supply the fig leaf' which the British say they need to cover their nakedness in withdrawing from Suez … providing they get out of the area at once." They did.[6]

It's worth dwelling on the humbling of the British government at Suez a moment more, if only to show the reaction of John Kennedy to the most serious test of Anglo-American amity since the Munich crisis eighteen years earlier. His response was complicated by two factors. Kennedy knew and personally liked both Anthony Eden and Britain's current foreign secretary Selwyn Lloyd. He was on terms of intimacy with Lloyd's protégé David Ormsby-Gore. Although Kennedy hadn't yet met Harold Macmillan, as a young man in London he'd read and admired Macmillan's 1938 book *The Middle Way* (calling for all classes to share in a "dynamic of social change"), which he thought "wonderful" and "full of hope."[7]

Apart from his British friendships, there was also the course of political events at home in America. In August 1956, as tensions came to the boil in Egypt, Kennedy was busy lobbying delegates at the Democratic Convention in Chicago to back his perhaps optimistic vice presidential bid. After that he embarked on a ten-week coast-to-coast speaking tour to support his party's preferred ticket. Since November 6 was the date both of the presidential election and the British decision to pull back from the Suez Canal Zone in a phased withdrawal, Kennedy had only limited time to devote to the active part of the crisis. While others were grappling with the intricacies of troop movements and currency crashes, Jack himself was barnstorming the United States to often delirious public response. The *New York Times* soon became the first but not the last of the major daily papers to compare his appearance to that of a "movie star," with an "instant appeal." At a women's college in Louisville, a group of some two hundred screaming students, providing "a clamor and crowding unusual for an academic setting," attempted to block his car as he left their campus, informing him that he was "a doll" and "better than Elvis Presley." These were not the standard accolades of a 1950s presidential election.[8]

It was one of the ironies of Suez, the event that threatened to violently breach the Atlantic alliance (and in the short term did), that a leading spokesman and declared vice presidential candidate of the American Democratic Party should continue to receive his private briefings on the crisis from a ranking minister at the British foreign office. Kennedy's confidence in David Ormsby-Gore during the critical weeks of late 1956 was heightened by his lesser faith in the "hot air [and] mental vapidity" he associated with many of the career diplomats in the US State Department.[9] The two pre-war friends continued to regularly speak and cable one another even as official channels of Anglo-American communication dwindled to a few mordant exchanges about the collapse of Britain's currency. By and large, both men distrusted the bureaucratic machinery of government.

Both distanced themselves from what Gore characterized as the "frock-coat brigade" of "over-qualified twits" who personified the foreign-affairs establishment in London and Washington. Both admired heroic men and heroic action. Both had a healthy suspicion of the Soviet Union, which they rightly believed to be supplying Nasser with arms and cash, not so much out of ideological fraternity but as an opportunistic means of agitating the West. Both accepted that the British had overreached themselves in Suez, and both took a passionate interest in restoring the allied status quo. Ormsby-Gore told Kennedy that the Russians loved nothing more than this sort of internecine squabbling among their foes, and that the West's first priority was to bury its differences and present a unified position on urgently needed disarmament negotiations with Moscow. Kennedy in turn called Gore "the most intelligent man [he] had ever met."[10]

In Chicago, Kennedy was rejected as Adlai Stevenson's running mate by a vote of 755½ to 589. He conceded gracefully, flew to London and the Riviera for a week, and then returned to the campaign trail. Given the scale of Stevenson's subsequent defeat by Eisenhower, Kennedy's was one of those political losses that was in fact a net gain. On November 2, four days before polling, the United States combined with the Russians for the first and to date only time in UN history to vote against her wartime allies Britain and France. The following day, Eisenhower's secretary of state John Foster Dulles, a stereotypical 1950s public official to look at and listen to, with some of the same general allure of an Old Testament prophet (and cordially loathed by the British), was rushed to the hospital for emergency cancer surgery. During this same febrile week in international affairs, the Soviet Union threatened Britain with atomic weapons unless she cease and desist in Egypt, and within twenty-four hours of that her troops and tanks moved to crush the Hungarian revolution at the cost of some twenty-two thousand casualties. From his seat on the Senate Foreign Relations Committee, Kennedy would soon come to invoke what he called "a new realism" in American policy, one with the twin goals of opposing both communism and "the prolongation of Western colonialism."[11] Insofar as he recognized they might prove mutually contradictory, he relied on the UN to sort things out.

There was another striking coincidence of events in January 1957. The same forty-eight-hour period that first brought Kennedy to a position of executive influence in American foreign affairs also saw the resignation of Anthony Eden and his replacement by Harold Macmillan as British prime minister. Macmillan in turn soon promoted or appointed to government several of his party's rising young stars, such as David Ormsby-Gore, Hugh Fraser, and Richard Wood, whom Kennedy had counted as friends for over twenty years.

When an interviewer later asked him about Kennedy's "Solomon-like wisdom [in reaching] a decision," Alastair Forbes said this: "I think he potentially did have that ability, and it was to do with his method of being instinctive and also being lazy. One of the reasons why one didn't notice the gift in him so much was because he preferred not to have to deal with something rather than to deal with it ... He was not a decisive man by nature. He would prefer to postpone matters. He would prefer the matters to settle themselves ... But when he saw that [a] decision was necessary, he took it."[12]

This same equivocal approach was at work in Kennedy's response at the height of the Suez crisis. His basic position was shaped by two key, if ill-defined, concepts. The first was national self-determination. "We have permitted our own attitude on colonial affairs to be tied too closely to the policies of our Western allies," Kennedy told an audience at Winston-Salem on October 5, 1956. "We have permitted millions of uncommitted people – people who hold in their hands the balance of power in the world in the next ten years – to believe this nation has abandoned its proud traditions of self-governance and independence."[13]

"Since 1945," Kennedy proceeded to tell telephone workers in Boston, turning up the rhetoric a notch, "we have been tremendously hampered by diplomatic ties with Britain and France, who wish to preserve their colonial ties. We have now taken a definite moral stand against colonialism for the first time since then."[14] Speaking with hindsight a year later, Kennedy said:

> The Suez episode and the events surrounding it illustrate the important impact of the dissolution of the old European empires. As nationalism triumphs in the former colonial states, a residue of defensive nationalism is left, [as the] ill-fated British attempts at national self-assertion in Egypt clearly indicate ... Americans quite properly must grasp the truth that a capacity for creating an ordered and peaceful society is within the grasp of any people, no matter what [their] stage of economic and social development ... It is not enough that we proclaim our anti-colonialism. We must also help these new states to find the means for accelerated economic growth and stable self-rule.[15]

Because Kennedy also recognized the potential for communist mischief making in these newly enfranchised countries, he relied on his other overreaching idea – the need for closer Anglo-American relations – to hold the line. "We all share the guilt," he later reflected of Suez, in terms that owed something to David Ormsby-Gore, "the United States not least of all for the course it pursued diplomatically ... There is little point at this date trying to assign exact responsibility," he continued. "What should concern us now is the question of why it was that it was easier to obtain a condemnation of the Suez invasion than it was of the far more brutal Russian intervention in Hungary ... Why, too, did Soviet influence rise in the Middle East at the very moment when the Soviet Union was exposing unmistakably its cast-iron grip on Eastern Europe?"[16]

It was the same story when Kennedy addressed a closed-circuit television audience in the final days of the 1956 campaign, when he spoke to Zionist groups in New York and Baltimore, and when he met with Democratic backers at a fundraiser in San Francisco. "At least the [Republicans] have learned – after once presenting him with the pistol he now holds at our head – that what is good for General Nasser is not necessarily good for us," Kennedy told cheering party loyalists.[17] Indeed, his whole latter-day theme was to blame the Eisenhower administration rather than the British for ineptly driving Egypt into the Soviet camp.

Four years later, while campaigning for president, Kennedy took the time to read Anthony Eden's somewhat embittered memoirs, *Full Circle*.

If the United States Government had approached this issue in the spirit of an ally, they would have done everything in their power … to support the nations whose economic security depended upon the freedom of passage through the Suez canal. They would have closely planned their policies with their allies and held stoutly to the decisions arrived at … It is now clear that this was never the [American] attitude. Rather did they try to gain time, coast along over difficulties as they arose and improvise policies, each following on the failure of its immediate predecessor.[18]

Eden's private assessment of John Dulles, who died in 1959, was if possible even less favorable. In his old age, the former prime minister remarked of the late secretary of state that he was "legalistic," "devious," and abandoning caution altogether, "a château-bottled shit." Eden's colleague Selwyn Lloyd both confirmed this appraisal on the part of his old boss and added that it was "Jack Kennedy's own view of Dulles, at least as it applied to Suez."[19]

What remains of the whole sorry affair is the damage it permanently inflicted on Britain's great-power pretensions and the fact that, from 1956 onward, her foreign policy would largely be a matter of decline management. The human cost of Suez, at least, was comparatively modest. Grotesque though it is to use the word "only" in connection to casualties, it might be applied on a relative basis here. The British and French lost 16 and 10 men, with 96 and 33 wounded, respectively. There were approximately 330 Israeli deaths. The Egyptians suffered roughly 3,000 casualties and won a considerable propaganda victory. Among other lessons of Suez, as specifically applied by Kennedy, was that "there was a deep division of opinion in Great Britain" on foreign affairs generally, and that from now on it would be to his friend David Ormsby-Gore rather than the formalized structure of the British government that he would primarily turn for information.[20]

Suez also continued, or extended, Kennedy's intellectual detachment from his father. The political tumult of 1956 reverberated in their personal relationship. Nearly five years earlier, Ambassador Kennedy had warned in a Mutual Broadcasting System radio speech from Chicago that America was "wasting her resources" in a futile support of her wartime allies. "In the Suez and on the Persian Gulf, we may soon become embroiled by the actions of the British," the ambassador continued – a notable feat of prediction, if not one to threaten his prevailing reputation as an only modestly gifted diplomat.[21] Later in the 1950s, Kennedy's friend Alastair Forbes would come to see the father-son relationship at unusually close quarters:

> I can remember sharing a room at Hyannis in his parents' house. Jack used to snore a lot, and there was a good deal of reason to sort of postpone the moment of actually dossing down. We would both sit up and chew the cud quite late. I naturally found myself totally out of sympathy with almost all of the ideas of old Joe, and I found that there was absolutely no embarrassment whatsoever on Jack's part in agreeing with many of my criticisms of his father's views. They did … in fact

have a kind of armistice in which they less and less discussed affairs because the father realized that the possibility of finding common ground diminished rather than increased with years.[22]

★ ★ ★

FOR ALL JOHN KENNEDY's British stylings and his personal fondness for men like Forbes and Ormsby-Gore, his keen grasp of his core constituency still led him to indulge in regular public effusions about his immigrant roots. Ireland remained a constant in Kennedy's politics. He never quite succeeded, much as he tried, in portraying himself as the sort of stereotypical, dirt-poor migrant to have been persecuted mercilessly in the old country before going on to enjoy only "outsider" status in the new. Kennedy's lot in life was significantly removed from that of the Boston "mick" still widely stigmatized for his alcoholism, feckless behavior, and at best rudimentary grasp of social decorum. Nonetheless, he often made the sentimental connection. "The special contribution of our people," Kennedy announced to an appreciative audience at the Irish Institute of New York in January 1957, "has been the constancy, the endurance, the faith that they displayed through endless centuries of foreign oppression – centuries in which even the most basic religious and civil rights were denied to them – centuries in which their mass destruction by poverty, disease, and starvation were ignored by their conquerors."

The historic suffering of the Irish was the result, therefore, not of any lack of individual enterprise or fortitude but rather the cruelty and indifference of their English oppressors. "For example," Kennedy told his audience in New York, "on February 19, 1847, it was announced in the House of Commons that 15,000 persons were dying of starvation in Ireland every day. Queen Victoria was so moved by this pitiful news that to the society for Irish relief she contributed five pounds." Combining both the tragic and the comic elements of the story, Kennedy continued: "Perhaps we should not be too quick to condemn the good queen, however – for in those days the English pound was no doubt worth more than it is today."★ From there he brought his oration to a close with an expression of his most fundamental political philosophy – the twin evils represented by colonialism and communism – which in due course would accompany him to the White House:

> In the [seventeenth century] the Irish people were hard put to keep alive the memory of their lost freedom. The education of their children and the preservation of their native language and customs were controlled by a foreign dictator in a manner no less ruthless than that demonstrated by the Soviets in Hungary today. Then, as now, priests were imprisoned, tortured and murdered, and the Catholic religion was all but totally suppressed. Then, as now, the lands and property of the people were confiscated, their legal rights denied, their meetings banned, their very existence regarded with contempt – and with fear. A secret court – the Court of Castle Chamber – imposed a so-called justice no less harsh than that imposed by the commissar courts operating today in Budapest.[23]

The preoccupation with the actual British miscalculation at Suez was short lived. Harold Macmillan's charm offensive to win back American friendship and support began at a summit meeting with President Eisenhower held in Bermuda in March 1957. Like a family feud patched up for the holidays, in the normal course of events the special relationship would still sometimes show signs of stress – as when Ike used the Bermuda talks to complain about "particularly vicious and coordinated attacks" made

---

★ The British currency had indeed been seriously devalued by the actions taken by the US government shortly before Kennedy spoke. The queen's gratuity would translate roughly as £650, or $950, in 2017 terms.

on him in the British press. But in general the Atlantic allies coexisted peacefully on colonial issues over the next four years. The post-Dulles era was one of nominal American sympathy for Western European possessions seeking an orderly transition to self-rule, but there were no further high-noon confrontations on the subject. In October 1957, a year after Suez, Macmillan felt sufficiently confident of the allied partnership while on a visit to Washington to raise the question of the Atomic Energy – or "McMahon" – Act, which prevented US administrations from sharing atomic information with even friendly foreign powers. During the discussions, Eisenhower remarked that he "personally felt ashamed" of the law as it applied to countries such as Britain, and he went on to hand his guests a document titled "A Declaration of Common Purpose."[24] Among other steps, this modified the McMahon Act so that the allies could again freely exchange scientific intelligence. Macmillan's confidential account of this breakthrough was ecstatic. The American proposal was "in effect, a declaration of inter-dependence," he reported to the cabinet on October 28. "The government and people of the United States had been greatly impressed by recent Soviet successes and above all by the spectacular success, in their launching of an earth satellite, of Soviet achievements in science and technology. They now recognised that no single country, however powerful, could alone withstand the Soviet threat … The prevailing mood in Washington had therefore been highly favourable to proposals for closer Anglo-American cooperation, and [this] had been achieved."[25]

In the midst of this euphoria, John Kennedy did not forget the central lesson of Suez – that the United States and her allies should actively offer the world's emergent nations the practical support and friendship they might otherwise find in Moscow. As chairman of the African Task Force of the Senate Foreign Relations Committee, Kennedy frequently portrayed the Eisenhower administration as asleep at the switch when it came to meeting the challenges of the postcolonial era. His specific comments in July 1957 on the desirability of "full and immediate" independence for Algeria caused alarm more in French official circles than British. But Kennedy's broader belief in the dismantling of empire led him to "extol the merits … of self-government among the countries [of] the new developing civilization" as a whole.[26] His personal taste both for English country-house life and the eighteenth-century Whig traditions of high-minded imperialism and forward morality, as detailed in David Cecil's *The Young Melbourne*, met with an equally strong conviction in "favor [of] liberty and self-determination of all the world's peoples."

It was perhaps fortuitous that Kennedy's term of high office coincided with that of Harold Macmillan, a foreign-affairs pragmatist whose February 1960 speech in Cape Town acknowledging that "the wind of change is blowing through this continent, and whether we like it or not, this growth of national consciousness is a political fact" provided one of the iconic moments of his premiership. In the meantime, the ambitious young senator would continue to enjoy his uniquely close and mutually congenial ties to the newly appointed minister of state at the British Foreign Office, his old pre-war carousing friend David Ormsby-Gore.[27]

★   ★   ★

THREE MONTHS AFTER the final British retreat from Suez, the representatives of the four major wartime allies met for disarmament talks in London. Kennedy was not impressed by the head of the US delegation, the fifty-year-old, perennial Republican presidential candidate Harold Stassen. "We sent a man who was not even active in the field," he later complained. "We also sent him without formulating an American position. Mr. Stassen was never able to get clear instructions at the meeting as to what our position was. We came close, and in part failed because the American line was never finalized."[28] Although Kennedy had good reason for deeming Stassen ill equipped to go toe-to-toe with the Russians over nuclear stockpiles, the London talks produced at least one notable initiative. In August 1957, President Eisenhower offered to suspend American high-explosive weapons testing for two years if the Soviets in turn agreed to halt production of "fissionable materials" for the same period. In a style familiar to observers of Cold War negotiations of the late 1950s and 1960s, the issue rumbled on inconclusively – although there was a decisive shift in superpower relations as a whole when, on November 27, 1958, Nikita Khrushchev issued a Soviet ultimatum on West Berlin. The divided city had become "a sort of malignant tumor," Khrushchev announced at a rare Kremlin news conference. Therefore, the USSR had "decided to do some surgery," as outlined in an accompanying twenty-eight-page note. As Kennedy immediately recognized, this was the end of the policy of "grudging co-existence" at the front line of the Cold War and the beginning of one that would lead to what Khrushchev coyly called "Operation Rose," and the erection of the communists' "anti-Fascist protection device" – or Berlin Wall, as others preferred to term it – some two-and-a-half years later.[29]

In September 1959, Khrushchev launched himself on a supposed "goodwill" tour of America, combining formal state events with somewhat surreal meet-the-people sideshows in New York City, San Francisco, Hollywood, and rural Iowa. There was a reception for the Soviet leader at the US Senate, where he exchanged handshakes with John Kennedy. Kennedy later invoked two late eighteenth-century British politicians when describing Khrushchev to William Douglas-Home. "Jack said he was rough ... And he repeated what he had often said to me, on previous occasions, about William Pitt [the Younger] and [Charles James] Fox, that you must be as strong as Pitt and a negotiating type like Fox at the same time, which is always a problem."[30] Kennedy privately told Home that Khrushchev also reminded him of his father. Although "brilliant in their own way," both men could blow hot and cold. "The plain people of America like me," Khrushchev exclaimed at one point on his tour. "It's just those bastards around Eisenhower that don't."[31]

Between times, Kennedy managed another of his regular visits to Britain and the French Riviera, where he took an uncontrived pleasure in mingling with friends respectively dressed in "superb English costume" and "almost no costume at all."[32] William Douglas-Home witnessed the odd and poignant moment when, after twenty-five years of admiring him from afar, Jack finally found himself face to face with Winston Churchill. The historic encounter came at a moonlit dinner party on board Aristotle Onassis's floating Xanadu of a yacht, the 325-foot shimmering-white *Christina*, as it lay at anchor off Cap d'Antibes. Kennedy wore a tan mess-jacket and black tie for the occasion, while the eighty-three-year-old former premier was dressed in a frayed white Panama hat and cruising suit, and was showing signs of his age. "We went down to Mr. Onassis's boat," Home recalled, "and Sir Winston wasn't recognizing people that evening much. And as we left, Mrs. Kennedy said, 'I think he thought you were the waiter, Jack.' That's about as far as it went. Churchill was his hero, and it was rather sad to think that that was the first time he'd ever met him."[33]

It's possible that at some stage in 1958 Kennedy also made the acquaintance of the forty-five-year-old Duchess of Argyll, the former Margaret Whigham, who divided her time between her husband's ancestral estate in Scotland and a thirteen-bedroom house near the American Embassy on Upper Grosvenor Street in London. "She lit up the room," it has been fairly said of her. Born into wealth, after an upbringing largely spent in New York, where she was relieved of her virginity at fifteen by the actor David Niven, Margaret had been launched on society as a glamorous if somewhat stony-faced pre-war debutante. In 1951 she'd married Ian Campbell, the eleventh duke of Argyll, but their happiness was short lived. As a British high court judge was later to remark, the duchess was "a highly sexed woman who has ceased to be satisfied with normal sexual activities, and has started to indulge in disgusting sexual exploits to gratify a debased sexual appetite."[34] Speaking under ground rules of anonymity, several people familiar with the Argylls' domestic arrangements suggested that Margaret had at some point bedded both Ambassador Kennedy and his second son, though not concurrently. It should be stressed that there's no evidence for this in the publicly released files, although it would not be entirely inconsistent with the known facts. Jack Kennedy had an acknowledged weakness for a certain kind of British bohemian-aristocratic type, and Margaret in turn seems to have been uninhibited in her selection of lovers. When in 1959 the duke came to consider the matter of possible co-respondents in his divorce proceedings against his wife, he was somewhat spoilt for choice. He and his advisers eventually narrowed the list down to eighty-eight, of whom four were named on the petition.[35]

Kennedy also used the summer 1958 congressional recess to publish a short but important booklet, *A Nation of Immigrants*. The historian John Roche later argued in a preface to this that the Kennedy family's commitment to "inclusiveness" in American society was bound up in their own struggle for acceptance in their adopted homeland. "John and his siblings grew up in an environment where the plight of the Irish, at the hands of the British and of the Americans whom they encountered in emigration was a vibrant cause," Roche wrote. "The great jump between Joseph P. Kennedy and his son was that the Ambassador's concern was purely for the Irish–Americans and their woes, while the Senator who prepared this primer had broadened his vista to include all immigrant peoples – including a number his father would have surely kept outside the pale."[36] Certainly the ambassador never quite reconciled himself to what he called the "Zionist curse" in American life, having, for example, insisted at a December 1940 meeting of Hollywood studio chiefs that "Britain was doomed ... that the Jews were on the spot, and that they should stop making anti-Nazi pictures, or using the film medium to promote or show sympathy to the cause of the 'democracies' versus the 'dictators.' He continued to underline the fact that ... the Jews would be in jeopardy if they continued to abuse that power."[37]

★ ★ ★

ALTHOUGH HIS informal mandate from Kennedy was only to advise on colonial affairs, by 1959 David Ormsby-Gore also began to assert himself in the area of general foreign policy. "The experience and the friendships JFK made [in the 1930s] were a permanent asset," the *Time* bureau chief and Kennedy family friend Hugh Sidey wrote. "In August of 1959 I was asked to telephone David Ormsby-Gore for Senator Kennedy, to seek Ormsby-Gore's opinion on the ending of nuclear weapons testing. Mr. Ormsby-Gore gave me the information I needed in a polite and crisp manner and then added he would be in touch with Senator Kennedy with further detail."[38]

As Gore himself recalled,

I was over for the United Nations Assembly meetings, and we met in New York. Kennedy asked me how the [disarmament talks] were going, and what I thought might come out of them, and I explained in great detail the situation I thought we had arrived at in that particular negotiation. I thought that if the United States could make certain changes in their position there was a real possibility that the Soviet Union might want a test ban treaty at that time. He was very interested and asked me to send him a memorandum, which I did, outlining this position.

He became more interested in it. We had some correspondence, and I noticed in certain speeches he made after that that he did make it quite a theme.[39]

Gore's uncredited role in helping shape a declared presidential candidate's position on national security matters continued through the early days of 1960. Hugh Sidey was only one of several Kennedy friends and advisers to be told at moments requiring a rapid foreign policy pronouncement: "Call David." Gore added that:

> the United States position [on disarmament] had not been very carefully worked out. They had a committee studying the problem and hadn't been very happy about the report which was produced by this committee ... While I was in Washington I again saw Kennedy at his house and we had a further discussion about this and I described the situation as I discovered it, and he was obviously very concerned. That was the first time I think I remember him wondering out loud whether there shouldn't be more machinery in the American government for studying all the arms control and disarmament problems.[40]

This was an unusual second act to a friendship that had evolved from the exchange of sexual gossip in subterranean London nightclubs into earnest discussions about nuclear deterrents and other high policy matters touching upon mankind's continued survival on the planet. In fact, the entire Kennedy-Gore connection was unprecedented in its human embodiment of the postwar "special relationship." The two men were sometimes closeted together for six hours or more, Sidey remembered, "completely enraptured" by the mutual intellectual challenge of the occasion. There was also the question of the shared personal characteristics and growing affection between the two. Kennedy's ferocious appetite for women was matched in turn by Gore's for fast cars and up-tempo jazz. Both men enjoyed being where the action was. Both brought an irreverent and often satirical wit to bear in their approach to matters of grave international concern.

Later in life, Gore was described as an "endlessly smooth eighteenth-century courtier who'd somehow listened to Miles Davis."[41] One of his immediate family members remembered him to me as "a highbrow with a finely tuned ear for all the bullshit in politics." Dark haired and toothy, with a beaky Stravinsky nose, striding about in his slightly over-florid ties, Gore was a prototypical swinging London figure set loose in the nunnery of international diplomacy. Like Kennedy, he was also impressively literate, historically minded, and a supremely able negotiator, one who could bring apparently irreconcilable foes to support a common position and ensure that all sides felt they had a stake in its success. It's another sign of the obvious warmth between the two men that Kennedy found time during the hectic days leading up to the formal announcement of his candidacy in January 1960 to visit Gore's country estate at Oswestry in Shropshire. "Local people were amazed," the *Shropshire Star* reported. "Kennedy and his wife were seen walking in the town, having attended a mass at the Catholic church ... It caused quite a stir at the time."[42]

On the campaign trail, Kennedy frequently soared to Churchillian heights, or quoted Churchill himself. More than once, he returned to an early theme – the state of British military and political unreadiness in the 1930s – and applied it to the modern world. Speaking in Milwaukee, on November 13, 1959, Kennedy began:

> Meeting in this historic perspective ... I suggest we look back 23 years, when, in a bitter debate in the House of Commons, Winston Churchill charged the British government with acute blindness to the menace of Nazi Germany, with gross negligence in the maintenance of the island's defense, and with indifferent, indecisive leadership of British foreign policy and British public opinion. The preceding years of drift and impotency, he said, were "the years the locusts had eaten." And it seems to me tonight that this nation has, since January 1953, passed through a similar period.[43]

That Kennedy continued to see the mileage in his own cautionary tale of British disarmament and appeasement at Munich was
underlined later that week, when he took the trouble to write
to the publisher Wilfred Funk to inquire about the progress of
Why England Slept. On November 30, Funk's president William
Roulet replied, "In answer to your letter, the records available
indicate that the total [us] sales of your publication are approximately 12,000 copies."[44]

Furthermore, Kennedy saw lessons to learn – or avoid – in
British domestic politics. "Socialized medicine" along the lines
of the National Health Service would be "quite impractical" in
America, at least for the present, he told Gore shortly before the
1960 election. Instead there should be targeted improvements
such as subsidized insurance services for the indigent or elderly
and eventually the creation of national institutes of health to
promote research into serious diseases. Nor could the candidate
realistically hope to imitate the wholesale British state education reforms, instead offering a limited federal aid package to
elementary and secondary schools.

Jack's MP friend Hugh Fraser was also sending him regular
reports from the London *Times*, as well as his own more personalized accounts of parliamentary and ministerial proceedings.
Kennedy was determined to establish a government that avoided
the sort of dual welfare expansion and military contraction of
the British model. As a whole, he observed, the United States
had spent its time since the war "collecting nuclear bombs, while
Europe had been rounding up gold," or at least significantly
inflating the social services quotas of its individual domestic
budgets.[45] It was time the continental allies adjusted their economic priorities to better contribute to their own defense, which
should not become "simply an American enterprise."[46] When a
reporter went on to ask him if his vision of a strong, militarily
self-sufficient Europe broadly under British leadership conflicted
at all with his father's views, Kennedy replied that after looking
at matters "as cold-bloodedly as I can," he was convinced he was

right. "That is my position," he added decisively. "I think you should ask my father directly as to his position."[47]

That would not prove easy. At seventy-two, Ambassador Kennedy continued his regular European fact-finding tours, though these now increasingly centered on the south of France rather than his former family base in London. But unlike the old days, when the difficulty had often seemed to be to restrain Joe's public remarks, now he had little to say to reporters. In the same week that Jack accepted his party's nomination for the presidency of the United States at the Democratic Convention in Los Angeles, his father flew to the Riviera for an extended summer holiday. A reporter from *U.S. News and World Report* found the older Kennedy uncharacteristically tight lipped. "I stood up and took them and batted them out for 25 years," he declared. "Now it's somebody else's turn. I called them as I saw them at the time, even when it got me in trouble, which is more than some people did." The reporter had slightly more luck when he came to interview the ambassador's golf caddy, "an attractive French girl named Françoise, about 21 years old … The blonde Françoise says her [boss's] fairway shots are 'short' but very straight … Mr. Kennedy speaks no French, but has been teaching Françoise English during the rounds."[48]

The counterpart to Ambassador Kennedy's reticence with the press was his son's snatching at anything that could bolster his public reputation as a man who understood the world and knew from experience what conditions were like in several foreign capitals. A small but telling example of this came in Kennedy's official 1960 campaign biography, which boasted that he "attended London School of Economics 1935–36." In fact, he had spent a total of twenty-two days enrolled at the LSE and been hospitalized for half of them. Conversely, Kennedy tactfully played down his religious beliefs and his successive visits to the Vatican, well aware that many progressive Democrats regarded traditional papal doctrine as a repressive absurdity. "I am not the Catholic candidate for President," Jack told an audience of three hundred in a Houston hotel and millions more watching on television. "I am the Democratic Party's candidate for President, who happens also to be a Catholic."[49]

The challenge was to persuade the American electorate that a forty-two-year-old, second-term senator with no hands-on executive credentials could master his nation's foreign affairs in the era of Khrushchev, Mao, and Castro. As Lyndon Johnson remarked of his rival contender for the Democratic nomination, "The forces of evil ... will have no mercy for innocence, no gallantry for inexperience."[50] Kennedy duly brought the liberal Democrat strategist and former US ambassador to India Chester Bowles into the campaign, and later in the summer he asked the failed presidential candidate Adlai Stevenson to head an advisory task force specifically on Soviet–American relations. As the election neared, they were sometimes joined in their deliberations by a thirty-seven-year-old Harvard professor and part-time National Security Council consultant named Henry Kissinger. Kennedy told Kissinger he wanted the "Churchill touch" to his foreign policy speeches. He studied newsreel films of the former prime minister and wanted to know everything about how Churchill had written his great wartime set pieces. "He seemed like a young man obsessed with a favorite old uncle, who might die at any moment," a Kennedy staffer recalled. "'Those great rolling phrases,' Jack used to say. 'Powerful and simple at the same time. How did he do that?'"[51]

Brilliant as Kennedy's advisers were in their own ways, they were not men with whom anyone could have a normal conversation. As a rule, either they talked and everyone else present listened, or the others talked and they sat lost in thought, only to then repeat their original position on the issue under debate. A member of the Kennedy staff who was familiar with the inner workings of the candidate's foreign affairs team recalled, "The Senator frequently complained how [they] addressed him as though they were conducting a high-powered university lecture, and he was just another young undergraduate."[52]

So Kennedy turned to the British. Precise dates are unavailable, but it seems that he either met with or spoke to David Ormsby-Gore roughly a dozen times in the period from March to October 1960. We know that they were together at Kennedy's Washington home on the evening of April 4, which was the day before the Wisconsin primary. Ormsby-Gore recalled that they discussed "arms control and disarmament issues" before the candidate hurriedly left in order to fly to Milwaukee "to be present at the factory gates [at] half-past five the next morning."[53] Kennedy viewed Gore with "great warmth," especially because of the caustic views of this supposedly conservative figure on some of the absurdities of the foreign affairs establishment on both sides of the Atlantic. The old friends consulted again the next month, when a summit meeting between the Western powers and the USSR ended in some disarray amid Nikita Khrushchev's heated protests about an American U-2 spy plane that had been shot down over Soviet soil. Those who witnessed the Russian's fury would long marvel at the scene, speaking of it like old salts recalling a historic hurricane. Harold Macmillan was sufficiently distressed at the collapse of the talks to contemplate resignation. "It was a terrible performance, reminiscent of Hitler at his worst," he wrote in his diary. "[Khrushchev] threatens, rants, uses filthy words of abuse."[54] In time, Gore passed on not only his views on the Soviet position – borne of "Mr. K's crushing awareness of his side's weakness" – but also Macmillan's own concerns, faced with this "brutal figure," about maintaining an independent British nuclear capability. Kennedy was not alone in seeing the ensuing challenges of formulating a united Western policy on strategic arms. As he later remarked, "I'm the President of the United States, but who's the President of Europe?"[55]

In July 1960, a Gallup poll recorded that "the overwhelming majority of [Americans] interviewed regard relations with Russia and the rest of the world as being the primary problem facing the nation today."[56] Indeed, Khrushchev's behavior at this time gave widespread cause for alarm. When not threatening to annihilate the West in general, the Soviet leader found time to abuse Eisenhower and Macmillan in what the latter called "agricultural" terms and to go on famously to bang first his fist and then his shoe on his desk at the United Nations Assembly, in order to mark his displeasure at the way the debate there was proceeding. Some wondered if in fact Khrushchev might be clinically schizophrenic.

Kennedy again spoke to Gore, who was familiar with the Soviet position on nuclear disarmament talks as a result of the long hours spent discussing the issue with their representatives in London, New York, and Geneva. "Eisenhower and vice-president Nixon knew that there was no 'missile gap' – that the US was actually far ahead of the Russians – but didn't care to advertise the fact so as not to provoke Khrushchev into a crash program of weapons building," Gore's friend and mentor Selwyn Lloyd recalled. "Kennedy knew this, too, in part thanks to David, but spoke about it nonetheless. I'm sure he was genuinely concerned about the [US] falling behind, but it was also an easy issue to sell to the voters."[57]

On November 8, 1960, Kennedy won the presidential race against Nixon by 303 electoral votes to 219, but only 118,574 (or 0.17 percent) out of the 68,837,000 ballots cast. Doubts remain about the integrity of some of the polling arrangements in Illinois and Texas. Not long afterward, Kennedy and Ormsby-Gore met again in New York. "We had lunch alone together," Gore recalled. "We mostly discussed United Nations affairs, but he did tell me that people like [Kennedy's science adviser] Jerry Wiesner were off to Moscow on disarmament talks."[58] The young Democrat had reached the pinnacle of power, in part by portraying himself as a sort of modern-day Churchill who well understood the need for constant vigilance toward his nation's real or potential enemies. Thousands of congratulatory telegrams and letters flooded in to Kennedy headquarters following the election result. Many were read by his staffers and then

destroyed; a few were passed on for the president-elect's attention; and one, dated November 11, he carefully preserved in his
personal files. It read, "On the occasion of your election to your
great Office I salute you. The thoughts of the Free World will be
with you in the challenging tasks that lie ahead. May I add my
own warm good wishes. Winston S. Churchill."[59]

In due course, Kennedy proposed his brother Bobby, who was
thirty-five, as us attorney general, a defensible choice but also an
act of nepotism that rivaled Harold Macmillan's promotion that
winter of his wife's nephew, the eleventh duke of Devonshire,
who as plain Andrew Cavendish had been one of the young men
hovering around the Kennedys in pre-war London. His primary
brief would be the British colonial affairs that had so taxed the
new president while on the campaign trail. Curiously enough,
Kennedy and the duke were also related by marriage. David
Ormsby-Gore's own appointment to the highest ranks of the
Anglo-American union would soon follow.

8

SPECIAL RELATIONSHIPS

ON JANUARY 20, 1961, a sunny but bitterly cold day, forty-three-year-old John Kennedy announced himself in his inaugural address as of that "new generation of Americans – born in this century, tempered by war, disciplined by a hard and bitter peace, proud of our ancient heritage." Like millions of others around the world, Harold Macmillan, listening on the wireless in London, was particularly struck by the president's call to a renewed sense of national duty and sacrifice. He later presented Kennedy with an elaborately framed inscription of the phrase, "And so, my fellow Americans: ask not what your country can do for you – ask what you can do for your country" and its lesser-known sequel, "My fellow citizens of the world: ask not what America will do for you, but what together we can do for the freedom of man." There was an unmistakably Churchillian ring to Kennedy's assertion, "Let every nation know, whether it wishes us well or ill, that we shall pay any price, bear any burden, meet any hardship, support any friend, oppose any foe to assure the survival and the success of liberty."[1] Vice President Johnson, sitting a few feet away, evidently took note of the rhetorical flourish, because once in office he immediately ordered his own speechwriters to "read everything about Churchill" to help give him a "more Churchillian twist."[2]

Later that afternoon, as the car with the president and first lady passed the reviewing stand, seventy-two-year-old Joseph Kennedy was seen to rise to his feet and doff his hat in a gesture of deference to his son. The younger man nodded back genially. Rose Kennedy said later that several people had reported seeing tears in her husband's eyes. "Perhaps so," she wrote.[3] The triumph of perseverance and reconstruction that had, almost incredibly, led to this scene had begun fifteen years earlier when the older Kennedy had launched his "talented but rather aimless boy" on the Eleventh Congressional District of Massachusetts.

If Ambassador Kennedy was understandably moved by the spectacle of his second son assuming the highest office in the land, one he himself had coveted, some of the president's old British circle were equally struck by the enormity of the occasion. "It was as though one had gone to sleep knowing Jack as a charming young student or promising political apprentice, and woken up to find him the most powerful man in Christendom," Selwyn Lloyd recalled.[4] There was more than one fashionable London house or English stately home where the primary emotions that day were a combination of pride and mild disbelief that the "talented but aimless boy" they had known either side of World War II had now become – overnight it seemed – the de facto leader of the free world. In July 1945, twenty-five-year-old Andrew Cavendish had been one of the impeccably smooth young British toffs who had regularly met for predinner cocktails and political gossip in Jack Kennedy's suite at London's Grosvenor House Hotel. Now, as the eleventh duke of Devonshire and undersecretary at the Foreign and Commonwealth Office, he and his wife, the former "Debo" Mitford, found themselves in the VIP seats at President Kennedy's inauguration. Among other indelible phrases, they heard their host refer to "those old allies whose cultural and spiritual origins we share," with the pledge of remaining their "faithful friends."[5] The Devonshires came bearing a warm personal note from "Uncle Harold," as they knew the British prime minister. It would be hard to think of any other foreign power with similarly relaxed access to the new American head of state. Kennedy in turn sent an effusive letter later that week thanking Andrew and Debo both for the message and for being present at "the changing of the guard." A second letter sent only a few days later, also handwritten and signed "Jack," wondered if Debo might care to accompany the prime minister when he came to Washington for official talks later that spring.[6]

Deborah Devonshire's own published notes touch on both the sublime and the ridiculous – almost surreal – aspects of the inaugural proceedings:

> The parade itself was an extraordinary mixture of Army, Navy and Air Force, with girls' bands, majorettes in fantastic uniforms with long legs in pink tights, crinolined ladies on silver-paper floats, horses from the horsy states all looking a bit moth-eaten, army tanks, missiles on carriers, bands everywhere. One man marching by in an air-force contingent broke ranks, whipped out a camera, took a photograph of the president and joined in again ... The informality was so queer – Jack drinking coffee and eating a biscuit as the parade moved by. But he stood there for over three hours.
>
> Later [at the inaugural ball] we watched his speech again on the telly. As Jack himself came back along the front row, fenced in as usual by humans, he saw us, broke away and climbed over seven rows of seats to say goodbye, to the utter astonishment of the people sitting either side of us. I told Jack about Unity [Mitford's] letter of twenty-one years ago, saying how he was going to have a terrific future.[7]

There was a sizeable Irish contingent (nicknamed "the Murphia" by Jackie Kennedy) among the kitchen cabinet of the new administration. Larry O'Brien and Kenny O'Donnell acted as congressional liaison and presidential gatekeeper respectively, while Dave Powers, a first-generation Irish–American, served as special assistant, sexual procurer, and a sort of court jester-cum-butler. ("You met Phil?" he once inquired of a colleague during an official visit to London, while beckoning cheerfully to the Duke of Edinburgh.) The distinctly non-Irish Ted Sorensen, who wrote most of Kennedy's key speeches, and Pierre Salinger, the press secretary, rounded out the presidential inner circle.

Kennedy's secretary of state, Dean Rusk, was a balding, compact figure whose air of scholarly detachment from events emphasized the aptness of his forename. Behind his back, Ormsby-Gore, among others, sometimes referred to Rusk as "Buddha." The secretary's closely argued – and often convoluted – way of speech was only to be expected, another British official reasoned, "in one who has his office in Foggy Bottom." Born in 1909, Rusk had served with the US Army in Burma during World War II and had apparently formed a poor opinion of British colonial rule as a result. Neither instinct nor experience had equipped him to be a natural cheerleader on behalf of the Atlantic alliance. But against this, it could be said that in the truest sense Kennedy acted as his own foreign minister, establishing broad policy and leaving only the fine detail to others. "There were bureaucratic jobs to be done which neither the president, nor anyone else, particularly wanted, and which Rusk was willing to take on," Selwyn Lloyd remarked. "Dean wasn't a remotely political person, despite being surrounded by political struggles. He spoke in a soft voice. Nothing was likely to shock him."

★   ★   ★

KENNEDY NOW HAD the opportunity for serious reflection on the Anglo-American alliance, having recorded within a few hours of taking office his intention to "strengthen the old firm, based on our assessment of the issues ahead."[8] Macmillan, for his part, had written to share some of his hopes and anxieties about the state of world affairs even before the inauguration. "There is indeed plenty to talk about," he cabled the president-elect on December 19, 1960, before lavishing praise on Kennedy's collection of speeches in *The Strategy of Peace*. In something of a role reversal, the sixty-six-year-old British Tory then spoke to the forty-three-year-old American Democrat about the need to "properly adjust [the] Western Alliance to the realities" of the new decade. As a priority, he said, "I think the first and most important subject is what is going to happen to us unless we can show that our modern free society – the new form of capitalism – can run in a way that makes the fullest use of our resources … If we fail in this, communism will triumph, not by war, or even suppression, but by seeming to be a better way of bringing people material comforts."[9]

A follow-up letter of January 9, 1961, attached what the prime minister half-jokingly called his "Grand Design," a scholarly *tour d'horizon* outlining the worldwide challenges facing the two leaders and proposing an early conference to discuss them. Kennedy was characteristically charming and noncommittal in his reply. "Dear Mr. Macmillan," he wrote on January 13, "Thank you for the suggestions in your letter. A meeting between us during the week of April 2 seems to me a good basis for planning. Would it be difficult for you to delay your [travel arrangements] until our Inauguration? It would be preferable for me not to confirm such plans before Jan 20 and we could handle the matter much more simply after that date."[10] The economist John Kenneth Galbraith later insisted that he had been summoned posthaste to the White House to discuss the "Grand Design" and that a flustered president, after ransacking his office, was forced to admit that the document had been "misfiled." It was eventually found stuffed under a crib in three-year-old Caroline Kennedy's nursery.

★ ★ ★

THE ATLANTIC ALLIES may have been bound together by their common "cultural and spiritual origins," as President Kennedy put it in his inaugural address. But there was a more material aspect to the "duality of purpose and mutual commitment to the liberty of man," to quote the president's later remarks, which went largely unsaid in public. As Harold Macmillan was at pains to confirm even in the week Kennedy took office, there was also a nuclear special relationship between Britain and the United States. Although the allies' continuing exchanges on the subject necessarily dwelt on technical factors such as launch procedures and second-strike capabilities, a significant subplot to the discussions was whether Britain was to maintain a credible national nuclear force or simply become a forward base for American assets, much as Nikita Khrushchev later envisioned, to such global disquiet, in Cuba.

On January 21, 1961, Macmillan's foreign secretary Lord (Alec) Home, the elder brother of Kennedy's playwriting friend William Douglas-Home, cabled Sir Harold Caccia, Britain's ambassador in Washington. Caccia was to extract firm commitments from the new administration "concerning Allied consultation before the use of nuclear weapons and the use of bases in the United Kingdom."[11] Despite several more such requests, there were to be no immediate American assurances on the subject. A hitherto unpublished paper from Undersecretary of State Livingston Merchant to his new boss Dean Rusk, dated January 27, suggests only that the British note "be reviewed by Mr. Kohler, Mr. Farley, and the Acting Legal Adviser, who thereafter could prepare a draft reply by President Kennedy to Mr. Macmillan for you to consider and, if you approved, to discuss with the President."[12]

Whether swayed by the legal niceties or some deeper sense of commitment to the Atlantic axis, Kennedy replied directly to Macmillan on February 6, 1961:

> Dear Mr. Prime Minister: You will recall that you sent a message through your Ambassador concerning the continuance

of Anglo-United States Understandings … I am writing now
to tell you that the three points of clarification [you] make are
entirely acceptable to me and reflect our own interpretation
of these Understandings. I am happy, therefore, to confirm to
you that these Understandings reflect the agreement in force
between our two Governments … Needless to say, I welcome
this continuing evidence of the intimacy with which our
countries work together in all matters.

Kennedy attached to these warm thoughts on the wider canvas
of the alliance some of the more specific details Macmillan had
requested. Before launching any US nuclear weapons from bases
in the United Kingdom, "the President and Prime Minister will
reach a joint decision by speaking personally with each other,"
Kennedy assured him, although in the case of a possible launch
from sites located within the United States or from submarines positioned anywhere outside British waters, the president
undertook only to "take every possible step to consult with
the UK and our other allies," making allowance for the "likely
demands" of such a contingency.[13] Washington, in other words,
would do its best to exchange views with London in the event of
an imminent nuclear strike, but there were no promises.

Although Kennedy's obsession with the sales figures of his
book *Why England Slept* on its initial publication in 1940 ("Going
like hotcakes," he'd purred to his friend Chuck Spalding, "Dad's
seeing to that") was natural enough in any first-time author, it
was striking that the new president of the United States – who
kept a copy of the work's first edition on his White House desk –
would continue to inquire about its performance even as he came
to grapple with a full agenda both of domestic affairs of state
and the nation's precarious relations with the Soviet Union.[14]

"Dear Mr. Salinger," the publisher William Roulet wrote on
December 12, 1961, in reply to the latest inquiry from the president's press secretary, "Thank you … This is just a brief note …
to give you the good news that the Contemporary Affairs Society

has selected *Why England Slept* as half of their dual selection for their members for the month of January. They have placed an initial order for 600 copies and will probably order another 200 a bit later, and perhaps even more copies beyond the total of 800."[15] Two days later, Kennedy's aide Fred Holborn wrote to the president, "I understand that you would be interested to have some British reviews of *Why England Slept*. Here is one by a Britisher – your friend Denis Brogan – but in an American publication. Nonetheless, the review on pages 10–11 may interest you."[16] (Holborn had chosen wisely. "This extremely intelligent book by an extremely intelligent young man," Brogan wrote, "was composed at a time when the survival of England was of the highest urgency ... Most of the problems that the author saw being handled with varying success by Baldwin and Chamberlain, President Kennedy now must handle himself."[17]) If Kennedy felt any lingering debt in the matter to *Why England Slept*'s original ghostwriter Arthur Krock, he seems to have contained it by the time he came to meet that winter with his new journalistic best friend, Benjamin Bradlee of *Newsweek*. "Bust it off in old Arthur," the president told Bradlee, urging him to attack Krock in print.[18]

As we've seen, Kennedy showed a similar interest in his standing with the British public as a whole, mobilizing the resources of the us Information Agency to conduct a poll on the subject. In time, the agency proposed – in all seriousness – that the "very gratifying" results be passed to a friendly British MP who could read them into the record of the proceedings of the next session of the House of Commons. Kennedy did not think it a good idea.[19]

★　★　★

ON MARCH 7, 1961, Harold Macmillan answered a question in the Commons about the current state of Anglo-American affairs by assuring MPs, "Of course, there are close consultations through diplomatic channels at various levels on [nuclear] matters. I am also hoping to discuss them personally with the President in a very few weeks' time."[20]

The opportunity to do so came sooner than he expected. On the morning of March 24, Macmillan and his modest five-man party flew to Trinidad, looking forward to a "not particularly testing time" in the West Indies prior to talks in Washington scheduled to begin eleven days later. However, despite the meticulous planning that had been underway on both sides of the Atlantic since even before the inauguration, it was to be another case of what Macmillan characterized as "Events, dear boy, events." On March 23, Kennedy gave a perhaps unintentionally dramatic press conference about the situation in Laos, where a simmering civil war, with the Soviet Union hanging overhead like a dark cloud, provided an early test of the president's inaugural promise to "pay any price" to protect the world's nonaligned countries. "Southeast Asia is far away," the president remarked, in another foreshadowing of the domino theory of world affairs, "but the world is small … The security of all [the region] will be endangered if Laos loses its neutral independence. Its own safety runs with the safety of us all," Kennedy added, before going on to privately tell the *Washington Post* that "if he had to [invade] and if it meant he would be around only one term, nonetheless he would do it."[21]

In the predawn hours of March 25, a Saturday, Macmillan was awoken by a cable from Kennedy asking to meet him at the US naval base in Key West for "urgent" talks the following day. This was the way the president's highly personal – and occasionally impulsive – style of leadership worked. Kennedy apparently didn't consider the possible difficulties the sixty-seven-year-old premier might face in making an unscheduled, five-hour flight on such short notice. But Macmillan at least came prepared. He had not only done his homework on his opposite number through the normal ministerial channels, but he had called on his wife's nephew Andrew Devonshire and others who had known Kennedy from pre-war days in London for what the PM called "more arcane" information. "There was plenty of advice, not to say gossip" available as a result.[22] Nor can the politician in Macmillan have failed to grasp the irony that this was a rare case of the president of the United States soliciting a meeting with his principal ally and not vice versa. After hurriedly consulting his colleagues, the premier phoned the number he had been given in Washington to confirm that he would be in Florida on the 26, "in time for Sunday lunch."[23]

The scene that followed "was at the same time one of the strangest and one of the most interesting among my experiences," Macmillan later wrote, in the course of reviewing some forty years of active politics.[24] The visitors' noisy, turboprop Britannia aircraft, where the PM counted himself lucky to be served "stale ham sandwiches, with soup and a swig of tea" en route, touched down in Key West a few minutes after the president had landed to some ceremony on *Air Force One*. Kennedy and Macmillan strode across the tarmac to greet one another as a marine band struck up the national anthems, after which a military detail provided a nineteen-gun salute. The handshake, the sight of the two beaming leaders, and their departure side by side in the back of an open-top car, which then bore them down palm-fringed streets crowded with saluting sailors and cheering men, women, and children – these news images instantly transformed the Special Relationship, in the minds of millions of mainly American television viewers, from a valued but somewhat abstract alliance into a living and breathing partnership. Macmillan himself lingered over the scene in his memoirs, adding the detail that "a large number of spectators, in a great variety of costume, or no costume, lined the route and applauded enthusiastically." The prime minister's military aide was in a following car, and later remembered, "amidst the general fanfare, an attractive young lady lowered the top of her dress as the motorcade sped by, an accolade it was generally thought the president took in his stride."[25]

Recalling his first impression of Kennedy, Macmillan told his diary of "a curious mix of qualities: courteous, quiet, quick, decisive – and tough."[26] On arrival at the naval administration headquarters where the talks were to be held, there was another poignant reminder of the relative strength of the two leaders as measured by each man's entourage. "On the one side," wrote Macmillan, "was the President of the United States and Commander in Chief of all American forces, surrounded by officers of every rank and degree in a great naval fortress, and receiving all the honour due to a head of state; on the other, [his private secretary] Tim Bligh and I, with Harold Caccia in support." Following a detailed presentation on Anglo-American options in Southeast Asia, Macmillan observed drily that the recurrent civil war in Laos was an "almighty mess" and that his one-word advice for any Western leader tempted to intervene there was *Don't*.[27] Kennedy graciously took the point, while paraphrasing from the central thesis of *Why England Slept* by warning that nonetheless "there would be no negotiations" in the event of Soviet aggression in the region.[28] That effectively concluded the discussion. While Macmillan's secretary hurriedly typed up minutes that used terms such as "monitoring" and "vigilance" and conspicuously retreated from the threat of an imminent US invasion, the two principals adjourned to a private room for Sunday lunch, which consisted not of the traditional English roast beef but what the premier fastidiously called "meat sandwiches" – or hamburgers, a dish with which he was not familiar.

Macmillan flew back to Trinidad later that afternoon, impressed that the "cocky young Irishman" with such an equivocal reputation was able to match wits with him on a basis of immediately accepted trust and confidence. "He carries the weight of his great office with simplicity and dignity," the PM felt.[29] Kennedy in turn remarked to aides on the plane returning to Washington that he thought the old boy and his few advisers "kind of slow" compared to the frenetic pace set by the

Americans, but he appreciated the Englishman's obvious acumen and dry turn of phrase. In contrast to the president's boyish good looks, the shuffling and baggy-eyed Macmillan, who spoke in a drawling voice unfashionable even in the 1930s, seemed almost to be playing a part in some Gilbert and Sullivan comedy. But there was a core of steel under the vaudeville exterior. "I'm lucky to have a man to deal with with whom I have such a close understanding," Kennedy later told Henry Brandon. Going to see the premier was like being "in the bosom of the family," he added.[30] After this, Debo Devonshire remarked, "Jack was soon referring to the PM as Uncle Harold like the rest of us."[31]

On April 5, Macmillan and his now expanded party of nine arrived in Washington, where he received a "nice handshake" and "endless flowers," but no official proclamation of welcome. Since it was the queen, not him, who was British head of state, he qualified only for the "friendly foreign dignitaries" protocol of a "few State Department chaps hanging about, nodding inanely at one," he recalled in later discussion with a party colleague.[32] From there Macmillan was driven away to be entertained at a formal White House lunch. This restored the more convivial mood of the previous visit. During a break in the first morning's talks, Kennedy took Macmillan upstairs to meet his wife, Jackie, which marked the unofficial beginning of an unlikely twenty-five-year-long affectionate friendship. The premier told the First Lady that he couldn't help but notice that several of his own books and articles were gratifyingly displayed in the family's living quarters, and Jackie replied in something of a non sequitur that they also employed an English nanny for their young daughter and infant son.

A State Department "biographic information note" prepared for the president earlier that week described Macmillan as "a clever fox" and his wife Lady Dorothy as "of a quiet and retiring disposition."[33] The former part was right but not the latter; recalled as "loud, banal and relentlessly jolly – on occasion swearing like a sailor" by one Conservative minister, Dorothy balanced her "fiercely loyal and protective" attitude toward her husband with the competing demands of a thirty-five-year-long affair with Macmillan's party colleague Robert Boothby.

The next day, Kennedy, Macmillan, and their staffs were taken on a cruise down the Potomac River on board the presidential yacht *Honey Fitz*. Seated in wicker chairs on the aft deck and fortified by more "dynamite-strength" cocktails, they discussed matters ranging from Berlin and nuclear tests to the continuing enigma of Southeast Asia. Peering out onto a ramshackle flotilla of pleasure boats floundering away on the opposite side of the river, Macmillan deadpanned, "Looks like the Laotian Navy." It cracked everyone up. At the end of the talks, Macmillan presented Kennedy with an effusively signed photograph, which hung on the wall of his White House West Wing office for the remainder of his presidency. Kennedy used the word "happy" eight times in as many minutes when subsequently briefing reporters on the trip.

The president's "gleaming façade" both charmed and faintly concerned Macmillan, who wondered if there were much "inner resolve" behind it. Although Kennedy listened politely to a long exposition of the "Grand Design," with particular stress on the need for European unity and the advantages it would present for cross-Atlantic trade, he did so "in a rather detached way," the premier was forced to admit. "It was as though he was going through the social motions," Macmillan later reflected. "When [in 1963] Kennedy rang to congratulate me on Britain's role in concluding a nuclear test-ban treaty, you had the curious sensation that his mind was elsewhere. He might have been complimenting one on bringing off a reasonably competent shot on the tennis court."[34]

Kennedy was also the subject of a certain amount of spirited gossip in the stately homes of England in a way that would have been difficult to imagine of previous presidents. "Andrew [Cavendish] says Jack is doing for sex what Eisenhower did for golf," Debo Devonshire reported.[35] As we've seen, Kennedy had a deep affinity and respect for British politics and politicians, and sufficient personal warmth for Macmillan's Labour Party opponent Hugh Gaitskell to invite him to his inauguration. When the august figure of Earl Mountbatten of Burma, Queen Elizabeth's cousin and the last viceroy of India, came to pay an official visit to Washington in April 1961, Kennedy immediately asked him if he remembered their meeting at a party in London in March 1939. "For the sake of Anglo-us amity I lied and said 'yes,'" admitted Mountbatten. Their White House talks ran an hour longer than scheduled. "I formed the highest possible impression of Mr. Kennedy," Mountbatten added, high commendation from one so sparing of praise. "He seemed to be realistic and sound on everything we discussed."[36]

Mountbatten was only one of several British establishment figures of their generation to be pleasantly surprised at how much the younger Kennedy "differed in every vital respect" from the older. At times it almost seemed that Jack was acting the part of one of those superbly controlled, phlegmatic British aristocrats he so admired. "This is your show, but I feel we ought to place our worries frankly before you," or "I believe that on the historic evidence it is not likely that Mr. Khrushchev would make changes at a summit from [his previous] position as you suggest" were about as far as he ever went in expressing annoyance or impatience with his ally in London. Similarly, Macmillan was fussy about his health, if not something of a hypochondriac, in a way that rather jarred with his "unflappable" image. As pm he invariably traveled with his private doctor in tow, was finicky about what he ate and drank, and frequently admitted to feeling exhausted or depressed. Kennedy, who had a whole series of truly debilitating illnesses, apparently thought it bad form to speak of such things in public. His aides were left to deduce from a scarcely perceptible grimace or a low sigh as he rocked to and fro in his chair that his back was giving him particular hell that day. In short, Kennedy was in some ways stereotypically

"British," while Macmillan, both by birth and temperament, was nearly an American.

Kennedy's sense of gentlemanly reserve even extended to his reluctance to tax Macmillan at either their Key West or Washington talks with the fine details of the aptly named Operation "Bumpy Road," as the April 1961, CIA-backed invasion of Cuba was known. Essentially the idea was to land a somewhat motley band of anti-Castro exiles by moonlight on a beach located on the island's Bay of Pigs, seemingly in the hope that it would encourage organized uprisings by armed members of the Cuban resistance. In retrospect it was a reasonable enough military plan, but it required competence in its execution, mainly in the form of US air support. It also shared some of the broad characteristics of one of Kennedy's favorite books, the James Bond adventure *Dr. No* – a yarn in which Bond disposes of the maniacal dictator of a small Caribbean island – and even after the event, Macmillan seems not quite to have known what to make of it. "The counter-revolution in Cuba doesn't look too good," the PM was forced to record in his diary, as reports came in of the swift surrender of some 1,200 of the 1,400 attackers, and Kennedy's refusal to use US planes to salvage the disaster.[37] It was arguably the worst American foreign policy blunder in the period from their forfeiture of Berlin to the Russians in 1945 up to the dramatic escalation of the US combat role in Vietnam twenty years later, and it goes some way to explaining why Nikita Khrushchev felt able to successively risk war over Berlin and Cuba in the course of the next eighteen months.

All in all, Macmillan took the Cuban debacle – in broad outline, America's own Suez crisis – commendably in his stride, apparently seeing it as the kind of thing a favored but headstrong young nephew was bound to get up to from time to time. His principal worry was that this "unhappy story," as he called it, might be poorly received by some of the Commonwealth countries in the West Indies – particularly Jamaica, where the ruling Labour Party was pressing for full independence from Britain.

On May 3, David Ormsby-Gore at the Foreign Office sent the cabinet what amounted to a damage-assessment report on the affair. "Mr. Arthur Schlesinger, one of President Kennedy's men, came to see me yesterday," Gore wrote. "He was in London on a rather curious assignment. He had come at the president's request to make contact with leaders of the Labour Party in order to explain to them the considerations which had led up to the Cuban invasion, and to try and reassure them that the US administration was not composed of blood-thirsty imperialists."[38] It's notable that Kennedy would have cared enough about the intellectual respect of British opposition MPs to send his special assistant on a six thousand-mile goodwill tour, a courtesy he denied his other principal Western allies. "The President evidently took the debacle with extraordinary calm," Gore wrote. "He immediately decided to take full responsibility … However, already a number of others are making attempts to escape their share of blame for the failure … The President has certainly lost confidence in the CIA, and although he has no wish to sack people hurriedly and make them appear scapegoats, Mr. Allen Dulles would have to leave his job earlier than planned, Mr. Schlesinger thought about July."[39] (In the end, Dulles survived as CIA director until November 1961.)

Macmillan shared Kennedy's need to ingratiate himself with his principal ally. His flattery soon extended to writing the president personal greeting cards. "I had always imagined that you were born on March 17," Macmillan quipped, congratulating his "dear friend" on his forty-fourth birthday. "But the boys in my back room tell me that it is not so and that it is May 29. This note comes with every good wish for the future to you and yours. I value our friendship and rejoice that relations between the US and my country are close and 'happy.' Harold."[40]

Kennedy's first and only summit meeting with Nikita Khrushchev, held in Vienna on June 4, 1961, already commands a wide literature. The young president described it as "the roughest thing in my life – he savaged me."[41] His private comparison of Khrushchev's hectoring, profanity-laced manner with that of his father struck insiders like Ormsby-Gore as "not insignificant." Once back in the United States, Kennedy swiftly applied the lesson of Munich by announcing that he would ask Congress for a supplementary $3.3 billion defense budget to counter the Soviet buildup.[42] Like Churchill before him, he saw his role as shoring up a fraying world power that had fallen behind its rapidly mobilizing adversary.

After his experience with Khrushchev and before him with Canadian premier John Diefenbaker (whom he thought an "SOB" and "a jerk"[43]), Kennedy must have welcomed the chance to decompress during a thirty-six-hour visit to London, his first there as president. Macmillan drove out to the airport to meet his guest, whom he found "impressed and shocked" by his mauling in Vienna. "It was rather like somebody meeting Napoleon (at the height of his power) for the first time," the PM reflected.[44] Red-uniformed British soldiers appeared to be stationed under "every lamp-post and over-hanging pair of crossed flags" as the party drew up in the rain at Admiralty House, just off Trafalgar Square. The Macmillans had moved into this nearby government building when it was discovered that the premier's official residence at 10 Downing Street was not so much in need of repair (a metaphor for the country at large, some felt) as in imminent danger of collapse; on his last visit to Number 10, President Eisenhower had seriously worried that the floor in the Cabinet Room might give way under the weight of his entourage. Kennedy's fleet of back-up cars, each weighed down by two tons of extra armor plating, had some difficulty negotiating the narrow central London streets. There was a good deal of shouting by members of the president's Secret Service detail, who were dressed identically in short tan raincoats and sunglasses. Kennedy himself struck a Press Association reporter named Tony Gill as "just past his film-star best, but still with a luxuriant crop of hair and a solid and forcible set to his jaw like a young Roman senator's."[45]

Just a week earlier, the Atlantic allies had exchanged notes addressing what Macmillan called the "distasteful" matter of the infiltration by communist agents of Britain's top-secret Underwater Weapons Establishment, only one of several such security breaches to come to light in the period 1960–1963. The subject may have briefly flashed through Kennedy's mind as he stepped from his car to wave to the cheering crowds (among them twenty-year-old John Lennon, on a brief visit home from performing in Hamburg with the still obscure Beatles) on the pavement outside Admiralty House. An unmissably large billboard above the Whitehall Theatre, immediately next door to the two leaders' meeting place, read, "Now in Its 4th Year – The Classic English Farce, *Simple Spymen*."

Kennedy used the opportunity of his visit to London not only to discuss what were called "pressing matters of grave international concern" but to rekindle old British relationships. Following their official welcome, he and Jackie were driven to the home of the First Lady's sister, Lee Radziwill, and later attended their niece Anna's christening. David Ormsby-Gore, Andrew Cavendish, and several Astors in turn came to call on the Kennedys. "The [president] was obviously in great pain at that time because his back was extremely bad," Gore remembered. "There is no doubt that Khrushchev made a very unpleasant impression on him. That's what he said to me [in] London, that it had been a most disagreeable interview, that Khrushchev obviously tried to browbeat him and frighten him. He had displayed the naked power of the Soviet Union."[46]

The two old friends met again later that night at a dinner given in the first couple's honor at Buckingham Palace, where Gore was able to pass Kennedy some notes with suggested talking points for the televised address he would make to the American people immediately on his return to Washington. Other hands also helped draft the text, but the president's line insisting "The Soviets and ourselves give wholly different meanings to the same words: war, peace, democracy, and popular will – we have wholly different views of right and wrong" emerged fully formed from what he called his "skull session" with the British minister over the palace brandy and cigars.[47]

Following the next morning's talks at Admiralty House, the president and premier went downstairs for a lunch that proved "almost a family affair" for Kennedy, crowded as it was with his Cavendish cousins and in-laws and a fair sprinkling of other dukes and duchesses. Writing to the queen about the visit, Macmillan could only confirm that "Mr. Kennedy [had been] completely overwhelmed by the ruthlessness and barbarity of the Russian ruler, [who was] quite impervious to his charm,"[48] but that the "social aspects" of the London visit had nonetheless been splendid. The only discordant note came when Dorothy Macmillan for some reason took exception to the president's secretary of state, Dean Rusk, and expressed her displeasure by installing an entire Royal Marines band immediately behind Rusk's head at lunch.

More importantly, the personal Special Relationship that Kennedy had forged over twenty-six years with the British was now paying off. The London college dropout found himself back amidst flag-waving crowds who shouted themselves hoarse at the sight of the president in his open car. Macmillan noted in cabinet that "one result, at least, of the visit would be a closer understanding and co-operation between the Governments of the United States and the United Kingdom."[49] The prime minister had taken one look at the president on his arrival at Admiralty House, put his arm round his shoulder, and offered him a stiff drink, "which was accepted." Macmillan admitted that he was not encouraged by Kennedy's talks with Khrushchev, who had "maintained a stubborn and unyielding attitude on almost all the questions aired," nor by the quality of all the traveling American officials.[50] But at the same time, he drew a sharp distinction between the set-piece discussions when the president was surrounded by his full court of advisers, principally Dean Rusk talking interminably about the fine detail of nuclear test restrictions, and the precious three hours he enjoyed alone with Kennedy. "It was really *most* satisfactory – far better than I could have hoped," the premier wrote.[51] Macmillan even took it in his stride when he heard that the president had found the time in his busy schedule for a private meeting with the leader of the British parliamentary opposition, Hugh Gaitskell. Kennedy, the PM reasoned, simply had one of those "artistic" minds that could remain "commendably loyal to a partner, while allowing for the possibility (in his case, the actuality) of showing interest in a rival suitor."[52]

Kennedy's own assessment of the Vienna debacle consciously avoided Neville Chamberlain's note of apparent optimism about the world situation following his meetings with the German leader at Munich twenty-three years earlier. The president told Macmillan at Admiralty House that in the event West Berlin became "a Danzig" (the "free city" whose return Hitler had demanded), then war with the Soviets was inevitable. Curiously, there was also a human link for Kennedy back to the 1930s, because Lem Billings discreetly joined his entourage in London. The "First Friend," as he was now known, traveled around Europe in an official limousine, which he sometimes shared with Dr. Max Jacobson, a New York practitioner who dispensed "happy pills" – a combination of amphetamines and steroids – to the president and Mrs. Kennedy, attended state dinners, and flew on a government jet. These were significantly different conditions than had prevailed on Jack and Lem's summer vacation in 1937. The reporter Tony Gill insisted that there had also been a more allusive connection back to Kennedy's younger, frequently bedridden days in Britain, in the form of a well-known society prostitute who had visited him, dressed in a nurse's uniform, while the First Lady was otherwise engaged.[53]

Despite both his bad back and the pressure of other commitments, Kennedy told aides he wanted to visit Winston Churchill while in England, offering to travel "anywhere the old man chose" so they could speak "even for a few minutes."[54]

Neither time nor the burdens of high office had diminished the president's respect for Britain's wartime leader. Kennedy kept a bound copy of Churchill's speeches in the Oval Office and carefully preserved their occasional exchange of letters or cables in his personal files. He had been Churchill's ardent admirer for thirty years. But Macmillan explained that his old chief's memory was shot, and that it would likely be a mistake to see him. Kennedy reluctantly accepted the premier's advice, which followed on a similar disappointment just six weeks earlier. On that occasion, Churchill had been sailing up the eastern seaboard of the United States as a guest of Aristotle Onassis. A storm had forced the *Christina* to briefly dock in New York, an event sufficient to merit a State Department memo to the president. Churchill's traveling secretary, Anthony Montague Browne, recalled that Kennedy was "markedly friendly" and offered to send a plane to bring the distinguished British visitor to Washington. In retrospect, it's striking that the president was willing to clear his schedule to meet with the mentally diminished eight-six-year-old former prime minister in the very week he was in near-continuous briefings about the imminent Bay of Pigs invasion. Like Macmillan, Browne was forced to explain that Churchill was not up to the challenge of holding even informal talks with the leader of the free world. "I understand your reasons, and I feared this would be the case," Kennedy replied.[55]

★ ★ ★

THE FIRST APPEARANCE of a crude but starkly effective barbed-wire and cement barrier between East and West Berlin in the predawn hours of August 13, 1961, achieved almost total surprise. When news of the event reached him later that hot Sunday morning, President Kennedy was setting off in his cabin cruiser, the *Marlin*, for a family picnic at Hyannis Port. Shortly before noon, the president's military aide, Major-General Chester Clifton, signaled the boat to advise that a "significant" cable had arrived from the White House. Among other things, it included a CIA wire with the news that "on 13 August the East German regime ... put into effect a series of decrees introducing severe new control measures designed to stop immediately the outward flow of refugees," a step apparently thought likely to cause "spontaneous outbreaks in East Berlin and East Germany of local disturbances such as strikes, riots, and other anti-regime activities."[56] Kennedy immediately ordered the *Marlin* to return to shore.

For his part, Harold Macmillan was then on a shooting and golfing holiday with his wife in Scotland. Despite this "unhappy news" from the Continent, he could see no compelling need to return to London. "A lot of telephoning, morning and evening, to Alec Home about the 'Berlin crisis,'" Macmillan noted in his diary. "The Foreign Secretary has behaved with admirable sang-froid, and continues to urge the importance of taking at least the preliminary steps to a negotiation."[57] Buttonholed by an insistent reporter on the eighteenth fairway at Gleneagles, Macmillan snapped, "Nobody is going to fight about Berlin," and "I think it is all got up by the press." For once, it was too great a show of public insouciance. The US ambassador to London cabled the State Department that, as a result, the "Foreign Office spent a 'ghastly' day trying to explain away ... the [golf] remark ... PM ... sent message to President saying in effect he goofed."[58]

Although nobody in the West was prepared for the reality of a Berlin Wall, nor had the special needs of that city – dubbed a "wilderness of mirrors" for its network of competing espionage activities – been completely ignored. In March 1961, the CIA briefed President Kennedy on its prosecution of "certain high-level covert-action operations [such] as planting of news and feature articles in a variety of media appropriate to the target audience, encouragement and distribution of statements by various world leaders ... stressing the illegitimacy of the East German regime and the police-state mechanism which maintains and controls it … We want to help West Germans to review the Nazi past objectively [and] to continue financial warfare."[59]

In Britain, too, the news that refugees were leaving East Berlin at the rate of some 1,800 a day – meaning that the German Democratic Republic could have been completely empty by 1989 – also found its way to the top of the cabinet agendas in the early summer of 1961. On June 20, the foreign secretary told his colleagues, "There [was] no sign of a serious desire on the part of Mr. Khrushchev to negotiate on Berlin, [and] the expectation [was] that he will proceed to sign a separate peace treaty with East Germany in the autumn."[60] Speaking in the House of Commons that month, Macmillan said of his recent discussions with Kennedy, "The situation in Germany was reviewed, and there was full agreement on the necessity of maintaining the rights and obligations of the Allied Governments in Berlin."[61]

Nevertheless, the idea that Khrushchev and his sock-puppet first secretary of East Germany's Socialist Unity Party, Walter Ulbricht, would overnight draw a line literally marking the new front in the Cold War – ultimately to form an impenetrable ten mile-long urban ring, complete with guard towers, floodlights, motion censors, landmines, metal spikes, and attack dogs – came as something of a shock in both Washington and London. After returning to shore at Hyannis Port that Sunday morning, Kennedy was met by General Clifton in a motorized golf cart and taken to the small, whitewashed oceanfront cottage he used as a weekend office. After briefly calling Dean Rusk and Secretary of Defense Robert McNamara, the president agreed to an official State Department response indicating that Ulbricht's "anti-fascist protection device" did not affect the "Allied position in West Berlin or access thereto," although it would be subject to "vigorous protests through appropriate channels." This was a more temperate immediate response than the Soviet leader had feared and indeed than might have been expected of the man who had once publicly excoriated the British for their inaction in the face of Nazi aggression. On reading Kennedy's statement, Khrushchev's son Sergei later wrote, "Father sighed with relief. So far, things had turned out all right."[62]

Over the next few days, Kennedy would have to make one of the most important decisions of his presidency. Should he order American troops to tear down what was still only a temporary barbed-wire palisade, as proposed by President Truman's secretary of state Dean Acheson? Acheson told a group of friends that week, "Gentlemen, you might as well face it — this nation is without leadership."[63] Or should he proceed more deliberately, issuing only notes of regret that affirmed the allies' support of West Berlin and their commitment to the ultimate prospect of a reunified Germany but meanwhile accepted an act that sliced the city in half and prevented movement between the two sides?

Kennedy's dilemma harshly reflected some of the more abstract musings of his wartime diary. "If a split among the Big Four develops [in Germany] as far as long-time administrative procedure," the young Hearst newspaper correspondent had written in July 1945, "it will be serious."[64] In the intervening years, he had lost some of the certainties of youth. It was widely known in Washington during the early days of the Kennedy administration that the president still turned to his father for advice at particular moments of crisis, if no longer invariably accepting the results. As the ambassador's previously stated position on postwar Germany had been to castigate Truman and Acheson for pouring "arms and money into the quixotic adventure" to defend Berlin, it's unlikely he would have advocated the military option now.[65] In time, the new administration's policy in the region raised 1930s "Munich" analogies from the political Right. West Berlin's mayor Willy Brandt wrote the president an open letter comparing the "arbitrary division" of his city to Hitler's occupation of the Rhineland in 1936. Ironically, a group of disaffected German students even saw fit to send the author of *Why England Slept* an umbrella, the symbol of Neville Chamberlain's "cowardice and appeasement [in] preserving the peace at any price."[66]

"I feel sure you will agree with me," Macmillan cabled Kennedy on August 28, 1961, "that the German problem must be settled ultimately by negotiation. The Communists can do great injury to our economies and to the life of our Western peoples by continuing alarms and pressures over a long period ... I therefore thoroughly share [the] view as to the importance of stating that we are ready to talk at the right time and in the right way."[67] But this was not merely a case of a tired and effete British premier urging a policy of appeasement on a thrusting young American president. Kennedy's instinct now was also to find a workable accommodation with the Soviets. Acknowledging to aides that "a wall is a hell of a lot better than a war," the president restricted himself in public to remarking that events in Berlin and a subsequent Soviet decision to resume nuclear testing showed a "sad disregard of the desire of mankind for a decrease in the arms race ... [and] a threat to the entire world by increasing the danger of a thermo-nuclear event."[68] (Kennedy's private remarks on the subject betrayed more of his old life in the navy. "Fucked again," he noted when told of the Soviets' initiative. "That fucking liar," he added of Khrushchev.[69])

On August 18, Kennedy dispatched Vice President Johnson and General Lucius Clay, the architect of the city's lifesaving 1948 airlift, on a goodwill tour of West Berlin. Johnson's instructions were to "show the flag [and] mollify Mayor Brandt," which he did with his customary finesse. Harold Caccia, the outgoing British ambassador to Washington, cabled Macmillan that "the VP spoke very severely to Brandt, upbraiding him for reacting so impulsively ... and for firing off in public impractical proposals and unwarranted criticisms of the Allies. The mayor was apparently very shamefaced."[70] One source who was present at the meeting later reported that Johnson had seized Brandt by the lapels, stared down at him, and advised, "Don't shit on your own doorstep, son."

Macmillan subsequently sent Kennedy a flurry of cables urging him to remain calm in his overall policy in the region, most notably late that October when Soviet and American tanks moved up to Checkpoint Charlie and faced each other, barrel to barrel, in a high-stakes game of chicken, ready to fire if either side encroached on the border. The standoff lasted for sixteen hours. That effectively ended the Berlin crisis of 1961, though it remained as a static issue – and a killer of innocent civilians – for many years to come. Although it's officially said that 136 individuals died as a direct result of violence at the Wall, the total is reliably put at nearly double that figure once those who were caught and executed for escape attempts are included. In August 1962, eighteen-year-old Peter Fechter was shot by East German guards while trying to scale what was then a ten foot-high razor-wire wall, fell to the ground in no man's land, and, in full view of a watching crowd on both sides of the border, slowly bled to death.

It remains debatable whether the Berlin Wall did much for the solidarity of the Eastern Bloc, as its primary architects had hoped, but it undoubtedly brought the British and American sides closer together. Kennedy had abandoned his initial attempts to draft a strongly worded communiqué on the subject between the three Western powers because of President Charles de Gaulle's preference for using "uncompromisingly bold" language, a resolve that did not extend to his sending a single extra French soldier to Berlin. Any substantive Allied response to the continuing challenges in the region would thus be down to the Anglo-American axis. As a symbolic if not always practical gesture of the Special Relationship, Kennedy ordered the installation of a primitive first "hotline" connecting the Oval Office to Macmillan's cramped upstairs study in Admiralty House. The apparatus was both unreliable and unwieldy, looking more like a field telephone of World War II vintage – each party shouted the word "Over!" when it was the other man's turn to speak – but still provided a direct link to the White House not afforded to any other leader.

Both instinct and political necessity led Macmillan to treat the Americans with what he called "the frankness which true partnership and comradeship requires."[71] He would support them "unstintingly" when they were right and tell them "unhesitatingly" when they were wrong. For his part, Kennedy understood the opportunities this opened up and was personally delighted. He was even more pleased when Macmillan agreed to help accommodate the renewed US nuclear testing program. The PM thought the arms race as a whole "at once so fantastic and retrograde, so sophisticated and so barbarous, as to be almost incredible."[72] He also knew that Kennedy would not ideally wish the American public to see news images of a mushroom cloud, even under test conditions, eddying up over the Nevada desert. Macmillan told the president in a "Dear Jack" letter in January 1962, "We [have reached] a moment in history when it is better to take a bolder choice, and put a larger stake upon a more ambitious throw," by which he meant holding a tripartite conference with the Soviet Union to seek a deal on general disarmament.[73] In the meantime, bowing to expediency, he would put Christmas Island, a sparsely inhabited Commonwealth dependency in the Indian Ocean, at his friend's disposal. The Americans duly dropped a total of twenty-four high-yield bombs there beginning in April 1962, causing the islanders to report seeing a huge, sunlike fiery ball regularly appear in the night sky.

It would be unwise to exaggerate the practical results of the obvious human warmth that developed between Kennedy and Macmillan. Considerations of mutual national interest – and specifically, a shared distaste for what the PM called "certain Russian excesses" – remained at the core of the Special Relationship.[74] But even so, Kennedy's personal sympathy for the British surfaced not only when it came to formulating policy between the West and the Soviet Union but also in a whole range of strategically important global sideshows. In December 1961, for instance, the president overruled both his ambassador at the United Nations, Adlai Stevenson, and several other top advisers, in order to adapt American policy on the rumbling crisis in the Congo to better align with Macmillan's wishes. This involved passing an emergency resolution preventing the UN peacekeeping forces stationed there from dropping bombs on Moise Tshombe's breakaway freedom fighters, a tactic that had already sparked a kind of ideological brush fire in Westminster about British colonial policy in central Africa. The premier was actually winding up a heated Commons debate on the subject when, with exquisite timing, he was able to announce the news that Washington was on board. Before sitting down, Macmillan casually added that Kennedy had similarly agreed to contribute to the financing of the Upper Volta Dam project in Ghana, apparently persuaded by the PM's argument that to do otherwise would be an invitation for the Soviets to step in. The result was a government majority of ninety-four in a debate they might easily have lost, thus triggering a vote of no confidence and an early general election.

This was not the only time that Kennedy intervened to effectively maintain the British Conservative Party in office. Suppressing his own family sympathies, he took a utilitarian approach to the seemingly insoluble "Irish Question" and specifically to the guerilla warfare campaign intended to bring a swift end to British rule in Ulster. Rather than express clearcut support for a united Ireland, the president still contented himself with rattling off a suitable folk poem or an emotive ballad such as "Danny Boy" at the annual St. Patrick's Day festivities. Similarly, Kennedy encouraged Macmillan's vaunting ambition – almost an obsession – to join what was then called the European Economic Community, the precursor to today's European Union, even if the "mutually distasteful" price for entry was for the Atlantic allies to help the French develop nuclear weapons, as General de Gaulle was pressing them to. So enthused was the PM by what Kennedy told him on the subject during their April 1961 talks in Washington that he went on to gush to George Ball, the US undersecretary of state for economic affairs, "Yesterday was one of the really great days in history. We're going to join Europe. We'll need your help, since we have trouble with de Gaulle, but we're going to do it."[75]

It's reasonable to ask whether these issues would have been handled differently if, as was so nearly the case, Richard Nixon, not John Kennedy, had won the 1960 presidential election. The answer, up to a point, must be "yes." Nixon, while blowing hot and cold on the question of European unity, in large part depending on the sympathies of his audience at the time, would have been unlikely to encourage the sort of phased withdrawal from her former overseas commitments that constituted the bedrock of UK foreign policy in the early 1960s. He would also likely not have shared Kennedy's personal empathy for Macmillan or for the latter's bowing to the inevitability of Britain's colonial subjects acquiring an increasingly large say in the conduct of their own political affairs. A decade later, speaking as president, Nixon revealed that he was particularly distressed by the British retreat from Asia, leaving the United States as the "civilizing force" there. "The Japanese are all over Asia like a bunch of lice," he noted. "We have to reassure the Asians that the Nixon Doctrine is not a way for us to get out of Asia at their expense but a way for us to stay in."[76]

Given the personalities involved, it's unlikely, too, that Macmillan would have developed the same avuncular relationship with Nixon he enjoyed with Kennedy. The PM had privately recorded his views on the subject following a well-received official visit to Washington in June 1958. About the only discordant note to the trip had come at a formal dinner hosted by then Vice President Nixon. Although characteristically tactful in public, Macmillan was more candid in his diary. Nixon, he wrote, "poured out a monologue which extinguished any spark of conversation from whatever quarter it might arise ... This spate of banalities lasted for three to four hours ... I felt sorry for the Americans, who were clearly hurt and ashamed."[77] Nixon "wasn't a man you'd buy a car off, as the Americans say," was Macmillan's verdict a year later. "Ike always hated him – regarded him as a sharp lawyer."[78]

★　★　★

IN OCTOBER 1961, the UK–US relationship took on a significant new player. During their first brief encounter over hamburgers in Key West, Macmillan had asked Kennedy if he had any particular views about his choice of a suitable British ambassador to follow Harold Caccia in Washington. The president had immediately given that "dazzling smile of his, like a boy in a toothpaste advertisement," and said, "I'd like David."[79]

Forty-three-year-old David Ormsby-Gore duly assumed his duties as ambassador six months later. It was the remarkable culmination of a friendship with Kennedy that had reportedly begun at the horse races, if not among the debris of a "squalid basement bottle-party" twenty-three years earlier in London. Even before he took up his appointment, Gore signaled that a new era in Atlantic relations had begun when, on May 18, 1961, he sent the president a five-page handwritten letter. "Dear Jack," it began, "I have been meaning for some time to write to you privately – ever since the PM told me that you had received with admirable fortitude the news that Alec Home wanted me to come over as Ambassador."[80]

"You see," Macmillan later reflected of this "invigorating new spirit" in Anglo-American relations, "the President had three lives; he had his smart life, dancing with people not in the political world at all, smart people, till four in the morning; then he had his highbrow life, which meant going to some great pundit, and discussing his philosophy; and then he had his political life. And David belonged to all three … That was unusual in an ambassador."[81]

Ormsby-Gore was the only diplomat, American or foreign, with whom the president "really had a close relationship at all," Robert Kennedy added. "My brother would rather have his judgment than that of almost anybody else ... He was part of the family, really."[82] It was later said, not always approvingly, that Gore had become more like a de facto member of the administration than merely the envoy of a friendly power. In time, Dean Rusk was to complain that the president saw more of "that man" than he did of his own secretary of state. We've noted Vice President Johnson's displeasure when relegated to a distant seat at a top-level White House briefing while "the limey" reclined at the president's side. This was proof, if it were needed, that "Jack Kennedy always loved any smooth-talking British SOB who appeared on the horizon."[83]

David Bruce, Washington's man in London, was a similarly happy fit to his host government. Born in 1898 and a combat veteran of World War I, he shared a number of experiences and characteristics with Macmillan. Both could be alternately tough and charming: "a man with a nice smile and iron teeth," it was said of Bruce. Both married into great wealth, and both showed a certain courage when it came to overcoming the depression and loneliness of a dead marriage. Like Macmillan, Bruce was also mannered, courtly, and intimidatingly literate – he'd been a Princeton classmate of F. Scott Fitzgerald and became a boon companion of Ernest Hemingway before himself going on to write a best-selling book of biographical essays on American presidents. It was said that he and Macmillan sometimes passed the time while sitting together at Admiralty House awaiting Kennedy's phone call during the depths of the missile crisis by taking turns reading aloud from Jane Austen. Bruce's witty and incisive reports on the British political scene – and more particularly the Profumo affair of 1963 – were eagerly received in the Oval Office. At least that was the case most of the time. Like many diplomats, Bruce could also be fulsome and sometimes a touch overblown in his judgments. Describing the course of Anglo-American relations in the early 1960s, he reflected as follows:

> The President's confidence in the 5th Baron Harlech [Ormsby-Gore] was fully justified by the transcendent qualities and

unimpeachable character of Her Majesty's Ambassador. As
regards Mr. Macmillan, the frequency and frankness of their
exchanges had few modern parallels in diplomatic intercourse ... Concomitantly, I was kept meticulously informed
through the State Department and sometimes directly from
the White House, or the Prime Minister's office, of all transactions between these heads of Governments. Moreover, the
confidence reposed by the Prime Minister in his Secretary
of State for Foreign Affairs, Lord Home, and by President
Kennedy in his Secretary of State, Dean Rusk, and, as
respects the White House, in his National Security Advisor,
McGeorge Bundy, was such that the resultant team work was
exceptionally satisfactory.[84]

Selwyn Lloyd once remarked affectionately that he suspected
Bruce of having "somehow swallowed a dictionary."[85]

★　★　★

IN EARLY DECEMBER 1961, President Kennedy's list of daily
burdens included the increasing US presence in Vietnam and
elsewhere in Southeast Asia, the resumption of global nuclear
testing, the challenges posed by the Marxist regimes in Cuba and
East Germany, several other potential or actual ideological flash-
points around the world, and a domestic agenda that was coming
to be dominated by black complaints about ongoing racial bias
in American society. It was thus a testament both to Kennedy's
ability to simply switch off when the occasion arose and to his
particular affection for his British friends that he was able to go
directly from an "intense" White House meeting on civil rights
to hosting a laughter-filled dinner for the visiting duchess of
Devonshire. For the next few hours, it was almost as though it was
1938 again. "We sat in the gallery for drinks," "Debo" Devonshire
wrote in her memoirs, "and when dinner was announced, being
the only woman and a foreigner, I went without thinking to the

open door. On the threshold Jack threw out his arm and said, 'No, not you. I go first. I'm Head of State.' 'Good heavens,' I said, 'so you are,' and we sat down to dinner."[86] For all the cares of office, Kennedy was still the mixture of "schoolboy and statesman" his guest remembered. After dinner, Debo recalled that "he kicked off his shoes and shrieked with delight" at her tales of upper-crust British country life, including a recent visit made to the home of her "eccentric chum" Airmyne Harpur Crewe, whose own best friend was a goose. There was another gentle reminder of Kennedy's changed status in life when he and the duchess both left for New York a day or two later. Turning to Debo as their respective cars pulled up at the White House door, Jack kissed her goodbye and said, "I go presidential, you go commercial."[87]

Later that week Kennedy showed the extent to which national interest could be tempered by personal friendship when, at another private White House dinner, David Ormsby-Gore told him that the government in London remained in danger of falling because of the continuing Congo crisis and that to avoid this, Macmillan needed to put a stop once and for all to the threat of UN sanctions against the broadly pro-British Moise Tshombe and his army. Kennedy listened to Gore's summary of events, immediately picked up the telephone at his elbow, and once again "spoke plainly" to Adlai Stevenson along the lines noted. The result was to affect an overnight U-turn in existing US policy in the region. Although it could be argued that no vital American interest was involved (other than continued access to the Congo's vast mineral resources) and thus that he could afford to be generous, Kennedy was "wonderful," Gore later enthused. "He threw the full weight of his authority behind getting the results that Harold Macmillan required."[88]

Anglo-American summits usually end in agreement; momentum and mechanics alike drive them in that direction. In the weeks before their principals meet, scores of impeccably trained functionaries exchange agendas, talking points, and drafts of speeches. Areas of disagreement are identified and then arbitrated or discreetly dropped from consideration. The actual encounter between the heads of government is only the public, or symbolic, enactment of extensive private rehearsals. Preparation is the rule and freewheeling spontaneity the exception on such occasions.

So, on previous form, the meeting between Kennedy and Macmillan scheduled to begin on December 20, 1961, in Bermuda ought to have passed off without too many surprises. However, despite the meticulous planning, it was to be another case of what the PM called "Events, dear boy, events" when later coming to assess the extent to which the "smooth running of the affairs of state [had been] perturbed by circumstance."[89] The day before the president was due to fly to Bermuda on *Air Force One*, his seventy-three-year-old father suffered a stroke. Later that night, Joseph Kennedy's condition was severe enough for both his children and a priest to be summoned to his bedside in Palm Beach. On hearing the news, Macmillan immediately sent the president a "Dear Friend" wire, offering to change their meeting place to "Florida or Washington – or any other plan which might suit you." It was a magnanimous gesture by the PM, who shared the generally low opinion prevalent among Britons of his generation of the former US ambassador. Privately, Macmillan also thought it "not entirely regrettable" that Joe Kennedy would apparently "no longer serve as a one-man kitchen cabinet to his son the president," just at the moment when "issues of real concern to the United Kingdom's national security" were to be discussed.[90]

Although the ambassador's stroke left him partially paralyzed for the remaining eight years of his life, in the end the allies' conference went ahead as scheduled. On the one side were Macmillan, his foreign and defense ministers, two political advisers, a scientist, a detective, and a doctor; on the other, Kennedy with an entourage of 141. The governor of Bermuda, Major-General Sir Julian Gascoigne, was also on hand in his "somewhat antique" military uniform, cocked hat, and gold spurs to greet Kennedy's party. He would long remember the poignant sight of the president, who was again suffering from an acutely painful back, "bound[ing] around on the tarmac, like a puppy fresh off the leash, and then, a half-hour later, once out of view of the press, slowly shuffling up the stairs at Government House one step at a time."[91]

The list of contentious items awaiting discussion was headed by Laos, where the continuing "Phoumi versus Phouma" debate, pitting a moderately pro-American leader against a mildly pro-Russian one – if not without its comic-opera aspects, Macmillan felt – exposed a difference not only in opinion but also in style between the two Western leaders. Kennedy came to the table with a voluminous briefing book that Gascoigne only half-jokingly said reminded him of a "large metropolitan telephone directory, though without its variety." Supported by a team of eight officials at his side and with literally dozens more waiting in adjacent rooms with additional data, if required, the president, "quite different from the cavalier figure of myth," was instead "a grey-faced man, seemingly transfixed by details." Kennedy in turn yielded the floor to his forty-five-year-old secretary of defense, Robert McNamara, looking steely eyed and supremely rational behind his wire-rim glasses, his center-parted, crisp brown hair and brusque, staccato manner giving one observer the impression of "a human computing machine."[92] "Bob could always sit down to dinner with twenty other people, and three hours later, when the bill came, remember exactly who had the soup and who had the house salad," a colleague remembered.[93] To Gascoigne, it was all:

Slightly redolent of a clash of political culture, and the British establishment's acknowledged touch of 'amateurism.' The president and his team diligently read off all the facts and figures of recent border skirmishes in this inhospitable region [Laos], down to the precise strengths of individual man-militia units, and the length of available dirt airstrips … In general, the British civil service looked down, at least officially, on such calibrations, regarding them as 'academic' and

uninteresting to their political masters. Given the choice, it's
possible Kennedy might have preferred the more impromptu
approach.

When Kennedy later spoke directly to Macmillan, with only
their foreign ministers present, the two leaders quickly reached
agreement on the logistics of nuclear testing, even if deploring
the fact that they found themselves "sit[ting] in an ordinary
little room four days before Christmas discussing these terrible things," as the PM put it.[94] Their talks then touched on the
European Common Market and the broader issues of world
trade. "At this point, having no financial advisers to hinder me, I
tried to expound some of my ideas on global monetary reform,"
Macmillan confided. At least one party in the room wondered if
the president had used the opportunity of the lengthy recitation
that followed to discreetly take a nap, although the PM's self-confidence was unimpaired: "My remarks well received," he wrote.

The British foreign secretary, fifty-eight-year-old Alec
Home, whose misfortune it was in the television age to resemble
a prematurely hatched bird (his Adam's apple danced up and
down his narrow neck) later admitted to qualms about the way
the president had conducted himself in the first half of 1961. "I
confess I was disquieted," Home allowed, "when, instead of
giving himself time to play himself in, [Kennedy] launched into
a meeting with Mr. Khrushchev. He made a very bad mistake
from which it took many months to recover."[95] By the time they
met in Bermuda, Home had come to believe the president "was
fighting a significant interior battle." One part of him "agreed
with the British side about the obvious horrors of a nuclear
war"; the other part "openly spoke about never yielding to, if
not actively confronting, Mr. Khrushchev."[96] Kennedy, in turn,
was privately amused that a pre-war appeaser and the brother
of his slightly disreputable literary friend William Douglas-
Home had so thoroughly assumed that "thin film of superiority

separating himself and the rest of the world" that always seems to accompany the British foreign secretary.[97]

Although Kennedy's mind was clearly elsewhere during the Bermuda conference, Macmillan "felt the president and I [now] became even closer friends than before." Even in the privacy of his diary, he called Kennedy "courageous, amusing … and *very* sensitive. He seemed particularly pleased by the present which I brought him (a copy of the William and Mary ink stand on the Cabinet table) and by Debo Devonshire's gift (silver buttons – of the footmen's coats – with ducal coronets and crest)."[98] It would be difficult to immediately think of another foreign leader who might have been quite as taken as Kennedy was by these tokens of Britain's aristocratic heritage. The two men made no bones about their liking for each other. It was their fourth personal meeting within a year, which was three more than Kennedy had managed with any other head of government and considerably more of his undivided time than he gave to his cabinet in the White House. Macmillan appeared touchingly worried about the younger man's back, finding him a rocking chair to sit on and fussing over his health generally. Kennedy thanked his host for his concern and repeatedly assured him he was fine, although at one point in Bermuda he turned to the sixty-seven-year-old premier and mildly inquired if, like him, he agreed that regular sex was a great preventer of headaches.[99]

9

"WE ARE ATTEMPTING TO
PREVENT WORLD WAR THREE"

1962 WAS THE YEAR that would settle for all time the question of how far Kennedy's political appreciation of Great Britain and his personal affinity for Harold Macmillan and other British leaders would be willingly allowed to influence American state policy. The strengths – and even more, perhaps, the limitations – of the Special Relationship can only be fully understood against the background of the thirteen active days of the Cuban Missile Crisis that October, an event that brought the world closer to thermonuclear warfare than ever before or since. Historians will argue whether the British government played a material role in helping to save the planet as much as it served as a friendly sounding board for the president's decisions. Few of those who actually witnessed the inner workings of the Atlantic partnership at what Macmillan called this "quite stressful" time were left in any doubt on the subject. Robert Kennedy, who often took the lead in determining the US response to unfolding events, was just one of the high-placed officials to pay tribute to the British contribution to the final outcome. In his later account of the affair (published by the Macmillan firm in London), he noted that his brother had relied on the "good sense of the English people" for their "strength and friendship" at the critical hour, and that, but for this support, "our position would have been seriously undermined." Dean Rusk, not one generally to overpraise the British, thought that "in terms of mobilizing the unanimity of NATO," the Macmillan government's role had been "very important."[1] When the PM himself later wrote to congratulate David Ormsby-Gore on his performance as a de facto member of Kennedy's cabinet during the crisis, Gore replied, "The President has, I know, already told you how much he appreciated your support and advice during that critical week. In this, he was being deeply sincere, and he has repeatedly said the same thing to his closest friends, adding that he has no similar contacts with any other ally. He was furious with newspaper commentators who suggest that recent events indicate that there is little value for the US in the special Anglo-American relationship."[2]

Rather than treat Britain as a subsidiary, Kennedy went out of his way to consult Macmillan and his colleagues at each decisive stage of the missile crisis. The president called London nearly nightly (sometimes twice nightly) in the period 21–28 October, and communication was even more intense between the two sets of ministerial aides; McGeorge Bundy, Kennedy's national security adviser, spoke to Macmillan's foreign affairs secretary Philip de Zulueta five times on the afternoon of October 27 alone. Unlike other European leaders, Macmillan loyally supported the fundamental American position throughout, though with the self-confidence to occasionally offer what he called "friendly but corrective" advice.[3] An example of this came in the course of a hotline call Kennedy placed to Admiralty House on November 14, 1962, to discuss the continued presence of Russian aircraft and other munitions in Cuba. "We might get the [planes] out," the president began, "but [Khrushchev] wants us to withdraw the quarantine and the over-flights … The question is whether we should do that or take some other action. I think what I will do, prime minister, is to send you a message about what we propose to do in Cuba. I should be grateful for your judgment. I will send you a message tomorrow, and we could perhaps have a telephone conversation on Friday."

Macmillan responded, "I would be grateful. You must not give in to him."[4]

★   ★   ★

IRONICALLY, WHAT MACMILLAN called the "pivotal year" for the Anglo-American partnership began with an "at once ludicrous and yet profound" disagreement over formulating Western policy toward the small, densely forested South American state of British Guiana, for two centuries a "sphere of influence" – or colony, if you prefer – of the British crown, but in recent years showing increasing signs of impatience with these arrangements. Although only a subplot in the wider Cold War, it was an event that significantly strained the Atlantic alliance. It's also notable that the only serious ideological falling-out between the US and UK governments that occurred when John Kennedy was president was one that arose as a residue from colonialism, not as an aspect of the East-West struggle.

The problem essentially began in October 1961, when Kennedy agreed to receive British Guiana's new prime minister, the communist-leaning Cheddi Jagan, in the White House. As a result of this meeting, the president offered his guest a $5 million aid package, a gift that was then abruptly withdrawn when Jagan unwisely chose to criticize the United States in a live television interview before the money was safely in the bank. Under the Atlantic Charter of 1941, the Western Allies had guaranteed "the right of all peoples to choose the form of Government under which they will live." But the Americans made an exception to this rule when threatened with the installation of another Castro-like regime in the Western Hemisphere. Dean Rusk went on to send the British a possibly intemperate note on the subject. "I must tell you," it began, "that it is not possible for us to put up with an independent British Guiana under Jagan.

The American public and congressional opinion would not tolerate it." The London government, he suggested, in something of a volte-face of previously stated US policy, had a "moral obligation" not to surrender possession of their overseas territory but actually to extend and strengthen it. Macmillan thought the note "pure Machiavellianism," wondering if perhaps Rusk was drunk when he wrote it. His foreign secretary Lord Home, abandoning his normal air of scholarly diffidence when dealing with his American peer, wrote to ask him, "You say that it is not possible for you 'to put up with an independent Guiana under Jagan.' How would you suggest that this can be done in a democracy?"[5]

Kennedy became more acutely aware of the problem when, in February 1962, he entertained the Conservative MP Hugh Fraser – one of his fellow adolescent carousers in London a quarter of a century earlier and now Britain's undersecretary of state for the colonies – at a private White House dinner. It was another occasion that showed the extent to which the rigid confines of national policy could be modified by personal friendship.

"You're trying to ask us to remain [in British Guiana] forever, which means keeping four or five battalions, maybe, in the place," Fraser briskly told his host. "This isn't on. You must see … fundamentally, Guiana is a mudbank, and really hasn't any contact with the rest of Latin America. It's surrounded by forests and mountains with no natural communications, except by air, and after all, Moscow's got good communications by air with Latin America. And I think we're going."[6]

While the allies continued to debate the future political arrangements of what Fraser called a "cricket-playing sugar colony of some 500,000 souls" (in May 1966 to become the new nation of Guyana), David Ormsby-Gore arrived to take up his duties as British ambassador in Washington. At the formal White House ceremony to present his credentials, Gore read out from a scroll beginning, "Elizabeth the Second, by the Grace of God of the United Kingdom of Great Britain and Northern Ireland

and of her other Realms, Queen, Head of the Commonwealth, Defender of the Faith, to the President of the United States of America Sendeth Greeting!" At length, he went on to express his own confidence that the Atlantic alliance would "flourish and prosper so long, in the words of Sir Winston Churchill, as we have 'faith in each other's purpose, hope in each other's future and charity towards each other's shortcomings.'"[7] Kennedy and Gore smiled broadly at one another at the conclusion of these sentiments. Selwyn Lloyd thought it a case of "a private joke enshrined in state policy."

"Dear Jack," Gore wrote the president on July 24, 1962, proving again that he enjoyed a level of intimacy with Kennedy unlike the more staid relations between other heads of government and foreign officers. "Thank you for the immensely enjoyable week-end at Hyannis Port. I do not know which was the more pleasurable, the brisk and invigorating Saturday or the warm lazy Sunday. There is no doubt that toying with the instinct of fear adds spice to life, and that is why one pretends [to be] smiling in a boat that may at any time tip over, [as] opposed to one that is relatively stable" – a metaphor, surely, for events to come. At times it almost seemed as if Gore was Kennedy's ambassador to Macmillan, rather than the other way around. After remarking that he was soon to visit London, he concluded his letter by telling the president, "It would be an immense help if I could come and have a talk with you sometime before I leave. The PM seems to be brooding over the world economic situation and may come up with some, I hope, bright ideas quite soon."[8]

★ ★ ★

IN ADDITION to being a shrewd political strategist, Kennedy was an acute political historian. *The Young Melbourne*, which he reread on roughly an annual basis, would have provided him with plenty of uplifting material with which to nourish his passion for the great issues that had shaped European and American democracy. It also supplied him with the template of a more distinctively English attitude to public service, at least as it existed in Melbourne's heyday in the early to middle years of the nineteenth century. This approach combined in one individual the "skills, propensities [and] virtues that [had] made the nation excel in peace and at war," he noted, along with a generous degree of personal license. Illustrating this latter point, the book quotes a letter written by Melbourne's colleague Lord Carlisle, a Tory-turned-Whig politician who achieved little in his role as Britain's first commissioner of Woods, Forests and Land Revenues, but who managed to father at least two dozen children with a variety of women. "I was afraid I was going to have the gout the other day," Carlisle remarks. "I believe I live too chaste: it is not a common fault with me." In 1836, Melbourne himself achieved the rare distinction of being sued while serving as prime minister by the aggrieved husband of one of his numerous mistresses. He survived the scandal, although as the historian Boyd Hilton remarks, "It is irrefutable that Melbourne's personal life was problematic. Spanking sessions with aristocratic ladies were harmless, not so the whippings administered to orphan girls taken into his household as objects of charity."[9]

Libidinous as they were, even Melbourne and his circle might have saluted the compulsive intensity of Kennedy's sex life (which, it should be stressed, showed no known predilection for corporal punishment). Nineteen-year-old Mimi Beardsley, a White House intern, was only one of those to enjoy a brief tenure as the designated presidential partner. In December 1962, Beardsley flew to Nassau as part of Kennedy's entourage during the latest Anglo-American heads of government conference and was later spotted crouching in the president's limousine while her boss concluded his talks with Harold Macmillan. Although officially described as a press-office secretary, Beardsley's employment conditions were not very demanding. She "had no skills," Pierre Salinger's aide Barbara Gamarekian recalled. "She couldn't type."[10] While Jacqueline Kennedy remained in Washington, the president was attended by Beardsley and as many as three other young women during his seventy-two hours in the Bahamas. "It was like the Rolling Stones on tour," a British official later said.[11] The drama critic Kenneth Tynan believed that Kennedy had also found the time earlier in 1962 to enjoy a brief White House tryst with the screen siren Marlene Dietrich. "I hope you aren't in a hurry," the president allegedly remarked on finding himself alone with the sixty-year-old actress. According to Tynan, Dietrich replied that, in fact, she was in a hurry, as "2,000 Jews were waiting to give her a plaque at 7pm, and it was now 6.30." As she left his bed fifteen minutes later, Dietrich said Kennedy asked her "just one thing … 'Did you ever make it with my father?' She assured him she hadn't. 'Well,' Kennedy replied, 'that's one place I'm in first.'"[12]

If all Kennedy's hectic womanizing was in some way an homage to the likes of Melbourne and Carlisle, and his impression that such men routinely conducted affairs of state before repairing to "protracted banquets [where] naked girls emerged from silver dishes" (as *Time* magazine summarized the plot of *The Young Melbourne*), it seems not to have found favor with Harold Macmillan, who later reflected bitterly on how much better an eventual nuclear test-ban treaty with the Soviet Union might have been but for the president's "weakness." "I mean weakened by constantly having all those girls, every day," the retired British premier told his biographer Alistair Horne. "He was weak in pressing the Russians for seven inspections instead of three. If we could have had that, it would have eventually led to no testing in the air at all … I feel this is a great opportunity that we missed, and I do blame Kennedy's weakness."[13]

★ ★ ★

APRIL 1962 SHOWED the Special Relationship at work on a number of levels, nurtured by the common ideal of international nuclear disarmament as well as the president's personal fondness for the more rakish members of the British ruling class. Early in a month already crowded with pressing official engagements, he found the time to successively host David Ormsby-Gore, William Douglas-Home, and his friend the duchess of Devonshire at the White House. A more strategic demonstration of the Atlantic alliance followed on April 9, when a joint Anglo-American communiqué on nuclear testing was handed to the Soviet government. The message broke down along national lines, with an emollient British first half and a harsher US warning in the tail. After expressing the hope that the Russians might yet accept the principle of independent verification, the cable added that, were this not possible, the Western allies would conclude that the current test-ban negotiations were at an end and thus that the Christmas Island detonations "scheduled for the latter part of this month will have to go forward." They did.

Macmillan himself followed, with an official visit to the man he now called his "great American friend" from April 26 to 28, 1962. In Washington, Kennedy pulled out all the ceremonial stops, with a marine guard of honor, effusive welcoming speeches, and a helicopter ride for Macmillan and himself back to the White House. A mark of the personal warmth of the alliance was that the First Lady then flew home from her extended Easter break in Palm Beach to join the two heads of government at a state dinner in the British Embassy. Jackie remarked of a subsequent White House lunch that she had "never seen Jack so relaxed outside his own family circle." The formal talks, which, in an unusual gesture, took place largely around the president's Cabinet Room table, were equally cordial, if offering little new on the issues. Macmillan again held forth on the twin perils of a faltering global economy and the "rogue elephant" of nuclear proliferation, before touching specifically on Cuba and Berlin, and concluding his remarks, a US observer recalled, "by giving a wolfish smirk … bar[ing] his teeth in a rather ingratiating way, apparently intended to underline the aptness or wit of his words."[14]

In the second session of talks, Kennedy delivered a speech that spoke in general terms about Laos and Vietnam and barely mentioned nuclear arms at all. "There is a marked difference between the President 'in action' on a specific problem ... and his attitude to larger issues," Macmillan had recently confided in his diary. "In the first, he is an extraordinarily quick and effective operator – a born 'politician' (not in a pejorative sense). On the wider issues, he seems rather lost."[15]

In other business, Macmillan told his host that he did not see any "present communist threat to British Guiana," and Kennedy replied that, nonetheless, the United States intended to pursue "a policy of getting rid of Jagan." Following that, words were exchanged on the subject of Britain's possible entry into the European Common Market. The president was guardedly enthusiastic, although worried that such a move might "accentuate the us balance of payments problem, severely affect agriculture, and could cause withdrawal of us forces from around the world."[16] This was the signal for Macmillan to begin coughing violently. After a short delay, Kennedy turned over the meeting to his undersecretary of state George Ball, who undid some of the goodwill engendered the previous year in Washington by lecturing the British on their historic responsibilities to the United States. As Macmillan listened, his facial expression passed from "polite and attentive, to quizzical and uncertain, to annoyed and enraged, with a rapidly rising flush to his cheeks."[17] The premier later wrote in his diary that he partly blamed Kennedy for allowing "Mr. Ball ... to go on with his intrigues against us in Europe and the Common Market negotiations."[18]

Macmillan cabled the president on May 25, 1962:

Dear Friend
I write once again to send you my best wishes on your birthday. [He was four days early.] Looking back on the past year, you must, I think, feel considerable satisfaction. Both in the

international field and, so far as I can judge, at home also, you have made a lot of progress in getting your policies accepted and respected. Of course, nothing is ever perfect, particularly in the eyes of the newspaper columnists. But from a rather long experience, I have found that when things are really bad the newspapers shut up, and when the chorus gets going it is a very good sign."[19]

Kennedy's forty-fifth birthday did not go unnoticed elsewhere in British circles. Eighty-seven-year-old Winston Churchill, mentally frail but still an MP, cabled his effusive best wishes for the occasion and received a wire by return: "I am especially grateful for your birthday greetings, Sir, in view of the high admiration for you which I have in common with free people everywhere."[20] The president even rated a two-page handwritten letter from the queen. "I have seen my prime minister," she confided, "and he has told me how much he value[s] the chance to speak to you personally ... It is a great comfort to me to know that you and he are so close, and that you have confidence in each other's judgement and advice." After some more in this vein, the queen mentioned in closing that her husband would soon have the honor of visiting the Seattle World's Fair, where his highness went on to narrowly miss Elvis Presley. "I envy him the chance of being in the United States again. We have had two such happy trips there," she concluded. "Your sincere Friend, Elizabeth R."[21]

Less than three months later, Macmillan sent the president a very different cable. Returning from an "exhausting" August afternoon's grouse shoot at one of his wife's country estates, the PM was handed a telegram from the US Embassy in London. In what must have seemed to him further proof of American diplomatic chutzpah, it apparently announced that the Pentagon was about to supply a consignment of "Hawk" strategic missiles to Israel, so reneging on a previous agreement between the Atlantic allies. As we've seen, Macmillan's promptly cabled response gave full rein to the emotional and impulsive side of his character. "I have just received the information [about the missiles]," he began, "and that the decision will be conveyed to the Israelis tomorrow … Dean Rusk gave a most categorical assurance to David Gore your Government would consult us … To be informed on Saturday afternoon that your Government are going to make an offer to supply on Sunday is really not consultation." Macmillan concluded by expressing his "disgust and despair" at the treachery of the US administration. "I [do not] see how you and I are to personally conduct the great affairs of the world on this basis," he added.[22]

Of course, it was all a misunderstanding. Macmillan soon realized that he had misread the original cable, which spoke ambiguously only of the Americans considering their options on Israel, and he went back to his office on Monday morning suffering from an acute ideological hangover. "My Dear Friend," his contrite letter to Kennedy began. "Since I sent my indignant message to you, Lord Hood [Gore's deputy in Washington] has telegraphed to put a different complexion on this affair … This is just to tell you how glad I am that my serious concern was all based upon a muddle … With warm regard. As ever, Harold Macmillan."[23]

Macmillan never forgot a slight, worked himself up into such a state before delivering his apparently semi-improvised and airily free-associating speeches that he was sometimes physically ill, and thought little of breaking down in tears in front of colleagues. As Alistair Horne writes, "Underneath the sharp wit and the love of 'fun' was a great gulf – especially in later years – of loneliness [and] melancholia."[24] Kennedy, by contrast, maintained his air of carefully controlled sangfroid even in what he called the "quite tricky" circumstances that marked the overnight arrival in August 1961 of the Berlin Wall or the discovery of the Cuban missile emplacements fourteen months later. Whether by training or instinct, he could often appear to be more "British," if that conveys a sense of ironic detachment from events, than the quintessential Englishman Macmillan.

Robin Douglas-Home, a jazz-playing Scottish laird (and the nephew of Britain's foreign secretary) happened to be a guest at the White House in the last week of October 1962. On the night of the 25th, amid the continuing flurry of threats and counterthreats of mutual annihilation flying between Washington and Moscow, Douglas-Home remembered Kennedy, puffing on a Cuban cigar, chatting "about such diverse subjects as Lord Beaverbrook's way of running his newspapers, Frank Sinatra's handling of women, and why *Queen* magazine had published a fashion picture of a nude model lying on a bearskin rug sucking her thumb."[25] As Home admiringly noted, the president's preferred technique for coping with the pressure of events was to retreat into himself, sometimes accompanied by a good book, sometimes by a few friends who shared his ability to speak, half in earnest, half in jest, about issues that ran the gamut from "sexual gossip up to the end of the world – and always with the lightest of touches."[26] Although known to salt his language with intensifiers reminiscent of his navy days, it seems fair to say that Kennedy was generally self-possessed, and that in the normal course of events he would have been unlikely to put his name to the sort of "disgust and despair" cable Macmillan fired off at him in August 1962.

★　★　★

DRAWING ON A CIGAR after dinner in his cottage at the Kennedys' Hyannis Port estate on Saturday, July 21, the president told those present – who included David Ormsby-Gore, the "first friend" Lem Billings, and astronaut John Glenn – that he wanted to do something "big" to improve the state of East-West relations.[27] For that matter, he added, the Anglo-American alliance itself "could be better presented" than was currently the case. There had been one or two "regrettable lapses" in the three months since Prime Minister Macmillan had visited him so enjoyably in Washington. Although Kennedy tactfully avoided mentioning it, he may have been thinking of the recent remarks by his secretary of defense, Robert McNamara, in his commencement address at the University of Michigan. McNamara, never Britain's favorite ally, had taken the opportunity to announce that all non-American nuclear weapons in Western possession were "dangerous, expensive, prone to obsolescence, and lacking in credibility as a deterrent."[28] On hearing this, Macmillan himself went ballistic. McNamara's "foolish speech" had "enraged [the Europeans]," he wrote. "In NATO, all the allies are angry with the American proposal that we should buy rockets to the tune of umpteen million dollars, the warheads to be under American control ... It is a racket."

There was an added poignancy to the sight of Kennedy casually discussing the state of the Special Relationship over dinner that July with his friend the British ambassador, because the president's wheelchair-bound father, once a man of such pronounced views on the subject, sat silently to one side of the room. Robbed by his stroke of the power to speak, the former ambassador to London could communicate only by a series of nods and grunts, although, if sufficiently moved, he signaled by stamping his foot to register either spirited agreement or, more often, violent dissent to the consensus opinion.[29]

★　★　★

NOT LONG BEFORE Kennedy's dinner with Ormsby-Gore, senior allied and NATO chiefs had met in Athens to review the future control and uses of the West's nuclear stockpile. Marked "Cosmic Top Secret," the minutes of the meeting reveal just how much the United States and United Kingdom relied on intercontinental rockets rather than conventional weapons. "The Soviet Union," Dean Rusk remarked, "should be certain that the alliance would not use nuclear bombs for trivial reasons, but *would* use them to defend vital interests … His country hoped that the cohesion of the Alliance would be further enhanced by President Kennedy's commitment to consult in the Council prior to the use of nuclear assets anywhere in the world" – "if time permitted," Rusk added. Harold Watkinson, Britain's defense minister, went on to note that he "particularly welcomed the commitment to NATO of Polaris submarines, [which] represented an immense gain to the Alliance … He pointed out that over-reliance on conventional weapons might be interpreted by the Soviet Union as a sign of unwillingness on the part of the West to use ones [of] mass destruction."[30] What neither Watkinson nor Rusk knew as they sat discussing the theoretical use of nuclear arms was that the USSR Central Presidium was also in secret session that week in Moscow and that, with Khrushchev's enthusiastic support, they unanimously endorsed a resolution "to deploy a group of assets on the island of Cuba consisting of all types of Soviet Armed Forces."[31]

In a keynote address in Philadelphia on the anniversary of the signing of the Declaration of Independence, Kennedy, also ignorant of Soviet designs, went on to explain that he saw a strong Atlantic alliance as "part of destiny." "We do not regard a united Europe as a rival but as a partner," he announced, an advance on his private remarks to Macmillan of just two months earlier. "To aid its progress has been the basic object of our foreign policy for seventeen years." Kennedy ended with a rhetorical flourish: "I say here and now, on this Day of Independence, that the United States will be ready for a Declaration of Interdependence, that we will be prepared to discuss with a United Europe the ways and means of forming a concrete Atlantic partnership, a mutually beneficial partnership between the new union now emerging in Europe and the old union founded here."[32] This same formula of a wise American superstate seeking to defend and sometimes to dictate the interests of the fragile, ancient democracies has been a staple fact of the Special Relationship ever since.

★ ★ ★

THE RESULTS OF Kennedy's long-running personal empathy for Britain and British political history were seen elsewhere that summer of 1962. "Dear Jack," Richard Cushing, archbishop of Boston, wrote on August 2:

> Pardon the familiarity, but I prefer it to the formal title of 'Mr. President' because of my affection for you and yours ... I write to acknowledge receipt of the gift of $7,662.77 that Tom O'Hearn presented to me representing the sales of WHY ENGLAND SLEPT. The check was made payable to Nazareth, Inc, our great child caring institution that serves every year over a thousand temporarily and permanently homeless children. It is the greatest institution of its kind in the east, but it has a monthly deficit of over $15,000 which I am glad to finance. You have lightened my burden by your princely check."[33]

As well as the satisfaction of contributing to a worthy cause, Kennedy would have been well aware that his precocious cautionary tale of British inertia when faced with a megalomaniacal tyrant in the 1930s resonated with the increasingly strained East-West relationship of thirty years later. As he wrote at the time, warning that it was necessary to first acknowledge the prospect of a war in order to subsequently win it, "A boxer cannot work himself into proper psychological and physical condition for a fight that he seriously believes will never come off."[34]

★   ★   ★

LIKE THE BERLIN CRISIS (as opposed to the Berlin Wall) before it, the construction of offensive missile bases in Cuba did not catch the West completely by surprise. The drama that brought the world closer to nuclear conflict than before or since did not begin with the US reconnaissance flight of Sunday, October 14, 1962, which produced 928 photographs of the weapons, nor did it begin when the evidence itself was brought to President Kennedy's

White House bedroom with his breakfast tray on the morning of the 16th. It had been building all summer, and the CIA had been fielding reports from operatives on the ground for several weeks before the first confirmed sighting of a missile convoy rumbling toward the coast of Cuba on September 21. Along with the briefings of his national security team, Kennedy had also received advance intelligence on the subject from Colonel Oleg Penkovsky, the deputy head of Soviet military planning who served as a double agent under the code name "Ironbark." Equipped with a Minox pocket camera and an apparently burning conviction that he must "tell people in the West what conditions in the USSR are really like," he would eventually hand over some ten thousand pages of classified data on Soviet rocket emplacements. A CIA station chief named Hugh Montgomery later recalled how he had arranged for Penkovsky to be one of the Russian officials invited to a July 4, 1962, party at the US ambassador's residence in Moscow. Penkovsky placed photos of top-secret Cuba documents in a sealed polythene bag hidden in the bathroom, where, with some difficulty, Montgomery was able to retrieve them from the toilet cistern. All the files circulated to the president and his advisers during the thirteen days of the active crisis bear the name Ironbark, indicating that they made use of that source. Penkovsky himself was arrested by the KGB on October 22, 1962, the day on which Kennedy publicly revealed the existence of the missiles in Cuba, and was executed by means of a bullet to the head the following May.[35] Along with US Air Force Major Rudolf Anderson, who was shot down and killed while on an aerial reconnaissance mission over Cuba, he was one of the two human casualties of the crisis.[36]

The excited and at times chaotic atmosphere that characterized foreign affairs in general that month already enjoys a wide literature. As just one individual subplot of the worldwide drama, there was the moment when the venerable former US secretary of state Dean Acheson, aged sixty-nine, was summoned from his Maryland farm at eight o'clock on Sunday morning and

told to be ready to take off for Paris two hours later in order
to brief the French government on the crisis. The banks were
closed, and he had to borrow $60 from his secretary. Acheson's
air force jet touched down for a fueling stop at ten that night,
local time, at Greenham Common, fifty miles west of London,
where it was raining heavily. David Bruce went out to meet the
plane. Acheson gave him a set of classified U-2 photographs
to present to Harold Macmillan, and Bruce in turn handed
Acheson a hip flask of scotch that he had thoughtfully brought
with him. Watching the two gray-suited diplomats silently conduct their exchange by the dim light of an airfield hut, a British
MI5 officer was reminded of "one of those classic espionage
swaps somewhere in the alleys of Berlin."[37] The presence of several heavily armed US Marines and Secret Service personnel only
added to the melodrama of the occasion. Before taking his leave,
the normally staid, sixty-four-year-old ambassador whispered
to Acheson, "Put your hand in my pocket." Acheson did so and
found that it contained a revolver. Bruce explained that he had
been issued it earlier in the evening by the security officer at the
American Embassy and told to keep it on him at all times for
the foreseeable future. Some "uneasy laughter" had followed,
Acheson remembered.[38] It is not known if Bruce was "pack-
ing heat" when he arrived at Admiralty House by appointment
early the next morning to confer with Macmillan.

For our purposes, the primary question to be answered about
Cuba is whether Kennedy's personal affinity for Macmillan
and other British men of affairs had any major impact on the
outcome of the crisis. Was the PM's role "passive" and "supine,"
further crushing proof that the UK, with an arsenal of Soviet
nuclear missiles aimed at it, had become "a wholly owned subsidiary [of] American interests," as Labour leader Hugh Gaitskell
claimed in the House of Commons? Or were some of the most
persuasive voices in Kennedy's ear that fateful week those with
a British accent? As far as the Special Relationship went, it has
to be immediately noted that the president said nothing direct

to the prime minister about the missiles in Cuba for five days after he had learned of them. Sidney Graybeal, a CIA expert on aerial photography, remembered that at the first White House meeting of the Executive Committee, or ExComm, of the president's National Security Council, the door of the Cabinet Room "suddenly burst open, and [four-year-old] Caroline Kennedy came in, and said, 'Daddy, Daddy, they won't let my friend in.' The President got up, went over, put his arm around her, took her out of the room, came back within a minute and said, 'Gentlemen, I think we should proceed.'" For that brief moment, Kennedy's young daughter had commanded more of ExComm's undivided attention than Macmillan or any of America's other allies thus far.[39]

Kennedy later referred to his "luck" in being able to draw on the lessons of recent British history when dealing with the Soviet Union. Others might call it diligence. On October 22, speaking to the American people about the missile crisis for the first time, the president again drew on the parallels to Munich. "The 1930s taught us [that] aggressive conduct, if allowed to grow unchecked and unchallenged, ultimately leads to war."[40] But Kennedy tempered this hard truth with other important lessons from the British experience. War was not only physically destructive, it often brought dislocating social change in its wake, as witnessed by the United Kingdom's "cataclysmic" general election of July 1945. There was much talk of mobilization and pre-emptive strikes that week around the White House Cabinet Room's coffin-shaped table, but little of it happened. It's possible that Kennedy feared the political aftermath of even a limited armed exchange more than he feared the hostilities themselves.

A significant theme running throughout the events of October 1962 was the president's repeated insistence on bringing diplomatic pressure to bear prior to any attack on Cuba – a position that not only put him increasingly at odds with his joint chiefs of staff but also the generally more placid figure of Dean

Rusk, the secretary of state. The Soviets had turned Cuba into "a powerful military problem" for the United States, Rusk told an October 18 meeting of ExComm, and a failure to strike now would "undermine our alliances all over the world."[41] Kennedy's more nuanced approach, which involved assembling a massive ground force of some 140,000 troops for a possible invasion of Cuba, while pursuing negotiations both through the UN and several other channels, official and unofficial, was undoubtedly taken first and foremost in the American national interest as he saw it. But it also owed something to the historical British model. As Arthur Schlesinger later wrote of the period, "Kennedy never tired of quoting Winston Churchill: 'We arm to parley.'"[42]

★ ★ ★

HAROLD MACMILLAN was working alone in his study at Admiralty House at around ten o'clock on Sunday night, October 21, when the duty clerk appeared with an "eyes only" teletype from Kennedy. A mark of its gravity was its use of the formal salutation. "Dear Prime Minister" it began, "I am sending you this most private message to give you advance warning of a most serious situation, and of my plan to meet it. I am arranging to have David Bruce report to you more fully tomorrow morning, but I want you to have this message tonight so that you may have as much time as possible to consider the dangers we will now have to face together."[43] After reading the clipped, 250-word account of the looming crisis in which "I have found it absolutely essential ... to make my first decision on my own responsibility, but from now on I expect that we can and should be in the closest touch," Macmillan replied with a "Dear Friend" cable just an hour later. "I am most grateful for your private message," he told Kennedy. "Naturally I am thinking about you and all your problems at this difficult time." The PM's emollient tone slipped only when he came to record the scene in his diary on the morning of the 22nd. "The first day of the world crisis!" he wrote.[44]

It was also the start of a period of unusually close collaboration between the heads of the British and American governments. Fifteen minutes after finishing his speech revealing the existence of the Soviet weapons in Cuba, Kennedy took the elevator down to the newly created Situation Room in the basement of the White House West Wing and picked up the hotline to Macmillan. It was the first of a dozen such calls he placed over the course of the next week, which often took place late at night, London time. The president was generally at his most alert (sometimes further stimulated by Dr. Jacobson's amphetamines) just as the sixty-eight-year-old premier was preparing to go to bed with a favorite volume of Jane Austen. Their first conversation reads almost like a continuation of Kennedy's scripted address to the nation. He spoke torrentially, while Macmillan limited himself to the occasional soothing platitude. At one point, the president remarked that "we are attempting to begin [our response] in a way to prevent World War Three," and the PM agreed that this was prudent. Macmillan later wrote in his diary that Kennedy "seemed rather excited, but very clear ... He was grateful for my messages and [our] help. He could not tell what Khrushchev would do. He is building up his forces for a *coup de main* to seize Cuba should that become necessary."[45]

The informal exchanges between Kennedy in his large, dimly lit underground bunker, furnished with satellite maps and futuristic steel chairs, and Macmillan, in his modest, book-lined upstairs den in Admiralty House, with a view across the London rooftops to the dome of St. Paul's Cathedral, continued throughout that week, in which ordinary Americans and Britons braced themselves for the possibility of a thermonuclear war. It's often been pointed out that the president was informing the premier rather than actively consulting him during most of these calls and, for that matter, that Britain acted not as a fully equal strategic partner but as "another arm of our defense forces," as Kennedy himself had said of it in the febrile atmosphere of December 1940.[46] But, in the opinion of Robert Kennedy among others, the president was doing more than merely extending a courtesy to an old and valued ally. "He needed to unburden himself and to listen" said Bobby, "to the man he'd come to privately know as 'Uncle Harold.'"[47]

Other than the attorney general himself, none of the other members of ExComm were aware of the regular transatlantic conversations, and Kennedy refrained from making any similar person-to-person calls to other allied heads of government. There was almost something of an illicit romance about the late-night exchanges of confidence. Nor was it Macmillan's role merely to grunt affirmatively to each of the president's proposals. On the evening of October 23, the premier pointedly asked if Kennedy was now "going to occupy Cuba and have done with it, or is it going to drag on?" The president admitted, "We are preparing a potential for that kind of action [if] necessary." Macmillan then wanted to know, "Is your blockade going to extend beyond the military and arms into things like oil and all the rest of it, in order to bring down the Castro government?" He later privately remarked that there seemed to him "something quite startling, perhaps even unique, about the comprehensiveness of the us government's blindness" when it came to the political future of a militarily conquered Cuba. Kennedy replied, "At the beginning we're going to confine ourselves to offensive weapons of war in order not to give [Khrushchev] cause [to retaliate in] Berlin."[48] During the week, Macmillan also took the opportunity to gently remind the president that "if you live on Vesuvius, you don't bother much about eruptions" – meaning that the British had long since learned to live with the reality of Soviet rockets being pointed at them – and successfully argued that the U-2 photographs of the missiles in Cuba should be published, contrary to the advice of the president's own chiefs of staff. "No one will believe this unless they see them," he said.[49]

There was another significant symbol of British influence that week when the US Strategic Air Command was ordered, for the first time in its existence, to move to Defcon 2, or "Code Red," and B-52s armed with hydrogen bombs circled continually over the Norwegian Sea, ready to move on the commander-in-chief's order to their preassigned targets in the Soviet Union. This was Kennedy's friend David Ormsby-Gore, notionally still the representative of a foreign power, but who acted throughout as a seated member of the US National Security Council, with unfettered access to the president and attorney general, and who arguably made a more tangible contribution to the outcome of the crisis than the likes of Dean Rusk or any other accredited member of the US government as a result. Given what was at stake for the world that week, it's worth repeating that this unprecedented working relationship between the American president and the British ambassador had been forged on the high-spirited round of English country-house weekends and morally dubious London bottle parties where the two young men had bonded some twenty years earlier.

Kennedy, then, may not have consulted Harold Macmillan for the first five days of the thirteen-day Cuban standoff – yet, in one sense, he was extraordinarily receptive to British counsel. Shortly before noon on Sunday, the 21st, the Ormsby-Gores arrived at the White House for a previously scheduled family lunch. After the meal, Kennedy took the ambassador aside and laid out his basic alternatives in Cuba as he saw them: "bomb the hell" out of the rocket sites, or impose a restrictive quarantine around the island and appeal to the United Nations. It was the essential dilemma of all postwar American foreign policy crises. "What would *you* do?" Kennedy then asked.

Although Gore, unlike the president's own cabinet, had previously seen the U-2 spy photographs, Kennedy's direct question forced him to improvise. Thinking well ahead of events, he replied that he saw "very serious drawbacks in the first course of action ... Very few people outside the United States would consider the provocation offered by the Cubans serious enough to merit an American attack ... I thought a bombing would not be understood in the rest of the world, and that some form of blockade was probably the right answer."[50] Kennedy then revealed that he had reached the same conclusion. This wasn't the first time that week that the president had confided in the ambassador before he did in any other head of government, let alone the American people. The First Lady would remember having learned of the crisis two days earlier, while entertaining the maharajah of Jaipur at a White House reception and finding "upstairs, David and Jack squatting on the floor, looking at the missile pictures."[51]

On October 23, the eve of the Cuban blockade going into effect, Ormsby-Gore was back at the White House for dinner. It sometimes seems surprising to learn that the British ambassador ever ate anywhere else during that week. Afterwards, Gore went upstairs into a little-used family office where the Kennedy brothers and he spoke further over brandy and cigars. The president wanted to know what he could do to spin public opinion in Western Europe, and Gore reiterated Macmillan's advice about releasing a selection of the U-2 photographs so that the evidence would be there for everyone to see in the newspapers. No one in the us government had previously considered this idea, and Kennedy had hesitated when Uncle Harold had first suggested it. His friend's intervention now proved decisive. "He quite understood," Gore wired Macmillan overnight, "and after he had sent for a batch of photographs, he gave instructions as to which of them should be published, and he emphasized the importance of clear explanatory notes being attached to them." Gore then went on to propose that, to give the Russians the maximum time to consider their position, the line of interception around Cuba should be reduced from eight hundred to five hundred miles – a concession the Kennedys immediately agreed to and that ExComm ratified at its meeting early the next morning.[52]

On the surface, Kennedy was completely focused that week on the twin problems of preventing the Russians from reinforcing their missiles in Cuba and then of removing the sites altogether without a full-scale war. But in the midst of the crisis, he still displayed his peerless ability to simply switch off from the pressure of events. To recreate the prevailing atmosphere in the private quarters of the White House late that October is seemingly to look through the pinhole of a souvenir charm at a Gilbert and Sullivan farce treating boisterously of English country-house life, with some vast and yet faintly ludicrous international calamity looming as a backdrop. As we've seen, thirty-year-old Robin Douglas-Home was a guest of the first family that particular week. On the same day as the US and Soviet representatives clashed furiously in the UN, Home remembered a "wonderfully relaxed" president who made no mention of the missiles, although at one point he compared negotiating with the Russians in general as "like trying to talk to people who've spent all their lives in a cellar." After an evening of studied gaiety, Kennedy then went to bed around 10:00 p.m., later returning in his monogrammed bathrobe to wish his houseguest good night.[53]

Undeterred by the prospect of global annihilation, the duchess of Devonshire was also in town that week for the opening of an exhibition of drawings on loan from Chatsworth House to the Washington National Gallery. On October 21, the night before his address to the American people about the crisis in Cuba, Kennedy gave "Debo" and some other British friends dinner in the White House. "He was his usual self, showing no outward signs of the strain he must have felt," she later said. "In the room where we met for drinks before dinner, photographs of the now infamous missiles were lying on a table and were being picked up and put down by Jack's guests as though they were holiday snaps." Three nights later, as the crisis intensified, Kennedy invited Debo back for a nostalgic chat "about the old days, about his sisters Kick and Eunice, and the girls he had met twenty-four years before. He asked about the home life of various politicians, including [former British minister for the colonies, and devout imperialist] 'Bobbety' Salisbury." At one point the duchess described how Vice President Johnson had tried to upstage Princess Margaret at the recent independence celebrations in Jamaica, "and told Jack that Hugh Fraser had been at the head of our delegation. 'Not *our* Hugh Fraser?' he said. 'Yes, of course it was our Hugh Fraser,' I replied. He roared with laughter at the idea."[54]

Shortly after 11:00 p.m. London time on October 24, an hour at which Macmillan had been known to be turning in with his cocoa and Jane Austen, Kennedy called again on the hotline. As the transcript of the conversation makes clear, the president was seeking advice as well as mere affirmation:

> MACMILLAN: Well, I'm all right. What's the news now?
> KENNEDY: Well, we have no more word yet on what's going to happen out there. As you have probably heard, some of the ships, the ones we're particularly interested in, have turned around – others are going on.... .
> MACMILLAN: You don't really know whether they're going back, or whether they're going to try and make it, do you?
> KENNEDY: Some of the ships that have turned back are the ones that we were most interested in, and which we think would have given us some material. Others are continuing ... I don't know whether we are going to be permitted to search them. That's still in question.

Also in doubt, Kennedy admitted, was what action he might take to remove the rockets already in Cuba.

"We're going to have to make the judgment as to whether we're going to invade Cuba, taking our chances, or whether we hold off and use Cuba as a sort of hostage in the matter of Berlin. Then any time [Khrushchev] takes an action against Berlin, we take action against Cuba. That's really the choice we have now. What's your judgment?"

Macmillan replied that, on the whole, he would like to think about it, and Kennedy then went on to speculate further on his options:

> If [the Russians] respect the quarantine, then we get the second stage of this problem, and work continues on the missiles. Do we then tell them that if they don't get the missiles out that we're going to invade Cuba? [Khrushchev] will then say that if we invade Cuba that there's going to be a general nuclear assault, and he will in any case grab Berlin. Or do we just let the nuclear work go on, figuring he won't ever dare fire them, and when he tries to grab Berlin, we then go into Cuba? That's what I'd like to have you think about.

As the conversation wore on, the picture emerged both of two chess grandmasters plotting their moves and of two battle-hardened politicians calculating the odds. In the midst of the strategic theorizing, each man took the time to ask the other one how he was coping with his domestic opposition. Macmillan then expressed the view that this was a "big issue" about which he felt "pretty sure we ought not to do anything in a hurry." Kennedy replied, "Right, prime minister," and went on to politely sidestep the PM's proposal that he fly personally to Washington to meet him. Whether reflecting sheer pressure of time or some deeper psychological facet of his charming but slightly detached manner even to close colleagues and friends, the president preferred to keep his distance. ("You know how Americans love telephones," Macmillan would later sigh.[55]) At close to midnight, having touched on the prospect of imminent global extinction, the conversation ended on an almost comically banal note:

> MACMILLAN: Well, we'll have a talk on Friday night. Is that the best we can do?

KENNEDY: That'll be fine, prime minister, unless you're going
to be away on Friday night?

MACMILLAN: I shall stay in London, but I think it very useful
if we can have a brief chat each evening if it's not incon-
venient to you, then we can just compare notes as to how
things are going on.

KENNEDY: Good, I will call you then, tomorrow evening,
prime minister, at 6:00 my time.

MACMILLAN: That'll do me fine. Good night.

KENNEDY: Good night, prime minister. Thank you.[56]

At 11:30 the following night, half an hour late, Kennedy duly
called. The first thing he said was, "How did you do with your
[parliamentary] debate?"

"We did very well, actually, very good, very good," Macmillan
assured him. "I sent you the text of what I said, and I think it
was very well accepted. I made all the points I could, and the
reception was good, very well received."

After some discussion about the possible role of the UN and
more particularly its new secretary-general U Thant in broker-
ing a truce between the two sides, Macmillan again proposed
that he immediately fly to Washington or, failing that, at least
take the initiative and call the president back the following day.
There was a lot of static on the line that night, and perhaps as a
result Kennedy apparently didn't hear this, or at any rate didn't
respond to it, and instead continued with his narrative:

KENNEDY: We will know tomorrow night whether
Khrushchev will accept U Thant's proposal to cease all
shipping going to Cuba during these talks, number one.
Number two, if he doesn't do that we will know what
their reaction will be to our searching of a vessel, so I think
that I could call you tomorrow night at the same time,
unless this is too late for you.

MACMILLAN: No, indeed. I am very much obliged to you. We will have a talk tomorrow night. Good night.

KENNEDY: Good night, prime minister. I'll send you Chairman Khrushchev's message of last evening. Good night.

After reading Khrushchev's note, Macmillan in turn wired Kennedy: "After much reflection, I think that events have gone too far." He could no longer countenance any American plan for "taking out" Cuba, he said. Instead, he wanted Kennedy to insist that, while the existing missile sites must go – and he, Macmillan, would do everything in his power to that end – "some system of inspection" should then take the place of the naval blockade. It was the "firmness with flexibility" approach that soon also found official favor in Washington.[57]

In a conversation on October 26, which again began at close to midnight, the British premier (born in 1894) showed his affinity for the broader historical perspective:

KENNEDY: There are some reports around, some Russian conversations … they might do something about withdrawing the weapons if they could get a territorial guarantee in Cuba. But that is so unofficial that I'm not in a position now to know whether there's anything to it or not… .

MACMILLAN: The idea that you've just mentioned is that Cuba might be made like Belgium [pre-1914] by international guarantee – an inviolable country, and all of us would guarantee its neutrality and inviolability. Is that a possibility?

KENNEDY: Well, that is a matter which seems to me we ought to be thinking about, and we will be thinking about that in the next 24 hours as to whether there is any room for a settlement on that basis. That would leave Castro in power, and it would leave the Russians perhaps free to ship in a good deal more offensive equipment."[58]

Although it could be argued from this exchange that Macmillan's role was essentially to listen sympathetically to Kennedy unburden himself, their conversation that night still produced some new ideas:

> MACMILLAN: There is just a third alternative that occurred to us. If we want to help the Russians save face, would it be worthwhile our undertaking to immobilise our Thor missiles which are here in England during the same period – during [a] conference?
>
> KENNEDY: Well, let me put that into the machinery, and then I'll be in touch with you on that.
>
> MACMILLAN: I think it is an idea that it might help the Russians to accept.
>
> KENNEDY: Sure, prime minister. Let me send that over to the Department.[59]

Kennedy's measured response fails to betray much enthusiasm for the temporary defusing of Britain's stockpile of sixty medium-range PGM-17 Thor missiles. Macmillan had accepted the weapons in a deal struck with President Eisenhower at their first fence-mending talks following the Suez affair, and they were due to be decommissioned anyway about a year later. Even so, the idea of dismantling allied rockets as a quid pro quo for Cuba clearly appealed to Khrushchev, too, because he made a similar proposal in a letter to Kennedy that Radio Moscow began broadcasting only a few hours later.

Meanwhile, having spoken of Belgium, the United Nations refugee camps in Nicaragua and Guatemala, the continued threat to Berlin, and all the other adjuncts to the main crisis, the principal Western leaders, still not knowing if a general war would start at any moment, brought their latest exchange to an end as gently as two old friends finalizing some social arrangements:

KENNEDY: Well, I will be in touch in [the usual] way with you
tomorrow on the matter, and I'll send you tonight the
memorandum on the U Thant conversation. Thank you.
And I hope all goes well.

MACMILLAN: Well, thank you very much, and of course Bundy
can always ring up de Zulueta here. They can speak to each
other, so it is quite easy to have a chat.

KENNEDY: Fine, prime minister. And I'll be in touch with you
very shortly. Thank you and good night.

MACMILLAN: Good night.[60]

The following morning, Khrushchev sent Kennedy a note,
which among other things agreed "to expel those weapons
from Cuba which you regard as offensive," provided the United
States in turn remove its "analogous" missiles in Turkey. This
was a reference to the wing of fifteen PGM-19 Jupiter long-
range rockets stationed at Izmir, about four hundred miles (or
two-and-a-half minutes' flight time) from the southern coast of
Russia. Kennedy replied, "The first thing that needs to be done is
for work to cease on offensive bases in Cuba." Only then would
it be possible to "mutually work toward a more general arrangement regarding 'other armaments.'" To emphasize that the
Americans meant business, Robert Kennedy summoned Soviet
ambassador Dobrynin to his office at the Justice Department
at nine that Saturday night and personally read him his brother's message. This was an unusual function for the US attorney
general to perform, and it clearly signaled the urgency of the
situation. Bobby concluded the interview by saying, "Time is
running out," and that the president "hoped that the head of the
Soviet government would understand what he meant."[61]

Khrushchev did understand. After a perfunctory meeting of
the Politburo at noon, Moscow time, on Sunday October 28, he
cabled the president to say that he had "given a new order to
disassemble the arms which you described as offensive, and to

crate and return them to the USSR." Macmillan had just finished a working lunch in Admiralty House when news of the deal came through, much like an old stock market report, on the upstairs ticker tape. He immediately slumped down in an armchair, then remarked that it was like the end of a wedding, "when there is nothing to do but drink the champagne and go to sleep."[62]

Macmillan revived to cable Kennedy that afternoon, "Whatever dangers and difficulties we may have to face in the future, I am proud to feel that I have so resourceful and so firm a comrade." Perhaps the "comrade" was ironic. Kennedy wired back, "Your heartening support publicly expressed and our daily conversations have been of inestimable value in these past days."[63]

★ ★ ★

DESPITE SUCH GOOD CHEER, the Cuban missile crisis did not end with Khrushchev's "disassemble … crate and return" order, which Kennedy read among his breakfast things on that unseasonably warm Sunday morning in Washington. Three weeks of hard negotiations followed about the continued presence of Soviet IL-28 bombers in Cuba, which the Kremlin had failed to include in the original protocol. Only then did the United States formally lift the five hundred-mile quarantine and return her troops to Defcon 4. It could be argued, too, that Kennedy had contributed to the advent of Soviet nuclear weapons ninety miles off the coast of Florida in the first place. Without the Bay of Pigs escapade, Castro might have had a quite different reaction to the Russian delegation that had arrived in May 1962 to quietly discuss using his country as an advance rocket base. As it was, he had told his guests only that if they wanted to "bolster the defensive power of the entire socialist camp," then he had no particular objection.[64] Some of the details of the Kennedy administration's Operation Mongoose, the ill-fated attempt to sabotage Castro's revolution by means such as supplying an exploding cigar, a poisoned wetsuit, or an LSD-spiked drink to the Cuban dictator, read like a luridly melodramatic James Bond movie script as interpreted by Woody Allen. Overall, these were not initiatives that conspicuously added to the reputation of American foreign policy for probity and high-minded principle. Of the four main players in the drama, Castro was the only one who remained in power two years later.[65]

For all that, it's hard to fundamentally disagree with the verdict of David Ormsby-Gore, in an effusive handwritten letter to Kennedy on British Embassy stationery, of October 30, 1962:

Dear Jack,

I have an aversion to tempting fate by offering congratulations before one can be completely certain of the final outcome, but as I know that older and wiser men have been prepared to take the risk, on this occasion I now do the same.

I am lost in admiration for the superb manner in which you handled the tremendous events of the critical week we have just lived through. I know what a mass of conflicting advice you received, and I can only say that looking back at it you acted at each stage with perfect judgement. I mean it quite sincerely when I say that America and all of the world must feel a deep sense of gratitude that you were President of the United States at this moment in history. I and countless millions are deeply in your debt.

Well done. With best wishes as always,

Yours ever,
David.[66]

Kennedy kept this testimonial from his closest British friend in his office desk for the remainder of his life.

★ ★ ★

IT TOOK ONLY A MONTH for the Anglo-American allies to plunge from their greatest collaborative triumph to their greatest mutual crisis of confidence. This was the Skybolt affair: on one level, about the technical capabilities of an air-to-ground missile system; on another, about whether Britain could still survive as an independent nuclear power or simply become a strategically positioned launchpad for American assets, much like a westernized version of what Khrushchev had envisioned with Cuba. During his visit to President Eisenhower in March 1960, Macmillan had agreed to purchase 144 of the Skybolt rockets at what he called an "advantageous" price. Essentially, the British contribution would be limited to the cost of adapting her fleet of "V" (Vulcan) bombers to take the new weapon, as well as providing the Americans with an advance nuclear submarine base at Holy Loch in Scotland. As part of the deal, Britain's Blue Streak surface-to-air missile, on which some £62 million had been spent in research and development, was scrapped. Reporting these arrangements in cabinet, Macmillan noted that a "static ballistic weapon system was [now viewed as] excessively vulnerable ... Our contribution to the nuclear deterrent must in future be based on some mobile means of delivery." The PM added that "during his recent trip to Washington, he had satisfied himself that we should be able in due course to obtain from the United States, on acceptable terms, supplies of [Skybolt], to be armed with a British warhead."[67]

Unfortunately, between July 1960 and August 1962 Skybolt's development costs had risen by more than a third of their original estimate, and by the time of the Cuban crisis the US Department of Defense was spending upwards of $30 million a month just to get the system operational. Nor were the weapon's initial tests encouraging – in its first six outings, the rocket either simply failed to launch or exploded prematurely.[68] Similar compatibility trials with the British Vulcan bomber were a disaster. The intimacy and mutual accord of previous allied exchanges on this strategic defense system evaporated as a result, to be replaced by a chilly formality. Some British commentators came to grow particularly indifferent to the "robotic" figure of Secretary McNamara, with his oiled hair and that faint air of condescension toward the rest of humanity that apparently came from having a $65 billion annual budget (more than half of total state expenditure) at his disposal. A former president of the Ford Motor Company, McNamara was not one to be swayed by woolly concepts of goodwill toward a foreign ally when there were hard questions of business efficiency and basic cost control to be considered. Older British observers were quick to note the similarities to the one-time American ambassador to their country. Macmillan's colleague Selwyn Lloyd thought, "at least with Jack Kennedy, a personal accommodation might have a chance of reasonable life, whereas his defense secretary was a cold-blooded adding machine."[69]

By late November 1962, it had finally become clear that McNamara had no intention of persevering with Skybolt, but that he was prepared to offer the British the AGM-28 – or "Hound Dog" – supersonic cruise missile as a substitute. The more you study the politics of allied rocket technology in the Kennedy administration, the more you find its distinguishing features (apart from the silly nicknames) to have been the tragicomic misunderstanding between the American conviction on the one side that it was all a straightforward commercial proposition between a supplier and a customer, determined solely by market forces, and the deep British sense of unease on the other that they were being kicked out of the nuclear club by the perfidy of an ally who had good reason to be grateful to them. To add insult to injury, neither McNamara nor Kennedy himself thought to inform the British of their decision to scrap the Skybolt program until the order confirming its cancelation was already on the president's desk. Typically, David Ormsby-Gore was to learn of the latest twist to American policy before Macmillan did. After being called in and told, in so many words, that the whole strategy of Britain's "independent nuclear deterrent" had at a stroke been made redundant, Gore returned to his office "in shock ... a colleague who saw him later in the day recalls that he 'was like a man who'd learned the Bomb was going to drop, the end of civilisation, and he doubted he could stop it.'"[70]

It was against this backdrop that Kennedy and Macmillan met for their previously scheduled conference in Nassau from December 18 to 21, 1962. Instead of coming together to offer mutual congratulations over their handling of the Cuban affair, the two leaders were forced to deal with a Special Relationship that – at least as it applied to strategic arms – had become dysfunctional. In an unusual arrangement, Ormsby-Gore sat next to the president during the two-hour flight to the Bahamas, "conversing as politicians," and patiently explained to him that, without the Skybolt option, the British "self-defense apparatus" would simply no longer exist.[71] This apparently came as a news flash to Kennedy. The two men had then hurriedly agreed to a compromise that they thought might adequately cover Macmillan's nakedness on the subject. According to their formula, jotted down on an *Air Force One* notepad, the Americans would forgo Skybolt for themselves but would continue to develop it for the British. The costs of the system would be split fifty-fifty. It was another example of the sort of sweeping, blue-sky initiative Kennedy was capable of when separated from his army of advisers and closeted, instead, with his oldest British friend. Unfortunately, even as Jack and David were fixing the terms of the deal over their in-flight martinis, on the ground in Nassau Macmillan had reached a quite different conclusion. After weeks of agonizing on the subject, he was now convinced that Skybolt was a dead duck – or that, "while the proposed British marriage with [the weapon] was not exactly a shotgun wedding, the virginity of the lady must be regarded as doubtful," as he put it in his inimitable style.[72] Skybolt, in other words, had simply failed in its tests too often for the PM to retain any faith in its arcane technology. It may have been purely a coincidence, but observers noticed that the welcoming Royal Marines band struck up a spirited version of an old English folk song, the chorus of which ran, "Oh, don't deceive me," when the American delegation touched down at Nassau on the morning of December 18.[73]

When *Air Force One* came to a stop, a smiling Kennedy strode briskly across the tarmac to embrace his "firm friend [and] comrade" Macmillan.[74] It was their first meeting in eight months, and they went out of their way to show the world their respect and affection for each other. Within only a few moments, they were no longer the bickering old couple they had played in public for several weeks beforehand. Macmillan warmly welcomed Kennedy, and Kennedy replied by noting the two men's affinity for Christmastime meetings in the tropics. Meanwhile, the British ambassador had taken the opportunity to discreetly leave the president's plane by a rear exit, the piece of paper with the scribbled nuclear-deterrent formula in his jacket pocket, and quietly position himself at his prime minister's back. When the moment came, Ormsby-Gore stepped forward into the receiving line and vigorously shook Kennedy's hand as though just now meeting him for the first time. The president then went to the microphone to announce that he had "benefitted greatly from the counsel and friendship you have shown to me, Prime Minister, to my predecessor, and also to the American people, who have a heavy claim laid upon you from earliest birth."[75] It was another one of those slightly overblown public declarations that might have been written for him by Winston Churchill.

That night, Macmillan and Kennedy took a long walk together under the palm trees, without secretaries or advisers. Again pulling rank, the PM spoke of the whole history of Anglo-American relations during his six years in office. "At Camp David in 1960, Eisenhower discussed with me both Skybolt and Polaris," he reminisced. "We accepted Skybolt because it seemed the best way for us to prolong the life of our bomber air force … But if Skybolt were definitely to fail us, Ike assured me we could rely on obtaining Polaris."[76] It was apparently only now that Kennedy fully appreciated that the British were concerned not so much with the nuances of solid-fuel rocket technology as they were with sustaining their role of influence in the post-war world. Although the president privately believed the whole concept of Britain's national deterrent "a political necessity but a piece of military foolishness," he called in his advisers before the full-scale talks began the next morning and told them in effect to give Macmillan what he asked for. "If you were in that kind of trouble, you'd want a friend too," Kennedy later remarked of Nassau. The premier got his Polaris missiles, which were to be armed with British warheads. The weapons would be formally under NATO control, "save where Her Majesty's Government may decide that the supreme national interests are at stake." It was widely recognized as a major coup for Macmillan, and one Kennedy personally orchestrated over the protests of senior members of his staff. On the last day in Nassau, someone took a photograph of McNamara and his newly appointed British peer, Peter Thorneycroft, sitting across the table from one another, looking as grumpy as a couple in divorce court.

Some days after the conference ended, the Pentagon mentioned for the first time that they expected Britain to contribute significantly to future research and development costs of Polaris. On hearing this, Macmillan wrote directly to Kennedy refusing to do so. "But," he noted in his diary, "I have offered, in lieu, to add five per cent to the retail cost. So, if we bought fifty million pounds of missiles, we would pay fifty two-and-a-half million pounds. Not a bad bargain. But it has caused me some sleepless nights."[77] Kennedy accepted Macmillan's offer.

Back in the grip of the worst British winter in a century, the PM wrote to tell the president (who was in Florida):

> I enjoyed our talks in the Bahamas. Although rather strenuous, I think they were very rewarding ... I feel certain that the dust will soon begin to clear, and that our agreement will become a historic example of the nice balance between interdependence and independence which is necessary if

Sovereign states are to work in partnership together for the defense of freedom.

If I may, I will send you some further thoughts on the question of money.[78]

For all the strategic and economic considerations involved, the Skybolt affair ultimately proved to be a case where Kennedy chose to accommodate the British interest in a way that it would somehow be hard to imagine him doing with the likes of France or Germany – let alone Canada, whose premier John Diefenbaker he deemed "a jerk," among other more anatomical epithets.[79] It was the single most significant example of the president's personal empathy for the country where he had come of political age. Once again embodying the Special Relationship, David Ormsby-Gore flew straight from the Bahamas to Palm Beach, where he spent that Christmas week as the Kennedys' houseguest.

By this stage, the president felt sufficiently relaxed around the British ambassador to occasionally reveal his inner reservations about members of his own cabinet. On December 22, just hours after the delegations had left Nassau, Secretary McNamara triumphantly announced to the world that Skybolt had at last passed a flight test, immediately after the executive decision had been made to scrap it. Kennedy "fl[ew] into a terrible rage," Gore recalled. "He went through the roof ... We were sitting by the pool at Palm Beach behind his house, ready to have a swim, when the crisis burst. He was having a manicure, the manicurist sitting beside him ... This wonderfully sunny scene beside the pool – and suddenly this vast explosion and this violent language going out via telephone while the wretched manicurist went on cutting his nails."[80] Like the rocket itself, the president had "simply gone into orbit." "Bob's normally so goddamned good at everything," he kept exclaiming, in a mixture of astonishment and rage. It was perhaps as well for McNamara that by then he happened to be at a remote ski lodge in Colorado and thus not immediately available to take Kennedy's call. Macmillan took a more measured view but still remarked, in pained terms, on this exquisite coincidence of events. "It was rather provoking that Skybolt should go off so well," he wrote to Kennedy on Christmas Eve. "It would have been better if it had been a failure. However, these are the chances of life."[81]

Ormsby-Gore was still enjoying the president's hospitality at Palm Beach when Kennedy exchanged nuclear-related messages with Nikita Khrushchev. The Soviet leader had quickly learned of the Polaris deal struck at Nassau and, coincidentally or not, now felt that a global test-ban treaty, including the provision of independent inspections, might be in order. It was a substantial advance on his previous position that had called any international scrutiny of Russian bomb sites "an act of espionage." In his cable, Khrushchev went on to assure Kennedy that a test ban need not be linked to any further "readjustment of controls" in Berlin. What was instead needed, he now informed the president, were urgent talks on "general and complete disarmament."[82] For whatever reason, the Soviet ruler had taken the first tentative step back from the brinkmanship that had nearly led to war over Cuba and declared it as his mission to "help avert [the] insanity" of nuclear proliferation.

10

HAROLD AND JACK

ON THE DAY KENNEDY AGREED to Macmillan's basic terms for the sale of Polaris missiles, President de Gaulle vetoed Britain's application to join the European Common Market. Macmillan did not conceal his anger about France's treatment of his country. The premier saw it as an act of almost Shakespearian treachery, and one that reflected a pervasive flaw in the French character. "Good at cooking and sex," he privately noted, they were not otherwise greatly gifted. Macmillan thought de Gaulle "did not want us in for two main reasons: 1. It will alter the character of the Community ... Now it is a nice little club [under] French hegemony. 2. Apart from our loyalty to the Commonwealth, we shall always be too intimately tied up with the Americans."[1] Between the reaction first of the Soviets and now the French to events at Nassau, Kennedy's personal gesture of solidarity with the British people was coming to have significant repercussions around the globe.

The problem was not only de Gaulle's sense of being the poor relation of the wartime Allies, Macmillan felt. There was a degree of personal rancor – even derangement – involved.

Immediately calling Kennedy on the hotline to complain, Macmillan sounded concerned for de Gaulle's mental health:

> MACMILLAN: Well, I think it's a very bad situation. I think this man has gone crazy – absolutely crazy.
> KENNEDY: Well, what do you think it is that's made him crazy?
> MACMILLAN: He's simply inventing any means whatever to knock us out.[2]

On January 30, 1963, Kennedy wrote back for the record:

> Dear Prime Minister,
> I am sure that you realize how sorry I am about the great disappointment you have suffered in recent days. My regret is compounded by my realization that part of your difficulties resulted from your country's historic association with the United States, and your own strong support of this alliance. I count on working closely with you in the coming days.
> John F. Kennedy.[3]

Several of the president's men were as distressed as Macmillan was at the outcome, precisely because it meant having to attune American foreign policy to a Great Britain that remained semidetached from the rest of Europe. McNamara had satisfied himself that the idea of a British nuclear deterrent was an expensive farce, and Rusk had satisfied himself of the policy advantages of moving away from a "special relationship" and toward a monolithic "system of … strict non-favoritism" to America's NATO allies. Only Kennedy himself consistently saw the twin Atlantic partners as bound together by more powerful ties of shared history and friendship.

In a private message to Macmillan, Kennedy wrote, "You will know without my saying so that we are with you, in feeling and in purpose, in this time of de Gaulle's great effort to test the chances for his dream world. Neither of us must forget for a moment that reality is what rules, and the central reality is that he is wrong … We are doing everything we can at this end, as our people will be telling yours. And if this is an unmentionable special relationship, so much the better."[4]

Kennedy's big idea was Britain at the head of a Western European union – the so-called Single Phone Call option – which would allow him to agree on the broad contours of policy with Macmillan and for the latter to then communicate the fine detail down the line to the subordinate allies. It was a pragmatic as well as a personally attractive formula for the anglophile American president. In February 1963, Kennedy again took the time to write to the publishers Wilfred Funk to inquire about sales of *Why England Slept*. The company's reply demonstrated the harsh commercial realities faced by even a celebrity author. The book now seemed simply to have run out of steam. "I enclose the statement covering the period from July 1, to December 31, 1962," Funk's manager Joseph McLaughlin wrote back. "As the figures show, in this period the number of copies returned exceeded the number sold. Hence there is, unfortunately, no royalty payable at this time."[5]

On April 9, 1963, twenty-three years after he published *Why England Slept*, John Kennedy announced that the United States was finally to grant Winston Churchill honorary citizenship. The eighty-eight-year-old wartime leader was too frail to travel, leaving his fitfully brilliant but alcoholic son Randolph to represent him at the White House ceremony. The latter fortified himself for the occasion by drinking a full bottle of Beefeater gin. Jacqueline Kennedy remembered that she had been especially nervous while listening to her husband speak "because every second was ticking closer to Randolph." However, he carried it off. The younger Churchill read out his father's remarks reminding the assembled company that Britain still had a leading role to play in the world. "Let no man underrate our energies, our potentialities and our abiding power for good," he boomed."[6] It seemed to some observers, as they listened first to Kennedy's words, then to Churchill's, and then in closing to Kennedy's again, that it was almost impossible to say which was which. When a reporter later asked if Congress would now erect a statue of Churchill in Washington, D.C., the president replied, "Well, he is still very much with us, and I think we ought to lay our wreath at his feet."[7] Churchill himself had hoped to respond to the proceedings by making a few televised remarks from his home in London, but he was forced to abandon this plan when the British satellite link broke down shortly before transmission.

Apparently inspired by the occasion, Kennedy took David Ormsby-Gore aside immediately following the ceremony and told him that he wanted to move ahead with "constructive steps" that might encourage the Soviet Union's recent proposals about a nuclear test-ban treaty. The next morning, the president picked up the hotline and told Macmillan that he had read his latest draft on the subject, and "I've only really got one change, and that would be on page five on the last version you sent me, where the words go, 'If we could make progress here, we might be able to envisage a meeting.'"[8] Kennedy still had misgivings about being seen to reward Khrushchev with a great international conference. The full 1,200-word text finally went off to the Kremlin on April 15. Khrushchev bridled once again at being asked to permit third-party inspections of his nuclear sites. But, following a conciliatory speech by Kennedy in Washington in which he noted, "We all inhabit this small planet, we all cherish our children's future, [and] we are all mortal,"[9] the Soviet leader agreed that perhaps it finally was time for a fresh start after all and that representatives of the United States and United Kingdom would be welcome to discuss "all such matters" at high-level talks in Moscow.[10] Even then, the State Department planners at Foggy Bottom responded cautiously, drafting what Arthur Schlesinger called "a debater's screed, dealing *seriatim* with Khrushchev's points."[11] It was left to Ambassador Gore to cut through the bureaucratic ramblings and go direct to the Oval Office, where he told his friend the president that this was the great chance that the West had been waiting for, and that they should immediately take Khrushchev up on his offer in "clear, concise terms, expressed in simple language." Kennedy "readily agreed," Schlesinger wrote.[12]

Before the Moscow talks began, Kennedy accepted Macmillan's open invitation to go to Britain to publicly demonstrate US solidarity with the NATO allies and, more narrowly, to show support for the embattled prime minister. The latter complained that he was then being "snubbed, attacked and ridiculed" by the press. Apart from the Common Market fiasco, a major sex scandal had blown up and threatened to topple Macmillan's entire government. Schlesinger had himself recently returned from London and told his chief, "It is hard to overstate the atmosphere of political squalor there nowadays."

Kennedy, who balanced his dedication to sober-minded public service with his lifelong enjoyment of gossip, seems to have taken the news more in his stride than did his fastidiously bow-tied special assistant. Earlier in the year, the president had instructed his press secretary, Pierre Salinger, to send him the daily newspaper reports of the divorce proceedings between the duke and duchess of Argyll, which got under way in London on February 26, 1963, and included a saga of aristocratic adultery that might have raised eyebrows at a Roman orgy. This was effectively to be the curtain raiser to the legendary Profumo scandal that shook the Macmillan government to its core throughout the spring and early summer. The president's friend Ben Bradlee later recalled him as having "devoured every word about the Profumo case; it combined so many of the things that interested him: low doings in high places, the British nobility, sex, and spying."[13] David Bruce was soon also wiring detailed daily accounts of the affair direct to the White House. One of these bears the handwritten notation, "This is not government, but chaos."

Kennedy may have enjoyed the more salacious aspects of the Profumo crisis, but he was wary enough of its consequences to ask that his visit to Macmillan take place at Birch Grove, the prime minister's family home in Sussex, rather than the febrile atmosphere of Westminster. In a spirit of even-handed bipartisanship, he also agreed to meet the new British Labour Party leader Harold Wilson when Wilson visited Washington. Kennedy's April 2, 1963, phone call on the subject with Ambassador Ormsby-Gore captures some of the true flavor of their relationship. What particularly drew the president to the Argylls' story, Gore remarked privately, was above all "the duchess's habit of wearing nothing but her pearls at the moment of coitus:"

KENNEDY: Hello?

ORMSBY-GORE: Yeah. Hello?

KENNEDY: David?

ORMSBY-GORE: Yeah.

KENNEDY: Good.

ORMSBY-GORE: I just thought I would have a word with you before you see Wilson.

KENNEDY: Sure. Right.

ORMSBY-GORE: One of the impressions he's got talking to senators, and even some people in the administration, is that there's no enthusiasm for the Multilateral Force [a European naval fleet to be armed with nuclear weapons, but under overall US control].

KENNEDY: Yeah. Yeah.

ORMSBY-GORE: The other impression he strongly got from talking to senators is that any question of doing away with the US veto of weapons in [the] Force is really not a political possibility.

KENNEDY: Yeah?

ORMSBY-GORE: Yeah.

KENNEDY: Yeah. Well, I think that's correct.

The conversation then turned to the matter of the transatlantic balance of payments and other commercial issues:

ORMSBY-GORE: Wilson happily goes on and thinks, you see, there will be a great conference at which all these [trade] barriers will come down and you will allow in lots of raw materials and temporary foodstuffs from the Commonwealth and the under-developed countries.

KENNEDY: Yeah.

ORMSBY-GORE: It's a nice picture, but I don't see it happening with the [Common Market].

KENNEDY: Yeah. Yeah. Yeah.

ORMSBY-GORE: Right.

KENNEDY: OK.

ORMSBY-GORE: Yeah.

KENNEDY: Yeah. Good. Thanks, David.[14]

Part of Kennedy's consuming interest in the Profumo saga may have been the fact that it seemed to mirror much of the heady late eighteenth-century British political landscape he had read about so enjoyably in *The Young Melbourne*. Both cases involved "England's genius for combining public probity with private tomfoolery," as he later summarized it to Macmillan's colleague Selwyn Lloyd.[15] This latest scandal to captivate the nation that had raised the luridly exposed "sex romp" to an art form centered on the balding but puckish figure of forty-eight-year-old John Profumo, Britain's secretary of state for war and thought by some to be a possible future prime minister. In July 1961, Profumo had attended a party given by a society osteopath and sexual procurer named Stephen Ward at the country estate where he rented a summer cottage. At some point, they had walked out to the swimming pool and there encountered an aspiring actress called Christine Keeler, a striking brunette, and her equally free spirited blonde friend, Mandy Rice-Davies, a dancer and showgirl. Both women were, as the jargon of the day had it, of doubtful reputation. Keeler, who emerged nude from the pool to demurely shake Profumo's hand, then happened to be in a relationship with Yevgeni Ivanov, the Soviet naval attaché to Britain and reportedly a confidant of the highest members of the Moscow Politburo. Somehow inevitably, Keeler had begun an affair with Profumo, which meant that she was sleeping both with the British war minister and an alleged Russian spy, thus bringing a national security dimension to the proceedings.

When challenged in parliament, Profumo (who was married to the film star Valerie Hobson) at first indignantly defended his honor but then admitted that perhaps he had slept with Keeler after all, and that he was resigning his ministerial portfolio with immediate effect. He got a "Dear Profumo" letter back from Macmillan, accepting his decision with alacrity.[16]

The British press was not slow to build the affair into a cause célèbre that linked not only the Tory government but also the ruling elite as a whole to an underworld of prostitutes, pimps, spies, topless go-go dancers, and exotic household practices. "The whole United Kingdom government has become a sort of brothel," *The Times* was left to sigh. One widely circulated story was said to have involved an eminent·politician who had waited on table at a fashionable London dinner party naked, masked, and wearing a placard that read, "If my services don't please you, whip me" – if true, a sorry lapse from the late-Victorian public etiquette Macmillan himself seemed to embody. ("Of course," the PM wrote in his diary, "all these people move in a raffish, theatrical, bohemian society where no one really knows anyone and everyone's 'darling.'")[17]

Although Macmillan's government survived Profumo, it failed to recover its former aura of respectability. Deference was never quite the same again. A Gallup poll published in June 1963 showed 71 percent of voters wanting either the PM's resignation or an immediate election. In late July, Stephen Ward – a scapegoat, some felt, for his more aristocratic clients – went on trial at the Old Bailey on a variety of morals charges. Following a harsh attack on his character in the prosecution's closing speech, Ward went home to his flat and took a fatal overdose of sleeping pills. His suicide note read, "I am sorry to disappoint the vultures."[18]

Although the Profumo scandal was a peculiarly British affair, there was a strong transatlantic element to it. As a senator, John Kennedy had communally slept with two society prostitutes who called themselves Maria Novotny and Suzy Chang. Both women had subsequently moved to London and become part of the Ward vice – or "V-girl" – ring. Novotny, whose real name was Stella Capes, had gone on to a colorful career that combined a degree of legitimate social assimilation with a fanatical pursuit of sexual partners, male and female, whose tempo rivaled that of the duchess of Argyll at her most prolific. It's widely agreed that she had attended, if not hosted, the notorious "man in the mask" dinner party in December 1961. Novotny would later tell reporters that she had serviced Jack Kennedy both before and after his election as president, and that his special predilection had been for her to dress up as a nurse, with him the patient. Suzy Chang, for her part, was at one time said to be anxious to sell her tale of nights with a "high-elected US official" to the *New York Journal-American*. According to the journalist Seymour Hersh, Robert Kennedy used his considerable influence with the Hearst family, who owned the *Journal-American*, to kill the story.[19] In June 1963, FBI director J. Edgar Hoover cabled Charles Bates, his man in London, and ordered him to "stay on top of this 'V-girl' case and … keep Bureau fully and promptly informed of all developments with particular emphasis on any allegation that U.S. nationals are or have been involved in any way."[20]

Though Kennedy was silent in public, he lapped up the details of the broader Profumo scandal, apparently regarding it as an enjoyable romp in itself and possibly also as a cautionary tale. "You've read about Profumo in the newspapers?" the president asked Martin Luther King Jr., who had come to the White House to discuss civil rights. "That's an example of friendship and loyalty carried too far. Macmillan is likely to lose his government because he has been loyal to his friend."[21] That was also the consensus of many of the daily briefings Kennedy's national security team brought him at the height of the scandal.

"[Macmillan's] days in power appear to be numbered; seems to have outlived his usefulness," the brief noted on June 12, 1963. "Party expected to seek a new leader before summer is out," was the next day's verdict. "Atmosphere of tension and uncertainty as dynamic as Suez," Kennedy read on the 14th. "Several ministers are on the point of resignation. Could start a landslide against Macmillan."[22]

On June 20, the Labour MP Marcus Lipton[23] got up amid some uproar in the Commons and asked, "Is the visit of the President still on? Doesn't the Prime Minister think that the president should be given the opportunity of exchanging views with a new Prime Minister, and not one under notice to quit?" At that, several members rose from their seats to wave their order papers at Macmillan and shout, "Out!"[24] He seemed suddenly to be a wretched and visibly older figure. Jackie Kennedy, who was pregnant and thus stayed home in Washington, later described her husband as "very depressed" at the prospect of Macmillan losing office. "So Jack wanted to do something really nice – to [visit]," she said, "and also to give him a nice present, and to hell with the State Department budget."[25] As at Nassau, the president ignored those of his subordinates who wanted him to keep his distance from Macmillan and Britain generally, telling a mutual colleague that, whatever happened, he would be "there for Harold."[26] But it was not loyalty alone that motivated Kennedy. Fear also played its part; fear that if Macmillan fell he would be replaced by the shifty Wilson, whose foreign affairs spokesman had been described to Kennedy as an "anti-nuclear alcoholic."[27]

So Kennedy was indeed "there for Harold," at least to the extent of spending a night under his roof. It would be an official visit, but also what Macmillan called a "slightly mad" house party. The reporter Tony Gill was on hand as part of the press pool, and believed it was all a "glorified photo-op skillfully managed by Harold." The PM was genuinely fond of his American guest, but he was also not averse to the prospect of being pictured conversing with the leader of the free world, enhancing as it did his own image of being at the forefront of international affairs. Given Macmillan's precipitous fall in the polls, it was less easy to see what was in it for Kennedy. "PM probably [will] quit later this year ... will resign to make way for a younger man," the president learned from "informed sources" quoted in his daily briefing on June 16.[28] Many observers still thought that Macmillan would be out of office in time to enjoy the grouse-shooting season in August. Kennedy may simply have liked the idea of putting himself on the fringes of a major British political sex scandal. Macmillan's naval aide later overheard some of the president's men conversing with him in hushed tones while standing in a small group just outside the garden door of Macmillan's home. "[Dean] Rusk made some sombre remark about how they all then found themselves in the thick of this terrible atmosphere of wanton sex and promiscuity tainting the entire British establishment, up to and including the very house they were staying in, and a second later I heard Kennedy's voice say: 'Well, one can but hope.'"[29]

On June 23, the president assured a welcoming crowd in Cologne, "The United States is here on this continent to stay. So long as our presence is desired and required, our forces and commitments will remain."[30] More than half a million people came out to listen to Kennedy speak on June 26 at West Berlin's City Hall. He was cheered deliriously when he told his audience, "*Ich bin ein Berliner*," one of the defining moments both of his presidency and the Cold War, notwithstanding that "ein Berliner" was colloquial German for a jelly roll. Standing behind the president, his speechwriter Ted Sorensen saw "a sea of human faces, chanting '*Kenne-dy, Kenne-dy*.'"[31] As John Lennon and Paul McCartney sat down that night in a small northern English hotel to write "She Loves You" – the best-selling single of the Beatles' career, and the song that thrust them full-tilt into the spotlight – and the reforming John Paul VI began his long reign as Pope, it's arguable that what we now call "the Sixties" really began in

the last week of June 1963.[32] Turning to Sorensen on the plane
taking them from Berlin to Dublin, Kennedy said, "We'll never
have another day like this one as long as we live."[33]

Kennedy's homecoming to Ireland had met with a frenzy of
local activity during the previous days and weeks. Unlike the
English, the Irish pulled out all the stops. Thousands of miniature American flags had been issued, shops and houses on the
route of the presidential motorcade had been given a fresh lick
of paint, and it was said that a thousand extra pints of beer had
been laid on at Mulligan's pub in central Dublin in order to
supply the press corps for the night. On the plane, Kennedy
reminisced with his aides about his visit to Dunganstown in 1947
together with the outspoken Pamela Churchill. "You'll be there
tomorrow," the president's friend and appointments secretary
Kenny O'Donnell told him. "This time in Ireland you won't be
mixed up with any members of the British nobility," he added.
It was the point where Kennedy's affinity for the historic world
of *The Young Melbourne* met with his sentimental attachment to
his ancestral home. "Good," he said.[34]

Kennedy touched down at Dublin Airport late on the damp
evening of June 26, and found eighty-year-old President Éamon
de Valera waiting for him on the tarmac. An aide led de Valera
forward to his guest, because he was now almost blind. Forty
years earlier, he had been a leader of the Irish guerilla war
against the hated British security forces but had since come to
regard himself as a "conservative moderniser" who could save
his people from the "two ugly sisters" – the Eastern and Western
blocs – in the Cold War. De Valera told the crowds at the airport that the American president was a "distinguished son of our
race" and a representative of the land of hope and opportunity
"in which our people sought refuge when driven by the tyrant's
laws from their Motherland." Kennedy in turn remarked that
he was glad to be back in "this green and misty island."[35] He had
politely turned down the offer of honorary Irish citizenship that
de Valera had recently made him. There were ecstatic scenes

along the streets, where a cavalcade of black limousines conveyed Kennedy with other dignitaries and honored guests to a
brief appearance at Phoenix Park, Dublin's natural affection for
its VIP guest merging with the characteristic exuberance of that
city at the time the pubs close on a summer's night. De Valera
later remembered a somewhat chaotic atmosphere, with Secret
Service officials trying to restrain the crowd while Kennedy
stood up to wave in the back of his car, "and it did pass through
my mind, curiously enough, what an easy target he would
have been."[36]

There followed four days during which the president's hosts
waited patiently for him to speak out on the charged matter of
Irish partition, much as he had on a similar issue in Berlin, but
which Kennedy himself evidently saw more as an exercise in
pure nostalgia. He was plainly not there to address the rights and
wrongs of the English suppression of 1649 or of the subsequent
period of more or less permanent war. He looked, instead, for a
break with traditional resentments to a society where "talent has
its own reward" and there was "prosperity and liberty" for all.
When Dublin's ambassador to Washington, Thomas Kiernan,
first raised the subject of a possible official pronouncement on
Irish reunification, Kennedy had "visibly winced ... he looked
as if [a] headache had struck him and asked me [if] he was
expected to say anything in public."[37] As it happened, he never
did. Kennedy was content to take his Irishness no further than a
few generic avowals of goodwill and somewhat hazy late-night
allusions to historic differences with the British. For him, the
highlight of the trip was clearly his return after sixteen years to
Dunganstown, where the president again took tea in his cousins'
farmhouse and posed for photographs in what had been a dirt
yard on his earlier visit but which had been hastily transformed
just a few days before into a concrete patio. Kennedy's relative
Josephine Ryan remembered, "Before he came everyone was
very tensed up. But I think he made them all just draw at their
ease ... A lot of the neighbours were in the kitchen and they

were supposed to keep in the background. But when [Kennedy] was going out they opened the door there. He went in and he chatted away with them. Some of them were shaking hands with him, for instance, three times."[38]

Kennedy caused a minor furor when he went on to teasingly remind the Irish National Assembly that it had once been thought "not to inspire the brightest ideas." Amid "some murmuring and shifting in seats," he had swiftly added, "That was a long time ago, however."[39] President de Valera later erased these remarks from the official parliamentary record of the visit.[40] Kennedy then paid his respects at the graves of some of the 485 victims of the six-day 1916 Easter Rising. At dinner that night, de Valera told his guest, "If you are weak in your dealings with the British, they will pressure you … Only if you are reasonable will they reason with you, and being reasonable with the British means letting them know that you are willing to throw an occasional bomb into one of their lorries."[41] Kennedy smiled and responded by singing some old sea shanties.[42]

Waiting to receive the president at his country estate on the edge of Ashdown Forest (the "100 Acre Wood" of the Winnie-the-Pooh stories), Harold Macmillan noted these events with some unease. The PM's view of Ireland, while not wholly unsympathetic, was tainted by his long experience of the Connolly Association and other radical mainland organizations that supported the aims of Irish republicanism. Macmillan himself had been targeted for special abuse from such groups over the years. To him, as to a large number of mainstream English politicians, Ireland was an odd, bog-covered little place whose inhabitants were a chaotic, scrappy people not to be entirely trusted around an open bottle. Speaking on June 28 outside the city hall in Cork, Kennedy enthused, "I come to this island which has been identified with that struggle [for self-determination] for a thousand years, which was the first country in the twentieth century to lead what is the most powerful tide of the century – the desire for national independence, the desire to be free, and I come here in 1963 and find that strong tide still beats, still runs."[43] Summarizing this oration in his diary, Macmillan called it "a rather foolish speech about Liberty."[44]

Thomas Kiernan, who accompanied the presidential party through Ireland, remembered, "Kennedy was constantly asking about places ... He was costing houses. How much would a place like that cost with a certain amount of land attached? I assumed he was wondering just what it would be like to live in Ireland, or to have a pied-à-terre where he could come or send the children."[45] Others believed the president might ultimately have gone on to become the US ambassador to Dublin. Perhaps the only certainty is that Kennedy was prepared to play up his Irishness when it suited him to do so, that he still never came close to explicitly endorsing a policy of reunification, let alone direct action against the British, and that the ultimate beneficiary of his June 1963 visit was Ireland's tourist industry, which saw a 40 percent increase in American visitors over the next two years. "The day Kennedy visited was the day Galway changed from being a sleepy town to a thriving city," a local journalist remarked.[46]

★ ★ ★

JOHN KENNEDY's thirteenth visit to the United Kingdom was, he said, "like going on a pilgrimage, for some of the friends here were also family."[47] It began in the early evening of June 29, 1963, a Saturday, in one of the most affecting scenes of the Kennedy presidency. While Harold Macmillan and the higher echelons of the British government awaited their guest's arrival at Birch Grove, Kennedy himself was 220 miles away to the north, in a US Army helicopter descending on the tiny churchyard at Edensor, a self-contained village set among the grounds of the Cavendish family's vast ducal seat at Chatsworth. The president's means of transport seemed to some to strike a note of absurd unreality against the backdrop of the medieval estate. He was met on arrival by Macmillan's nephew Andrew, the eleventh duke, whose people had owned Chatsworth since the sixteenth century. The duke's wife, the former Deborah Freeman-Mitford – "Debo" – followed behind, struggling to control several dogs straining on their leashes, to greet the president with a kiss. It had been a damp, English early summer's day, but pale sunshine now played off several of the main house's four hundred windows. A number of Secret Service personnel had spent the previous night up nearby trees, and now they looked down as the duke and duchess escorted Kennedy over a small wooden bridge and into the estate's private cemetery, where he went on alone in order to kneel at the plain stone grave of his favorite sister. Their father had personally chosen the phrase on the marker: "In loving memory of Kathleen, 1920–1948, widow of Major the Marquess of Hartington, killed in action, & daughter of the Hon. Joseph Kennedy, sometime Ambassador of the United States to Great Britain. Joy she gave – joy she has found."[48]

In May 1948, Jack Kennedy, then a thirty-year-old first-term congressman, had gone to the airport in New York that now bears his name on the first leg of a journey intended to take him across the Atlantic to his sister's funeral in London. Apparently too distraught to continue, he had changed his mind and instead flown home to Washington. Now, fifteen years later, Kennedy was at last able to pay homage, praying for several minutes as a steady rain returned before laying a simple wreath of local flowers on the ground. When he straightened up again, his hosts noticed that he kept his right arm stiffly to his side. "He was obviously suffering from the back pain that plagued him but was never mentioned," Debo remembered. The Cavendish family later placed a small stone tablet in front of Kathleen's burial place with this inscription: "In memory of John F. Kennedy, President of the United States of America, who visited this grave, 29 June 1963."

Kennedy's ability to swing rapidly from the somber to the playful, and sometimes back again, surfaced as he joined the duke and duchess in their waiting Bentley and quickly agreed with their proposal that they repair for a "beano" in the main house. As Debo wrote in her memoirs, "This was against the wishes of the Secret Service who said they could not ensure his security because [Chatsworth] was open to the public." On the short drive to the house, Jack, having been gently deterred from taking the wheel of the car, described the helicopter that had brought him. "It's even got a bathroom," he said proudly. "When we arrived," Debo continued, "we joined the public who were making their way up the stairs. They looked at Jack, looked back at each other and looked at him again in a classic double-take, astonished to see the President of the United States sharing their staircase."[49]

Along with the tourists, the Devonshires were also playing host to several houseguests, including the violinist Yehudi Menuhin. They now joined Kennedy for tea in Chatsworth's state drawing room, which was decorated by a painted ceiling and woven wall tapestries depicting what Menuhin called "biblical scenes side-by-side with attractive and colorful female figures. I noticed that the president's eye travelled towards the latter."[50]

Kennedy was in his element. It wasn't just a matter of creature comforts, which were always readily available to the president wherever he went. It was a question of quality. Kennedy knew of the horrors of boredom and fatigue attendant upon an existence spent in Washington among often intensely serious and almost exclusively white, male government employees who for the most part feared, suspected, and despised each other. Upper-class English country life may have held its own peculiar terrors, but these had nothing to do with excessive solemnity or the suppression of eccentric behavior. Fresh from the wrenching scene at his sister's gravesite, Kennedy was soon enjoying a "spirited natter" over tea and crumpets with the Devonshires and their set, "emitting loud peals of laughter, some of them helplessly protracted" as they discussed the finer points of the

Profumo affair and its implications for the man they called Uncle Harold.[51] The president "loved the world of heroes, myths, antiquity, great houses, and above all the failings and foibles of the English nobility," Menuhin recalled years later.[52] "I can see him now, sprawled back in his chair, teeth flashing, wrinkling up his nose at a room filled with wet dogs and cigar smoke."[53] In September 1963, the duchess's twenty-one-year-old niece Constancia ("Dinky") Romilly wrote home of a recent visit to Chatsworth, "They keep referring to the President as Jack, and there is a wonderfully autographed portrait of him in Debo's drawing room."[54] Selwyn Lloyd later remembered that Kennedy had inquired about possibly renting a summer home at Chatsworth, too, but had worried how "the local people might react to the prospect of 'security men blocking off their streets and climbing up onto their roofs with rifles.'"

The president's Tory MP friend (and now Britain's air minister) Hugh Fraser joined him on the last leg of his evening's jet-and-helicopter ride to Macmillan's home, where the heads of government were to confer about the nuclear test-ban negotiations due to begin in Moscow, and the PM's belief that these could lead to a general treaty on disarmament. Despite the weighty agenda, Kennedy remained in a nostalgic mood. "I remember almost the last time I saw him, when we were travelling in the presidential helicopter," Fraser said, "and Jack did an imitation of me being made a member of parliament [in 1945] near Stoke-on-Trent, and did a perfect imitation of the chairman and everyone introducing me."[55] This wasn't the only time on which Jack used humor to spice up the general sentimentality. "I remember he recalled a fact that must [have been] eight or ten years back," Fraser added. "We'd been late up one night in New York and gone to a late movie. It must have been one of those movies that begin at 2 a.m. And we had gone to a shooting match, you know, one of those booths down Broadway where you're talking about trying to shoot horses. And he laughingly recalled this instance. Now this showed an incredible memory of just a purely social occasion. The fact that he was president of the United States seemed to make no difference at all."[56] To judge from his dinner conversation that night, Kennedy was "ecstatic to be in England, showed a complete grip of Westminster politics and [the] larger society, and did brilliant impersonations of all the leading personalities except those actually seated around the table with him and of course Winston Churchill, whom he revered."[57]

Kennedy's pre-war traveling companion Lem Billings, who now mixed advertising work with various honorific government appointments, provided – along with the likes of Fraser and the Devonshires – the human link back to the president's early visits to Britain. "It's kind of different now," the "first friend" was heard to remark as he deplaned from *Air Force One* and headed toward a waiting bulletproofed limousine. "I was the only civilian on the trip with absolutely no protocol status," Billings later acknowledged, and after having him under his roof overnight Harold Macmillan would admit to "think[ing] the chap was a food-taster or valet of some sort."[58] Kennedy enjoyed sending Billings off on local shopping trips to pick up trinkets that he would later present to Jackie. In Rome this involved his buying several hundred dollars' worth of statuettes and jewelry on the president's behalf.[59] The immediate area around Macmillan's rural home on a Sunday morning offered a more limited range, and Billings later complained that he had found only one village shop open for business, "and even that trafficked solely in string, cheese flavor potato chips, and *Farmer's Almanac*." He eventually located "a scarf with patterns of horse heads on it," and that constituted Kennedy's British gift for his wife. Some wondered if Billings's real role in the president's entourage was to remind Kennedy of just how far he had come since their first budget-conscious European summer in 1937.

Unlike Kennedy's hosts elsewhere in Europe, Harold Macmillan went out of his way to give the impression of staging a "slightly loopy" house party rather than a great political rally – shuffling around in his ancient tweed suit, collar askew, surrounded by a cast of comic gardeners, cooks, and butlers to act as a backdrop to what appeared to be less a grave international conference than a performance of one of those bucolic P. G. Wodehouse sketches the president so enjoyed. There was considerable advance fuss, even so, in the surrounding countryside. Restaurants and pubs in the neighboring villages had been requisitioned to feed the president's 120-strong retinue, while large crowds of the curious or the obsessed began to form outside the prime minister's front gates, some with flags, others with banners protesting the visit. Macmillan wrote of the "fantastic, even romantic atmosphere that prevailed during these thrilling hours," before again noting in his diary that it had been like wandering onto the set of some "mad play."[60] Shortly after seven on a now-overcast Saturday evening, amid new frenzies of excitement, an enormous olive-green helicopter descended onto a nearby park. Macmillan's memory of the event was rhapsodic: "I can see [the president] now, stepping from the machine, this splendid, young, gay figure, followed by his team of devoted adherents. Never has a man been so well or so loyally served. Until he left, the whole of our little world was dominated by the sudden arrival and equally sudden departure of leading figures in the drama."[61]

At Birch Grove, Macmillan added, "There was none of the solemnity which usually characterizes [high-level] meetings. After all, we were friends … The President seemed in the highest spirits and was particularly charming to [my wife] and the children. None of his disabilities seemed to have the slightest effect upon his temperament. Of our party, as doubtless of many others, he was what is called 'the life and soul.'"[62] The free world's two principal leaders made an amusing pair, almost as if intentionally contrasted for comedy – Macmillan, superficially dotty and benign, wearing an egg-stained cardigan under his jacket, occasionally licking at his much-parodied cavalryman's mustache; Kennedy, taller and now bulkier, clean-cut and clad in an elegant Savile Row suit, the unconscious echo of his older peer, or in a more jaundiced opinion, "a sort of MGM version of an English gentleman." One of their first orders of business was to go out together for a predinner drink in the lounge bar of the Crown Inn, in nearby Chelwood Gate. In a joint Anglo-American security operation, the Sussex police had provided two unarmed men on bicycles to patrol the route, while the twenty-four Secret Service agents traveling with the president "operated upon somewhat cruder lines," Macmillan noted.[63] Once inside the pub, the PM enjoyed his familiar glass of dry sherry, while Kennedy bravely ordered a martini – a drink he finished with gusto, but which he later privately conceded had "tasted like anti-freeze."[64]

Dinner at the premier's house was a truly spirited affair. "Everybody loved it," one nonpolitical guest remembered. "Or at least most of them did. It was all like a pantomime that night ... Masses of people sort of screaming, running in and out of each other's bedrooms, applying make-up, while these crew-cut security men in black suits squatted around in corners staring at one." Kennedy merely smiled at this latest demonstration of the British establishment's ability to combine the exercise of political and cultural power with a generous degree of personal buffoonery. He had seen it all before. Local rumor insists that the president had continued to actively explore the limits of his wedding vows while in England, and that as a result his advance men had arranged for him to be joined by a "typist" in his bedroom at Birch Grove. A source familiar with the domestic arrangements for the trip assured the author that he had come across Kennedy late that evening dandling a young woman on his knee and giving renditions of his favorite Irish folk songs, though this detail has proved impossible to corroborate.

The talks themselves were studiously informal and quickly reached agreement on a joint Anglo-American position for the test-ban negotiations with the Soviets. Having disposed of the set agenda in little over an hour together, Kennedy and Macmillan called in their respective teams and went through the charade of pretending to have a detailed discussion on the future of NATO. This took place over the Birch Grove drawing-room table and, Macmillan thought, appealed to his guest's "puckish humour."[65] Kennedy listened attentively, answered questions with a friendly smile, and then looked the premier full in the face and said he was prepared to discuss any possible formula for accommodating the Russians so long as he wasn't personally required "to spend more than five minutes with Chairman Khrushchev." "Khrushchev!" said Macmillan, excited for the first time. "When we were in Moscow in '59, he stuffed Selwyn Lloyd into a picnic hamper, and then spun him across a frozen lake. Quite an unusual posture for the British foreign secretary." Kennedy laughed, although no one else in his party quite seemed to know what to make of this story, which happened to be true. A slight pause ensued. The president, who sat in a rocking chair, then pretended to consider rival candidates to be the new supreme allied commander in Europe, and the PM in turn pretended that they should appoint a Russian to the post. A senior State Department official, not known for his light touch, helpfully observed, "that would require very considerable serious consideration, Prime Minister."

The president was driven to Mass later on Sunday morning and showed that he had not lost his acute sense for the workings of British domestic politics. According to Philip de Zulueta, "He turned [to me] in the car, and enquired if a test-ban treaty would be of assistance to the Prime Minister. I said that it would … but that the fundamental point was the economy. He quite agreed with this."[66] Kennedy went on to press one of Macmillan's other advisers on the current state of the political opinion polls and to accurately quote the result of the parliamentary debate on the Profumo affair, which had taken place twelve days earlier. "It seems the worst attack came from some of Harold's own MPs," the president truthfully noted.[67]

After that, all that remained was the ritual exchange of presents. Kennedy gave Dorothy Macmillan a gold dressing-table set and distributed signed photographs down the family. The president had also brought with him a copy of *Why England Slept*, which he signed, "To Elizabeth (II) with affection, John F. Kennedy," before adding the slightly curious PS, "We must not fear to negotiate!" Unfortunately, the queen was in Scotland that weekend, and as a result the book went back to Washington, D.C., where it remained in private hands before being sold at auction some fifty years later. Perhaps relishing the symbolism, Macmillan in turn presented his guest with a pair of bone-china blue jays. The official catalog lists the birds as "perched on tree stumps, with backs glazed blue, breasts pink, staring fondly into each other's eyes." The owlish features of one of the pair subtly suggest Macmillan. The PM kept the president's rocking chair in his study for the rest of his life. The next day, he told his cabinet that it had been "an international meeting of a quite unique character because it could only have taken place between the British and American Governments. It is inconceivable that a series of agreements could have been reached on such a wide range of difficult topics, except by people who regard themselves as partners, and even as brothers."[68]

Kennedy's private note to Macmillan was only slightly less effusive: "I think we did good work together, and proved again the value of our informal meetings. Certainly we have never met in more agreeable or comfortable circumstances. I shall not forget ... With renewed thanks, JFK."[69] Four days later, Kennedy cabled again to thank the Macmillans for their hospitality and particularly to praise the quality of his three meals with them. From now on, he would consistently use the same "Dear Friend" prefix Macmillan did.[70]

Having first set foot on British soil in October 1935 as an eighteen-year-old student, fresh off a rough ferry crossing during which "everyone began to yawk," Kennedy wrote at the time, "leaving me covered from tip to toe with hot vomit," the man who was now president of the United States and commander in chief of all American forces left again in June 1963 under markedly different circumstances.

"Before he said goodbye," wrote Macmillan, "we discussed once more our plans for frequent communication, by telegram or telephone; with another meeting before Christmas or, at the latest, in the New Year. Hatless, with his brisk step, and combining that indescribable look of a boy on a holiday with the dignity of a President, he walked across the garden [and] went, as he came, by helicopter" – to Macmillan, leaving an indelible image of his young friend ascending into a now-cloudless English summer sky. Having arrived at the exact moment his host had most needed a balm for his soul, the president's visit now struck Macmillan in quasi-spiritual terms. "He was gone," he wrote. "Alas, I was never to see him again. Before the leaves had turned and fallen, he was snatched by an assassin's bullet from the service of his own country and the whole world."[71]

Just ten days after Kennedy's departure, an Anglo-American delegation arrived in Moscow to hold talks on the continuing test-ban problem. Averell Harriman led the US side, Lord Hailsham (the former Quintin Hogg) led the British, and between them they effected something of a role reversal of the usual national stereotypes. The seventy-one-year-old Harriman was a spare, ascetic figure who reminded many of a Victorian schoolmaster. Like his father, a fabulously successful businessman who became an outstanding statesman, he had gone on to serve as secretary of commerce, among other senior positions in Washington, where his negotiating skills had helped to broker the Lend Lease exchanges of 1940–1941. (Harriman was also a future husband of Pamela Churchill.) Hailsham, by contrast, was the fifty-five-year-old sometime minister for science, currently with a roving brief in Britain's northeast, a stocky and pugnacious character perhaps chosen for the role less for his diplomatic finesse than in the hope he might prove compatible with the more flamboyant of his Russian hosts. On July 23, Khrushchev himself unexpectedly appeared at the talks and ended up taking Hailsham and Harriman out to an extended dinner. After months of stonewalling about on-site inspections, the Soviet leader now not only wanted to conclude a comprehensive test ban, but he pressed his guests for a general "non-aggression pact" to be hammered out as well.[72]

Early the next day, Kennedy called in David Ormsby-Gore and spelled out his "frank misgivings" about the current state of the Moscow negotiations. In particular, there was the trying matter of the French. "The President has just heard," Gore cabled Macmillan, "that de Gaulle [may] try to do a deal with the Soviet Union to obtain nuclear information in order to rid himself of his hateful Atlantic links."[73] Kennedy went on to reiterate that he wanted a stand-alone test ban, without any further wishful talk about a so-called general peace treaty. If the French were foolish enough to side with the Kremlin, there would be a clear "line of demarcation" between the four wartime allies, he added, a rift that would come gradually into sharp focus and that would see the final triumph of freedom over tyranny.

"Dear Friend," the president then cabled Macmillan, "the one question which might prevent accord this week would appear to be the handling of the non-aggression pact issue. The communiqué language suggested by Hailsham in Moscow seems to me to go too far."[74] Among other things, Kennedy wanted the words "proliferation" and "intercourse" removed from the text, because, he told Gore with a straight face, "these might provoke thoughts of Miss Keeler and her circle."[75]

After intense three-way maneuvering, the breakthrough came about on July 25. The outcome was in doubt up to the last moment, with Hailsham squabbling with the Americans and cabling back that morning that he foresaw "a struggle and perhaps a breakdown."[76] Four hours later, Kennedy himself was on the line to tell Macmillan that he had authorized Harriman to sign a limited test-ban agreement and that the deal was in fact being initialed as he spoke. The treaty, which barred tests underwater, in the atmosphere, and in space (but not under-ground) and allowed up to seven annual on-site inspections by each side, would be widely hailed as a significant thaw in East–West relations, if not the beginning of the end of the Cold War. In a televised address, Kennedy told the American public that "for the first time, a shaft of light [had] cut into the dark-ness" of the arms race. The US Senate would go on to ratify the treaty by a vote of eighty to nineteen. Perhaps with just a touch of color, Jacqueline Kennedy later called the agreement "the only thing that matters in this whole century."[77] It may at least be the one truly imperishable event of the Kennedy and Macmillan administrations.

On hearing the news from Moscow, the two Western leaders had reacted in character: Macmillan, as we've seen, burst into tears, while Kennedy went about his normal daily schedule in the White House, holding a meeting with Edwin Reischauer, his ambassador to Japan, discussing the state of the economy, and hosting a reception for visiting Ethiopian dignitaries.[78] None of those who saw the president at around the time the flash came in from Moscow would recall him being visibly moved, although it's remembered that he privately repeated the line from his June 10 speech remarking, "If we can't end our differences, at least we can help make the world a safe place for diversity" while enjoying a celebratory cigar that night.

Two days later, Kennedy went off on a long weekend at Hyannis Port, accompanied only by his immediate family, his childhood friend Chuck Spalding, and the Ormsby-Gores. The pictures of the president and the British ambassador sitting bare-chested over their drinks on the aft deck of the *Honey Fitz* as the yacht cruised lazily off Cape Cod again testi-fied to the closeness of the Special Relationship. During the coming weeks, it received a good deal of play in the press. "Dear Jack," Ormsby-Gore wrote in his thank-you note of August 2, 1963, by which time he was back home on holiday, "You were so kind to have me at Hyannis Port last week-end.

They were two glorious days." After some more in this vein, Gore added one of those personalized briefings that left Kennedy so well informed about the workings of British domestic politics. "The Prime Minister is in such a state of euphoria after the Test Ban agreement that Alec [Home] doubts whether he now has any intention of ever resigning. This may lead to trouble, as an overwhelming majority of the Conservatives in Parliament are convinced he should make way for a younger man in the shape of [Chancellor of the Exchequer] Reggie Maudling this autumn."[79]

Although Kennedy didn't visit England again after June 1963, it was not the last time his friends there heard from him. "Jack sometimes telephoned with a question about Uncle Harold or another member of the government or just for a chat, usually in the early hours of the morning," "Debo" Devonshire recalled. "On one occasion he sounded exasperated. 'I was put through to a tavern called The Devonshire Arms,' he said. 'It was closed.' He was always full of Uncle Harold and ready for any stories I could tell about him."[80] Often Kennedy leavened an official cable to Macmillan mentioning NATO or SEATO or some other such acronym by signing off: "How's DEBO?"[81]

Kennedy's personal affection was sometimes tested by events. Even before the ink had dried on the historic treaty with the Soviets, the allies had again turned to the chronic problem of British Guiana. "Here we are in a great mess," Macmillan glumly cabled Kennedy. "The situation gets worse and worse. The strike continues. Industry is at a standstill, and food is running out. Yet the [government] is not overthrown." (He was referring to Georgetown, not to London.)[82] Kennedy went on to tell Ormsby-Gore that he wanted "this shitstorm in Guiana" at the top of the agenda in his future talks with Macmillan. The State Department note of a subsequent heads of government exchange on the issue concluded, "The President said he agreed with the analysis of all the difficulties, but that these still paled in comparison with the prospect of a communist regime in Latin

America."[83] At that, Macmillan adopted his fallback position and called for an international conference.

On August 3, it was the turn of Indonesia to be the cause of an anxious cable from Kennedy to Macmillan, who was then staying at Chatsworth. "I am quite worried that hopefully successful Manila summit will be torpedoed unless August 31 date for Malaysia can be postponed briefly to give [President Achmed] Sukarno a fig leaf," Kennedy wrote. "I well realize that kowtowing to Sukarno is a risky business, but a little give now may be worth the risk, especially if the likely alternative is a further step-up of subversive pursuits. This is your show," Kennedy added, displaying a gift for British idiom, "but I feel we ought to place our worries frankly before you."[84]

"Uncle Harold was staying with us," Debo Devonshire recalled, "and read [out] the message he was proposing to send to Jack. It began with a long, flowery account of the day's shooting (something the president had never done) and was larded with such phrases as 'sunlit heather,' 'birds plentiful,' and 'strong north-west wind.' The point of the message came right at the end of this poetic description."[85] Luckily, David Ormsby-Gore also happened to be staying at Chatsworth that weekend and was able to suitably edit the cable before it went off to Washington. "Dear Friend," the final draft read. "Thank you for your note. I share your grave concern about the outcome of this Malaysia meeting, but I do not believe that Sukarno can be bought off with a fig leaf. He would need something much bigger to cover him effectively."[86]

Kennedy's reply, if perfectly civil, betrayed some of the lightly mocking tone with which he occasionally met Macmillan's emotional high and low extremes, if not his specific concerns about Sukarno. "I have telegraphed our Indonesian friend," he said. "I told him that I could not believe he wanted to carry matters to the point where a showdown might become inevitable ... He has agreed, and is even willing to attend a summit meeting without preconceptions. This move suggests that he is quite loath to burn all his bridges."[87] Some advisers close to the president wondered if "the old boy," as one official referred to Macmillan, might be "just a touch loco" on the subject of Indonesia. David Bruce had provided the White House an only mixed report on Sukarno's official visit to Britain earlier in the year. "I do not think it exaggerated to say he is regarded here as a bombastic rabble-rouser, an over-heated jungle Hitler, whose greed for political power is as insatiable as his private appetites," the ambassador wrote.[88] A State Department briefing note to Kennedy on October 4 read, "The British regard Sukarno as their Castro … They fear that the US is not going to press him hard enough to force him to behave."[89]

Then events took a hand. In the week beginning October 7, 1963, Lord Home (soon to be plain Sir Alec Douglas-Home), Britain's Atlanticist foreign minister, was in the United States to address the UN Security Council before going on to a private dinner with the president and his family. We've seen that Home's younger brother William had been a friend of Kennedy since their days in pre-war London and that the Homes' nephew Robin had been a guest in the White House during the depths of the Cuban missile crisis. Back in London, on October 8, Harold Macmillan fell ill in the course of a cabinet meeting and was later found to be suffering from the not-uncommon condition of an enlarged prostate. It wasn't immediately known if cancer was involved. Over the next few days, Macmillan came to accept that it was the end of his career. The first Kennedy heard about the matter was when Randolph Churchill, who was traveling in America with Home, turned up one afternoon in the White House "with a severe list to port" and collapsed into a chair in the Oval Office, where the president then happened to be posing for Christmas photographs with his young children. Kennedy was understandably anxious to prevent his British visitor from appearing in any of the pictures. Following this, Churchill slurred out the news that "Uncle Harold" was finished – even before his illness, a seemingly anachronistic figure in a fast-developing era of beads, miniskirts, and the flying pudding-bowl haircuts of the Beatles hollering "She Loves You" – and "would probably be dead within the year."[90] According to Selwyn Lloyd, the president had shown no outward emotion at the prospect of losing his chief partner in the Western alliance. Kennedy "took it in his stride," expressing only the view that the Special Relationship was one forged by many generations of mutual trust and shared principle, before suggesting that Churchill might care to make use of a guest bedroom for a brief nap.[91]

Macmillan duly underwent surgery later that week. There was no cancer. Having resigned his office, he was left to ruefully refer to the remaining time left to him as his "life after death." Once predicted to be a matter of weeks, or at best a few months, Macmillan's retirement lasted for nearly a quarter of a century – he died in December 1986, in his own bed, just six weeks short of his ninety-third birthday.

When the queen took the unprecedented step of going to visit her departing (and heavily sedated) prime minister as he lay in the hospital in October 1963, Macmillan groggily advised her on whom to appoint as his successor. This proved to be neither "Rab" Butler, the PM's long-serving deputy, nor the heir-apparent Reggie Maudling, but the same sixty-year-old Alec Home who had been born into a titled Scottish family with a three thousand-acre ancestral estate, and, as we've seen, who happened to have been Neville Chamberlain's principal assistant at the time of Munich. His selection was not noticeably a step in the direction of modernizing Britain. Having come to office in January 1957, following a series of Tory backroom maneuvers, Macmillan left it again in similar fashion nearly seven years later. There was just time for Kennedy to send an eloquent but brief note of farewell saying, "I believe that the world is a little more safe and the future of freedom more hopeful than when we began," before a security officer appeared in the outgoing PM's hospital room to remove his special scrambler link to the White

House – at once both a symbolic and a tangible end to the "Dear Friend" partnership.[92]

★　★　★

IN WASHINGTON, Vietnam pressures were producing more anxious moments. Kennedy, while promising to withdraw one thousand troops from the area by the end of 1963, had privately concluded that the Saigon regime of President Ngo Dinh Diem was incapable of defeating the communist incursion from the north. Some of Diem's generals felt the same and engineered a coup against him on November 1. Neither Washington nor London intervened. The next day, the deposed president was placed in an armored car, told that there was no US plane available to fly him to safety, as he had asked, and then brutally shot and stabbed to death in an act of carnage that might have shocked the Manson family at its worst. Taping a statement for the record two days later, Kennedy was contrite: "I feel that we [at the White House] must bear a good deal of responsibility for it," he said, "beginning with our cable of early August in which we suggested the coup. In my judgment, that wire was badly drafted, and should never have been sent on a Saturday. I should not have given my consent to it."[93]

Historians are left to speculate whether a continued Kennedy presidency, with Harold Macmillan's uninterrupted advice and support, might have approached the situation in a different way than that of their successors in office. We'll never know; but it's worth remembering that within minutes of their first meeting at Key West in March 1961, Macmillan had warned Kennedy against any American military intervention in Southeast Asia of the type the Pentagon was then urging. Asked for his advice about sending even a token force to the area, the PM's answer came back like a bullet – "*Don't.*"[94] By 1963, Macmillan was shocked to learn that the United States nonetheless had sixteen thousand "advisers" on the ground. He had been neither consulted nor informed about their deployment. According to Kenneth O'Donnell, it was a case where the president's political calculation trumped considerations such as loyalty to his British ally, or to any other foreign power. O'Donnell later wrote of a White House meeting in which Kennedy had said he "now agreed with [the] thinking on the need for a complete withdrawal from Vietnam. 'But I can't do it until 1965 – after I'm reelected.'"[95] Kennedy had told O'Donnell in private, "If I tried to pull out completely now, we would have another Joe McCarthy scare on our hands, but I can do it after I'm reelected. So we had better make damned sure I am reelected."[96] For all their differences on the issue, Macmillan continued to believe that Kennedy would never have left American ground forces in Vietnam beyond 1965 nor tolerated the final unraveling of that country into a decade of full-scale war.

Instead, just twenty days after Diem's murder, the echo of an assassin's rifle in Dallas reverberated around the world. One of the hardest things to accept about President Kennedy's death at the age of forty-six, and surely a factor in the proliferation of conspiracy theories about the events of November 22, 1963, is how a "lone nut" could have succeeded where a lifetime of critical illnesses, debilitating surgeries, and violent contact with hostile Japanese warships – let alone the subsequent burdens of office – could have failed. The news was as profoundly shocking to Kennedy's British friends as it was to everyone else. The president's murder was "a staggering blow," Harold Macmillan wrote in his diary that night. Merely hearing the newscaster's words on the radio was "overpowering, incredible," he added, telling a political adviser it felt as if he'd been struck an "actual blow – the breath just went out of me."[97] Macmillan was too distraught to make any public comment over the course of that weekend and physically not up to the challenge of flying to Washington for the funeral. For Alec Home, who did go, it was "almost beyond comprehension" to now find himself helping to bury a man who had been "so exuberant and vital" at their meeting just six weeks earlier.[98]

Winston Churchill, who turned eighty-nine the following week, spent the miserably wet and blustery evening of
November 22 sitting in his London home, a blanket over his
knees, watching the flickering news images from across the
Atlantic. He appeared to be pitifully diminished and literally
mute with sadness at the death of his young American admirer.
"Tears streamed down his face as he watched the reports on television," recalled his granddaughter Celia Sandys.[99] By the next
morning, Churchill had composed himself sufficiently to send
a message to the president's widow. "Never have I been so filled
with revulsion, anger and sorrow as when I heard of your husband's death," he wrote. "On this great and good man were set
the hopes of humanity ... Nothing can be of consolation to you
at this time. But I would like you to know that throughout the
world, and in England especially, all men who prize Freedom
and hope for Peace share your loss and partake of your grief."[100]
Randolph Churchill paid his own tribute to the fallen president in the pages of the London *Evening Standard*. "If it is not
presumptuous to say so, I not only admired John Kennedy as a
statesman, but loved him as a brother," he wrote.[101]

On November 25, at the same hour as Kennedy's funeral
procession was leaving the White House, Harold Macmillan unexpectedly appeared on the floor of the House of Commons. It was
his first time there since his illness, and the chamber was uncharacteristically silent as he rose slowly to his feet. Like many others
present, the former prime minister wore a plain, dark suit, while
The Times reported that his "drawn face and trembling hands testi-
fied to the emotion of the moment." His voice faltering, Macmillan
nonetheless was at his most vivid – starting quietly, "like the rus-
tling of a few leaves," it seemed to Selwyn Lloyd, before "welling
up with a power that was like an organ filling a church."

Macmillan began:

> My only purpose in rising is to add a few sentences as a friend
> and, in a true sense, a colleague ... In this country, we shall

always remember Jack Kennedy as a sincere and loyal friend of Britain. To the whole world without distinction his life and words and actions were a constant inspiration. He did not regard it as a statesman's duty to yield to public opinion, but to strive to lead it. Subjected to great pressures on many conflicting issues, he seemed sometimes to be almost a rather lonely figure, but always true to his own integrity and his own faith. What he said, he meant, and he did his best to accomplish. To him the words "peace and progress" were not just a phrase for a peroration, but a living and burning faith.[102]

During the previous years, some of the gilt had occasionally flaked off the Atlantic Special Relationship when the two sides clashed about the likes of Skybolt, or when the us national security adviser McGeorge Bundy once made an unguarded remark to the effect that all the United States wanted out of Britain was "a government" – the cause of a hurried note of apology from Kennedy to Macmillan. But these were more typical of the bureaucratic dealings between London and Washington than of the relationship at the top. "Jack *loved* you," the president's widow told Macmillan in the course of an effusive and often deeply moving correspondence that lasted for the next twenty-three years. In June 1965, the retired premier wrote to express the view that "Jack and I ran the affairs of our two countries better than they are being managed now," and deploring the lack of "finesse" in their successors.[103]★ In September, another letter came from Jackie, extolling the recent joys of horseback riding and barbecues on the beach – it had all been a glorious summer, she said, "except that Jack didn't come on weekends."[104] Maurice

★ It was possibly this defect the courtly Macmillan had in mind when he later told the story of President Johnson having summoned Ambassador Ormsby-Gore and his deputy for a briefing in the White House. The Britons had arrived to find their host sitting in his private lavatory, "whose door he left open for them to survey him during his oration."

Macmillan believed that his father had had an affectionate or intellectually romantic attachment to the president.[105] "Unlike me, Jack never disappointed him," he remarked. The former premier later spent some weeks negotiating the purchase of the rocking chair Kennedy had used during their June 1963 talks at Birch Grove. After several inconclusive exchanges on the subject, the Home Office Internal Audit Agency, acting in concert with Government Hospitality, finally agreed to sell Macmillan the chair for six guineas, or roughly $30 at the exchange rate of the day.[106]

In May 1965, Macmillan and his wife hosted several of the Kennedys when they came to England for the unveiling of a memorial stone to the president at Runnymede, close to the site where 750 years earlier King John had signed the basis of modern constitutional government, the Magna Carta. By royal proclamation, three acres of surrounding British land was ceded in perpetuity to the United States. The queen spoke warmly of Kennedy, "whom in death my people still mourn and whom in life they loved and admired."[107] Harold Macmillan echoed the sentiments. The president's widow had been due to respond, but when the moment came she was overcome with grief. Jacqueline Kennedy later released a statement affirming her husband's love for the country to which he had spoken of retiring. "Your literature and the lives of your great men shaped him, as did no other part of his education," she said. "In a sense, he returns today to the tradition from which he sprang."[108] In a long thank-you note to Macmillan, Jackie wrote candidly of her in-laws: "All that family, and all the confusion – you cannot travel with them without it." Speaking of her two young children, she added: "You have to have something that makes you want to live – and now I have them … I don't know why I inflict you with all this – probably because I don't keep a diary or go to a psychiatrist – I pour it all out on you." For the first time, she now signed herself off to her seventy-one-year-old correspondent "With love."[109]

Harold Macmillan and Jacqueline Kennedy Onassis died at the ages of ninety-two and sixty-four respectively. She was married and widowed a second time and worked as a book editor and a global celebrity-without-portfolio until succumbing to cancer in May 1994. Ambassador Joseph Kennedy died in 1969, aged eighty-one, having never fully recovered from his stroke. His wife Rose outlived him by twenty-five years, dying at the age of 104. Three of their four sons and one of their five daughters predeceased them. John Kennedy's British friend Hugh Fraser was an unsuccessful candidate in the Conservative Party's leadership contest of 1975, which was won by Margaret Thatcher. He survived an IRA attack on his life and died in 1984, aged sixty-six. Winston Churchill passed away in January 1965 at the age of ninety. Churchill's son Randolph succumbed to a heart attack on June 6, 1968, which also happened to be the day of Robert Kennedy's death; he was fifty-seven. Randolph's former wife Pamela died in February 1997, aged seventy-six, while serving as US ambassador to France. John Kennedy's pre-war friends William and Alec Douglas-Home lived to be eighty and ninety-two respectively, the latter having lasted less than a year as British prime minister. The Homes' nephew Robin committed suicide at the age of thirty-six. Deborah Mitford, Duchess of Devonshire, died in 2014, by which time she was the last surviving of the six Mitford sisters whose behavior had variously entertained and scandalized polite society for much of the twentieth century. To the end of her life she often spoke of the "gay, irrepressible, honey-voiced" president and the excitement of the "new America" he embodied.

David Ormsby-Gore resigned as Britain's ambassador to the United States at an early stage in the Johnson administration, heartbroken after the death of his friend President Kennedy. "The sun has gone down and Washington seems desolate and dull in comparison with the still so recent past," he wrote to Macmillan shortly after the events in Dallas.[110] There were subsequent rumors that Ormsby-Gore, by then widowed, would marry Jacqueline Kennedy. According to the author Sarah Bradford, the retired ambassador later "admitted under pressure" that he and the former First Lady had slept together.[111] Gore went home to a second career as a successful British television executive and national film censor. He died in January 1985 at age sixty-six, like both his elder brother and his wife before him, the victim of a car crash.

Had he lived and been reelected to a second term, John Kennedy would still have been only fifty-one when he left the presidency. Historical speculations are by nature inexact. No one can say for sure what Kennedy might have done in retirement, nor, given his history of truly crippling illnesses, how much longer he might have lived. We've seen that some of the president's hosts during his June 1963 tour of Ireland took him at his word when he spoke of possibly returning to live there, either as an ambassador or a private citizen, although it's also possible that they mistook what was a friendly and sentimental interest in their country for some deeper kinship. Those inclined to take seriously Kennedy's image as a native son of the green countryside around the banks of the River Barrow – and by extension as an implacable foe of the Westminster political elite – saw his apparent recognition of Irish suffering under the yoke of English oppression as an integral part of his political philosophy. On the other hand, Éamon de Valera later remembered, "Once [Kennedy] left, we didn't hear from him and there was no real sense of connection. I think that what we saw [in 1963] was the president's charm and good manners rising to the occasion, not him preparing the groundwork to live here."[112] Only a day or two later during that same European visit, Kennedy left a member of the Cavendish family with the clear impression, "Jack [would] spend more of his time in England when he left office. Personally, I could see him living here as a battered old roué, shuttling around between town and some great country pile like a much brighter Uncle Galahad [of P. G. Wodehouse fame], and still with a gleam in his eye."[113] As early as 1947,

recalling Kennedy's excessive fondness for visiting London, Sean
Nunan, the Irish ambassador to the United States, portrayed the
thirty-year-old congressman as "an English American." "Many
people made much of Jack's Irish ancestry," one of Kennedy's
family friends added. But he was "a European … more English
than Irish."[114]

★ ★ ★

AS PRESIDENT, John Kennedy rarely if ever allowed his personal empathy for Great Britain to significantly modify the
course of American foreign policy. His essential pragmatism
in office checked and balanced his belief that Britain deserved
credit for having resisted Hitler in 1940, and that in Winston
Churchill the nation had produced a leader who lifted the spirits of freedom lovers on both sides of the Atlantic, roused the
isolationists in Congress and elsewhere in America (Kennedy's
own father among them), and had in fact saved the world for
democracy. This was a "not insignificant legacy," the president
once remarked.[115] Perhaps the one exception to Kennedy's consistent pursuit of his own national interest came at Nassau in
December 1962, when in defiance of his senior advisers he agreed
to provide the British government led by Harold Macmillan
with her own independently controlled Polaris missiles. Even
then, he proceeded with due caution. The president set the sales
discussions in motion with the British in a memorandum dated
January 30, 1963. Among other things, he "emphasized that in
the course of the talks, US should not become engaged in such a
way that failure to achieve agreement would seriously damage
US prestige."[116] He was well aware that Macmillan's euphoria
following their initial deal reflected "elemental relief" on the
Briton's part that his country would remain at the nuclear table.
Kennedy later spoke of the Nassau accord as his "roughest [for-
eign policy] fix since meeting Khrushchev."[117] It's not known if
he deliberately omitted the Cuban missile crisis when he made

the comparison. During that same week of January 1963, in the course of a hotline conversation, Kennedy and Macmillan had an exchange that seemed to suggest that whereas the British had battled for their independent nuclear weapon as a point of vital principle, the American side had seen it as a bureaucratic process that had simply needed to be resolved before both parties could move on to other matters:

MACMILLAN: I say, did you enjoy Nassau? I loved it, didn't you? I thought it was awfully good.
KENNEDY: Oh, which is that?
MACMILLAN: The Nassau meeting.
KENNEDY: Oh, yes – very good, very good.[118]

For all that, Kennedy was a true Anglophile, one whose youthful reading of books like *The World Crisis* instilled in him ideals that would color the rest of his life. He profoundly admired warrior-politicians like Churchill, long envied the cut-and-thrust of the House of Commons, which in contrast to its Washington model he once described as "a chamber of the most brilliant intellectual debate, undertaken in the atmosphere of a college food fight,"[119] and personally identified with the sort of bohemian and endlessly urbane British aristocratic statesman like his historical role model Lord Melbourne. In David Ormsby-Gore, Kennedy found an attentive and good friend who served as much as an unofficial foreign policy adviser and critical sounding board for the president's ideas as he did the accredited representative of a foreign power. Their uniquely close working relationship and personal rapport helped to put a human face on the otherwise warmly valued but somewhat abstract Special Relationship.

As a result of all this, Kennedy never gave up on Britain, even when others in his administration sometimes took a more coldly detached view of their historic Atlantic ally. Unlike them, he had a profound personal stake in the continued strength of the Anglo-American partnership.

"Together with his family, John Kennedy had many ties with our country," Queen Elizabeth said during the course of the May 1965 ceremony at Runnymede, overlooking the River Thames, to honor the fallen president. "He and they lived among us in that doom-laden period which led up to the outbreak of war," the queen continued. "His elder brother, flying from these shores on a hazardous mission, was killed in our common struggle against the evil forces of a cruel tyranny. A dearly loved sister lies buried in an English churchyard."[120]

As several of those around her struggled to contain their emotion, the queen concluded her account of the late president and his mutual regard for the British people. "His abiding affection for Great Britain engendered an equal response from this side of the Atlantic," she said, looking up for a moment at the lush springtime fields, and the river beyond, before adding simply, "Bonds like these cannot be broken." It is hard to believe that many of those who heard the queen's speech either then or later would have seriously disagreed with her remarks.

NOTES

1. "Father Does Not Always Know Best"

1.   Among the many variants on this remark by John F. Kennedy (hereafter "JFK") to Harold Macmillan is the report of Bobby Baker to US Senate Democrats, attributing more direct words to the president: "I get a migraine headache if I don't get a strange piece of ass every day," as quoted in Seymour Hersh, *The Dark Side of Camelot* (Boston: Little, Brown, 1997), p. 389. Others cite Macmillan's press secretary Harold Evans as the primary source.

2.   Quoted in Theodore C. Sorensen, *Kennedy* (New York: Bantam Books, 1966), p. 566.

3.   Richard Neustadt, as quoted in Alistair Horne, *Harold Macmillan*, vol. 2 (New York: Viking, 1988), p. 439.

4.   *Boston Sunday Globe*, November 10, 1940.

5.   Quoted in David Nasaw, *The Patriarch: The Remarkable Life and Turbulent Times of Joseph P. Kennedy* (New York: Viking Press, 2012), p. 433.

6.   Ibid., p. 474.

7.   Ibid., p. 417.

8.   Joseph P. Kennedy (hereafter "JPK") to President Franklin D. Roosevelt, July 20, 1939. See President's Secretary's File 37, Franklin D. Roosevelt Presidential Library and Museum, Hyde Park, NY.

9.   David Nasaw, *The Patriarch*, p. 365.

10. Ibid., p. 356.

11. David Ormsby-Gore (Lord Harlech) Oral History, p. 59, John F. Kennedy Presidential Library and Museum, Boston, MA (hereafter cited as "JFKL").

12. Quoted in Thomas Maier, *When Lions Roar: The Churchills and the Kennedys* (New York: Crown Publishers, 2014), p. 274.

13. Private political source close to both Harold Macmillan and David Ormsby-Gore, interview of July 2, 2009.

14. JFK letter to JPK, December 6 1940. See Thomas Maier, *When Lions Roar*, p. 274.

15. Alistair Horne, *Harold Macmillan*, vol. 2, p. 280.

16. Ibid., private political source, July 2009.

17. Rose Kennedy letter, April 1938. U.S. National Archives, as retrieved from JFKL, File No. NLJFK-KFC-23–22P.

18. JPK letter dated February 2, 1942. Box 234, Joseph. P. Kennedy Personal Papers, JFKL.

19. Quoted in Edward Renehan Jr., *The Kennedys at War, 1937–1945* (New York: Random House, 2002), p. 183.

20. Ibid., p. 180.

21. Ibid., p. 200.

22. Surgeon Rear Admiral Cyril McClintock, RN, to author, November 1992.

23. Harold Macmillan, *Tides of Fortune* (London: Macmillan, 1969), p. 622.

24. *Boston Globe*, April 10, 1941. See also Robert Dallek, *An Unfinished Life: John F. Kennedy 1917–1963* (New York: Little, Brown, 2003), p. 408.

25. Rear Admiral Cyril McClintock, RN, to author, November 1992.

26. Quoted in Nigel Hamilton, *JFK: Reckless Youth* (New York: Random House, 2002), p. 398.

27. Ibid., p. 403; see also *Boston Globe*, April 30, 1941.

28. David Shields, *Kennedy and Macmillan: Cold War Politics* (Lanham, MD: University Press of America, 2006), p. 117.

29. *Daily Mail* (London), March 5, 2009.

30. "Personal Reminiscences – Private: Robert F. Kennedy Papers," as quoted in Nigel Hamilton, *JFK: Reckless Youth*, p. 648.

31. JFK Personal Papers, Box 4A, JFKL. The letter was written to Kathleen Kennedy on March 10, 1942.

32. Nigel Hamilton, *JFK: Reckless Youth*, p. 594.

33. See *Hansard Parliamentary Report*, 3 September , 1939. hansard.millbanksystems.com/commons/1939/sep/03/prime-ministers-announcement.

34. Ibid.

35. JFK diary entry, August 1, 1945, quoted in *Prelude to Leadership: The European Diary of John F. Kennedy*, Hugh Sidey, ed. (Washington, DC: Regnery, 1995), pp. 73–74.

36. Ibid.

37. See "UK: Security, 1962," File No. JFK-POF-127–018, JFKL.

38. John F. Kennedy Personal Papers, JFKL.

39. See Thomas J. Kiernan, Oral History Interview, May 8, 1966, JFKL.

40. See Hugh Sidey, *Prelude to Leadership*, p. xxxvii.

41. David Nunnerley, *President Kennedy and Britain* (London: Bodley Head, 1972), p. 16.

42. Private political source, interview of February 12, 2006.

43. David Cecil, *The Young Melbourne* (Indianapolis, IN: Bobbs-Merrill, 1939), p. 5.

44. Timothy Naftali and Philip D. Zelikow, eds., *The Presidential Recordings: John F. Kennedy*, vol. 2: *The Great Crises* (New York: Norton, 2001), pp. 578–595.

45. Private political source, interview of February 12, 2006.

46. Arthur Schlesinger Jr., *A Thousand Days* (Boston: Houghton Mifflin, 1965), pp. 302–303.

47. Robert Dallek, *An Unfinished Life*, p. 340.

48. Published minutes of National Security Council meeting of July 19, 1961, and president's remarks at the State Department of the same date; US State Dept. Archives.

49. Presidential cable via State Department, February 6, 1961; US State Dept. Archives.

50. David Nunnerley, *President Kennedy and Britain*, p. 10.

51. US Information Agency Report to the President, March 3, 1961, "UK: Security, December 1960–March 1961," JFKL.

52. Source familiar with David Ormsby-Gore (Lord Harlech) to author; see also Christopher Sandford, *Harold and Jack* (Amherst, NY: Prometheus Books, 2014), p. 125.

53. Quoted in Henry Brandon, *Special Relationships: A Foreign Correspondent's Memoirs from Roosevelt to Reagan* (London: Arrow Books, 1989), p. 160.

2. My Trip Abroad

1. Martin Gilbert, *Winston S. Churchill: The Prophet of Truth*, vol. 5 (London: Heinemann, 1977), pp. 456–457.

2. Richard Lamb, *Mussolini and the British* (London: John Murray, 1997), p. 98.
3. Col. Burton C. Andrus, US Army, to author, August 12, 1976.
4. Joseph Kennedy Jr. to JPK, April 23, 1934, quoted in Amanda Smith, *Hostage to Fortune: The Letters of Joseph P. Kennedy* (New York: HarperCollins, 2008), pp. 130–131.
5. Ibid., pp 133–135.
6. See *Documents on German Foreign Policy, Series D*, vol. 1 (Washington, DC: US Government Printing Office, 1949) pp. 713–718.
7. Nigel Hamilton, *JFK: Reckless Youth*, p. 93.
8. Ibid., p. 107.
9. Ibid., p. 106.
10. Quoted in Joan and Clay Blair, *The Search for JFK* (New York: Putnam, 1976), p. 35.
11. Choate graduate source to author, November 2014.
12. Kirk LeMoyne Billings Papers, JFKL.
13. Nigel Hamilton, *JFK: Reckless Youth*, pp. 67–68.
14. Ibid., p.116.
15. Private source, interview of May 15, 2008.
16. Personal Papers of the President, JFKL.
17. "JFK: 50th Reunion of 1000 days at School, June 1985," Choate School Archives, Wallingford, CT.
18. Private source, interviewed on May 2, 1999.
19. Nigel Hamilton, *JFK: Reckless Youth*, pp. 112–113.
20. David Nasaw, *The Patriarch*, p. 147.
21. Nigel Hamilton, *JFK: Reckless Youth*, p. 104.
22. Rose Kennedy, *Times to Remember* (New York: Doubleday, 1974), p. 93.
23. Kirk LeMoyne Billings Oral History Project, JFKL.
24. Nigel Hamilton, *JFK: Reckless Youth*, p. 105.
25. Ibid.
26. Quoted in Edward Klein, *All Too Human: The Love Story of Jack and Jackie Kennedy* (New York: Simon and Schuster, 1996), p. 318.
27. Private source, interview of July 12, 1994.
28. JFK letter dated June 19, 1934, Kirk LeMoyne Billings Papers, JFKL.
29. JFK to Lemoyne Billings, June 27, 1934, Kirk Lemoyne Billings Papers, JFKL.
30. JFK letter dated July 25, 1934, Kirk LeMoyne Billings Papers, JFKL.
31. Ibid.
32. Personal Papers of the President, JFKL.
33. Quoted in John Kenneth Galbraith, *A Life in Our Times* (Boston: Houghton Mifflin, 1981), p. 53.

34. Rear Admiral Cyril McClintock to author, November 1992.
35. JFK letter dated September 29, 1935, Kirk LeMoyne Billings Papers, JFKL.
36. JFK letter dated October 9, 1935, Kirk LeMoyne Billings Papers, JFKL.
37. Undated JFK letter (October 1935), Kirk LeMoyne Billings Papers, JFKL.
38. Undated Billings letter, ibid.
39. Ibid.
40. James Lees Milne, *Ancient As the Hills* (London: John Murray, 1997), p. 113.
41. Rear Admiral Cyril McClintock, quoting family letter, to author, November 1992.
42. Selwyn Lloyd interview with author, November 1972.
43. Quoted in David Pitts, *Jack and Lem: John F. Kennedy and Lem Billings, the Untold Story of an Extraordinary Friendship* (Philadelphia: Da Capo Press, 2008), p. 41.
44. Kirk LeMoyne Billings Oral History Project, JFKL.
45. Harold Laski to Joseph P. Kennedy, August 20, 1940, quoted in Max Freedman, *Roosevelt and Frankfurter, Their Correspondence, 1928–1945* (Boston: Little, Brown, 1967), p. 590.
46. Undated JFK letter (January 1936), Kirk LeMoyne Billings Papers, JFKL.
47. Letter dated October 16, 1936, Kirk LeMoyne Billings Papers, JFKL.
48. Letter dated January 27, 1937, Kirk LeMoyne Billings Papers, JFKL.
49. Kirk LeMoyne Billings Oral History Project, JFKL.
50. JFK letter dated February 28, 1936, Kirk LeMoyne Billings Papers, JFKL.
51. "Diary of European Trip 1937" (hereafter "DET"), JFK Personal Papers, Box 1, JFKL.
52. Ibid. Entries for August 10–11, 1937.
53. Ibid. Entry for August 9, 1937.
54. Nigel Hamilton, *JFK: Reckless Youth*, p. 190.
55. Kirk LeMoyne Billings Oral History Project, JFKL.
56. DET, August 20, 1937.
57. Ibid., August 26, 1937.
58. Rear Admiral Cyril McClintock to author.
59. DET, August 27, 1937.
60. Ibid.
61. Kirk LeMoyne Billings Oral History Project, JFKL.
62. DET, August 28, 1937.

63. James Lees Milne, as quoted to author by Selwyn Lloyd, MP, November 1972.

64. DET, September 2, 1937.

65. Alan Burrough, CBE, interview with author, December 12, 1992.

66. Kirk LeMoyne Billings Oral History Project, JFKL.

67. David Kelly interview with author, October 2007.

68. Ibid.

69. Joseph P. Kennedy to Carmel Offie, May 13, 1938, JPK Papers, JFKL.

70. Boake Carter to JFK, December 28, 1937, Box 90, JPK Papers, JFKL.

71. Ted Morgan, *FDR: A Biography* (New York: Simon and Schuster, 1985), p. 549.

72. David Nasaw, *The Patriarch*, p. 286.

73. Hermione Baddeley interview with author, July 1983.

74. Seymour Hersh, *The Dark Side of Camelot* (Boston: Little, Brown, 1997), p. 258.

75. Priscilla Wear interview, March 16, 1965, Oral History Project, JFKL.

76. Hermione Baddeley interview with author, July 1983.

77. William Douglas-Home interview with author, April 1973.

78. JPK to JFK, May 2, 1938, Box 1, Joseph P. Kennedy Papers, JFKL.

79. Arthur Krock Oral History Project, JFKL, and also cited in Nigel Hamilton, *JFK: Reckless Youth*, p. 233.

80. Paul Johnson, *A History of the American People* (New York: HarperPerennial, 1997), p. 849.

81. See *New York Times*, 20 October 1938.

82. David Nunnerley, *President Kennedy and Britain*, p. 20.

83. Auberon Waugh interview with author, June 5, 1994.

84. David Ormsby-Gore (Lord Harlech) Oral History Project, JFKL.

85. William Douglas-Home interview, October 28, 1966, Oral History Project, JFKL.

86. Auberon Waugh interview, June 5, 1994.

87. Nigel Hamilton, *JFK: Reckless Youth*, p. 236.

88. Private source, interview of February 12, 2007.

89. Deborah Mitford, Duchess of Devonshire, *Wait for Me!: Memoirs* (New York: Picador, 2011), p. 90.

90. Arthur Krock Oral History Project, JFKL.

91. Henry Morgenthau Diaries, entry for September 1, 1938, vol. 138, Library of Congress Manuscript Division, Washington, DC.

92. Harold Nicolson, *Diaries and Letters* (New York: Athenaeum, 1966–1968), vol. 1, pp. 370–371.
93. David Nasaw, *The Patriarch*, p. 346.

3. Why England Slept

1. JFK letter to LeMoyne Billings, March 23, 1939, Kirk LeMoyne Billings Papers, JFKL.
2. Joan and Clay Blair, *The Search for JFK*, p. 68.
3. "Personal Papers and Telegrams," File no. JFKPP-004–138, JFKL.
4. Undated JFK letter (March 1939) to LeMoyne Billings, Kirk LeMoyne Billings Papers, JFKL.
5. Selwyn Lloyd interview with author, November 1972.
6. Ibid.
7. Selwyn Lloyd interview with author, November 1972.
8. W. Walton Butterworth Oral History interview, May 28, 1970, JFKL.
9. HM King George VI diary entry, March 9, 1939, quoted in Robert Rhodes James, *A Spirit Undaunted* (London: Little, Brown, 1998), p. 173.
10. David Ormsby-Gore remarks conveyed to author by Selwyn Lloyd, MP.
11. "Press Conference of Senator Kennedy, Portland, Maine, September 2, 1960," John F. Kennedy Speeches, JFKL.
12. Torbert Macdonald interview, CBS Interviews, Audio-Visual Archives, JFKL.
13. Ormsby-Gore, as quoted by Selwyn Lloyd, MP.
14. Ibid.
15. James M. Landis (hereafter JML), draft manuscript for unpublished memoirs of Ambassador Joseph P. Kennedy, Library of Congress, Washington, DC.
16. See Alexandra Richie, *Faust's Metropolis* (New York: Carroll and Graf, 1998), p. 483, which book also deals at length with general conditions in Berlin.
17. Hermione Baddeley interview with author, July 1983.
18. See Minute Book, September 1939, FO 371/2287, United Kingdom National Archives (hereafter "UKNA").
19. JFK letter to LeMoyne Billings, August 20, 1939, LeMoyne Billings Papers, JFKL.
20. Nigel Hamilton, *JFK: Reckless Youth*, p. 270.

21. Tony Rosslyn letter to JFK, November 18, 1940, JFKL.

22. JFK letter to LeMoyne Billings, July 17, 1939, Kirk LeMoyne
     Billings Papers, JFKL.

23. Quoted in Hank Searls, *The Lost Prince: Young Joe, the Forgotten
     Kennedy* (New York: New American Library, 1969), pp. 115–116;
     and private political source.

24. JML, chapter 34, p. 1.

25. Ibid., p. 3.

26. Rose Kennedy, *Times to Remember*, p. 252.

27. The former Molyneux premises still stand, if much reduced
     by both the Luftwaffe and the subsequent demands of postwar
     town planning.

28. The *Boston Globe*, September 26, 1939.

29. Selwyn Lloyd interview with author, November 1972.

30. The *Daily Telegraph* (London), September 8, 1939.

31. Ibid.

32. Ibid.

33. Cudahy telegram of September 11, 1939; see Personal Papers of the
     President, File no. JFK-PP-004–019, JFKL.

34. Cudahy cable of October 2, 1939, ibid.

35. *London Evening News*, September 7, 1939.

36. JPK diary entry, June 17, 1943, Box 101, Joseph P. Kennedy
     Papers, JFKL.

37. See "The *Athenia* Affair," Box 1, John F. Kennedy Personal
     Papers, JFKL.

38. JML, chapter 34, p. 5.

39. JFK to JPK, undated (September 1939), John F. Kennedy Personal
     Papers, Box 1, JFKL.

40. *Harvard Crimson*, October 9, 1939.

41. Rose Kennedy interview, CBS Interviews, Audio-Visual
     Archives, JFKL.

42. David Ormsby-Gore, as quoted to author by Selwyn Lloyd, MP.

43. See John F. Kennedy, *Why England Slept* (New York: Wilfred Funk,
     1940), passim.

44. Herbert S. Parmet, *Jack* (New York: Dial, 1980), p. 70.

45. JFK to James Seymour, January 11, 1940, Box 1, James Seymour
     Papers, JFKL.

46. Seymour reply to JFK, ibid.

47. JFK to JPK, n.d. (1940), John F. Kennedy Personal Papers, Box
     4B, JFKL.

48. John F. Kennedy, nationally televised address, July 25, 1961.

49. JPK to Cordell Hull, August 2, 1940, File 700.0001, US National Archives, Washington, DC.

50. Ibid.

51. JPK to Cordell Hull, September 27, 1940. See Rogers P. Churchill, et al., eds., *Foreign Relations of the United States, 1940*, vol. 3 (Washington, DC: US Government Printing Office, 1958), pp. 48–49.

52. JPK to JFK, 2 August, 1940, as quoted in Rose Kennedy, *Times to Remember*, pp. 261–262.

53. David Nasaw, *The Patriarch*, p. 463.

54. Paul Johnson, *A History of the American People*, p. 850.

55. Harold Laski to JPK, August 20, 1940, as quoted in Max Freedman, *Roosevelt and Frankfurter*, p. 590. See also Felix Frankfurter, recorded interview by Charles McLaughlin, June 19, 1964, Oral History Project, JFKL.

56. Selwyn Lloyd interview.

57. JPK to President Roosevelt, April 11, 1940, President's Office Files, Box 229, Franklin D. Roosevelt Presidential Library and Museum. For FDR reply of May 3, 1940, see Joseph P. Kennedy Personal Papers, File no. JPKPP-071–007, JFKL.

58. Quoted in Joseph P. Lash, *Roosevelt and Churchill 1939–1941* (New York: Norton, 1976), p. 146.

59. Quoted in Hugh Sidey, *Prelude to Leadership*, p. xxvii.

60. JPK to JFK, September 10, 1940, Joseph P. Kennedy Personal Papers, File no. JPKPP-004–030, JFKL.

61. Quoted in David Nasaw, *The Patriarch*, p. 445.

62. Breckenridge Long diary entry, June 24, 1940. Breckenridge Long Papers, Library of Congress, Manuscript Division, Washington, DC.

63. David Nasaw, *The Patriarch*, p. 468.

64. See "The Roosevelt Legacy and the Kent Case," Institute for Historical Review, introduction by Mark Weber, published in *Journal of Historical Review* vol. 4, no. 2 (summer 1983), p. 3.

65. JFK to JPK, December 5, 1940, "Joseph P. Kennedy Letters from John F. Kennedy, 1939–1942," JFKL.

66. JFK letter to LeMoyne Billings, November 14, 1940, Kirk LeMoyne Billings Papers, JFKL.

67. Quoted in Nigel Hamilton, *JFK: Reckless Youth*, p. 379.

68. JFK undated (December 1940) letter to JPK, John F. Kennedy Personal Papers, Box 4A, JFKL.

69. David Nasaw, *The Patriarch*, p. 512.

70. Harold Ickes diary entry, January 19, 1941, Harold J. Ickes Papers, Library of Congress, Washington, DC.

71. JFK to JPK, December 6, 1940, as quoted in Amanda Smith, *Hostage to Fortune*, pp. 499–503.

72. JPK radio address, January 18, 1941, Box 253, Personal Papers of Joseph P. Kennedy, JFKL.

73. Winston S. Churchill, *The Grand Alliance* (Boston: Houghton Mifflin, 1950), p. 128.

74. Quoted in Thomas Maier, *When Lions Roar*, p. 267.

75. Selwyn Lloyd, MP, to author.

76. Cited in C. L. Sulzberger, *The Last of the Giants* (New York: Macmillan, 1970), p. 630.

77. Franklin D. Roosevelt to his son-in-law John Boettiger, March 3, 1941, FDR Personal Papers, Franklin D. Roosevelt Presidential Library and Museum.

78. JPK diary entries, November 30 and December 1, 1940, quoted in Amanda Smith, *Hostage to Fortune*, pp. 494–497.

79. Selwyn Lloyd interview.

80. Anthony St. Clair-Erskine to JFK, December 4, 1940, John F. Kennedy Personal Papers, JFKL.

81. Selwyn Lloyd interview.

82. John Simon to JPK, October 21, 1940, "Joseph P. Kennedy General Correspondence, 1940–1946," JFKL.

83. See *New York Journal-American*, February 2, 1941.

84. Edward J. Renehan, *The Kennedys at War*, p. 183.

85. JFK to LeMoyne Billings, December 12, 1941, Nigel Hamilton Papers at Massachusetts Historical Society, Boston, MA.

86. See online source, "Inga Arvad, girlfriend of JFK," available at www.findadeath.com/forum/showthread.php?14135-Inga-Arvad -girlfriend-of-JFK&p=526195; and Bjorn Westergaard, "B.T. fandt de smukke piger" [in Danish] *B.T.* [Copenhagen daily newspaper], June 24, 2006.

87. *Washington Times-Herald*, 27 November, 1941.

88. Robert J. Donovan Oral History Project, JFKL.

89. JFK aide-mémoire, "Dinner at Mrs. Patterson's" – "Speech or Book Materials November 10 1941– January 23 1942," JFKL.

90. Barbara Leaming, *Jack Kennedy*, p. 123; and Selwyn Lloyd interview.

91. "Mrs. Paul Fejos, alias Inga Arvard," file no. 100–3816, February 9, 1942, "Hoover Confidential Files: JFK," FBI Archives, obtained by Freedom of Information request.

92. Arvad to JFK, February 14, 1942, John F. Kennedy Personal Papers, Box 4A, JFKL.

93. Arvad to JFK, April 23, 1942, ibid.

94. See "Speech or Book Materials," John F. Kennedy Pre-Presidential Papers, Box 11, JFKL.

95. Joan and Clay Blair, *The Search for JFK*, p. 156.

96. Ibid., p. 229.

97. See Theodore Sorensen, *Kennedy*, p. 18.

98. JFK to LeMoyne Billings, May 19, 1944, Kirk LeMoyne Billings Papers, JFKL.

99. Captain Charles Waterhouse interview with author; see also Barbara Leaming, *Jack Kennedy*, p. 161.

100. JFK to dowager duchess of Devonshire, September 21, 1944, John F. Kennedy Personal Papers, file no. JFKPP-063–044, JFKL.

101. Quoted in Lynne McTaggart, *Kathleen Kennedy* (New York: Dial Press, 1983), p. 146.

102. Rose Kennedy, *Times to Remember*, p. 285.

103. Cavendish family source, interviewed on 5 May, 2015.

104. Kathleen Kennedy to Family, February 27, 1945, John F. Kennedy Personal Papers, Box 4A, JFKL.

105. Quoted in Theodore Sorensen, *Kennedy*, p. 14.

106. See "John F. Kennedy Articles 1941–1949," JFKL.

107. Herbert Parmet, *Jack*, pp. 129–130.

108. Joe Kane interview, Ralph Martin and Ed Plaut Papers, Boston University Archives; see also Peter Holleran, *Irish America Magazine*, October 1989.

109. JFK to LeMoyne Billings, February 20, 1945, Kirk LeMoyne Billings Papers, JFKL.

110. Quoted in Merle Miller, *Plain Speaking: An Oral Biography of Harry S. Truman* (New York: Putnam, 1973), p. 186.

111. "John F. Kennedy Articles 1941–1949," JFKL.

4. A Very Broad-Minded Approach to Everything

1. JFK to Harold Tinker, February 9, 1945, Harold Tinker Papers, Brown University, Providence, RI.

2. Hugh Sidey, *Prelude to Leadership*, p. xxxv.

3. See Thomas Maier, *When Lions Roar*, p. 406.

4. Kathleen Kennedy to JFK, 27 February, 1945, John F. Kennedy Personal Papers, Box 4A, JFKL.

5. Quoted in Nigel Hamilton, *JFK: Reckless Youth*, p. 684.
6. Accessed from "John F. Kennedy Articles 1941–1949" (article of April 3, 1945), JFKL.
7. *Chicago Herald-Tribune*, May 2, 1945.
8. Quoted in Barbara Leaming, *Jack Kennedy*, p. 170.
9. Kathleen Kennedy to JFK, April 1945, John F. Kennedy Personal Papers, Box 4A, JFKL.
10. Ibid.
11. Kathleen Kennedy to JFK, February 27, 1945, John F. Kennedy Personal Papers, Box 4A, JFKL.
12. *Chicago Herald-Tribune*, May 28, 1945.
13. See Thomas Maier, *When Lions Roar*, p. 397; and author interview with Harold Pinter, November 1999.
14. Barbara Leaming, *Jack Kennedy*, p. 178.
15. See Martin Gilbert, *Winston S. Churchill*, vol. 8: *Never Despair, 1945–1965* (London: Heinemann, 1988); also Michael Dobbs, *Six Months in 1945* (New York: Knopf, 2012), p. 335.
16. *New York Journal-American*, June 24, 1945.
17. Selwyn Lloyd, MP, interview.
18. Kathleen Kennedy undated (1945) letter to JFK, John F. Kennedy Personal Papers, Box 4A, JFKL.
19. Joan and Clay Blair, *The Search for JFK*, p. 384.
20. Veronica Fraser undated (1945) letter to JFK, John F. Kennedy Personal Papers, file no. JFKPP-004–132, JFKL.
21. Fraser family source, interviewed on January 3, 2015.
22. Ibid., quoting JFK.
23. Ibid.
24. *New York Journal-American*, June 24, 1945.
25. *New York Journal-American*, May 28, 1945.
26. *The Daily Telegraph* (London), May 21, 2005.
27. Ibid.
28. Alastair Forbes, quoted in Nigel Hamilton, *JFK: Reckless Youth*, p. 709; and Selwyn Lloyd, MP, to author.
29. David Ormsby-Gore, as quoted to author by Selwyn Lloyd.
30. William Douglas-Home Oral History Project, JFKL.
31. Quoted in Barbara Leaming, *Jack Kennedy*, p. 177.
32. Ibid.
33. Ibid., p. 178.
34. *New York Journal-American*, July 10, 1945.
35. See Hugh Sidey, *Prelude to Leadership*, pp. 23–24.

36. Ormsby-Gore, as quoted by Selwyn Lloyd, MP.
37. Ibid.
38. Hugh Sidey, *Prelude to Leadership*, p. 10.
39. Ibid., p. xxxiii.
40. See Michael Dobbs, *Six Months in 1945*, p. 335.
41. Selwyn Lloyd, MP, to author.
42. JFK diary entry, July 27, 1945, as quoted in Hugh Sidey, *Prelude to Leadership*, p. 37.
43. Ibid., p. 38.
44. Quoted in Thomas Maier, *The Kennedys: America's Emerald Kings* (New York: Basic Books, 2004), p. 371.
45. Selwyn Lloyd to author.
46. *New York Journal-American*, July 29, 1945.
47. Ibid.
48. Ibid.
49. Quoted in Michael Dobbs, *Six Months in 1945*, p. 334.
50. See Walter Millis, ed., *The Forrestal Diaries* (New York: Viking Press, 1951), p. 79.
51. JFK diary entry, July 29, 1945, as quoted in Hugh Sidey, *Prelude to Leadership*, pp. 46–47.
52. Ibid., p. 58.
53. Major John R. Riley, MC, to author, December 1985.
54. JFK diary entry, quoted in Hugh Sidey, *Prelude to Leadership*, Appendix C.
55. Major John R. Riley, MC, to author, December 1985.
56. Ibid.
57. Quoted in Robert Dallek, *An Unfinished Life*, pp. 132–133.
58. Quoted in Hugh Sidey, *Prelude to Leadership*, p. 73.
59. Ibid., p. 74.
60. Quoted in Nigel Hamilton, *JFK: Reckless Youth*, p. 722.
61. Selwyn Lloyd, MP, to author.
62. Quoted in Nigel Hamilton, *JFK: Reckless Youth*, p. 722.
63. The *New York Times*, August 7, 1945, p.1.
64. JFK speech, November 11, 1945. See Pre-Presidential Papers, Boston Office Speech Files, 1946–1952, JFKL.
65. Quoted in Nigel Hamilton, *JFK: Reckless Youth*, p. 727.
66. JFK to Lannan, September 23, 1945. See J. Patrick Lannan Papers, Lannan Foundation, Los Angeles, CA.
67. Confidential political source, interviewed by author on March 7, 2015.

68. Ibid.; and Nigel Hamilton, *JFK: Reckless Youth*, pp. 724–725.

69. Quoted in Amanda Smith, *Hostage to Fortune*, p. 622.

70. Ibid.; and see "Joseph P. Kennedy, memorandum of conversation, 31 January, 1946," JPK Papers, JFKL.

71. *Boston Globe*, April 10, 1946, p. 4.

72. Accessed from Pre-Presidential Papers, Box 96, JFKL.

73. Political source, interviewed on March 7, 2015.

74. This is a very widely quoted tribute to the late Pamela Churchill (see, for example, "Ambassador Harriman Dead," CNN Interactive, World News Report, February 5, 1997), although it remains difficult to establish its exact provenance.

75. In a letter to her parents dated March 10, 1945 (see John F. Kennedy Personal Papers, Box 4A, JFKL), Kathleen Kennedy remarks that it was she herself whom Lady Anderson thought could go on to "straighten out Anglo-American relations." Another source familiar with Lady Anderson believes that Kathleen may have been mistaken in this and that the party in question was in fact her brother Jack.

76. See "John F. Kennedy Independence Day Oration 1946," JFKL.

77. Ibid.

78. Kathleen Kennedy to JFK, July 13, 1946, John F. Kennedy Personal Papers, JFKL.

79. Ibid.

80. Selwyn Lloyd, MP, to author.

81. "John F. Kennedy Speech at Red Feather Fundraising Event," October 14, 1946, JFKL.

82. Selwyn Lloyd, MP, to author.

83. Ibid.

84. See Joan and Clay Blair, *The Search for JFK*, p. 384.

85. Nigel Hamilton, *JFK: Reckless Youth*, p. 737.

86. Quoted in Peter Collier and David Horowitz, *The Kennedys: An American Drama* (New York: Summit Books, 1984), p. 183.

87. The *Boston Globe*, November 21, 1946; see also Nigel Hamilton, *JFK: Reckless Youth*, p. 791.

88. "John F. Kennedy Radio Address on USSR," Pre-Presidential Papers, Box 94, JFKL.

89. See Arthur Krock, *Memoirs* (New York: Funk and Wagnalls, 1968), p. 338; also the *New York Times*, March 12, 1947.

90. Quoted in William O. Douglas, *Go East, Young Man* (New York: Random House, 1973), p. 200.

5. Europe's New Order

1. John F. Kennedy statement for the record, March 1947, Pre-Presidential Papers, JFKL; also as quoted at www.airpower .maxwell.af/mil.

2. See Doris Goodwin, *The Fitzgeralds and the Kennedys* (New York: Simon and Schuster, 1987), pp. 725–726.

3. Victor Lasky, *J.F.K.: The Man and the Myth* (New York: Macmillan, 1963), p. 117.

4. David Ormsby-Gore, as quoted by Selwyn Lloyd, MP.

5. Quoted, in very slightly amended form, in Alistair Horne, *Harold Macmillan*, vol. 2, p. 280.

6. Peter Catterall, *The Macmillan Diaries*, vol. 2: *1957–1966*, passim.

7. LeMoyne Billings, undated (January 1947) letter to JFK, Kirk LeMoyne Billings Papers, JFKL.

8. Kathleen Kennedy letter, May 16, 1947. See "Family Correspondence File, 1910–1994," JFKL.

9. Auberon Waugh interview, June 5, 1994.

10. See Evelyn Waugh letters of November 1940 and May 19, 1945, in Mark Amory, ed., *The Letters of Evelyn Waugh* (London: Weidenfeld and Nicolson, 1980).

11. Auberon Waugh interview, June 5, 1994.

12. The exact phrase is quoted in David Nasaw, *The Patriarch*, p. 619. There was perhaps less of the bounder about the marquess of Hartington than the 8th earl Fitzwilliam.

13. See Barbara Leaming, *Jack Kennedy*, p. 191.

14. Arthur Krock, *Memoirs*, p. 338; see also the *New York Times*, March 12, 1947.

15. JFK speech of November 20, 1947, as quoted in *Congressional Record: Proceedings and Debates of the 80th Congress, First Session* (Washington, DC: US Government Printing Office, 1947).

16. JFK note, as quoted by Selwyn Lloyd, MP.

17. Deborah Mitford, *Wait for Me!* p. 158.

18. Anthony Eden to Kathleen Kennedy, January 10, 1948; see Joseph P. Kennedy Personal Papers, JFKL.

19. Leslie family source to author, November 30, 2014.

20. Kathleen Kennedy to Family, June 22, 1947; Joseph P. Kennedy Personal Papers, JFKL.

21. Leslie family source, quoting Hugh Fraser.

22. Leslie family source.

23. See, for instance, transcript of "Kennedy Called to the Bar" transmission of Irish RTÉ radio program at *Liveline* www.rte .ie/radio1/liveline (repeated, August 2014), which suggests that JFK went to Mulligan's pub in 1947. While there seems no reason to doubt that Kennedy did at some stage enjoy a drink on the premises, it is just as likely to have been on a subsequent visit to Ireland.

24. Quoted in Doris Goodwin, *The Fitzgeralds and the Kennedys*, p. 731.

25. See Ryan Tubridy, *JFK in Ireland: Four Days That Changed a President* (Guilford, CT: Lyons Press, 2011), p. 30.

26. Ibid., p. 31.

27. Doris Goodwin, *The Fitzgeralds and the Kennedys*, p. 732.

28. Barbara Leaming, *Jack Kennedy*, p. 192.

29. See Herbert Parmet, *Jack*, pp. 167–168.

30. Sir Daniel Davis, as quoted in Joan and Clay Blair, *The Search for JFK*, and in Barbara Leaming, *Jack Kennedy*, p. 191.

31. Ormsby-Gore private family source to author.

32. Dinah Bridge Oral History Project (interview of October 30, 1966), JFKL.

33. Ormsby-Gore family source.

34. JFK undated (1939) letter to Joseph P. Kennedy, Presidential Office Files, Box 135, JFKL.

35. David Ormsby-Gore (Lord Harlech) Oral History Project, JFKL.

36. Selwyn Lloyd, MP, repeated this story to the author, quoting the experience of a young female relative.

37. Doris Goodwin, *The Fitzgeralds and the Kennedys*, p. 541.

38. Kathleen Kennedy undated (1927) letter to family. See Kathleen Kennedy Hartington Correspondence File, JFKL.

39. Ted Reardon letter, May 17, 1948. See "John F. Kennedy Passport Application File, 1936–1956," JFKL.

40. Barbara Leaming, *Jack Kennedy*, p. 194; see also David Nasaw, *The Patriarch*, pp. 621–622.

41. Quoted in Peter Collier and David Horowitz, *The Kennedys*, pp. 207–209.

42. Ormsby-Gore family source to author, December 21, 2009.

43. JFK radio address, November 14, 1951, Box 102, Pre-Presidential Papers, JFKL.

44. Revised Standard Version, 1946.

45. Quoted in Thomas Maier, *When Lions Roar*, p. 444.

46. See Winston S. Churchill, *In the Balance: Post-War Speeches* (New York: Rosetta Books, 2014).

47. See "John F. Kennedy China Statement," February 1949, *Congressional Record: Proceedings and Debates of the 81st Congress, First Session* (Washington, DC: US Government Printing Office, 1949).

48. JPK speech, December 12, 1950, Joseph P. Kennedy Personal Papers, JFKL.

49. JFK speech, undated (1950), see Box 7, John F. Kennedy Personal Papers, JFKL.

6. John F. Kennedy Slept Here

1. Churchill made a number of broadly similar remarks on being unexpectedly returned to power in 1951. This particular comment was recorded by Selwyn Lloyd, MP, who passed it to the author.

2. Ormsby-Gore family source to author, December 21, 2009.

3. See "Mutual-Yankee Radio Transcript, January 1951," JFKL.

4. Harold Wilson interview with author, November 1992.

5. See "John F. Kennedy Travel Journal, January-February 1951," JFKL.

6. Ibid.; and Ormsby-Gore family source to author.

7. The charge that Joseph P. Kennedy was ever tied to illegal liquor trafficking is discussed in David Nasaw, *The Patriarch*, pp. 79–81.

8. Auberon Waugh interview, June 5, 1994.

9. Alastair Forbes Oral History Project, interview of 19 October, 1966, JFKL.

10. See *US Congress, Senate, Hearings Before the Committee on Foreign Relations, 82nd Congress, First Session* (Washington DC: Government Printing Office, 1951), pp. 434–435.

11. *Congressional Record*, August 25, 1950 (Washington, DC: US Government Printing Office, 1950).

12. Joseph P. Kennedy, Virginia Law School Forum Speech, December 12, 1950, Joseph P. Kennedy Papers, JFKL.

13. "The World and Democracy," *Time* magazine vol. 49 no. 12 (March 24, 1947).

14. Joseph P. Kennedy, "The Churchill Memoirs," *New York Times*, September 26, 1948.

15. The furnishings of President Kennedy's office are itemized by the JFKL.

16. See Henry Brandon Oral History Project, JFKL.

17. Ibid.

18. Kay Halle Oral History, JFKL.

19. David E. Koskoff, *Joseph P. Kennedy: A Life and Times* (Englewood Cliffs, NJ: Prentice-Hall, 1974), p. 393.
20. Henry Brandon Oral History Project, JFKL.
21. See David Nunnerley, *President Kennedy and Britain*, pp. 180–181.
22. Ibid., p. 195.
23. See "The Edwin Martin Personal Papers, JFK Interview," JFKL.
24. Alastair Forbes Oral History Project, JFKL.
25. Winston S. Churchill, *Triumph and Tragedy*, vol. 6: *The Second World War* (Boston: Houghton Mifflin, 1953), passim.
26. See, for instance, Athan Theoharis, *The Secret Files of J. Edgar Hoover* (New York: Rowman and Littlefield, 1993), p. 44.
27. Ormsby-Gore family source.
28. Ibid.
29. *New York Journal-American*, July 27, 1945.
30. See "John F. Kennedy Personal Papers, Boston Office, 1940–1956," JFKL.
31. Ibid.
32. Ibid.
33. Ibid.
34. See *Pakistan Today* (Karachi), April 17, 2015, p. 2.
35. Transcript of radio address, November 14, 1951, Box 135, President's Office Files, JFKL.
36. Quoted in Robert Dallek, *An Unfinished Life*, p. 209.
37. See Edward Klein, *All Too Human* (New York: Simon and Schuster, 1996), passim; Christopher Sandford, *Harold and Jack*, p. 99; and numerous online biographical entries citing Ambassador Kennedy's fondness for his daughter-in-law, including, for instance, *New World Encyclopedia*, "Jacqueline Kennedy Onassis."
38. Peter Collier and David Horowitz, *The Kennedys*, p. 233.
39. Quoted in David Nasaw, *The Patriarch*, p. 669; see also "The Rise and Fall of John Fox," *Time* magazine, July 7, 1958.
40. See *Congressional Record*, 83rd Congress, January 1953–January 1955.
41. Joseph P. Kennedy to "Torb" Macdonald, July 22, 1953, Box 229, Joseph P. Kennedy Papers, JFKL.
42. Selwyn Lloyd, MP, interview with author.
43. See "All the President's Women," *New York Post*, November 10, 2013.
44. Ibid.
45. Ormsby-Gore family source.
46. JFK St. Patrick's Day address, 17 March, 1954, John F. Kennedy Speech Files, 1953–1960, JFKL.
47. Hugh O'Neill interview with author, May 2012.
48. Liam Cosgrave Oral History Project, JFKL.

49. Hugh O'Neill interview with author, May 2012.

50. Quoted in Doris Goodwin, *The Fitzgeralds and the Kennedys*, p. 774.

51. Ormsby-Gore family source, December 21, 2009.

52. Hugh Fraser Oral History Project, JFKL.

53. Quoted in R. A. Butler, *The Art of the Possible: The Memoirs of Lord Butler* (London: Hamish Hamilton, 1971), p. 173.

54. Ryan Tubridy, *JFK in Ireland*, p. 36.

55. JFK address to Annual New England Air Reserve Review, South Weymouth, MA, October 28, 1955, John F. Kennedy Speech Files, JFKL.

56. Doris Goodwin, *The Fitzgeralds and the Kennedys*, p. 790.

57. JFK speech to Irish Fellowship Club, March 17, 1956, Pre-Presidential Papers, JFKL.

58. JFK, "Imperialism: The Enemy of Freedom," July 2, 1957, Compilation of Speeches, JFKL.

59. William Douglas-Home Oral History, JFKL.

60. Ibid.; see also Nigel Hamilton, *JFK: Reckless Youth*, p. 718.

61. Quoted in Kenneth O'Donnell and David Powers, *Johnny, We Hardly Knew Ye* (Boston: Little, Brown, 1972), p. 138.

62. Selwyn Lloyd, MP, interview.

63. Quoted in Peter Collier and David Horowitz, *The Kennedys: An American Drama*, pp. 246–247.

64. "John F. Kennedy Interview, Martin Papers," Library of Congress, Washington, DC.

7. Family Feud

1. Harold Macmillan to cabinet colleague Selwyn Lloyd; Lloyd interview with author.

2. See Robert Murphy, *Diplomat Among Warriors* (New York: Doubleday, 1964), p. 379.

3. Macmillan diary entries of July 30 and 31, 1956; see Peter Catterall, *The Macmillan Diaries*, vol. 1: *1950–1957*.

4. Harold Macmillan, *Riding the Storm* (London: Macmillan, 1971), p. 157.

5. Quoted in Charles Williams, *Harold Macmillan* (London: Weidenfeld and Nicolson, 2009), p. 263.

6. See Nina J. Noring, ed., *Foreign Relations of the United States, Suez Crisis, July 26–December 31, 1956*, vol. 16 (Washington, DC: US Government Printing Office, 1990), p. 1040.

7. Harold Macmillan, *The Middle Way* (London: Macmillan, 1938), passim.

8. See Victor Lasky, *J.F.K.: The Man and the Myth*, p. 251.
9. Private comments of John F. Kennedy, ca. January 27, 1961, to US Defense Department audience including Admiral Arleigh Burke, US chief of naval operations, and Commander S. R. Sandford, RN, author's father.
10. Quoted in David Nunnerley, *President Kennedy and Britain*, p. 41.
11. See JFK, "A Democrat Looks at Foreign Policy," *Foreign Affairs*, October 1957, pp. 1–16.
12. Alastair Forbes Oral History Project, interview of October 19, 1966, JFKL.
13. JFK speech, October 5, 1956, Pre-Presidential Papers, JFKL.
14. Quoted in David Nunnerley, *President Kennedy and Britain*, p. 22.
15. JFK speech, November 1, 1957, Pre-Presidential Papers, JFKL.
16. Ibid.
17. JFK remarks at Fairmont Hotel, San Francisco, September 21, 1956, Pre-Presidential Papers, JFKL.
18. Lord Avon (Anthony Eden), *Full Circle* (London: Cassell, 1960), pp. 458–459.
19. Selwyn Lloyd, MP, interview with author.
20. JFK remarks of November 1, 1957 ("The New Dimensions of American Foreign Policy"), Pre-Presidential Papers, JFKL.
21. Joseph P. Kennedy radio address, as quoted in David Nasaw, *The Patriarch*, p. 660.
22. Alastair Forbes Oral History Project, JFKL.
23. JFK speech at Irish Institute, New York, January 12, 1957, Pre-Presidential Papers, JFKL.
24. Harold Macmillan diary entry, October 24, 1957, Peter Catterall, *The Macmillan Diaries*, vol. 2: *1957–1966*.
25. UK Cabinet minutes, 28 October, 1957, Cabinet Papers, UKNA.
26. Macmillan initially referred to "the new developing civilisation" in March 1960 follow-up remarks to his "Wind of Change" speech, and according to Selwyn Lloyd and others, JFK seems to have borrowed the phrase, which he frequently used in discussion with British officials in the period January 1961–November 1963.
27. David Ormsby-Gore served under Britain's foreign secretary Selwyn Lloyd until July 1960 and then under Lloyd's replacement Lord (Alec) Home.
28. JFK speech at Milwaukee, WI, October 23, 1960, Pre-Presidential Papers, JFKL.
29. JFK remarks to Selwyn Lloyd, MP, as reported by Lloyd to author.
30. William Douglas-Home Oral History Project, JFKL.

31. Quoted in William Taubman, *Khrushchev: The Man and His Era* (New York: W. W. Norton & Co., 2004), p. 433.
32. Author interview with Selwyn Lloyd, MP.
33. William Douglas-Home Oral History, JFKL.
34. See "The Scarlet Duchess of Argyll," The *Independent on Sunday* (London), 17 February, 2013.
35. Margaret, duchess of Argyll, went on to feature in the 1963 Profumo scandal, when as part of the general air of dissolute sexual practice surrounding the case a court was shown thirteen Polaroid photographs depicting the duchess, naked save for a string of pearls, in two separate encounters with men, framed so that they were headless but who are now widely assumed to have been the actor Douglas Fairbanks Jr. and then British secretary of state for the colonies (and Winston Churchill's son-in-law) Duncan Sandys. Margaret, duchess of Argyll died in 1993.
36. See JFK, *A Nation of Immigrants* (New York: Harper and Row, revised edition 1986, with preface by John P. Roche), passim.
37. Quoted in David Nasaw, *The Patriarch*, p. 501.
38. See Hugh Sidey, *Prelude to Leadership*, p. 90.
39. David Ormsby-Gore (Lord Harlech) Oral History Project, JFKL.
40. Ibid.
41. Jacqueline Kennedy Onassis to Selwyn Lloyd, MP, as reported by Lloyd to author.
42. See "Revealed: JFK's Secret Visit to Shropshire," *Shropshire Star*, November 20, 2013.
43. JFK remarks to Annual Convention of Democratic Party of Wisconsin, Milwaukee, November 13, 1959, Pre-Presidential Papers, JFKL.
44. Roulet letter of November 30, 1959, "*Why England Slept* Correspondence and Reviews," JFKL.
45. Quoted in Douglas Brinkley, ed., *John F. Kennedy and Europe* (Baton Rouge, LA: LSU Press, 1999), p. 284.
46. Remarks by JFK in the US House of Representatives, February 22, 1951, Pre-Presidential Papers, JFKL.
47. Barbara Leaming, *Jack Kennedy*, p. 207.
48. See "A Talk with the Silent Kennedy," *U.S. News & World Report*, August 22, 1960.
49. JFK remarks of September 12, 1960, Box 1061, Pre-Presidential Papers, JFKL.
50. Quoted in Robert Dallek, *An Unfinished Life*, p. 264.
51. Private political source, May 6, 2016.

52. Ibid.
53. David Ormsby-Gore Oral History Project, JFKL.
54. Harold Macmillan diary entry, May 18, 1960, Peter Catterall, *The Macmillan Diaries*, vol. 2: *1957–1966*.
55. Quoted in Douglas Brinkley, *John F. Kennedy and Europe*, p. 284.
56. Gallup Poll no. 1676, published July 1960.
57. Selwyn Lloyd, MP, to author.
58. David Ormsby-Gore Oral History Project, JFKL.
59. Barbara Leaming, *Jack Kennedy*, p. 257.

8. Special Relationships

1. JFK Inaugural Address, January 20, 1961, Speeches of President John F. Kennedy, JFKL.
2. See David Halberstam, *The Best and the Brightest* (New York: Random House, 1972), pp. 431, 531.
3. Rose Kennedy, *Times to Remember*, p. 388.
4. Selwyn Lloyd, MP, interview with author.
5. JFK Inaugural Address.
6. Deborah Mitford, Duchess of Devonshire, *Wait for Me!* p. 208.
7. Ibid., pp. 318–319.
8. US Navy source to Commander (later Rear Admiral) S. R. Sandford, RN.
9. Harold Macmillan letter to President-Elect Kennedy, December 19, 1960, Harold Macmillan Archives, Radcliffe Science Libraries, Bodleian Library, Oxford, UK; and as quoted in Alistair Horne, *Harold Macmillan*, vol. 2, p. 283.
10. Accessed from "UK: General, January–May 1961," Box 127, JFKL.
11. UK Cabinet minutes January–February, 1961, passim, Cabinet Papers, UKNA.
12. Livingston T. Merchant, Memorandum to the State Department, January 27, 1961, US State Department Archives.
13. Presidential cable via State Department, February 6, 1961, US State Department Archives.
14. Chuck Spalding's memory of his friend JFK's remark is quoted in Seymour Hersh, *The Dark Side of Camelot*, p. 24.
15. William Roulet to Pierre Salinger, December 12, 1961, "*Why England Slept*: Correspondence and Reviews," JFKL.
16. Memorandum for the President, December 14, 1961, "*Why England Slept*: Correspondence and Reviews," JFKL.

17. Ibid.
18. Quoted in Joe McGinniss, "Stomping on Camelot," *New York Times*, March 14, 1982.
19. US Information Agency Report to the President, March 3, 1961, "UK: Security, December 1960–March 1961," JFKL. Private political source to author.
20. *Hansard Parliamentary Report*, March 7, 1961.
21. Quoted in Robert Dallek, *An Unfinished Life*, pp. 351–352.
22. Harold Macmillan, *Pointing the Way*, p. 308.
23. Macmillan later gave this perhaps comic account of his response to JFK to his Conservative party colleague Selwyn Lloyd, MP. Lloyd interview with author.
24. Harold Macmillan, *Pointing the Way*, p. 335.
25. Rear Admiral Cyril McClintock, RN, to author, November 1992.
26. Macmillan diary entry, 26 March, 1961, as cited in Alistair Horne, *Harold Macmillan*, vol. 2, pp. 292–293.
27. Alistair Horne, *Harold Macmillan*, vol. 2, p. 293.
28. Barbara Leaming, *Jack Kennedy*, p. 275.
29. See, for example, Nigel Fisher, *Harold Macmillan: A Biography* (London: Weidenfeld and Nicolson, 1982), p. 288.
30. Henry Brandon diary entry, June 9, 1961, Henry Brandon Papers, Library of Congress, Washington, DC.
31. Deborah Mitford, Duchess of Devonshire, *Wait for Me!* p. 208.
32. Selwyn Lloyd, MP, to author.
33. US Department of State Biographical Division note to the President, March 1961, "UK: Security, January–June 1961," JFKL.
34. Ibid., Selwyn Lloyd.
35. See Mary S. Lovell, *The Sisters* (New York: Norton Paperback, 2003), p. 471.
36. Hugh Sidey, *Prelude to Leadership*, p. 92.
37. Harold Macmillan diary entry, April 19, 1961, as quoted in Alistair Horne, *Harold Macmillan*, vol. 2, p. 299.
38. Ormsby-Gore memorandum to UK Cabinet, May 3, 1961, Cabinet Papers, UKNA.
39. Ibid.
40. Accessed from Prime Minister's Correspondence File, May, 1961, UKNA.
41. See, among others, the *New York Times*, June 5, 1961, and David Halberstam, *The Best and the Brightest*, pp. 95–97.
42. JFK televised address, July 25, 1961, accessed from the *New York Times*.
43. See Robert Dallek, *An Unfinished Life*, p. 389.

44. Nigel Fisher, *Harold Macmillan*, p. 263.

45. Tony Gill interview with author, May 1988.

46. David Ormsby-Gore Oral History Project, JFKL.

47. JFK televised address, June 6, 1961, accessed from the *New York Times*.

48. Harold Macmillan letter, September 15, 1961, Macmillan Papers, Bodleian Library, University of Oxford, UK; and quoted in part in Alistair Horne, *Harold Macmillan*, vol. 2, pp. 303–304.

49. Minutes of UK Cabinet meeting, June 6, 1961; see Cabinet Papers, UKNA.

50. Ibid.

51. Harold Macmillan used this phrase in his diary entry of April 6, 1961, following a round of talks with President Kennedy in Washington; according to Selwyn Lloyd and others, he repeated the words "most satisfactory" or "highly satisfactory" when coming to describe his Admiralty House meeting with Kennedy two months later.

52. Rear Admiral Cyril McClintock, RN, to author, November 1992.

53. Tony Gill interview with author, July 16, 1999.

54. Selwyn Lloyd, MP, to author.

55. See Anthony Montague Browne, *Long Sunset: Memoirs of Winston Churchill's Last Private Secretary* (London: Cassell, 1995), pp. 220 and 290.

56. CIA/OCI to President Kennedy, filed as "DTG: 131317Z, Cable to White House, Hyannis, August 13, 1961," JFKL.

57. Harold Macmillan, *Pointing the Way*, pp. 392–393.

58. US Ambassador, London, to the State Department, "UK: General, National Security Files, August–September 1961," Box 170, JFKL.

59. US National Archives, Identifier 6035203, March 1961 discussion paper: "Clandestine Action in Support of United States Berlin Policy."

60. Minutes of UK Cabinet meeting, June 20, 1961, Cabinet Papers, UKNA.

61. *Hansard Parliamentary Report*, June 6, 1961.

62. Quoted in Sergei N. Khrushchev, *Nikita S. Khrushchev*, vol. 2 (Moscow: Novosti, 1991), pp. 133–135.

63. See Honore M. Catudal, *Kennedy and the Berlin Wall Crisis* (Berlin: Berlin Verlag-Arno Spitz, 1980), p. 182.

64. JFK diary entry, 29 July, 1945, as quoted in Hugh Sidey, *Prelude to Leadership*, pp. 43–45.

65. David Nasaw, *The Patriarch*, p. 746.

66. See Arthur Schlesinger Jr., *A Thousand Days*, p. 395; and Theodore Sorensen, *Kennedy*, pp. 593–594.

67. The correspondence is quoted in "UK: Security 1961," JFKL.

68. Kenneth O'Donnell and David Powers, *Johnny, We Hardly Knew Ye*, p. 343.

69. David Halberstam, *The Best and the Brightest*, p. 84.

70. Harold Caccia note to the Foreign Office permanent secretary, August 21, 1961, Cabinet Papers (PREM 11/3350) UKNA.

71. Quoted in Alistair Horne, *Harold Macmillan*, vol. 2, p. 24. Although Macmillan was speaking in March 1957 specifically of the Suez crisis, the words stand as a reflection of his sentiments toward the US right up to his resignation from office in October 1963.

72. Macmillan letter to JFK, January 5, 1962, quoted in Harold Macmillan, *At the End of the Day*, p. 155.

73. Ibid.

74. Macmillan portrayed his reaction to Khrushchev in these words to Selwyn Lloyd, MP, later interviewed by author.

75. See George W. Ball Oral History Project, JFKL; also Macmillan diary entries, April 1961, passim, as quoted in Peter Catterall, *The Macmillan Diaries*, vol. 2: *1957–1966*.

76. See "The President's Private Meeting with Prime Minister Edward Heath," President's Office Files, Box 86, Nixon Presidential Materials Project, National Archives, Washington, DC.

77. Harold Macmillan diary entry, June 7, 1958, Peter Catterall, *The Macmillan Diaries*, vol. 2: *1957–1966*.

78. Quoted in Alistair Horne, *Harold Macmillan*, vol. 2, p. 132.

79. Selwyn Lloyd to author.

80. David Ormsby-Gore letter to JFK, 18 May, 1961, "UK: General, January-May 1961," JFKL.

81. Alistair Horne, *Harold Macmillan*, vol. 2, p. 307.

82. See Thomas Maier, *The Kennedys: America's Emerald Kings*, p. 369.

83. Selwyn Lloyd, MP, to author.

84. David Bruce Oral History Project, JFKL.

85. Selwyn Lloyd to author.

86. Deborah Mitford, Duchess of Devonshire, *Wait for Me!* p. 209.

87. Ibid.

88. Alistair Horne, *Harold Macmillan*, vol. 2, p. 402.

89. Harold Macmillan's "Events, dear boy …" is one of those widely quoted political truisms whose exact provenance continues to baffle his many biographers; Macmillan's remark about "the smooth

running of the affairs of state …" came in his speech to the Tory Reform Group, London, November 1985.

90. A source familiar with the diary notes of Major General Sir Julian Gascoigne (1903–1990) put these comments at author's disposal on November 7, 2000.

91. Ibid., Gascoigne.

92. Rear Admiral Cyril McClintock to author, November 1992.

93. Ibid.

94. Arthur Schlesinger, Jr., *A Thousand Days*, p. 452.

95. Oral Statement by Sir Alec Douglas-Home (Lord Home), March 17, 1965, JFKL.

96. Douglas-Home to his colleague Selwyn Lloyd, MP, interviewed by author.

97. Selwyn Lloyd (himself British foreign secretary 1955–1960) to author.

98. Harold Macmillan, *At the End of the Day*, pp. 147–148.

99. JFK comments to Macmillan, as quoted in Alistair Horne, *Harold Macmillan*, vol. 2, p. 290.

9. "We Are Attempting to Prevent World War Three"

1. Oral History Interview, Secretary of State Dean Rusk, JFKL.

2. Alistair Horne, *Harold Macmillan*, vol. 2, p. 384.

3. Harold Macmillan remark to his colleague Selwyn Lloyd, MP. Lloyd to author.

4. For the Kennedy-Macmillan exchange of 14 November, 1962, see Harold Macmillan, *At the End of the Day*, p. 215.

5. Lord Home, note to Dean Rusk, 26 February, 1962, Cabinet Papers (PREM 11/3666), UKNA.

6. Hugh Fraser Oral History Project, JFKL.

7. Transcript of credentials ceremony, File FO 371/156510, UKNA.

8. David Ormsby-Gore letter to JFK, July 24, 1962, "UK: General 1962, President's Office Files," JFKL.

9. Much of what remains of the British aristocracy can trace its roots to the sixth earl of Carlisle (1773–1848). Through his twelve legitimate children, he's the ancestor of the present dukes of Hamilton and Brandon, Argyll, Leinster, and Westminster, the present marquesses of Hertford and Londonderry, the present earls of Selkirk, Lichfield, and Cromartie, and the present

viscount Dilhorne, among many others; he was also a direct forbear both of Kathleen Kennedy's husband "Billy" Cavendish, marquess of Hartington, and of Lady Dorothy Macmillan, wife of Harold Macmillan.

10. Quoted in Robert Dallek, *An Unfinished Life*, p. 476; see also "The World Knows What He Was Like," the *Age* (Melbourne, Australia), 17 May, 2003.

11. Political source, interview with the author, London, May 2013.

12. ABC News Report, August 4, 2000, "JFK, Marlene Dietrich Trysted in 1962"; and see Kenneth Tynan diary entry, 4 April, 1971, quoted in John Lahr, ed., *The Diaries of Kenneth Tynan* (London: Bloomsbury, 2001).

13. Alistair Horne, *Harold Macmillan*, vol. 2, p. 525.

14. A US official familiar with the White House discussion that took place on 28 April, 1962, made this remark to Selwyn Lloyd, MP. Lloyd to author.

15. Harold Macmillan, *At the End of the Day*, pp. 146–147.

16. See "The Papers of Arthur Schlesinger, Jr., White House Files, Box WH-36, Great Britain," JFKL.

17. This description of Macmillan was made by a well-positioned British official, who mentioned it, inter alia, to his Conservative Party colleague Airey Neave, MP (1916–1979). Airey Neave interview with author, July 1973.

18. Macmillan diary entry, May 6, 1962, Peter Catterall, *The Macmillan Diaries*, vol. 2: *1957–1966*.

19. Harold Macmillan "Dear Friend" cable to JFK, "UK: General, January–June 1962, President's Office Files," JFKL.

20. Ibid.

21. Ibid.

22. For Harold Macmillan's outburst to JFK of August 18, 1962, see Cabinet Papers (PREM 11/4052), UKNA.

23. For Macmillan's apology, ibid.

24. Alistair Horne, *Harold Macmillan*, vol. 2, p. 611.

25. See Robin Douglas-Home's leading article in the defunct magazine *Now*, March 1967.

26. Douglas-Home original draft of same, made available to author, May 2015.

27. Quoted in Barbara Leaming, *Jack Kennedy*, p. 390.

28. Robert McNamara commencement address at University of Michigan, Ann Arbor, June 16, 1962, US Department of Defense Archives.

29. For an account of Ambassador Kennedy's physical condition in 1962, see David Nasaw, *The Patriarch*, p. 778.

30. See the Summary Record, C-R (62) 25, declassified 1997, US National Intelligence Archives.

31. For a discussion of the fateful USSR presidium meetings of May 1962, see Andrei A. Gromyko leading article, *Izvestia*, April 15, 1989; and Raymond L. Garthoff, "New Evidence on the Cuban Missile Crisis," *Cold War International History Project Bulletin* no. 11 (winter 1998), pp. 255–257.

32. JFK's Philadelphia address, July 4, 1962, *Public Papers of the Presidents, 1962* (Washington, DC: US Government Printing Office, 1964), item 278.

33. Archbishop Cushing letter, August 2, 1962, "*Why England Slept*: Correspondence and Reviews," JFKL.

34. Quoted in Nigel Hamilton, *JFK: Reckless Youth*, p. 331.

35. See Christopher Andrew, "The Edge of Destruction," the *Spectator* (London), December 1, 2012; and Tom Bower, *The Perfect English Spy* (New York: St. Martin's Press, 1995), p. 286.

36. Major Anderson, a fourteen-year veteran of the US Air Force, and the same pilot who took the first incriminating photographs of the Soviet missile sites, was aged thirty-five at the time of his death. The wreckage of his aircraft remains on public display in Cuba.

37. Airey Neave, MP, to author.

38. See "Dean Acheson Oral History Project, UK: General, 1962," JFKL.

39. See Sidney Graybeal, interview for US National Security Archive.

40. JFK Speech, October 22, 1962, *Public Papers of the Presidents, John F. Kennedy 1961–1963* (Washington, DC: US Government Printing Office, 1964).

41. For Rusk's comments, see Timothy Naftali and Philip Zelikow, eds., *The Presidential Recordings: John F. Kennedy*, vol. 2: *The Great Crises*, pp. 516–570.

42. See Arthur Schlesinger Jr., *Robert Kennedy and his Times* (Boston: Houghton Mifflin, 1978), p. 427.

43. JFK-Macmillan exchange of 21 October, 1962, Cabinet Papers (PREM 11/3689), UKNA.

44. Macmillan diary entry, 21 October, 1962, Peter Catterall, *The Macmillan Diaries*, vol. 2; and Alistair Horne, *Harold Macmillan*, vol. 2, p. 364.

45. Harold Macmillan, *At the End of the Day*, p. 194.

46. JFK to Joseph P. Kennedy, undated (December 1940), John F. Kennedy Personal Papers, Box 4A, JFKL.

47. Selwyn Lloyd interview.

48. See Cabinet papers (PREM 11/3689), UKNA.

49. For the varying reaction of the Western allies to the initially top secret U-2 photos, see Dean Acheson Oral History Project, JFKL.

50. David Ormsby-Gore (Lord Harlech) Oral History Project, JFKL.

51. As quoted by Macmillan's biographer Alistair Horne, Jacqueline Kennedy seems to have mistaken the date of her entertaining the maharajah to dinner, which the official White House record gives as October 23, as opposed to the 19 or 20. It's possible that, speaking some twenty-five years after the fact, Mrs. Kennedy simply confused the sequence of affairs. If so, she was not the only person to be confounded by the fast-breaking events of that week.

52. Nigel Fisher, *Harold Macmillan*, p. 297.

53. Robin Douglas-Home, *Now*, March 1967.

54. See Deborah Mitford, Duchess of Devonshire, *Wait for Me!* pp. 210–211.

55. Alistair Horne, *Harold Macmillan*, vol. 2, p. 367.

56. JFK-Macmillan conversation, October 24, 1962, "Presidential Telephone Transcripts, October 1962," JFKL.

57. See "UK: Security, 1962," file no. JFKPOF-127–018, JFKL.

58. Quoted in Harold Macmillan, *At the End of the Day*, pp. 209–212.

59. Ibid., pp. 212–213.

60. Ibid.

61. Quoted in Aleksandr Fursenko and Timothy Naftali, *"One Hell of a Gamble": Khrushchev, Castro, and Kennedy, 1958–1964: The Secret History of the Cuban Missile Crisis* (New York: Norton, 1997), pp. 281–283.

62. Harold Evans, *Downing Street Diary: The Macmillan Years 1957–1963* (London: Hodder & Stoughton, 1981), p. 224.

63. JFK cable to Macmillan, "Presidential Transcripts, files T524/62 and T525/62," JFKL.

64. William Taubman, *Khrushchev*, p. 545.

65. For details of the October 4, 1962, meeting at the US Justice Department, at which Robert Kennedy opened by "saying that higher authority is concerned about the progress of the MONGOOSE programs, and that more priority should be given to trying to mount sabotage operations," see "Memorandum for the Record, Task Force Meeting of 10.4.62," declassified February 23, 2006, US National Security Archives. For some of the tragicomic

initiatives that distinguished the long campaign to unseat Castro,
see, for instance, David C. Martin, *Wilderness of Mirrors: Intrigue,
Deception, and the Secrets That Destroyed Two of the Cold War's Most
Important Agents* (Guilford, CT: Lyons Press, 2003), p. 130.

66. David Ormsby-Gore letter to JFK, October 30, 1962,
     "UK: General, 1962, President's Office Files," file no.
     JFKPOF-127–008, JFKL

67. UK Cabinet minutes, April 13, 1960, Cabinet Papers
     (CAB/128/34), UKNA.

68. Harold Brown Oral History Project, interview of 9 July,
     1964, JFKL.

69. Airey Neave, MP, to author.

70. See Richard Neustadt, *Report to JFK: The Skybolt Crisis in Perspective*
     (Ithaca, NY: Cornell University Press, 1999), p. 37.

71. Ibid., pp. 86–87.

72. Harold Macmillan, *At the End of the Day*, p. 358.

73. Quoted in Alistair Horne, *Harold Macmillan*, vol. 2, p. 437.

74. See "UK: Security 1962, Nassau," passim, JFKL.

75. Ibid.

76. A very close approximation of these remarks, also privately reported
     to the author, appears in Harold Macmillan, *At the End of the Day*,
     p. 357.

77. Harold Macmillan diary entry, 28 January, 1963; see also Macmillan,
     At the End of the Day, p. 363.

78. See "UK: General," file no. JFKPOF-127–008, JFKL.

79. Robert Dallek, *An Unfinished Life*, p. 389.

80. David Ormsby-Gore Oral History Project, JFKL.

81. Quoted in Alistair Horne, *Harold Macmillan*, vol. 2, p. 441.

82. William Taubman, *Khrushchev*, pp. 582–585.

10. Harold and Jack

1. Harold Macmillan, *At the End of the Day*, p. 120.

2. Quoted in Alistair Horne, *Harold Macmillan*, vol. 2, p. 446.

3. JFK cable to Harold Macmillan, January 30, 1963, "UK: General
    1963," file no. JFKPOF-140–007, JFKL.

4. JFK private note to Harold Macmillan, quoted in "Kennedy-
    Macmillan Relations," *Euro-Atlantic Studies*, 2012 (Belgrade), p. 30.

5. Pierre Salinger (on behalf of JFK)-Joseph McLaughlin exchange,
    February 1963, "*Why England Slept*: Correspondence and
    Reviews," JFKL.

6. For details of the April 9, 1963, ceremony conferring honorary US citizenship on Winston Churchill, see File FO371/168490, UKNA.

7. President Kennedy news conference, US State Department auditorium, May 8, 1963, President's News Conferences, 1963, JFKL.

8. See "UK: Transcripts of President's Telephone Calls, 1963," file no. JFKPOF-127–022, JFKL.

9. Cited in Michael Beschloss, *The Crisis Years: Kennedy and Khrushchev, 1960–1963* (New York: HarperCollins, 1991), pp. 598–599.

10. Ibid.

11. Alistair Horne, *Harold Macmillan*, vol. 11, p. 510; and see Harold Macmillan diary entry, May 20, 1963.

12. Ibid.

13. Benjamin C. Bradlee, *Conversations with Kennedy* (New York: W.W. Norton, 1975), p. 230.

14. JFK–Ormsby-Gore call, April 2, 1963; see Transcripts of President's Telephone Calls, 1963, JFKL.

15. Selwyn Lloyd, MP, interview.

16. John Profumo made his public admission on June 4, 1963. Since parliament wasn't sitting, and Macmillan himself was golfing in Scotland, the disgraced war minister came clean to Government Chief Whip John Redmayne. Profumo then disappeared from public life and spent some forty years working as a full-time volunteer at Toynbee Hall, a welfare center for down-and-outs in the East End of London. His award of the CBE (Commander of the Most Excellent Order of the British Empire) in 1975 for services to charity signaled a partial return to respectability. John Profumo died in March 2006 at the age of ninety-one.

17. Harold Macmillan diary entry, March 22, 1963, Peter Catterall, *The Macmillan Diaries*, vol. 2: *1957–1966*.

18. See, among numerous other published sources, Christopher Sandford, "Sex, Spies, and the 1960s," *American Conservative*, May-June 2013.

19. Quoted in Seymour Hersh, *The Dark Side of Camelot*, pp. 390–397.

20. Ibid.

21. Quoted in David J. Garrow, *The FBI and Martin Luther King, Jr.: From "Solo" to Memphis* (New York: Penguin, 1983), pp. 61–63.

22. Daily reports of UK press coverage, collated in "UK: General," file no. JFKPOF-127–009, JFKL.

23. Marcus Lipton (1900–1978) was one of those maverick public figures who combined left-wing rhetoric with a strong vein of

British traditionalism. Scandalized by the scenes of "young girls screaming deliriously with heaving bosoms" at a 1970s concert by the bubblegum group the Bay City Rollers, Lipton announced in parliament, "If pop music is going to be used to destroy our established institutions, then it must be destroyed first." Earlier, in visiting a Brixton youth center where the future prime minister was in residence, he inspired the teenaged John Major to get into politics.

24. *Hansard Parliamentary Report*, June 20, 1963.
25. Quoted in Sarah Bradford, *America's Queen: The Life of Jacqueline Kennedy Onassis* (New York: Viking, 2000), p. 259.
26. Airey Neave, MP, interview, July 1973.
27. A reference to George Brown (1914–1985), a trade union agitator and rogue Labour politician (whom Kennedy knew and liked) with a well-publicized drink problem. In November 1963, Brown's slurred public tribute to the fallen president later led him to issue an apology for his "emotional" state.
28. See "UK: General," January-June 1963, JFKL.
29. Senior Royal Navy source, quoted to author by Rear Admiral Cyril McClintock, RN.
30. For JFK's full remarks in Cologne, June 1963, see *Public Papers of the Presidents: John F. Kennedy 1963*, pp. 498–529.
31. Ibid.
32. See Christopher Sandford, *McCartney* (New York: Carroll and Graf, 2006), among many other published Beatles chronologies.
33. Quoted in Ryan Tubridy, *JFK in Ireland*, p. 88.
34. Kenneth O'Donnell and David Powers, *Johnny, We Hardly Knew Ye*, p. 362.
35. See "Events, June 1963, Dublin, Ireland," JFKL.
36. Eamon de Valera Oral History Project, interview of September 15, 1966, JFKL.
37. Thomas J. Kiernan Oral History Project, interview of May 8, 1966, JFKL.
38. Josephine Grennan Oral History Project, interview of August 7, 1966, JFKL.
39. See Ryan Tubridy, *JFK in Ireland*, p. 194.
40. Ibid.
41. Quoted in Kenneth O'Donnell and David Powers, *Johnny, We Hardly Knew Ye*, p. 368.
42. In Ryan Tubridy's account of the occasion, "President Kennedy called across to Dave Powers and asked him to regale the company with a few Boston Irish jokes"; Selwyn Lloyd, who heard of it

through David Ormsby-Gore, added the detail that "sea shanties [had] definitely been involved."

43. Ryan Tubridy, *JFK in Ireland*, p. 173.
44. Harold Macmillan diary entry, July 7, 1963, Peter Catterall, *The Macmillan Diaries*, vol. 11: *1957–1966*.
45. Thomas J. Kiernan Oral History project, JFKL.
46. Stan Shields, quoted in the *Evening Herald* (Dublin), October 26, 2010.
47. Airey Neave interview.
48. See, for instance, image located in Wikimedia Commons: "St. Peter's churchyard, Edensor, Grave of Kathleen Kennedy, Marchioness of Hartington, 1920–1948."
49. Deborah Mitford, Duchess of Devonshire, *Wait for Me!* p. 213.
50. Yehudi Menuhin interview with author, May 23, 1976.
51. Ibid.
52. Ibid.
53. Ibid.
54. See "The Jessica Mitford Collection," Ohio State University, Columbus; and several published Mitford family obituaries, including that in the *Daily Telegraph* (London), September 24, 2014.
55. Hugh Fraser Oral History Project, JFKL.
56. Ibid.
57. Private political source, interview of May 6, 2015.
58. Ibid.; see also David Pitts, *Jack and Lem*, p. 223.
59. David Pitts, *Jack and Lem*, pp. 223–224.
60. Harold Macmillan, *At the End of the Day*, p. 472.
61. Ibid., pp. 472–473.
62. Ibid., p. 473.
63. Airey Neave to author; Harold Macmillan also used the same phrase when referring to the president's press secretary, Pierre Salinger.
64. Rear Admiral Cyril McClintock, RN, to author, November 1992.
65. Harold Macmillan, *At the End of the Day*, p. 474.
66. De Zulueta memorandum, June 30, 1963, Cabinet Papers, UKNA; see also Alistair Horne, *Harold Macmillan*, vol. 2, pp. 516–517.
67. Ibid., private political source to author.
68. Harold Macmillan to cabinet, 1 July, 1963, Cabinet Papers (PREM 11/4586), UKNA.
69. See "UK: General," 1963, file no. JFKPOF-127–009, JFKL.
70. JFK cable to the Macmillans, July 5, 1963 "UK: General, President's Office Files 1963," JFKL.
71. This is a fusion of two valedictory remarks by Harold Macmillan, sometimes quoted separately and at other times given as one. For

specific references, see Macmillan, *At the End of the Day*, p. 473 and p. 475.

72. See Charles S. Sampson, ed., *Foreign Relations of the United States, 1961–1963*, vol. 6: *Kennedy-Khrushchev Exchanges* (Washington, DC: US Government Printing Office, 1996), pp. 301–302.

73. David Ormsby-Gore cable to Harold Macmillan, July 24, 1963, Cabinet Papers, UKNA; see also Alistair Horne, *Harold Macmillan*, vol. 2, p. 521.

74. JFK cable to Harold Macmillan, July 23, 1963, "UK: General," July–November 1963, JFKL.

75. David Ormsby-Gore family source, December 21, 2009.

76. Hailsham cable to Foreign Office, July 25, 1963, UKNA.

77. Jacqueline Kennedy in private correspondence to Harold Macmillan, Macmillan Deposit, box 553, Radcliffe Science Libraries, Bodleian Library, University of Oxford, UK.

78. See President's Daily Schedule 1963 (Evelyn Lincoln Papers), JFKL.

79. Ormsby-Gore letter to JFK, August 2, 1963, "Ormsby-Gore, David (Lord Harlech), June 1962–November 1963," file no. JFKPOF-031–032, JFKL.

80. Deborah Mitford, Duchess of Devonshire, *Wait for Me!* p. 212.

81. Ibid., p. 211.

82. Harold Macmillan note to JFK, May 30 1963, Cabinet Papers (PREM 11/4593), UKNA.

83. For the State Department note of June 30, 1963, see "Profile: Philip de Zulueta," HistoryCommons.org, historycommons.org/entity.jsp?entity=philip_de_zulueta.

84. JFK cable to Harold Macmillan, August 3, 1963, "UK: Security, 1963," file no. JFKPOF-127–021, JFKL.

85. Deborah Mitford, Duchess of Devonshire, *Wait for Me!* p. 195.

86. Harold Macmillan to JFK, August 3, 1963, "UK: Security, 1963," file no. JFKPOF-127–021, JFKL.

87. JFK to Harold Macmillan, ibid.

88. For the David Bruce cable from January 15, 1963, see "UK: Security, 1963," file no. JFKPOF-127–019, JFKL. Added by an unknown hand to the ambassador's wire are the words, "Bundy … Did Sukarno get Bruce's watch, too?"

89. US State Department paper on Sukarno, October 4, 1963, "UK: Security, 1963," JFKL.

90. Selwyn Lloyd, MP, interview.

91. Ibid.

92. Final JFK–Harold Macmillan cable exchange, October 18, 1963, "UK: General, 1963," file no. JFKPOF-127–010, JFKL.

93. See Edward C. Keefer, *Foreign Relations of the United States, 1961–1963*, vol. 4: *Vietnam, August–December 1963* (Washington, DC: US Government Printing Office, 1991), pp. 526–527; see also Robert Dallek, *An Unfinished Life*, pp. 683–684.

94. Quoted in Alistair Horne, *Harold Macmillan*, vol. 2, p. 293.

95. See "Conversations with John A. McCone," Institute of International Studies, University of California, Berkeley (spring 1988); see also Kenneth O'Donnell and David Powers, *Johnny, We Hardly Knew Ye*, p. 16.

96. Ibid.

97. Harold Macmillan diary entry, November 22, 1963; see also Alistair Horne, *Harold Macmillan*, vol. 2, p. 574.

98. Airey Neave, MP, interview.

99. See Robin Weaver, "Celia Sandys – Chasing Churchill," November 15, 2010, www.womanaroundtown.com/sections/ woman-around-town/celia-sandys-chasing-churchill, accessed October 26, 2016.

100. Winston Churchill letter to Jacqueline Kennedy, Kay Halle Personal Papers and Oral History, JFKL.

101. Thomas Maier, *When Lions Roar*, p. 602.

102. *Hansard Parliamentary Report*, November 25, 1963.

103. See Alistair Horne, *Harold Macmillan*, vol. 2, p. 579.

104. Quoted in Sarah Bradford, *America's Queen*, p. 310.

105. See Alistair Horne, *Harold Macmillan*, vol. 2, p. 579; and political source to author.

106. Harold Macmillan would have paid approximately $225 for the chair in 2017 prices.

107. See, among many other published sources, The *Times* (London), May 15, 1965.

108. The *Daily Telegraph* (London), May 15, 1965, p. 1.

109. Jacqueline Kennedy and Harold Macmillan's exchange, cited in Alistair Horne, *Harold Macmillan*, vol. 2, pp. 576–579; and as quoted to the author by a source familiar with the Macmillan Deposit, box 553, Radcliffe Science Libraries, Bodleian Library, University of Oxford, UK.

110. David Ormsby-Gore to Harold Macmillan, February 1, 1964, as quoted in Barbara Leaming, *Jack Kennedy*, p. 440.

111. Sarah Bradford, *America's Queen*, p. 324.

112. Éamon de Valera remarks, given to Airey Neave, MP. Airey Neave to author.

113. Cavendish source to Rear Admiral Cyril McClintock, RN.

114. Quoted in Robert Dallek, *An Unfinished Life*, p. 3.

115. Selwyn Lloyd, MP, interview.
116. See "Presidential Action Memorandum 218, January 30, 1963," Papers of President Kennedy, National Security Files, JFKL.
117. Source familiar with Kennedy-Neustadt discussions, interview with author, May 2013.
118. For the JFK–Macmillan exchange of January 19, 1963, see "Presidential Telephone Transcripts, 1963," file no. JFKPOF-127–022, JFKL.
119. Selwyn Lloyd interview.
120. See Thomas Maier, *When Lions Roar*, p. 607. The queen's remarks at Runnymede can also be viewed on a number of readily available film archives, including British Movietone News, May 1965.

SELECTED BIBLIOGRAPHY

Abel, Elie. *The Missile Crisis*. New York: Lippincott, 1966.

Acheson, Dean. *Present at the Creation: My Years in the State Department*. New York: W. W. Norton, 1969.

Adler, Bill, ed. *The Eloquent Jacqueline Kennedy Onassis: A Portrait in Her Own Words*. New York: William Morrow, 2004.

Alford, Mimi. *Once Upon a Secret: My Affair with President John F. Kennedy and its Aftermath*. New York: Random House, 2012.

Bradlee, Benjamin C. *Conversations with Kennedy*. New York: W. W. Norton, 1975.

Bundy, McGeorge. *Danger and Survival: Choices about the Bomb in the First Fifty Years*. New York: Random House, 1988.

Butler, R. A. *The Art of the Possible: The Memoirs of Lord Butler*. London: Hamish Hamilton, 1971.

Catterall, Peter, ed. *The Macmillan Diaries*, vol. 2: *1957–1966*. London: Pan Books, 2012.

Cecil, David. *The Young Melbourne*. Indianapolis, IN: Bobbs-Merrill, 1939.

Clifford, Clark. *Counsel to the President: A Memoir*. New York: Random House, 1991.

Clymer, Adam. *Edward M. Kennedy: A Biography*. New York: William Morrow, 1999.

Collier, Peter, and David Horowitz. *The Kennedys: An American Drama*. New York: Summit Books, 1984.

Colville, John. *Footprints in Time: Memories*. London: Collins, 1976.

Crankshaw, Edward. *Khrushchev: A Career*. New York: Viking, 1966.

Dallek, Robert. *An Unfinished Life: John F. Kennedy, 1917–1963*. New York: Little, Brown, 2003.

Denenberg, Barry. *John Fitzgerald Kennedy: America's 35th President*. New York: Scholastic, 1988.

Dietrich, Marlene. *Marlene*. New York: Grove/Atlantic, 1987.

Dulles, Allen W. *The Craft of Intelligence: America's Legendary Spy Master on the Fundamentals of Intelligence Gathering for a Free World*. New York: Harper and Row, 1963.

Eden, Anthony. *Full Circle: The Memoirs of Anthony Eden*. London: Cassell, 1960.

Evans, Harold. *Downing Street Diary*. London: Hodder and Stoughton, 1981.

Fisher, Nigel. *Harold Macmillan: A Biography*. London: Weidenfeld and Nicolson, 1982.

FitzSimons, Louise. *The Kennedy Doctrine*. New York: Random House, 1972.

Fursenko, Aleksandr, and Timothy Naftali. *"One Hell of a Gamble": Khrushchev, Castro, and Kennedy, 1958–1964: The Secret History of the Cuban Missile Crisis*. New York: W. W. Norton, 1997.

Gaddis, John Lewis. *The Cold War: A New History*. New York: Penguin, 2005.

Goodwin, Richard. *Remembering America: A Voice from the Sixties*. Boston: Little, Brown, 1988.

Halberstam, David. *The Best and The Brightest*. New York: Random House, 1972.

Hamilton, Nigel. *JFK: Reckless Youth*. New York: Random House, 1992.

Hersh, Seymour. *The Dark Side of Camelot*. Boston: Little, Brown, 1997.

Hess, Stephen. *Organizing the Presidency*. Washington, DC: Brookings Institution, 1988.

Horne, Alistair. *Harold Macmillan*, vol. 1: 1894–1956. London: Macmillan, 1988.

– – – . *Harold Macmillan*, vol. 2: 1957–1986. New York: Viking, 1989.

Hughes, Emrys. *Macmillan: Portrait of a Politician*. London: Allen and Unwin, 1962.

Hunt, David. *On the Spot*. London: Peter Davies, 1975.

Hutchinson, George. *The Last Edwardian at Number 10: An Impression of Harold Macmillan*. London: Quartet, 1980.

James, Robert Rhodes. *Robert Boothby: A Portrait of Churchill's Ally*. New York: Viking, 1991.

Johnson, Haynes. *The Bay of Pigs: The Leaders' Story of Brigade 2506*. New York: W. W. Norton, 1964.

Johnson, Paul, *A History of the American People*. New York: HarperPerennial, 1997.

Judt, Tony. *Postwar: A History of Europe since 1945*. New York: Penguin, 2005.

Kennedy, John F. *Why England Slept*. New York: Wilfred Funk, 1940.

Khrushchev, Nikita S. *Khrushchev Remembers*. Boston: Little, Brown, 1974.

King, Anthony. *The British Prime Minister*. London: Macmillan, 1985.

Klein, Edward. *All Too Human: The Love Story of Jack and Jackie Kennedy*. New York: Simon and Schuster, 1996.

Koenig, Louis W. *The Chief Executive*. New York: Harcourt, Brace and World, 1964.

Krock, Arthur. *Memoirs: Sixty Years on the Firing Line*. New York: Funk and Wagnalls, 1968.

Lasky, Victor. *J.F.K.: The Man and the Myth*. New York: Macmillan, 1963.

Leaming, Barbara. *Jack Kennedy: The Education of a Statesman*. New York: W. W. Norton, 2007.

Macmillan, Harold. *At the End of the Day*. London: Macmillan, 1973.

– – –. *Pointing the Way*. London: Macmillan, 1972.

– – –. *Riding the Storm*. London: Macmillan, 1971.

Maier, Thomas. *The Kennedys: America's Emerald Kings*. New York: Basic Books, 2003.

– – –. *When Lions Roar: The Churchills and the Kennedys*. New York: Crown Publishers, 2014.

Manchester, William. *The Death of a President*. New York: Harper and Row, 1967.

– – –. *Portrait of a President*. Boston: Little, Brown, 1962.

Matthews, Christopher. *Kennedy and Nixon: The Rivalry That Shaped Postwar America*. New York: Simon and Schuster, 1996.

Mitford, Deborah, Duchess of Devonshire. *Wait For Me!: Memoirs*. New York: Picador, 2011.

Morgan, Kenneth. *The People's Peace: British History, 1945–1989*. Oxford: Oxford University Press, 1990.

Nasaw, David. *The Patriarch: The Remarkable Life and Turbulent Times of Joseph P. Kennedy*. New York: Penguin Press, 2012.

Nathan, James, ed. *The Cuban Missile Crisis Revisited*. New York: St. Martin's, 1992.

Navias, Martin S. *Nuclear Weapons and British Strategic Planning, 1955–1958*. Oxford: Oxford University Press, 1991.

Neustadt, Richard. *Report to JFK: The Skybolt Crisis in Perspective*. Ithaca, NY: Cornell University Press, 1999.

Nunnerley, David. *President Kennedy and Britain*. London: Bodley Head, 1972.

Nutting, Anthony. *No End of a Lesson: The Story of Suez*. London: Constable, 1967.

Parmet, Herbert S. *JFK: The Presidency of John F. Kennedy*. New York: Dial Press, 1983.

Pitts, David. *Jack and Lem: John F. Kennedy and Lem Billings, the Untold Story of an Extraordinary Friendship*. Philadelphia, PA: Da Capo Press, 2008.

Public Papers of the Presidents of the United States: John F. Kennedy. Washington, DC: US Government Printing Office, 1962–1964.

Raison, Timothy. *Power and Parliament*. London: Blackwell, 1979.

Raneleagh, John. *The Agency: The Rise and Decline of the CIA*. New York: Simon and Schuster, 1987.

Reeves, Thomas C. *A Question of Character: A Life of John F. Kennedy*. New York: Free Press, 1991.

Renehan, Edward J. *The Kennedys at War, 1937–1945*. New York: Random House, 2002.

Rostow, Walt W. *The Diffusion of Power: An Essay in Recent History*. New York: Macmillan, 1972.

Rusk, Dean. *As I Saw It: A Secretary of State's Memoirs*. New York: W. W. Norton, 1990.

Salinger, Pierre. *With Kennedy*. New York: Doubleday, 1966.

Sampson, Anthony. *Macmillan: A Study in Ambiguity*. London: Allen Lane, 1967.

Schlesinger, Arthur, Jr. *A Thousand Days*. Boston: Houghton Mifflin, 1965.

Schwarz, Urs. *John F. Kennedy, 1917–1963*. London: Paul Hamlyn, 1964.

Seitz, Raymond. *Over Here*. London: Weidenfeld and Nicolson, 1998.

Shields, David Brandon. *Kennedy and Macmillan: Cold War Politics*. Lanham, MD: University Press of America, 2006.

Smith, Amanda. *Hostage to Fortune: The Letters of Joseph P. Kennedy*. New York: HarperCollins, 2008.

Sorensen, Theodore C. *Kennedy*. New York: Bantam Books, 1966.

Taubman, William. *Khrushchev: The Man and His Era*. New York: W. W. Norton, 2003.

Taylor, Frederick. *The Berlin Wall: 13 August 1961–9 November 1989*. London: Bloomsbury, 2006.

Taylor, Maxwell D. *Swords and Ploughshares*. New York: Norton, 1972.

Thorpe, D. R. *Selwyn Lloyd*. London: Jonathan Cape, 1989.

Tubridy, Ryan. *JFK in Ireland: Four Days That Changed a President*. Guilford, CT: Lyons Press, 2011.

Weiss, Richard. *The American Myth of Success: From Horatio Alger to Norman Vincent Peale*. Urbana: University of Illinois Press, 1988.

Williams, Charles. *Harold Macmillan*. London: Weidenfeld and Nicolson, 2009.

Wills, Garry. *The Kennedy Imprisonment: A Meditation on Power*. New York: Mariner Books, 2002.

Wilson, Harold. *A Prime Minister on Prime Ministers*. London: Weidenfeld and Nicolson, 1977.

Wofford, Harris. *Of Kennedys and Kings: Making Sense of the Sixties*. New York: Farrar, Straus and Giroux, 1980.

Wright, Michael. *Disarm and Verify*. London: Chatto, 1964.

Younger, Kenneth. *Changing Perspectives in British Foreign Policy*. London: Collins, 1964.

INDEX

Acheson, Dean, 254, 283
Act to Promote the Defense of the
    United States, 103
Addison's disease, 168–9
Admiralty House:
    Bruce, David, 261, 284
    hotline, 29, 256, 269, 287,
        292–7, 307, 310, 345
    JFK, 249
    "skull sessions," 248
    Trafalgar Square, 247
    "Uncle Harold," 288
AGM-28 Hound Dog (supersonic
    cruise missile), 301
agranulocytosis, 48
Algeria, 218
Alsop, Joseph, 31, 169
Americanism, 175–6
American Red Cross Club, 126
Anderson, Eva, 150
Anderson, Rudolf, 283
Argyll affair, 220, 221, 311, 315

Arvad, Inga (Inga Marie Arvad
    Peterson), 107
Ashdown Forest, 320
Asquith, Raymond, 113–5, 119
Astor, John Jacob, 20
Astor, Nancy, 149
As We Remember Joe, 116
Athenia, SS, 83–6
Athens, 280
Atlantic Charter of 1941, 270
Atlantic partnership, 11, 144, 200,
    340
    See also Special Relationship
atomic bomb, 120, 144, 176, 210
atomic energy, 147, 217
atomic test ban, 222
Attlee, Clement, 28, 48, 124, 134,
    138

Ball, George, 258, 276
Bates, Charles, 315
Bay of Pigs, 245–6

Beardsley, Mimi,273
Beatles, 317, 336
  See also Lennon, John
Beatty, David Field (2nd Earl
    Beatty),163
Beatty, Dorothy Rita Furey, 163
Berlin, 141, 175, 219, 251–2, 317
Berlin speech ("*Ich bin ein*
    Berliner"),317
Berlin Wall, 14, 251–5
Bermuda meeting, 264–5
Biddle, Margaret, 159
Big Four, 254
Billings, LeMoyne ("Lem"):
  1934, 41
  1939, 73–5, 81
  1945, 107
  1962, 282
  1963, 324–5
  bisexual,39
  Choate Alumni News, 159
  "First Friend," 250
  "Fresher's Social," 51–2
  grand continental tour, 55–62
  on Jackie Kennedy, 193
  and JFK, 38, 44–7, 77, 117, 156
  and Joe Kennedy, 115
  and Kathleen Kennedy, 112, 172
  military service, 102
  Normandie, 49
Birch Grove, 321, 325–6, 341
Blair, Tony, 12
Bligh, Tim, 241
blitz (bombing of Britain), 15,
    82, 93
Bloodhound (rocket), 13
Blue Streak (surface-to-air missile),
    300
"Boofy," 68, 75

Boothby, Robert John Graham
    (Baron Boothby), 243
Boston Boot and Shoe Club, 154
Bouvier, Jacqueline, 193
  See also Kennedy, Jacqueline
Bowles, Chester Bliss, 227
Bracken, Brendan (1st Viscount
    Bracken), 104
Bradlee, Benjamin Crowninshield
    ("Ben"), 238, 311
Brandon, Henry, 185, 242
Brandt, Willy, 254
Bridge, Dinah, 169
brinkmanship, 142, 306
British Guiana, 34, 270–1, 276,
    333
British Labour Party, 124
Brogan, Denis William (Sir), 238
Bronxville, New York, 41
Brown, Gordon, 12
Browne, Anthony Arthur Duncan
    Montague, 251
Bruce, David Kirkpatrick Este,
    261–2, 284, 311
Bundy, McGeorge, 269
Bush, George Walker, 12
Butler, Richard Austen (Baron
    Butler) ("Rab"), 79, 208
Butterworth, William Walton, 76

Caccia, Harold Anthony (Baron
    Caccia), 236, 241, 254–5
Calder, James, 61
Campbell, Ian Douglas (11th Duke
    of Argyll), 220
Cannon, Frances Ann, 73–4
Capes, Stella, 315
Cape Town, 218
Carlisle, Lord, 273–4

Carter, Harold Thomas Henry
  ('Boake'), 63–4
Castle Hot Springs, 115
Cavendish, Andrew Robert
      Buxton (11th Duke of
      Devonshire), 131, 232, 243
Cavendish, Elizabeth, 161
Cavendish, William John Robert
      (Marquess of Hartington)
      ("Billy"), 24, 25, 69, 80, 131,
      160
    See also Hartington, William
      John Robert Cavendish
      (Marquess of Hartington)
Cavendish family, 14, 322
Cecil, David (*The Young
      Melbourne*), 30, 272–3, 318
Cecilienhof Palace, 134, 141
Chamberlain, Arthur Neville, 27,
      71, 82
Chang, Suzy, 315
Chatsworth House, 24, 112, 321
Checkpoint Charlie standoff, 256
China, 148, 178, 198
Chinese communist threat (1949),
      178
Choate (school), 38–40, 44, 47,
      55, 159
Christina (yacht), 220
Christmas Island, 257, 275
Churchill, Pamela (Pamela Beryl
      Digby Churchill Harriman),
      149–50, 164–6, 330, 342
Churchill, Randolph, 174, 188,
      309, 335, 339, 342
Churchill, Winston (Sir):
    1945, 120–5, 134, 188, 190
    1948, 176
    1954, 199
    and Buckingham Palace, 124

death in, 1965, 342
death of JFK, 338
honorary U.S. citizenship, 309
"Iron Curtain," 123
and Johnson, Lyndon B., 231
and Kennedy, Joe Sr., 20, 71,
      82, 92, 93, 105, 146–7, 184
and Kent, Tyler, 99
and Kissinger, Henry, 227
and Lloyd, Selwyn, 168
and Macmillan, Harold, 157
Mussolini, Benito, 35
Potsdam conference, 134, 138
and Roosevelt, Franklin D.,
      103–4, 165
and Truman, Harry S., 28
V symbol, 124
visits to US, 143, 163, 176–7
The World Crisis, 47
Churchill, Winston, and JFK
      admiration:
    books, 70, 94–5, 105, 186, 250
    face-to-face, 99, 147, 220, 251
    praise, 25, 100, 168, 176, 324,
      344
    quotes, 27, 142, 188, 224–5,
      273, 286
Clark, Alfred Corning, 189
Clay, Lucius Dubignon, 175, 255
Clifton, Chester, 251–3
 "Code Red" (Defcon 2), 289
Coldstream Guards, 113
Coleman, Bill, 115
communist threat, 178
    See also Soviet Union
Congo, 258, 263
Connally, Thomas Terry ("Tom"),
      183
Contemporary Affairs Society, 238
Cosgrave, Liam, 197

Crewe, Airmyne Harpur, 263
Cuba:
    Bay of Pigs, 245, 262
    missile crisis, 14, 29, 268–9,
        282–8, 290, 293–6, 298
Cudahy, John Clarence, 86
Cummings, A. J., 18
Curley, James Michael, 117
Cushing, Richard, 282

Dallek, Robert, 42
Darr, Alicia, 189
Davis, Daniel, 169
"Dear Friend," 246, 264, 276, 278,
    286, 329–31, 334, 336
Deborah, Duchess of Devonshire
    ("Debo"), 174, 232, 242,
    243, 262, 267, 291, 322–4,
    333
    See also Mitford, Deborah
    ("Debo")
Defcon 2, 289
Defcon 4, 298
de Gaulle, Charles, 256, 258, 307
de Valera, Éamon, 137, 318, 343
Devonshire, Andrew Robert
    Buxton (11th Duke of
    Devonshire), 239
Devonshires, 323
de Zulueta, Philip, 269, 328
Diefenbaker, John George, 247,
    305
Diem, Ngo Dinh, 337
Dietrich, Maria, 81
Dietrich, Marlene, 81, 274
disarmament, 67, 90, 116, 210, 218,
    222, 225, 228–9, 257, 274,
    306, 324
Dobrynin, Anatoly, 297
domino theory, 157, 162

Dr. No, 245
Dulles, Allen, 245
Dulles, John Foster, 210, 213
Dunganstown, 166–7, 319
Dunkirk, 97

Earhart, Amelia, 85
East Germany, 262
East–West relations, 116, 121, 269,
    279, 282, 332
Eden, Anthony, 11, 66, 163, 198,
    208, 211, 213
Edensor, 174
Eisenhower, Dwight David, 11, 28,
    140, 194, 216
Elizabeth (II), the Queen Mother,
    19, 74, 194, 271, 277, 329,
    346
Erskine, Anthony St. Clair, 52
European Common Market, 266,
    276, 312
European Economic Community,
    258
Evans, Reginald ("Reg"), 26
ExComm, 285, 288, 290

Fay, Paul, 204
Fechter, Peter, 256
Fine Gael Party, 197
Fitzgerald, John Francis ("Honey
    Fitz"), 42
Fitzgerald, Mary, 42
Fitzwilliam, Olive ("Obby"), 160
Fitzwilliam, Peter Wentworth, 25,
    160, 163
Forbes, Alastair, 129, 174, 182,
    187–8, 211–4
Forrestal, James, 108, 124,
    139–41
Fox, John, 194

Fraser, Hugh:
  1939, 34
  in British Guiana, 270
  in Jamaica, 292
  and JFK social life, 69, 127–8,
    149–51, 164, 199, 211,
    324–5, 341
  and Kathleen Kennedy's
    funeral, 174
  and socialized medicine, 225
  at Stafford, 134
Fraser, Veronica, 126
Freeman-Mitford, Deborah
  ("Debo"), 322
  See also Deborah, Duchess of
    Devonshire ("Debo")
Friedrich, Carl, 90
Fuel Order, 180
Funk, Wilfred, 92, 225, 309

Gaitskell, Hugh, 180, 224, 250,
  284
Galbraith, John Kenneth, 48, 235
Gamarekian, Barbara, 273
Gascoigne, Julian, 264
Gascoyne-Cecil, Lady Mary, 131
Gascoyne-Cecil, Robert, 168
Gathering Storm, The, 184
George, David Lloyd, 35
Ghana, 23, 258
Gill, Tony, 247, 250, 316
Glenn, John, 279
global test-ban treaty, 306
Gore (Ormsby-Gore), David (5th
  Baron Harlech):
  admiration of JFK, 17, 129, 158,
    178, 210, 280, 300
  as ambassador, 260, 271, 312,
    342
  appearance, 68, 77

arms control, 228
Bahamas meeting, 303, 305
British Guiana, 333
Congo crisis, 263
Cuban missile crisis, 289–90,
  300
de facto cabinet member, 269
foreign office, 246
Grosvenor House, 126
Hyannis Port visits, 332
friendship with JFK, 169, 172,
  272
Kathleen Kennedy's requiem
  mass, 174
JFK illnesses, 144, 248
military service, 87
nicknames, 36, 68, 75
Oswestry, 224
personal philosophy, 90, 133,
  139, 153, 168, 210, 214, 223,
  312, 333
and President Sukarno, 334
Prince's Gate, 81
UN delegate, 197
Gore (Ormsby-Gore), Sissy, 136
Grand Design, 243
Grandi, Dino, 35
Graybeal, Sidney, 285
Gromyko, Andrei, 122

Hailsham (Lord) Hogg, Quintin,
  330
Halifax (Lord) Wood, Edward
  Frederick Lindley, 79, 109,
  118, 151
Halle, Kay, 186
Hamilton, Nigel, 43, 44, 153
Harlech (Lord) *see* Gore (Ormsby-
  Gore), David
Hawk (missile), 13, 277

Harriman, Averell, 20, 331
Hartington, William John
    Robert Cavendish (Marquess
    of Hartington) ("Billy"),
    110–3, 119
Harvard Crimson, 88, 92
Hearst (newspaper), 123, 204, 254,
    315
Heath, Edward Richard George
    (Sir) ("Ted"), 12
"Hebrew lobby," 16
Hersh, Seymour, 315
Herstmonceux Castle, 60
Hieroglyphic Mountains, 115
Hillman, Bill, 98
Hilton, Boyd, 273
Hiroshima, 143
Hitler, Adolf, 15, 22, 28, 35–6, 79,
    82, 107, 109, 138, 141–3, 344
Hobson, Valerie, 314
Hogg, Quintin (Lord Hailsham),
    330
Holborn, Fred, 238
Holy Loch, 300
Home, Alexander Frederick
    (Baron Home of the Hirsel)
    ("Alec"), 69, 131, 236, 252,
    266, 335–6, 342
Home (Douglas-Home), Cecil
    Robin, 279, 291, 342
Home (Douglas-Home), William,
    65, 69, 126, 130, 202, 219,
    266, 342
"Honey Fitz" Fitzgerald, 42
Honey Fitz (yacht), 243
Hood (Lord), 278
Hoover, John Edgar, 108, 189, 315
Hopkins, Harry, 47
Horne, Alstair, 274, 278
Horton, Ralph Jr. ("Rip"), 39

"hotline" calls, 29, 256, 269, 287,
    292–7, 308, 310, 345
Hound Dog (missile), 301
Hull, Cordell, 56
Humphrey, George Magoffin, 208
Hyannis Port:
    1934, 40
    1937, 55
    1961, 252–3
    1962, 272
    Forbes, Alastair, 214
    The Gathering Storm, 184
    Glenn, John, 279
    Jack vs. Joe, 115
    Kennedy, Joe, 144–6
    Ormsby-Gore, David, 197, 332
    Spalding, Chuck, 332
Hyde-White, Wilfrid, 203

illnesses of JFK:
    1931, 38
    1934, 46
    1935, 52, 53
    1941, 106
    Addison's disease, 168
    agranulocytosis, 50
    Arizona respite, 143
    back surgery, 111, 198
    general unease, 143
    in Korea, 192
    Lahey Clinic, 168
    leukemia, 44
    London Clinic, 168
Indochina War, 198
Irish-Kennedy roots:
    Ancient Order of the
      Hibernians, 165
    bad blood, 106
    Catholic republic, 134
    Dungastown, 167, 318–9

family tradition, 29
historic suffering, 215
"kiss my ring," 96
and Liam Cosgrave, 197
Lismore Castle, 162
and Sean Nunan, 344
self-determination, 320
St. Patrick's Day, 196, 201
unification, 138
Irish National Assembly, 320
"Irish Question," 258
Ironbark, 283
Israel, 171, 277–8
Ivanov, Yevgeni Mikhailovich
      ("Eugene Ivanov"), 313
Izmir, 297

Jacobson, Max ("Miracle Max"),
      250, 287
Jagan, Cheddi Berret, 270
Jerusalem, 171
Jewish question, 16
Johnson, Herschel Vespasian, 98
Johnson, Lyndon Baines, 12, 200,
      231, 255, 261
Johnson, Paul Bede, 95
Journal-American, 125, 132, 137
Jupiter (long-range rockets), 297

Kane, Joe, 117
Keeler, Christine Margaret, 313
Kennedy, Caroline, 285
Kennedy, Edward ("Ted"), 23
Kennedy, Jacqueline, 14, 241–3,
      275, 332, 341
   See also Bouvier, Jacqueline
Kennedy, John ("Jack") Fitzgerald:
   As We Remember Joe, 116
   Athenia, fact-finding, 83–6
   Berliner, 317

Britain, 24, 74, 128, 132, 183,
      282, 307, 344–6
Cuba, 269, 294, 298, 344
de Gaulle, Charles, 307–8
Eisenhower, Dwight D., 141
European politics, 154, 183–4,
      312
Harvard, 54
Kennedy, Joseph Sr., 22,
      100–1
Korea, 178
Khrushchev, Nikita, 22, 228,
      246–9, 255
"Let's Try an Experiment for
      Peace," 116
military service, 25, 107, 109
A Nation of Immigrants, 221
presidential ambitions, 31, 33,
      145, 158, 202, 209, 224–7,
      229, 231
Princeton, 53
Profiles in Courage, 199
senator from Massachusetts,
      148, 155–6, 171
Suez, 11, 157, 199, 202, 206–9,
      211–7, 220, 245, 316
test ban, 306, 310
travel, 56, 80, 191–2, 199, 327
Vienna, 121
Why England Slept, 27, 54, 199,
      225, 237, 241, 254, 282, 309,
      329
   See also illnesses of JFK; Irish-
      Kennedy roots; lady friends,
      JFK
Kennedy, Joseph Jr., 22–3, 36, 43,
      114
Kennedy, Joseph Sr.:
   Asia, 178
   Buckingham Palace, 76

build up to war, 14, 19, 72, 80, 92, 219
career, 45, 67, 110
Churchill, Winston, 146, 184
Europe, 225
import business, 36
stroke, 264, 280
Suez, 214
US-Britain relations, 184
See also lady friends, Joseph Kennedy Sr.
Kennedy, Kathleen ("Kick"):
Arvad, Inga, 107
Austin Seven, 126
Britain, 80, 116, 121–5, 148, 151, 194
Cavendish, William, 112–5, 131
Chatsworth House, 24
Churchill, Pamela, 150, 166, 168
Eden, Anthony, 163
Fitzwilliam, Peter Wentworth, 160, 173
Forbes, Alistair, 129–30
Freeman-Mitford, Deborah, 175
Kennedy, Rose, 174
Lismore Castle, 162
siblings, 24, 59, 108, 111, 159, 172, 291
station wagon, 166
Kennedy, Robert ("Bobby"), 23, 137, 229, 259–60, 268, 296, 315, 342
Kennedy, Rose:
Catholicism, 74, 112
early life, 41–6, 49
death, 341
JFK 38–40, 42–5, 88, 115, 193, 231

Kennedy, Kathleen, 24, 41–5, 162, 175
travel, 41, 44
visit to Windsor castle, 19
war years, 82–5
Kennedy, Rosemary, 21, 110
Kennedy family properties, 42
Kennedy–Macmillan partnership, 17, 22, 32, 151, 158, 205–8, 231–67, 275, 286–344
Kent, Tyler Gatewood, 98–100
Key West, 239–40, 245, 260, 337
Khrushchev, Nikita:
appearance, 150
behavior, 228, 328
Berlin, 253, 288, 292
Cuba, 236, 245, 281, 287, 292, 296–8
goodwill tour, 219
JFK, 22, 120, 229, 247–9, 254
non-aggression pact, 331
Operation Rose, 219
Ormsby-Gore, David, 312
Soviet threat, 89, 226
Strategic Arms Limitation Talks, 21
U-2 spy plane, 228
Vienna, 92
See also Russia; Soviet Union; Stalin, Joseph
Khrushchev, Sergei, 253
"Kick" *see* Kennedy, Kathleen
Kiernan, Thomas, 29, 319–21
King, Martin Luther, Jr. 315
Kissinger, Henry, 227
Klemmer, Harvey, 15
Kopzynska, Alicja, 189
Korean War, 180, 184, 192
Krock, Arthur, 66, 71, 92, 116, 161, 238

Labour Party, 33, 48, 124, 129–32, 134, 182, 244–5, 285, 312, 316

lady friends, JFK:
Arvad, Inga, 107–9, 122
B. D. 62
Beardsley, Mimi, 273
Bouvier, Jacqueline, 193
bragging, 50, 64, 69, 81, 168, 169, 209, 224, 240, 273, 275
Bridge, Dinah, 169
Cannon, Frances Ann, 73–4
Chang, Suzy, 315
Churchill, Pamela, 149, 164–7
Dietrich, Marlene, 81, 274
Freeman-Mitford, Deborah, 67–8, 333
Gascoyne-Cecil, Mary, 131
Halle, Kaye, 186
Keeler, Christine, 331
Kopzynska, Alija, 189
Latham, Patricia, 60
Laycock, Angela, 114
Mitford, Unity, 71
Novotny, Maria, 315
"playboy" 62, 157
rumors, 46, 51, 57, 64, 70, 78, 84, 95, 117, 154, 251, 327
Ruth, 47
Stammers, Kaye, 127
Suydam, Jayne, 74
Veronica, 127
von Post, Gunilla, 195, 199
Whigham, Margaret, 220

lady friends, Joseph Sr.:
Françoise, 226
rumors, 51
Ryan, "Toodles" 43
Swanson, Gloria, 40, 43
Whigham, Margaret, 220

Lannan, Patrick, 143–5
Laos, 239, 265, 276
Laski, Frida, 48
Laski, Harold, 29, 47, 51, 53, 96, 132, 153
Latham, Patricia, 60
Latham, Paul, 60
Laycock, Angela, 114
Lebensraum, 16
Lees-Milne, James, 60
LeMay, Curtis, 31
Lend-Lease policy, 20, 103, 104
Lennon, John, 248
See also Beatles
Leslie, Marjorie, 165
Leslie, Shane, 165
"Let's Try an Experiment for Peace," 116
Lindbergh, Charles Augustus, 77, 103
Lipton, Marcus, 316
Lismore Castle, 162

Lloyd, Selwyn:
Bruce, David, 262
Churchill, Winston, 97
Eden, Anthony, 213
first impression of JFK, 195
JFK, 195, 208, 232, 272, 324, 336
Khrushchev, Nikita, 328
Macmillan, Harold, 339
McNamara, Robert Strange, 301
missile gap, 229
Profumo, John Dennis, 313
Rusk, Dean, 234

Lodge, Henry Cabot, 194
London School of Economics, 29, 36, 40, 47, 50, 52, 53, 91, 96, 226

Long, Samuel Miller Breckinridge, 99
Lothian (Lord), 15
Luce, Henry Robinson, 176

Macaulay, Thomas Babington, 122
MacDonald, Bob, 115
Macdonald, Torbert, 195
Macmillan, Andrew, 322
Macmillan, Dorothy, 158, 242, 328
Macmillan, Harold:
    Berlin, 252, 255
    Britain-US 32, 236, 239
    Churchill, Winston, 339
    Cuban missile crisis, 268, 286–9
    de Gaulle, Charles, 307
    Eden, Anthony, 211
    Eisenhower, Dwight D., 216
    health, 316, 335
    hotline, 292–308
    Ireland, 320
    McNamara, Robert Strange, 280
    missile scandal, 13, 277–8, 301, 304
    Murphy, 205
    Nassau, 302–4, 344
    nuclear test ban treaty, 310
Macmillan, Harold, personal relationship with JFK:
    Crown Inn, 327
    "Dear Friend," 246
    "Debo," 333
    deep affection, 34
    gifts, 334
    Great American Friend, 275
    Hawk missile, 277
    Honey Fitz, 178
    JFK-Joe Kennedy Sr., 21
    McMahon Act, 217
    The Middle Way, 208
    non-aggression pact, 331
    nuclear testing, 257, 331
    The Strategy of Peace, 234
    Thant, U, 297
    "Uncle Harold," 233, 242, 288, 333, 335
    Upper Volta, 23
    Vienna, 249
    Vietnam, 337
Macmillan, Maurice, 158, 341
Maher, Jack, 38
Maier, Thomas, 176
Manchester, William Raymond, 64
Manila summit, 334
Mao Tse-tung, 178
Martin, John, 204
Maudling, Reginald, 333
May, Theresa, 14
Mayo Clinic, 46
McCarthy, Joseph, 187
McCullough, David Gaub, 139
McLaughlin, Joseph, 309
McMahon Act, 217
McNamara, Robert Strange, 253, 265, 280, 301, 304–5
Menuhin, Yehudi, 323–4
Miliband, Edward Samuel ("Ed"), 33
missile gap, 229
Mitford, Deborah ("Debo"), 68, 71, 232, 342
    See also Deborah, Duchess of Devonshire ("Debo")
Mitford, Unity, 71, 233
Molyneux, Edward Henry, 83
Montgomery, Hugh, 283
Moran, Charles, 134
Morgenthau, Henry, 72

Mountbatten, Earl, 244
Muckers Club, 38
Murphia, the, 233
Murphy, Robert, 205
Murphy, William, 51
Mussolini, Benito, 35, 57

Nasaw, David George, 15, 63
Nassau meeting, 14, 302
Nasser, Gamal, 11, 206
National Security Council, 285
Nazareth, Inc., 282
New England Baptist Hospital, 65
New Realism, 211
News Chronicle (London), 18
Ngo Dinh Diem, 337
Nicolson, Harold James, 72
Nixon, Richard Milhous, 78, 229, 259
North Atlantic Treaty Organization (NATO), 269, 281, 303, 330
Novotny, Maria, 315
nuclear proliferation, 275
nuclear test treaty, 222, 266, 310, 329, 331
Nunan, Sean, 344
Nunnerley, David, 30, 32

Obama, Barack, 12
O'Brien, Larry, 234
O'Donnell, Kenneth, 204, 233, 318, 338
Ohabei Shalom, 23
O'Hearn, Tom, 282
Onassis, Aristotle, 220, 251
Operation "Bumpy Road," 245
Operation Mongoose, 298
Operation Rose, 219

Orizaba, USS, 87
Ormsby-Gore *see* Gore (Ormsby-Gore), David (5th Baron Harlech)
Oswestry, 224

Pact of Four, 35
Pai, Baj, 191
Palm Beach, 41
Patterson, Cissy, 108
"Peace in Our Time," 88
Penkovsky, Oleg Vladimirovich, 283–4
Peterson, Inga Marie, 107
PGM-17 Thor (missile), 296
PGM-19 Jupiter (long-range rocket), 297
"Phoumi versus Phouma," 265
Pierrepont, John, 95
Polaris (missile), 303–7, 344
Pope John Paul VI, 317
Pope Pius XI, 57
Pope Pius XII, 77
Powers, David Francis ("Dave"), 234
Profiles in Courage, 200
Profumo, John Dennis, 313
Profumo affair, 311–3
PT 109, 25–7, 110–1
Purloff, Hyman, 51

Queen Elizabeth, 19, 74, 194, 271–2, 227, 328, 346

racial issues (domestic US), 262, 316
Radziwill, Caroline Lee (Bouvier), 248
Ramsay, Archibald Maule, 98–100

Reagan, Ronald, 12
Red Chinese, 178
Reischauer, Edwin Oldfather, 332
Rice-Davies, Mandy, 313
Riley, John Roland, 141
Riverdale, 41
Roberts, Andrew, 23
Romilly, Constancia ("Dinky"), 324
Roosevelt, Franklin Delano, 11, 71
Roosevelt, James ("Jimmy),"36
"RossKennedy" team, 81
Rosslyn, "Tony," 81, 149, 163
Roulet, William, 225, 237
Runnymede memorial stone, 341
Rusk, Dean:
British Guiana, 270
"Buddha," 234, 317
Hawk missile, 277
Johnson, Lyndon B., 253
Macmillan, Harold, 236
NATO, 269
nuclear deterrence, 249, 280–1, 308
Ormsby-Gore, David, 262, 289
Russia:
aggression, 176–8, 188, 191, 210–2, 249
arms control talks, 116–9, 121, 219, 274, 328
Berlin, 176–9, 245
brutality, 120, 140
Cuba, 270, 283, 290–9, 306
distrust, 116–20, 122, 228, 257, 265
European resistance, 98, 142, 148, 176–8, 210–2, 245, 257
Hungary, 210–2

Nazi resistance, 90
Phoumi vs. Phouma, 265
Profumo, 314
Turkey, 297
See also Khrushchev, Nikita; Stalin, Joseph; Soviet Union; Union of Soviet Socialist Republics
Ryan, "Toodles," 43
Ryan, Mary Josephine, 166, 319

Salinger, Pierre Emil George, 234, 237
Salisbury, Robert Gascoyne-Cecil (5th Marquess of Salisbury) ("Bobbety"), 292
Sandys, Celia (Perkins), 339
Sarnoff, David, 20
Schlesinger, Arthur, Jr., 136–8, 246, 286, 310–1
Senate Foreign Relations Committee, 1955, 200
sex, 13, 64, 108, 267
See also lady friends
Seymour, James, 91
"She Loves You" (Beatles song), 317, 336
Sheridan, Richard, 137
Shropshire, 224
Sidey, Hugh, 30, 121, 133, 222
Simon, John Allsebrook (1st Viscount Simon), 105
Single Phone Call option, 309
Skybolt affair, 300–3
socialized medicine, 225
Solomon Islands, 111
Somerset Importers, 35–6
Sorensen, Theodore Chalkin ('Ted'), 234, 317

Southeast Asia Treaty
    Organization (SEATO), 198
Soviet Union:
  accommodation, 162, 184, 257
  aggression, 248
  ambition for world domination,
    31
  arms control negotiations, 198
  atomic threat, 210, 218, 247,
    280–4
  Berlin, 175, 250, 255
  British Guiana, 333
  bulwark against, 200
  compared to Irish, 201
  containment, 170, 204
  Cuba, 285–8, 298
  de Gaulle, Charles, 331
  disarmament, 306
  Egypt, 206
  Europe, 118–20
  expansionism, 156, 201
  Ghana, 23
  goodwill tour, 219
  Hungary, 216
  interference, 178
  intransigence, 122
  JFK 77, 147
  Khrushchev, Nikita, 22, 141
  Laos, 239
  Middle East, 212–3
  nuclear treaties, 228, 274, 290,
    298, 310, 327, 331
  opinion poll, 178
  Potsdam, 28
  Profumo, 313
  Stalin, 134, 138
  territorial ambitions, 145
  test ban, 327, 331
  threat, 14, 22, 89, 140, 154, 176,
    181, 188, 199, 241, 258

  slave state, 142, 154
  Soviet-American relations, 227,
    238, 257
  strategic arms limitation talks,
    20
  See also Khrushchev, Nikita;
    Russia; Stalin, Joseph;
    Union of Soviet Socialist
    Republics
Spalding, Charles ("Chuck"), 174,
    237, 332
Special Relationship, 11, 240, 249,
    268, 274, 280, 302, 345
St. Clair-Erskine, Anthony Hugh
    Francis (6th Earl of Rosslyn)
    ("Tony"), 105
St. John, George, 38, 41
Stalin, Joseph, 138, 141
    See also Russia; Soviet Union
Stammers, Kay, 127, 153
Stassen, Harold Edward, 218
Stevenson, Adlai, 193, 203, 210,
    227, 257
Stimson, Henry, 101
Suez, 11, 157, 199, 202, 206–9,
    211–7, 245, 316
Suez Canal Company, 11, 206
Sukarno, Achmed, 334
Surloff (Prince), 52
Suydam, Jane, 74
Swanson, Gloria, 39, 40, 43
Swope, Herbert, 108

Thant, U, 294
Thatcher, Margaret, 12, 342
Thompson, Frank, 169
Thor (missiles), 296
Thorneycroft, Peter, 304
Time-Life, 176
Tinker, Harold, 120

Tooth, Hugh (Sir Hugh Vere Huntley Duff Munro-Lucas-Tooth), 134
Trafalgar Day speech (1938), 66
Trinidad, 239
Truman, Harry S., 28, 117
Trump, Donald, 12
Tshombe, Moise, 258, 263
Turkey, 297
Tynan, Kenneth Peacock, 274

U-2 spy photographs, 228, 289
Ulbricht, Walter Ernst Paul, 253
"Uncle Harold," 232, 242, 288, 333, 336
Underwater Weapons Establishment, 248
Union of Soviet Socialist Republics (USSR), 32, 78, 116, 218, 227, 281, 282, 298
See also Khrushchev, Nikita; Russia; Soviet Union; Stalin, Joseph
United Nations, 170
Upper Volta Dam project, 23, 257

Vienna, 92, 121, 246, 250
Vietnam, 12, 262, 276, 337
von Dirksen, Herbert, 37
von Post, Gunilla, 195–6, 199
Vulcan bomber, 300–1

Ward, Stephen, 313–4
Warfield, Thomas, 111
Waterhouse, Charles, 113
Watkinson, Harold, 281

Washington Times-Herald, 194
Waugh, Evelyn, 67, 149, 160
Wear, Patricia ("Fiddle"), 64–5
Welles, Sumner, 91
Wheeler, Burton, 108
Whigham (Duchess of Argyll) Ethel Margaret Campbell, 220
See also Argyll affair
Why England Slept:
    Churchill's remarks, 76, 82, 89, 98–106, 109
    Curley, James Michael, 117
    described, 27
    Kennedy, Joe Sr., 238
    Krock, Arthur, 238
    Laski, Harold, 54
    Macmillan, Harold, 242
    Profiles in Courage, 199
    Queen Elizabeth, 329
    reception by peer scholars, 238
    sales, 225, 282, 309
    umbrella incident, 254
Wiesner, Jerome Bert ("Jerry"), 229–30
Wilson, Harold, 12, 182, 312
Wilson, Pat, 127
Wodehouse, Pelham Grenville ("P. G."), 42, 326, 344
Wohlatt, Helmut, 76
Wood, Richard Frederick (Baron Holderness), 151

Young Melbourne, The, 30, 272, 274, 318

Zelig, Leonard, 27